RATIONAL MAN and
IRRATIONAL SOCIETY?

RATIONAL MAN and IRRATIONAL SOCIETY?

An Introduction and Sourcebook

Edited by
Brian Barry and Russell Hardin

SAGE PUBLICATIONS
Beverly Hills / London / New Delhi

For information address:

SAGE Publications, Inc.
275 South Beverly Drive
Beverly Hills, California 90212

SAGE Publications India Pvt. Ltd.
C-236 Defence Colony
New Delhi 110 024, India

SAGE Publications Ltd
28 Banner Street
London EC1Y 8QE, England

Printed in the United States of America

Library of Congress Cataloging in Publication Data

Main entry under title:

Rational man and irrational society?

  Bibliography: p.
  Includes index.
  1. Social choice. I. Barry, Brian M. II. Hardin, Russell, 1940-
HM271.R37   302   81-21508
ISBN 0-8039-1850-X   AACR2
ISBN 0-8039-1851-8 (pbk.)

FIRST PRINTING

Contents

Acknowledgments

We wish to thank David Shively for tracing relevant articles; Lori Gilman for working on the bibliography; Joanna Barry for keeping the project moving even when the editors weren't; Mancur Olson and Thomas Schelling for chivvying their publishers on our behalf; our own publishers for stoicism in the face of ever-receding deadlines for the completion of the manuscript; and Brian Downing for sorely needed help in checking the proofs and preparing the index.

B. B.
R. H.

Preface

I. WHAT THIS BOOK IS ABOUT

The book falls into two parts, each of which takes up one topic bearing on the overall theme of rationality in society.

Part I is designed to introduce the idea of the prisoner's dilemma and to show how this basic idea has been used to throw light on a whole variety of social phenomena. As will be explained more fully in the introduction to Part I, a prisoner's dilemma situation arises whenever two or more actors, (which need not be individual human beings), find that the consequence of each pursuing its own individual interests produces an outcome that all parties regard as worse than some alternative outcome that could have been achieved had they acted differently.

The name "prisoner's dilemma" arises from the story with which this kind of situation was first illustrated in the literature of the theory of games. (The history of the prisoner's dilemma is discussed in the Introduction to Part I.) In this story, two prisoners suspected of a serious crime are put in separate cells and each offered the same deal by the District Attorney. The terms of the deal are as follows: if you confess to the serious crime then you will be freed if the other prisoner does not confess, and you will receive a moderate sentence (along with the other prisoner) if he confesses too. If you don't confess, and if the other prisoner doesn't confess either, then you will both be convicted of a lesser crime that the D.A. has enough evidence to prosecute without a confession; however, if you don't confess and the other prisoner does, you will get a maximum sentence (one that is much more severe than that which you would have received had you both confessed).

What makes this a dilemma is that the payoffs from the alternative courses of action that face the prisoners have the following form: *each* prisoner gets a shorter sentence by confessing, *whichever* action the other prisoner takes. Suppose prisoner B is going to confess: then A's choice is, in effect, between a moderate sentence (if he himself confesses) and a maximum sentence (if he doesn't). Suppose, on the other hand, that B is not going to confess: then A's choice is, in effect, between going scot free (if he confesses) and the light sentence that they both get on the lesser charge (if he does not confess either).

Thus, taking each prisoner's calculation separately, it is clear that each is better off by confessing than by not confessing. Yet the outcome when both follow this strategy (moderate sentence on the serious crime) is worse for *both* than the outcome if neither confesses (conviction on the lesser crime).

There is clearly, at least on the surface, some sort of paradox of rationality at work here: the parties, by pursuing their interests rationally, finish up with less satisfactory results than they might have achieved by sacrificing their interests. One of the questions that will have to be considered later is whether or not the appearance of paradox is illusory. But wherever we come out on that issue, we will still have to acknowledge that the problem itself is, in practical terms, real enough, and ubiquitous in society, economy, and polity. We must therefore also ask how societies actually cope with prisoner's dilemma problems. What are the devices that typically emerge to cope with the fact that what is to each person's individual advantage may at the same time make everybody a loser? Much of the work presented in Part I is devoted to trying to answer that question.

Part II is devoted to Kenneth Arrow's "general possibility theorem" and the implications that it may (or, again, may not) have for the feasibility of basing social decisions on the aggregation of individual preferences. The basic issue here may be stated, in the simplest terms, as follows. Suppose we wish to take some decision that affects a number of us (e.g., where to go for a picnic) and we wish, reasonably enough, to arrange that the decision we arrive at should somehow reflect the preferences of the people concerned. What we want, in other words, is some method for aggregating our preferences so as to produce a consistent ranking of the alternatives. The striking claim put forward by Arrow in his general possibility theorem is that, if there are at least three of us whose preferences are to be counted, and if the choice has to be made among more than two alternative picnic spots, there is no formula for aggregating consistent (transitive) individual preferences into a consistent (transitive) ranking that will satisfy certain apparently very weak and reasonable conditions.

The theorem will be stated more precisely in the introduction to Part II, and the conditions stipulated by Arrow will be set out and discussed there. The robustness of the result—how far the impossibility depends on peculiar features of the conditions—will also have to be considered. For the present, however, let us simply take it that Arrow has indeed produced a disconcerting and counterintuitive proof. Again we have, at first glance anyway, a paradox of rationality. If we take even a minimal conception of rationality as including the notion of consistency, then we can paraphrase Arrow's result by saying that, in a different way from that presented by the prisoner's dilemma, we have once more a way in which individual rationality fails to guarantee collective rationality.

As before, the caution must be entered here that this way of talking may be suspect. We shall take up this question in the Epilogue, after the issues have become clearer in the body of the book. We shall there ask whether there is really any "paradox of rationality" in either the prisoner's dilemma or in Arrow's theorem, or whether the appearance of such a paradox derives from an overextension of the concept of rationality. We may meanwhile note that the Arrow theorem, like the prisoner's dilemma, has undeniable practical significance, whatever its precise philosophical significance.

Voting is the method by which we attempt to ensure that what gets decided on bears some systematic relation to the preferences of a group of people—a committee, an electorate, or whatever. It has been realized for a long time that, under some conditions, voting can have curious and even perverse characteristics. Thus, Pliny the Younger recounted in a letter a case that had arisen in the Roman Senate. The debate concerned "the freedmen of the consul Afranius Dexter; it being uncertain, whether he killed himself, or whether he died by the hands of his freedmen; and again, whether they killed him from a spirit of malice, or of obedience. One of the senators (it is of little purpose to tell you, I was the person) declared, that he thought these freedmen ought to be put to the question, and afterwards released. The sentiments of another were, that the freedmen should be banished; and of another, that they should suffer death" (Farquharson 1969, p. 57).[1] Since there was no majority for any of the three proposals, the result could turn, not on the distribution of opinion in the Senate, but on the voting rules adopted and on the strategies used by senators. Pliny noted in his letter both that the way of dividing the question was crucial and also that the situation lent itself to strategic manipulation. One senator, he said, "had given his voice for capital punishment" but "desisted from his first opinion, and voted for banishment; fearing, that, if the several votes were taken separately, . . . those who had voted for an entire acquittal would have been most numerous, the numbers being much greater on that side than either of the other two" (Farquharson 1969, p. 60).

A mid-Victorian Oxford don, Charles Lutwidge Dodgson (better known to the world as Lewis Carroll), analyzed the problem of votes between three or more alternatives in the context of decisions on fellowship elections and building plans in the Governing Body of Christ Church. He saw the possibilities of strategic manipulation inherent in the usual voting methods, and in answer to the question "Am I bound in honour to vote for the one whom I should *really* prefer?" in a series of separate votes between candidates, he replied no. "I think it desirable that all should know the rule by which this game may be won. It is simply this: 'In any division taken on a pair of issues neither of which you desire, vote against the most popular'" (Black 1958, p. 238).[2] This remains good advice.

Only in the wake of Arrow's general possibility theorem was the problem of strategic manipulation given a completely general treatment, when Allan Gibbard and Mark Satterthwaite proved that no procedure is immune to the potentiality for strategic manipulation. So long as there are at least three propositions to choose between and at least three voters, there is no way of guaranteeing that one voter will not be able to enhance his or her chance of getting a more desired outcome than would otherwise occur by deliberately voting for a less favored option at some point. The manipulability of voting schemes is thus an irreducible feature of politics at all levels. The papers by Vickrey and Gibbard in Part II discuss the implications for actual voting systems.

II. SOCIAL SCIENCE AS A THIRD CULTURE

This section is directed primarily toward that perhaps mythical being, the "general reader." Let us explain at once that we do not expect this book to be picked up by someone in mistake for the latest Joyce Carol Oates. But we do believe that it is worth the time and attention of others besides professors of social science and their students.

That is not to say that we in any way discount its pedagogic value: indeed, the idea for the present collection grew out of the frustrating experience of attempting to teach courses in the topics covered by this volume in the absence of a suitable collection of source materials. We think, however, that the case for the book can be made to the reader with a professional interest in the field without any difficulty. The materials brought together here were originally published in a wide range of journals in philosophy, economics, and political science, and in a number of books, some of which are quite hard to get hold of. The convenience of having them between two covers is manifest to anyone with academic interests in the subjects covered.

We are then left with the question raised at the start of this section: are the topics discussed in this book such as should interest anyone who does not have some kind of special reason for worrying about them? We should like to make the case for saying they should.

When in 1959 C. P. Snow gave a lecture in Cambridge on *The Two Cultures and the Scientific Revolution* (Snow 1963), he expressed an outlook to be expected in one of his generation and background (Cambridge University and the British civil service) in limiting the number of cultures to two. Snow's lecture was devoted to pressing the claim that two cultures—the humanistic and the scientific—should be regarded as essential mental furniture for anyone with pretensions to intellectual cultivation. In this, he was, of course, taking issue with the equation of "culture" with literature and the arts. That battle has, it would seem, been won to a great extent. The idea that anyone can claim to be well-educated while professing entire ignorance of what the physical sciences tell us about the universe seems almost as archaic today as the earlier notion that a decent familiarity with the chief Latin and Greek authors was all that any gentleman needed in order to pass in the world as a model of accomplishment. However, the third culture—that of the social sciences—still has a long way to go before it achieves a similar status to that now accorded to the physical sciences.

Anyone in the United States who reads the New York *Times* or watches public television is liable to be exposed to quite serious efforts to explain, say, quarks, black holes, or recombinant DNA. "Social science" is represented, however, as if it had no intellectual structure, but was simply common sense plus statistics, a matter of public opinion polling and economic forecasting. When has "Nova" or the science page of the New York *Times* ever tried to present some theoretical issue in the social sciences with the same seriousness as is taken for granted when the subject is physics or biology? Yet, as we believe this book illustrates, the social sciences contain disciplined speculation of a high order, worthy of serious attention on the part of anyone with a modicum of intellectual curiosity.

It should perhaps be said, in fairness to Snow, that in some further thoughts added four years later (Snow 1963, pp. 53-92), he did mention "what, in the terms of our formulae, is becoming something like a third culture" (Snow 1963, p. 67). Its carriers are, he says, a "mixed bag" of "intellectual persons in a variety of fields—social history, sociology, demography, political science, economics, government (in the American academic sense), psychology, medicine, and social arts such as architecture" (Snow 1963, pp. 66-67).

We have no wish to pillory Snow, especially since he was unjustly attacked even for daring to suggest that the physical sciences constituted a culture. But what he said about his "third culture" is so different from anything he would have said about the culture of physical science as to illustrate with particular vividness how limiting preconceptions about social science can be, even in one making every attempt to be broadminded. The essence of a scientific culture lies in two things: an intellectual structure and a scholarly community. Snow gives no sign of attributing either to social science. The bearers of his "third culture" (which he doubts really is one, so inchoate does he believe it to be) are "a body of intellectual opinion" whose main interest to Snow is that they are less hostile to (real) science than the literary intellectuals. Their distinguishing characteristic is that they are "concerned with how human beings are living or have lived" (Snow 1963, p. 67)—which would not distinguish social science from journalism, antiquarianism, or gossip. Snow would not, we can be sure, have defined physical science by its concern with the natural order, since this, again, would not distinguish, say, a biologist from a sharp-eyed enthusiast for long country walks.

However, the most persuasive evidence that Snow really held the view—a very widespread one, as we have suggested—of social science as an assemblage of information rather than as a body of theory, is provided not by his statements on the topic, but by his practice. In his original lecture, Snow made a whole series of claims about the conditions of economic development that would make any social scientist squirm by their simple-mindedness. Yet at no time did Snow reveal any appreciation of the fact that he was putting himself in the same position as someone with no training in physics who made equally dogmatic assertions about, say, the conservation of parity.

The best way of arguing for the worth of the "third culture" is to present examples of it at its best. That is what this volume is intended to do. We would, indeed, be inclined to claim that the two ideas dealt with here, the prisoner's dilemma and the Arrow theorem, are the two most challenging and fruitful ones to have arisen in the social sciences since World War II. Both are, at their core, quite simple and abstract notions, capable of being grasped in a fairly short time by anyone willing to concentrate. Yet they both turn out to have unlimited ramifications. In one direction they raise, as we have seen, philosophical problems about the concept of rationality. In other directions, they raise difficulties for the justification of democracy and throw light on arguments about the virtues of the market and of state intervention. In yet other ways, they can help us to look with fresh eyes at some central issues in the interpretation of classic political philosophers such as Hobbes and Rousseau.

There is a different reason for taking an interest in the topics discussed in this book, and that is self-defense. The only protection against being blinded by science is to know some yourself. The physical sciences again provide an apt analogy. As a consequence of the extremely low level of scientific literacy among the "educated public" in the interwar period, it was possible for charlatans to get away with outrageous claims about the implications of, for example, the theory of relativity ("everything's relative") or Heisenberg's uncertainty principle ("everything's indeterminate"). We can see a similar tendency just beginning to creep in with respect to the prisoner's dilemma and the Arrow theorem. In scholarly journals within such fields as political science and philosophy, the vocabulary of game theory and collective choice theory is more and more frequently being thrown around—very often misused—by people who obviously have a very insecure grasp on what they are talking about. The only way of ensuring against being hornswoggled by this kind of thing is to have studied the subjects oneself to the point at which one can tell when others are talking through their hats. We believe that this book can provide a useful starting place.

III. HOW THIS BOOK IS ORGANIZED

We have endeavored to make the book as usable as possible, even by those with no previous experience of the subjects covered, by providing a variety of aids to the reader. The readings are divided into two sets, and each of the sets of readings is preceded by an introductory essay, which sketches the way in which thought on the topic has developed to its present point, reviews the themes to be covered by the readings, and offers a brief guide to them that seeks to show their interrelations. Each of the individual readings is prefaced by an introduction, which provides whatever background is needed, explains unfamiliar terminology or notations, and indicates where later developments may be found. In making our choices of pieces to reprint in this book, we have found that on many topics, the most suitable treatments come relatively early on (by which we mean a decade or two ago) because these discussions tend to concentrate on the basic issues and to have less technical complexity than those that come later. Anyone who wishes to carry the story up to the present and to find out about refinements to the basic ideas presented in the readings should therefore consult the introductions to the individual readings. Following the readings is an Epilogue which asks what we may be able to learn about rationality—and about society—from the prisoner's dilemma and Arrow's general possibility theorem. There then comes a Guide to Further Reading, which is designed to offer suggestions to those who wish to study systematically the various fields drawn on in the readings collected here.

Finally, there is a consolidated Reference section that includes in a single list all works cited, whether in our own editorial material or in the readings. Our own contributions and a number of the readings employ the author-date method of citation which, of course, requires a bibliography. Two articles using a variant, with items in a bibliography identified in the text by number, have been converted to the author-date system. Some selections are, however, from articles and books that use the traditional method of citation in footnotes, giving full information on works cited. We have left these in the original form, since we have not felt that it would be justifiable to rewrite them in a different style. Although these references are self-contained, we have decided to include the works cited in the References, so as to make it comprehensive.

NOTES

1. The letter is printed in its entirety in Farquharson 1969, pp. 57-60 as an Annexure. Farquharson used the example throughout the book.

2. The text of Dodgson's three pamphlets on voting procedures is given in Black 1958, pp. 214-34. Black discusses the context in which they came to be written in a very entertaining way on pp. 189-213.

I

INDIVIDUAL ACTIONS AND COLLECTIVE CONSEQUENCES

I. THE PROBLEM

The issue in the readings in this section has come to be known as the problem of collective action, the prisoner's dilemma, the free-rider problem, and the condition of common fate, depending on the context (or discipline) in which it arises.[1] The multiplicity of names is indicative of a failure to generalize the nature of the problem, which has been recognized in a remarkable variety of contexts over many centuries. It has been generalized only recently, most notably in the game theoretic prisoner's dilemma and in Mancur Olson's (1965) logic of collective action. Because earlier writers failed to abstract from particular examples, they often failed to grasp the significance of the problem. They also often failed to recognize other instances of it. (Baumol [1952, p. 143] notes that "Writers, sometimes even those who had considered these ideas elsewhere in their writings, continued to make mistakes and omissions which greater familiarity with the analysis in question might have prevented.")

Suppose with Pareto (1935, vol. 3, pp. 946-947) "that if *all* individuals refrained from doing A, every individual as a member of the community would derive a certain advantage. But now if all individuals *less one* continue refraining from doing A, the community loss is very slight, whereas the one individual doing A makes a personal gain far greater than the loss that he incurs as a member of the community." This is the logic of collective action: if I am narrowly self-interested, I would presumably not refrain from doing A. I would plausibly refrain only if my not refraining would adversely affect the behavior of enough others to reduce my advantage from communal refraining more than the cost (to me) of my refraining. For example, suppose smog in our metropolis could be prevented if all of us would voluntarily pay to have certain antipollution devices installed in our cars, and suppose further that a referendum to require such devices would pass by a nearly unanimous vote. Voluntary action would not solve our smog problem if too many of us were narrowly rational.

Evidence of this logic at work is seemingly everywhere. We do not voluntarily clean up our car exhausts or stop burning wood in our fireplaces. We seldom join our neighbors to clean up our blocks or to shovel snow from our alleys and sidewalks. We contribute at most trifling sums to collective causes we support, and most of us contribute nothing. Most of us in the United States generally do not vote in elections. Fishing nations collectively destroy open-sea fisheries.

Oddly, however, the most pervasive and important instance of this logic is probably overwhelmingly beneficial. The logic of collective action is in another guise merely the logic of the efficiency of market exchange: the existence of large numbers of sellers makes collusive agreements to raise prices virtually impossible (unless they are backed by state sanctions). It is in this guise that Smith most clearly saw the logic. If the amount of capital of the grocery trade sufficient to meet demand in a town "is divided between two different grocers, their competition will tend to make both of them sell cheaper, than if it were in the hands of one only; and if it were divided among twenty, their competition would be just so much the greater, and the chance of their combining together, in order to raise the price, just so much the less" (Smith 1937, p. 342 [bk. 2, ch. 5]). It is the incapacity for collusion that makes sellers finally efficient, causes better products to drive out poorer, and leads to most of what Smith holds dear in capitalism: economic growth and progress. Of course, that incapacity also prevents sellers from earning the greater profits they would dearly love to have.

The argument of the logic of collective action is based on the strong assumption that individual actions are motivated by self-interest, or on the assumption of what is commonly called narrow rationality or, more briefly, rationality. Obviously, individual actions are motivated by concerns other than self-interest. But collective action for mutual benefit is, in an analogous sense, narrowly rational for a group or organization. Hence, it should not surprise us to find that many of those who want their collective interests to be served may weigh their own self-interest heavily, even too heavily to cooperate in serving their collective interests.

Part of the appeal of the assumption of narrow rationality is almost methodological: it is easy to accommodate in analysis and it is relatively easy to assess in generalizable behaviors. An additional appeal might be, as is sometimes claimed, that it explains a very large fraction of behavior in certain realms. One can too easily overrate the size of that fraction even in the most explicitly economic contexts. But often the assumption of narrowly rational motivation yields predictions that are the most useful benchmark against which to assess the extent and the impact of other motivations. Occasionally it yields predictions that so nearly fit behavior that investigation need go no further to satisfy us that we have understood why certain outcomes occur and others do not.

The logic of collective action does just this in many contexts, although not in others. It yields a notoriously poor explanation of voting behavior since it suggests almost no one would voluntarily vote in, say, American national elections. It helps us to understand why half of eligible Americans do not vote in presidential elections, but it does little to help us understand the other half. But the logic of collective action is overwhelmingly successful in predicting negligible voluntary activity in many realms such as, say, the contemporary environmental movement. Then what about the Sierra Club and other environmental organizations? The answer is that environmentalists contribute woefully little to their cause given the enormous value to them of success and given the repeated survey results that show high commitment by a large percentage of Americans to that cause. Environmentalists annually spend less on their apparently great cause than 25,000 two-pack-a-day smokers spend on cigarettes. It is a trivium, and one might find it inconceivable except that it makes clear sense on a narrowly rational analysis. One could go on to note even more embarrassing statistics on how little Americans have spent on such honored causes as civil rights, the contemporary women's movement, gun control (as opposed to anti-control), and so forth.

II. OLSON'S LOGIC OF COLLECTIVE ACTION

In his simplest statement of the logic of collective action, Olson presents the straightforward equation of costs (C), gross benefits (V_i) to the individual i, and net benefits (A_i) to the individual from i's own contribution to a group's collective good: $A_i = V_i - C$. If $A_i > 0$ for some i, the group is *privileged* and presumably will succeed. If $A_i < 0$ for *all* i, the group is *latent* and will fail unless other noncollective good (selective) incentives are available to induce contributions (Olson, 1965, pp. 23, 49-50).

Olson then applies this arithmetic analysis to various classical interest groups: industry lobbies, unions, farm lobbies, and professional associations. He concludes that these groups are generally latent and must therefore depend for their success on selective incentives to induce contributions from their members. For example, unions often benefit from union shop rules that compel workers to join or at least to pay dues. Professional associations depend on their private goods, such as journals, low-cost group insurance, investment counseling, and, most importantly for many associations, restrictive licensing. Industry groups depend on asymmetries among their member firms to obtain cooperation in lobbying on general interest issues that have some special, even firm-specific, implications (Hardin 1982, ch. 5). Of course, industry groups are often also privileged. For example, Exxon's interest in industry-wide tax benefits is great enough to justify Exxon's activities independently of the industry-wide group.

In his analysis, Olson sets out to do two things. First, he wishes to show that the rational incentive to an individual in a latent group is not to contribute to the group's provision of its collective good to itself. Because this is a strictly logical point, it is obvious once the definition of the case is clearly seen. Second, he wishes to show that large groups are less likely to succeed than small ones. Here the point is not so obvious, as our discussion of the prisoner's dilemma should make clear (in section 3 of this introduction).

Return for a moment to Olson's first point. It is an important point that seems to have been as surprising to many as Olson's presentation of it is compelling. Yet it was well understood before Olson's account, indeed before Samuelson's discussion of public goods. Among others, William Baumol had already spelled out the general argument with great clarity. However, his account is undercut in its effect by its being an account of several examples—farmers seeding clouds to cause rain, neighbors draining meadows, military preparedness, general education, public parks, public health facilities. The example he considers at greatest length is more general and might readily have been generalized. He discusses the problem of investment in the future, noting that risk aversion might deter individuals from making investments that would be socially beneficial. An individual's investment might prove to be unwise, and even if wise, its benefits might go to someone else because the individual had died or lost title to the fruits of the effort. Counter to this explanation of the tendency to underinvest in the future, Baumol then offers the far more general argument that

> the individual as a citizen, having his share of local pride, may desire an improvement in the general future state of welfare in the community. If, however, he alone directs his activities in a manner conducive to it, the effects of his action may be quite negligible. It is true that in the process he may also be improving the value of his own assets, but his private return must be discounted by a risk factor which does not apply in the calculation of the expected gain to the community. Thus neither private interest nor altruism (except if he has grounds for assurance that others, too, will act in a manner designed to promote the future welfare of the community) can rationally lead him to invest for the future, and particularly the far distant future, to an extent appropriate from the point of view of the community as a whole. Taken as a commodity,

improvement in the future state of the community as a whole is one that must serve a group demand and not just the demand of isolated individuals [Baumol 1952, p. 92].

The impact of Olson's account may be due in part to his having addressed political interest groups, so that he attracted the attention of social scientists other than economists. But Anthony Downs had already fully grasped the logic of collective action in the context of one of the most commonplace of political goods: electoral victory (see further the selection by Barry reprinted in Part I; Downs 1957). Hence, the impact of Olson's account must be due for the most part to the greater generality or abstractness of his presentation. He stops speaking of draining meadows, seeding clouds, winning elections, restricting wheat production to raise prices and profits, investing in the future, and so forth, and presents an abstract equation relating costs and gross benefits to net benefits. Henceforth, discussion has not depended on anyone's particular examples but on the best imaginable examples.

Olson's main conclusion that latent groups will fail is modified by three important considerations: extrarational behavior, entrepreneurship, and selective incentives (including solidary incentives) as argued by Olson in his by-product theory (Olson 1965, ch. 6) and as sometimes arise independently of organizational efforts, especially in ongoing relationships (Taylor 1976; Hardin 1982, chs. 9-13). The by-product theory is discussed by Barry in his selection, and we will discuss it further here (in section 4). The fact that some groups receive political representation of their interests despite their being latent has been the subject of a substantial literature not represented in our readings, and we will briefly discuss it here as well (in section 5). Finally, we will very briefly take up the claim that many logically latent groups may well succeed in collective actions because they have ongoing relationships which, in a sense, give their members selective incentives to cooperate. However, this claim can best be seen as the claim that in ongoing (that is, iterated) prisoner's dilemmas, continuous defection is not a dominant strategy so that cooperation may be the best strategy for every player (see section 7, "Caveats and Extensions").

III. THE PRISONER'S DILEMMA

The algebraic statement of the logic of collective action given previously and the graphic representation of it in part of Olson's book not reprinted here (Olson 1965, p. 32) may be augmented by a game theoretic representation. Since its presentation virtually whole cloth by von Neumann and Morgenstern (1944), game theory has been one of the dominant frameworks for analyzing social interactions. Its greatest strength is that it makes the strategic aspects of such interactions explicit, even emphatic. Since it also renders them algebraically, it makes them seem incontrovertibly clear and compelling, so that it becomes second nature even for casual students of game theory to take strategic interactions into account. Oddly, the principal gain from game theory in this respect for social scientists derives not from the abstruse theory, but merely from the form in which individual games are represented, especially from the payoff matrix, or strategic, game form. In strategic form, the strategic structures of some games are sufficiently compelling to remake the thinking of those who have once comprehended them.

On the evidence of the sheer volume of publications, the most interesting of all strategic structures is that of prisoner's dilemma. In its simplest form, prisoner's dilemma involves two players in interaction, each facing two possible strategies. Since each player can choose independently of the other, their two pairs of strategies produce four possible outcomes. Prisoner's dilemma is represented in strategic form in Matrix 1. Each outcome is a payoff pair, such as the lower left outcome $(3, -1)$ in which the first payoff goes to Row and the second to Column (according to the mnemonic Roman Catholic convention). In two prisoner's dilemma there are two players, Row and Column, each facing two strategy choices, cooperate and defect. If both cooperate, they receive positive payoffs of 1 each. If both defect, they receive payoffs of 0 each. If one cooperates and the other defects, the cooperator

		Column	
		cooperate	defect
	cooperate	1,1	$-1,3$
Row			
	defect	3,-1	0,0

Matrix 1

receives an even worse payoff, -1, while the defector does very well with a positive payoff of 3. There is therefore strong incentive to defect. Indeed, defection is a *dominant strategy* for each player: if Row's choice does not influence Column's, then Row is better off defecting *no matter what Column does.* As is clear from a glance at only Row's payoffs in the game matrix, Row gets more in each column from choosing defection than from choosing cooperation.

The prisoner's dilemma was discovered around 1950 by Merrill Flood and Melvin Dresher, who were concerned with testing Nash's solution for noncooperative games (games in which players are not allowed to collude). The game they created was strategically equivalent to the game of Matrix 1

(Flood 1952). It was later named the prisoner's dilemma by A. W. Tucker, who invented the story of the two prisoners (see the Preface to this volume). The further history of the game is recounted by Rapoport in his selection reprinted in Part I.

The appeal of the prisoner's dilemma, as of the logic of collective action, has been its generality and its apparent power in explaining manifold social interactions. Indeed, the problem of collective action and the prisoner's dilemma are essentially the same, as is shown by Hardin in his selection. Again, whereas numerous specific prisoner's dilemma interactions were commonly understood centuries, even millennia before game theory, the understanding has now been generalized in such a clear manner than it can no longer be easily put aside when we turn from investigating one specific interaction to another.

We can restate the logic of collective action in game theoretic terms as follows. In prisoner's dilemma games there is an outcome that is individually rational but collectively deficient. It is individually rational because it is the outcome that results when all players choose their dominant strategies, that is, when all defect. It is collectively deficient because it is not Pareto-optimal: there is at least one other outcome (that in which all cooperate) in which *all* players are better off than in the all-defect outcome. This is precisely the logic of collective action: it may be in everyone's individual interest not to cooperate in a collective effort even though everyone would be better off if everyone cooperated.

There are certain advantages to viewing the problem of collective action as a prisoner's dilemma. First, as we will discuss immediately, the prisoner's dilemma representation clarifies Olson's claim that large groups are latent and small groups are privileged. Second, it is easily fitted to the analysis of ongoing or repeated interactions, as will be discussed briefly in section 7, "Caveats and Extensions," of this introduction. Finally, it also allows easy generalization to considerably more complex interactions as in the selection by Schelling (see further, section 8, "Guide to the Readings," of this introduction).

Olson concludes that small groups are more generally privileged in his sense (as defined in section 2, "Olson's Logic of Collective Action"), while large groups are generally latent. Against this claim, consider the following examples. We have already seen an instance of the smallest of all possible latent groups in the prisoner's dilemma matrix above. It represents a symmetric group each of whose two members would be willing to pay up to three units for a collective good that costs four units to supply. Hence, the total value of the good to the group is six for a *group* advantage of two (total benefit minus total cost). In the lower right cell of Matrix 1, with no one paying, the good is not provided. In the other cells, the good is provided through payments of one player only or, in the upper left cell, through equal payments from both. The payoffs represent benefits minus contributions. By Olson's logic, this is a latent group because A_i is less than 0 for both members. Therefore, if there are no sanctions against noncooperation, and if there are no benefits to be gained from cooperation other than the enjoyment of the greater or lesser completion of the project, the group will fail.

Examples of exceedingly large privileged groups are also easily devised. One could simply add to the game above thousands of players who value the collective good of that group at, say five units. Now there are many people for whom $A_i > 0$, so that this very large group is privileged.

These logical conclusions are not without substance. It is easy to spot actual instances of two-person latent groups. Less common, no doubt, but still around, are very large privileged groups. For example, when Howard Hughes, whose tastes ran to watching westerns and aviation movies on television from midnight to 6 a.m., moved to Las Vegas, local station KLAS-TV regularly went off the air at 11 p.m. Hughes's aides badgered the station's owner to schedule movies through the night until the owner impatiently challenged a Hughes emissary: "Why doesn't he just buy the thing and run it the way he wants to?" Hughes obliged, paid $3.8 million for the station, and ran movies until 6 a.m. (*Time,* April 8, 1974, p. 42). The potential audience for Hughes's movies was a quarter of a million people.

Hence, Olson's logical conclusion can only concern whether groups are privileged or latent, not whether they are large or small. The size effects are far more complex than this logic for a narrowly defined realm of collective action problems as John Chamberlin notes in his selection, and as discussed more fully in Hardin (1982, especially ch. 3).

IV. THE BY-PRODUCT THEORY

Previously organized groups can occasionally cooperate to promote their interests. However, over the long term, the essential difference between the actions of such groups and the actions of traditional organized interest groups (whose political activity Olson characterizes as a by-product), is that the narrowly defined spontaneous groups commonly require some coordinating event to stimulate group-oriented behavior. Once the event is past, the individual's activities are no longer coordinated and the group returns to its latent state even though its interest may not yet have been secured. The occasional instantaneous successes of such groups can then frequently be dissipated over time, as Edelman (1964) argues.

Many traditional interest groups succeed in providing their collective goods as by-products of organization based on other, selective (that is, private rather than collective good) incentives. Such a group remains organized over a long period of time and can put a fraction of its resources into providing such collective goods as higher wages, political lobbying, public relations, and so forth. The incentives that encourage, sometimes even compel, membership and support range from nominal incentives such as low-cost group insurance and professional journals, to such potentially coercive incentives as union shop rules and restrictive licensing (Olson 1965, ch. 6). Some of the most important traditional interest groups, industry groups, may require no selective incentives because they are privileged groups (as, say, the oil industry and the industries dominated by General Motors, Dupont, AT&T, IBM, and so forth clearly are with respect to certain of their industry-wide interests). Other industry groups have selective incentives, such as a given firm's incentive to participate in lobbying on tariffs that could otherwise be deviously designed to benefit other firms in the industry preferentially (Stigler 1974).

Many traditional forms of selective incentives used by groups to encourage membership, however, are no longer available. In part because of the success of traditional groups, government has taken over the provision of many of the goods used as selective incentives, such as group insurance, pensions, even club houses (public reservoirs and parks with easy access highways undercut the attractions of group outing lodges). An attractive incentive sometimes still available to many of the middle-class qualitative issue groups is group air travel at attractively lower prices than individuals outside groups can obtain.

There are other, perhaps less obvious but often more important, forms that selective incentives can take. For example, there are clear benefits of group participation in many contexts. There is a vast organizational literature on the extent to which individual members of an organization tend to become committed to the organization independently of commitment to its goals or values (Selznick 1957; Starbuck 1965). Among the sources of commitment to an organization are its social life with friendship ties and shared experiences, the sunk costs that one may have invested in mastering its structure, and so forth. Furthermore, one may simply enjoy activities which for the organization are merely means to its ends. On Helen Gouldner's account, the League of Women Voters benefits from strong commitments to its local chapters brought on by the pleasure members find in chapter activities. Many members evidently place high value on belonging to *some* organization, and the League is the one (Gouldner, 1960). The success of the national organization in even trying to affect the general level of political discussion seems to depend in large part on its federated structure which provides valued local activities. If it merely solicited funds for its national purposes, it would not benefit from local selective incentives. Of course, it is in the nature of the League's national goals that local chapters serve those goals directly—to raise the level of political discussion and awareness nationally means to raise it everywhere locally.

The more recent movement for women's liberation has also no doubt benefited substantially from selective incentives, especially perhaps from the uniquely interesting incentive of individual consciousness-raising. This incentive is best provided by local, ongoing groups, so that the women's movement, like the League, has a natural federated structure of local chapters. The chief difference on this point may be that the movement is not so formally organized. If, as many now assert, the women's movement has gone into decline since its peak in the early to mid-seventies, a principal reason may be that there is little more to be individually gained by very many committed women from continued consciousness-raising. Hence, the federated structure of the movement is less able to motivate action, because action increasingly depends on public-spirited (collective good) motivation and decreasingly on the personal benefits to be gained from an improved self-image.

There are two important shortcomings of the by-product theory. The first and lesser of these is that many of the selective incentives commonly associated with groups are not very powerful motivators. This is not true of solidarity, restrictive licensing, or union shop rules, but it is true of access to recreational facilities, receipt of journals, group insurance, and so forth. These latter are essentially private goods that often display increasing returns to scale as the number of "purchasers" increases, so that one might think a large group organization could provide them at a "price" somewhat above marginal cost and thereby rake off a surplus for group-oriented activity. But if this is plausible, then markets should often develop to supply such goods more cheaply without any rake-off. As a perverse example, a union member would get a better price for group insurance sponsored by the company if the union were padding its price to include the equivalent of dues. If the origin of unions were principally explained by the by-product theory, one would probably have to conclude that their success was the result of employers' failure: if American industrialists had been as quick witted as the Fuggers of Augsburg, they might never have had to face unions on such nearly equal footing (but see the next paragraph). The Fugger family provided its workers with housing and other benefits whose unit costs must have been substantially lower than any "market" alternatives because they were all provided on such a large scale. Certain postwar American electronics firms have openly attempted to undercut the appeal of unions through similar devices.

The most obvious weakness of the by-product theory, however, is that, although it can make sense of contributions to an ongoing political organization, *it does not seem to explain how many groups come to be organized in the first place.* This would not be a problem if it seemed that organization for selective benefit reasons preceded organizational pursuit of collective benefits. But even limited knowledge of early efforts to organize labor or to organize professionals such as doctors (Berlant, 1975, pp. 225-234) strongly suggests the contrary: many organizations were built in order to pursue collective benefits and many of the selective incentives commonly discussed (such as union shop rules, restrictive licensing, group insurance, club houses, professional journals, and so forth) must generally have followed organization. *They were the result, not the source of group success.* As Samuel Gompers (1905) said, the union shop naturally follows organization—not vice versa.

Hence, Olson presents a compelling rational explanation of the survival of some organizations that provide their members with collective goods, but leaves the origin of many such groups—and therefore, the explanation of the success of their collective actions—in question. This was immediately seen as a major weakness of Olson's theory (Wagner, 1966). An easy answer to it is that early organizers of various interested may not have been primarily self-interested. An alternative answer, more in keeping with the assumptions of Olson's theory, is that organizers often are self-interested; indeed, they are political entrepreneurs whose payoff for organizing the provision of collective benefits is the individual reward of a political career.

V. POLITICAL ENTREPRENEURSHIP

The by-product theory generally, although not exclusively, explains how groups may maintain organization despite their being apparently latent. There is another argument that, through political entrepreneurship, groups may obtain collective benefits despite latency and even despite failure to organize at all. Political entrepreneurs are people who, for their own career reasons, find it in their private interest to work to provide collective benefits to relevant groups.

Political entrepreneurs work to the benefit of groups in two fundamentally distinct ways. First, they may be candidates for elective office who recognize that, even though a group may not be organized, it may nevertheless exist as a latent group and that its members might be more inclined to vote for candidates who seek to provide the group some collective benefit (Wagner 1966; Frohlich, Oppenheimer, and Young 1971; Barry 1970, pp. 37-40). Edmund Muskie and even Richard Nixon may have received some of their electoral support in the late sixties and early seventies from environmentalists who thought Muskie and Nixon would further their collective interests in various environmental policies. One may object to this explanation of latent group success in obtaining collective benefits that the group members must often be stimulated to vote at all by extrarational motivations having nothing to do with individual gain from the provision of collective benefits. Hence, narrowly rational behavior does not determine the result. This is a valid complaint against any claim that strictly self-interested behavior explains the whole outcome. But it does not undercut the argument that political entrepreneurship may lead to political action on behalf of a latent, unorganized group. More generally, it is not surprising that an admixture of individually extrarational moral behavior will produce collective benefits.

Second, they may work, just as entrepreneurial business leaders do, to found and expand organizations and to seek collective benefits for organization members in part because their own careers will be enhanced by the size and prosperity of their organizations (Frohlich, Oppenheimer, and Young 1971). On the analog of entrepreneurial business leaders, early union organizers and Nathan Smith Davis, an early and energetic organizer of the American medical profession (Berlant 1975, pp. 225-234), may have been partly motivated by their own career interests. But, as with the by-product theory, the personal career incentive may seem more suited to explaining ongoing rather than newly emerging organizations. Jimmy Hoffa owed his great power in the Teamsters Union in large part to his efforts to strengthen and expand the union, thereby enhancing the prosperity of its members. One may be less inclined to suppose that, say, Joe Hill was motivated by his own career prospects as an eventual union leader. Hoffa's efforts on behalf of the Teamster members might make rational sense independently of any extrarational concern he may have had for their well-being. In this respect, he is similar to Nixon and Muskie in their environmentalist policies, since they might sensibly have taken their stances even if they personally did not care about the issues. In the cases of both the politician and the leader of an ongoing union, action is heavily influenced by the fact that an electoral process is already organized and funded, so that neither the politician nor the union leader need pay the greater part of the costs for successful election. The later union leader's success and the leader's efforts at provision of collective benefits can plausibly be seen, however, as overwhelmingly the result of self-interest motivations by everyone concerned—the leader and the union membership—because there may be an extensive system of individual incentives to cause members to vote and the career interest might plausibly be the principal motivation of the leader.

In sum, political entrepreneurship probably helps to explain the fact that certain unorganized interests receive benefits, especially from government. Put together with the distribution of propensity to vote, it may even help to explain certain biases in government programs toward the upper middle class, as is traditionally argued. For organized groups, however, political entrepreneurship as an explanation generally suffers weaknesses similar to those of the by-product theory: it is most clearly a compelling rational explanation in the context of ongoing organizations and is not well suited to explaining the origin of many organizations that serve collective interests.

VI. PUBLIC GOODS AND COLLECTIVE ACTION

Olson bases his analysis of the logic of collective action on the notion of public goods, and much of the subsequent literature has followed his example. As it happens, however, most actual examples of collective action in the social science and philosophical literature are not concerned with goods that are public in the technical sense intended by Olson. Groups can as easily seek collective provision of ordinary private goods as of public goods. Furthermore, most of those goods which actually provoke groups to action in contemporary politics seem to be private rather than public goods. However, because so much of the collective action literature focuses on public goods and seems to assume that it is publicness that leads to collective action problems, we have included two selections here (by Samuelson and by Head) to clarify the notion of public goods, as well as one selection (by Chamberlin) with an analysis of collective action based on that notion.

The theory of public goods was almost exclusively European in its beginning, but it culminated in a few pages of notation and comments by Samuelson (reprinted in Part I) that have been the centerpiece of discussion since. Public goods are defined by two properties: jointness of supply and impossibility of exclusion. If a good is in *joint supply,* then one person's consumption of it does not reduce the amount available to anyone else. Such nonphysical goods as ideas may often plausibly be seen as joint, but it is not easy to think of physical goods that are fully joint. For example, air might historically have seemed like a good in joint supply, but it is hard to miss the fact today that, if enough people consume it in various ways, what is left available to others is drastically altered.

If a good is characterized by *impossibility of exclusion,* then it is impossible to prevent relevant people from consuming it. Again, it is not easy to think of pure cases of goods characterized by impossibility of exclusion, although one can easily think of goods from which de facto no relevant person is excluded (for example, most interstate highways in the United States are open to all legally qualified drivers and vehicles). Large bodies of law have as their purpose to erect exclusionary barriers where the naive might have thought exclusion impossible.

It is instructive to consider Samuelson's actual definition of public goods as contrasted with private consumption goods. For a private good, total consumption is the sum of individual consumptions, whereas for a public good, consumption is the same for every individual. If X is total consumption of a good, and x_i is individual i's consumption, then for a private good we have $X = \Sigma_{x_i}$, and for a public good, $x_1 = x_2 = \ldots = x_i = \ldots$ (Samuelson, ch. 9, pp. 175-176).

Conceptually, it would generally not make sense to speak of the sum of individual consumptions of a public good, unless it were a strictly physical good in de facto infinite supply, as one might have described, say, air in pre-Columbian America. One might say that Proust and his publishers offered up a public good when they published *A la recherche du temps perdu,* but one would be reluctant to claim either that the relevant public consume it in equal measure or that there is any "sum of individual consumptions" of it. It could make sense, however, to say that my consumption of it does not impair yours. Nevertheless, we may often impute a "collective value" to the collective consumption of a public good in the crude sense that a group enjoying a public good might be thought willing to pay some amount for the privilege. In this case, if the good is a *pure public good* in the sense that additional consumers do not detract at all from the consumption of previous consumers, then the value of the good is a function of the number of consumers, whereas the cost of providing the good is constant. If too few people would enjoy such a public good, it might be too costly for its "collective value."

Because it is hard to imagine pure cases of Samuelson's public goods, Mishan (1969, p. 334) ruefully comments that "we are left with the problem of reconciling ourselves to a neat definition of collective goods that is apparently inapplicable to nearly all the familiar instances of collective goods." Although it is not easy to think of examples of physically consumed pure public goods, it is easy to think of many cases of goods that seem similar to public goods over some range of the number of consumers. For example, a large swimming pool is often called a *shared good.* For most purposes, however, the finer distinctions are unnecessary. But since very few of the goals or goods that groups seek can accurately be described as pure public goods, it is probably best not to confuse the analysis of collective action by treating it as a problem in the provision of public goods.

There is a further reason for avoiding the technical issues of public goods in the analysis of collective action. Samuelson's account of public goods is concerned entirely with *consumption.* He was contributing to the theory of public finance. The issue of whether groups succeed or fail in providing themselves some collective good is rather a concern with *provision.* Their goods need to be collective only in the sense that they are collectively provided. Hence, the notion of public goods might seem irrelevant, and strictly speaking, it is. But the problem of collective provision has probably been clarified by conceiving of the goods that groups seek as public goods (although it has also often been thereby confused). Often it is technically wrong to do so except in some abstract sense. For example, unions seek better pay for their members. Clearly, more money every week for every worker is not a public good in joint supply, because one worker's wages are available to no other. But the higher *wage rate* that the union seeks might be seen as a public good if, once the rate is established, it benefits all the relevant workers, so that one worker's receipt of the higher rate does not reduce the rate available to others.

Olson's analysis of collective action depends not on jointness, but only on the impossibility of exclusion, or rather more accurately, on the de facto infeasibility of exclusion. For example, if the law says that wage rates in a factory must be uniform for each job category, nonunion workers cannot easily be excluded from enjoying the benefits of union negotiated wage increases. The central relationship between the analysis of public goods and the problem of collective action, then, is that the costliness or de facto infeasibility of exclusion from consumption of a collectively provided good commonly eliminates any direct incentive for individual consumers to pay for the good. (The issues discussed here are taken up more fully in the introductions to the selections by Samuelson, Head, and Chamberlin.)

VII. CAVEATS AND EXTENSIONS

Most of the discussion of collective action in the literature is relatively static in the following sense. Each individual faces a choice problem, each alternative of which is associated with its own costs and benefits, as in the passage from Pareto quoted previously, and this choice problem is unrelated to any other. The discussions in the selections reprinted here are almost entirely static in this sense. Social life is sometimes, but not always, captured in static analyses. In particular, many of the most interesting collective action problems are clearly dynamic in the sense that they recur or that they are ongoing. There is not a single choice, but rather, a sequence of choices to be made. Hence, each person's future choices may be contingent, indeed, may be *made* contingent on others' choices now.

The dynamic analysis of collective action has almost entirely been done either qualitatively or in the context of repeated plays of the prisoner's dilemma, or iterated prisoner's dilemma. Barry argues forcefully that much of political life is analogous to an iterated, and not to single-play, prisoner's dilemma (Barry 1965, pp. 254-255). Iterated prisoner's dilemma, which is often called the prisoner's dilemma "supergame," has been studied extensively both experimentally and analytically, especially by Rapoport and Chammah (1965), Taylor (1976), and Hardin (1982, ch. 9-13). The most striking result of iteration is that two players, who should rationally defect (that is, not cooperate) in a two-person single-play game, commonly should cooperate in iterated play. In general, in an n-person single-play prisoner's dilemma, defection is narrowly rational. In iterated play it may not be. Whether it is depends on how many others' choices are likely to be affected by one's own. As n becomes very large, it is increasingly implausible that cooperation will be narrowly rational even in iterated play. Hence, in the dynamic analysis, narrow rationality can lead to cooperation in prisoner's dilemma (or collective action), whereas in the static analysis, narrow rationality logically rules out cooperation. Still, cooperation becomes less likely as n increases in iterated play. Hence, in either analysis, the logic of collective action militates against cooperation in large enough groups.

A central issue in group theories of politics is the difference between an interest group and an organization that represents an interest, although the vocabulary of political science commonly runs the two together. The logic of collective action is not a theory about interest group organizations, rather *it is a theory of whether there will be interest group organizations or any other kind of collection action.* A group theory of politics might take interest group organizations for granted and go on from there to explain certain political outcomes. The general explanation of collective action starts from individual motivations in determining what kinds of collective actions are likely to be undertaken and what kinds are not. Hence, in the latter there is no reason to separate analysis into two substantive realms—those of groups and of group organizations. Rather, certain aspects of that split are to be explained. There is not a uniquely different motivational theory for explaining why people join political organizations. Indeed, our understanding of group politics is likely to be enhanced by the general understanding of motivations to action that is not political in the obvious sense of trying to influence government decisions.

In analyzing the internal incentives that motivate groups to action, it is necessary to know something about the cost functions to the groups for the provisions of their goods. These functions will obviously turn on, say, whether the groups have to buy their own goods or whether they can use government to force others to buy the goods. Many contemporary groups could achieve little or nothing without the help of government. But the issue of internal incentives turns not on how much the final provision costs, but on *how much a collective action that can cause such provision costs.* Some kinds of collective action are relatively cheap today because they need only be directed at influencing government. Similar actions might have been outrageously expensive in the past because government could not easily have been influenced to adopt relevant policies.

Finally, we should note that, if it is not already obvious, analyses of collective action such as those that follow are generally concerned with groups whose members share a common interest. All Americans do not comprise a group on such issues as protective tariffs, environmental regulations, civil rights policies, and so forth. Presumably, they do form a group on the issue of whether American nuclear weapons should be used to devastate American cities. It is often but not always the case that collective action is of interest to a group primarily because some other group has an ongoing interest that is being served to the detriment of the first group. Sometimes, however, as in Hume's example of the thousand neighbors who would benefit from draining a meadow (Hume, 1978, p. 538 [bk. 3, part 2, sect. 7]), there is no antagonistic interest, and nevertheless there is an obstacle to collective action: individual rationality in the pursuit of self-interest.

VIII. GUIDE TO THE READINGS

The readings in this section fall into four groups. The first includes selections by Olson and Barry that discuss the significance and nature of the logic of collective action. Olson's selection is a brief bit of the book that set off an enormous wave of work, both theoretical and applied, on collective action. Barry's selection relates Olson's theory to Downs's earlier, narrower economic theory of democracy, or rather, to the part of Downs's theory concerned with the individual's choice of whether to vote. Barry also surveys evidence for and against the narrowly economic explanation of participation in collective action. Even when the evidence weighs against the theory, it is instructive to note that our understanding is nevertheless enhanced even if merely from having a clear theory against which to analyze the relevant phenomena.

The second group of readings includes selections by Rapoport, Gauthier, Schelling, and Hardin. These are all concerned with the prisoner's dilemma. Rapoport gives an account of the history of research on the prisoner's dilemma, which he notes took off about 1965, the year in which Olson's book was published (and in which Rapoport's work with Chammah on iterated prisoner's dilemma was also published [Rapoport and Chammah 1965]). Prisoner's dilemma has since become a central model of—some would say metaphor for—social interactions of extraordinary variety in all disciplines concerned with the analysis of social problems. (As though to give evidence of the cross-disciplinary appeal of the prisoner's dilemma, these four contributions are by a mathematical biologist turned social psychologist, a philosopher, an economist, and a political scientist, in that order.) Rapoport was perhaps the major figure in stimulating prisoner's dilemma research, both in experimental settings and in application to actual contexts. In his selection, Gauthier discusses the general implications of game theoretic or economic reasoning for our notions of practical rationality and for moral theory. He finds that the prisoner's dilemma plays havoc with these.

Schelling's selection generalizes the prisoner's dilemma from the original two-person binary choice to many-person binary choice situation. They are binary choice in the sense that each person may choose either L or R (for left or right). In many of the generalized interactions that he discusses, choosing L is conspicuously equivalent to choosing to defect and R to cooperate in an ordinary prisoner's dilemma. But Schelling's generalization is concerned not with the specific nature of the choices so much as with the nature of the possible outcomes of the combined choices. That is to say, he generalizes the defining conditions for prisoner's dilemma roughly in the following way: An interaction is a (binary choice) MPD (multiperson prisoner's dilemma) if in it there is an optimal outcome that will not be reached by individually rational choices, and if *all* people involved in the interaction would prefer to achieve the optimal outcome rather than the outcome resulting from individually self-interested choices. Clearly, this condition could fit even situations in which the optimal outcome occurs when not everyone makes the same choice. Hence, the "cooperative" outcome might involve having some choose L and some choose R.

In his selection, Hardin demonstrates the equivalence of the logic underlying the prisoner's dilemma and Olson's logic of collective action. The demonstration is not particularly difficult. Given this equivalence, not only in the simplest form of the problem, but also in more generalized forms such as Schelling's, we can bring together evidence from remarkably varied contexts to test the logic of their interactions.

The third group of readings includes selections by Baumol and Hirsch. These authors are concerned with the wider implications of problematic social interactions for the kind of society such interactions bring about. Baumol discusses the conflict between individual interests and collective interests and the relevance of the conflict to welfare economics. Much of welfare economics takes for granted that individually rational choices will produce Pareto-optimal outcomes, that is, outcomes in which no one can be made better off without making someone else worse off. Anyone who has grasped the logic of the prisoner's dilemma or of collective action must reject any such assumption—hence, in Baumol's words, the wreck of welfare economics. Hirsch discusses a host of interaction problems that arise especially in an affluent society. Many of these problems are more thoroughly interactions of conflict than of potential cooperation, but many of them have prisoner's dilemma characteristics.

The final group of readings includes selections by Samuelson, Head, and Chamberlin, all of which are concerned with public goods. Given the nature of public goods one might suppose that they must be provided through some kind of collective action (including state action) rather than through narrowly self-interested individual action. Indeed, it was a recognition of vaguely public-good characteristics of certain goods that contributed to early development of an economic theory of the state. (Various writings on the economic theory of the state are surveyed by Baumol in part of his book not reprinted here [Baumol 1952, ch. 12].) In its more modern guise, economic concern with the theory of the state has turned to concern with the theory of public finance. Samuelson argues (partly by implication—note the title of his selection here) that the latter is essentially the problem of the provision of public goods. Head then tries to set straight the general conception of public goods. Finally, Chamberlin shows that Olson's argument for the logic of collective action is largely flawed to the extent that it relies on the notion of public goods. If collective action is motivated, as Olson implies in the final paragraph of his selection (and more extensively in parts of his book not reprinted here), primarily by the desire for purely public goods, then the failure or success of groups is not a function of their size as Olson's theory asserts it is. One can infer from Chamberlin's demonstration and from the nature of the prisoner's dilemma more generally that the problem of collective action does not depend on group demand for pure public goods in Samuelson's sense.

NOTE

1. This discussion borrows from Hardin (1982, ch. 1, 2, and 3).

1 • Introduction

The following selection is a small part of *The Logic of Collective Action* by Mancur Olson, Jr. The book has become a classic and should be read whole by anyone serious enough to be reading the present book. It is an unusual bit of social theory in its combinations of brevity and sweep and of theory and applications. Olson lays out the logic of collective action, deduces several implications of his logic, goes on to apply his general and remarkably simple theory to numerous categories of interest group activity and (more importantly) inactivity, and then proposes his by-product theory to explain the actual workings of the admittedly commonplace extant interest group organizations, organizations that one might have thought should not exist if his theory were correct.

It is not possible to do justice to such a work with a brief selection. We have, however, selected passages from Olson's introductory remarks to give some sense of just how sweeping his claims are. Despite its vast implications, Olson's argument has been so persuasive that the title of his book has become a standard part of the vocabulary of social theorists. Nevertheless, economists tend to find it more persuasive than do political scientists and we will here address the question of why this might be the case.

Olson is an economist and he tends to find evidence for and analogies to his theory in examples drawn from economic contexts. One of the most persuasive claims he makes for his theory is that it is little more than a generalization of a principle which is taken for granted by economists and which lies at the heart of economic theory at least since the time of Adam Smith. This principle (discussed in the opening section of our introduction to this section of readings) is that markets are efficient when the number of sellers in them is large enough to prevent collusion. A thousand wheat farmers independently striving to prosper will have to sell their grain at the price that clears the market—or it will rot in their hands. With large numbers of sellers prices will be minimized. Why? Because no seller will be able to get away with setting a higher price with so many others around to sell lower. But this argument depends on the expectation that the sellers will not get together and agree to force prices up. (If they did, the market would not clear and some grain would be left over. But the rise in prices would commonly more than offset the fall in demand, so that farmers would actually increase their incomes despite the leftover wheat.) That expectation is widely taken for granted in any industry that is not an oligopoly—that is, in any industry in which the number of firms is relatively large. *If that expectation were generally false,* market economics would not likely have come to be the highly articulated theoretical enterprise it is. Therefore, to persuade an economist that the logic that underlies market theory is the logic that underlies group action far more generally is to convince the economist of the theoretical power of the logic of collective action.

   To convince political scientists of that power has been much harder for the simple reason that political science has no powerful central doctrines to which the logic of collective action could be persuasively related. Indeed, political science has no powerful central doctrines at all. Worse still, one of its more widely accepted doctrines—the group theory of politics—was based on an unarticulated presumption that is contradicted by Olson's theory: that a group of people with a common interest will take action to further that interest. This presumption is probably an instance of the fallacy of composition:

> We are committing the fallacy of composition when we argue from the premise that every man can decide how he will act to the conclusion that the human race can decide how it will act (for example, with regard to the rate of increase of population or the choice between war and peace). . . . This, or a similar fallacy, is committed whenever we assume, without adequate reason, that we can speak about groups in the same ways in which we can speak about their members, that we can speak of a nation having a will or interests. . . . Of course, it may be possible to do this; there may be predicates applicable (in the same sense) to a group and to its members, but this cannot be assumed without evidence [Mackie 1967, p. 173].

Virtually everyone seems too ready to assume that if an action is in the collective interest of a group and if the members of the group are rational, then the group must be (in the same sense) collectively rational, which is to say that the group must act in its interest just as each of its rational members would do (see further, our Epilogue). An understanding of Olson's logic and of the prisoner's dilemma should block this fallacious conclusion.

   But this is not the whole of the difference between economists and political scientists in their grasping of Olson's logic. Against Olson's analogy of the general problem of collective action with the argument that underlies claims of market efficiency when the number of sellers is large, note the following significant differences between a group of sellers in a market on the one hand, and typical political interest groups on the other. Suppose there are not even very many sellers, say only ten. If nine of them agree to hold prices high and to divide the market among themselves, the tenth may wreck their effort by underpricing them and seizing a large part of their market. Even if all ten successfully collude, a new firm may be enticed into their market and might easily wreck their collusive effort. Hence, successful collusion in a market *even with a small number of sellers* may require virtually one hundred percent cooperation by all sellers and still it may fail simply because its success will attract new sellers.

Cooperation among the members of an interest group is not commonly so prohibitively difficult as among these sellers. Cooperation by ten percent or even one percent of the members may be sufficient to secure desired collective benefits. There are at least two important, interrelated reasons for the difference. First, and perhaps most obvious, is the relative lack of internal competitiveness in a typical interest group. I may wish to free-ride on the efforts of other group members, but I will not have incentive to take further advantage of them. As a seller, however, I may not merely free-ride on the higher prices and therefore, on the higher profits made possible by the collusion of my "colleagues"; I will also have incentive to increase my production and to go after the colluders' market shares. It is this aggressive action that destroys cartels. If other firms in my industry seek a tax break for the industry, I may benefit from their effort even though I do not contribute to their political campaign for the tax break. But there is no meaningful sense in which I am further enabled to take self-seeking aggressive action against them because of their lobbying success.

The second difference is that, because the actual cost of securing the interest group's collective benefit may be *very* small compared to the size of the benefit, a very small percentage of the group's members may be able to gain enough from providing it to justify their bearing the full cost. No small percentage of wheat farmers can affect the price of wheat nor, if they are all of comparable size, could any few of our ten sellers long affect the price of their goods in the market. The political expenditures of all interest groups in all of American history, however, are dwarfed by the scale of many of the benefits lavished upon them by the American government for their politicking. For example, milk producers contributed a mere $300,000 to Nixon's 1972 reelection campaign in return for his administration's increasing price supports for milk by 26 cents per hundredweight. According to a New York *Times* account, "that meant $500 million to $700 million more for dairy farmers in the *new marketing year*" alone (Frohlich and Oppenheimer 1978, p. 40, emphasis added). If a handful of the largest Wisconsin dairy farmers had gotten together to make this $300,000 donation, they would have gotten their money back with a large bonus. And this involves only milk.

With such opportunities available, trying to organize a cartel is a poor use of energy.

In sum, there is a significant difference between the problems faced by cartels and those faced by typical interest groups: cartels have a much harder problem and should be expected to fail even more than interest groups should. Yet even cartels occasionally succeed—the enduring success of the Organization of Petroleum Exporting Countries (OPEC) has surprised many economists.[1] Similarly, interest groups succeed remarkably often given Olson's thesis, and much of the success does not seem to fit either the by-product theory or the theory of political entrepreneurship (both discussed in our general introduction to this section of readings). Hence, political scientists are accustomed to seeing interest groups succeed and therefore often do not know how to respond to a theory that says such groups must generally fail. Nevertheless, Olson is clearly right to demolish "reasoning" from the fallacy of composition in this realm. One who wishes to understand how a particular group succeeds in cooperative action for collective benefit can no longer merely assume that the *group's* success is rationally motivated in the sense that *individual* actions can be rationally motivated.

This selection should present no technical difficulties to the reader. However, note that Olson's final remarks seem to imply that collective action is principally concerned with public goods. This is generally not true. One should therefore read his term "collective goods" as meaning simply "goods which are collectively sought or provided." (See further our introduction to the selection by Head and our general introduction to this section of readings.)

NOTE

---

1. There is a significant difference between OPEC and most other cartels which may explain its success and the consequent annoyance of many economists. An OPEC member that reduces its price to capture a larger part of the market may earn more in the short run, but in the long run its supply of oil underground will be exhausted sooner as a result. Hence, the producer would not merely be undercutting the OPEC cartel, it would also be undercutting its own future earnings. The sense in which an oil producer can "increase" its production is quite different from the sense in which a manufacturing firm or a wheat farm can increase its production.

1

THE LOGIC OF COLLECTIVE ACTION

Mancur Olson, Jr.

I. INTRODUCTION

It is often taken for granted, at least where economic objectives are involved, that groups of individuals with common interests usually attempt to further those common interests. Groups of individuals with common interests are expected to act on behalf of their common interests much as single individuals are often expected to act on behalf of their personal interests. This opinion about group behavior is frequently found not only in popular discussions but also in scholarly writings. Many economists of diverse methodological and ideological traditions have implicitly or explicitly accepted it. This view has, for example, been important in many theories of labor unions, in Marxian theories of class action, in concepts of "countervailing power," and in various discussions of economic institutions. It has, in addition, occupied a prominent place in political science, at least in the United States, where the study of pressure groups has been dominated by a celebrated "group theory" based on the idea that groups will act when necessary to further their common or group goals. Finally, it has played a significant role in many well-known sociological studies.

The view that groups act to serve their interests presumably is based upon the assumption that the individuals in groups act out of self-interest. If the individuals in a group altruistically disregarded their personal welfare, it would not be very likely that collectively they would seek some selfish

Reprinted by permission of the author and publishers from *The Logic of Collective Action* by Mancur Olson, Jr., Cambridge, Mass.: Harvard University Press, Copyright © 1965, 1971 by the President and Fellows of Harvard College.

common or group objective. Such altruism, is, however, considered exceptional, and self-interested behavior is usually thought to be the rule, at least
when economic issues are at stake; no one is surprised when individual
businessmen seek higher profits, when individual workers seek higher wages,
or when individual consumers seek lower prices. The idea that groups tend to
act in support of their group interests is supposed to follow logically from
this widely accepted premise of rational, self-interested behavior. In other
words, if the members of some group have a common interest or objective,
and if they would all be better off if that objective were achieved, it has been
thought to follow logically that the individuals in that group would, if they
were rational and self-interested, act to achieve that objective.

But it is *not* in fact true that the idea that groups will act in their
self-interest follows logically from the premise of rational and self-interested
behavior. It does *not* follow, because all of the individuals in a group would
gain if they achieved their group objective, that they would act to achieve
that objective, even if they were all rational and self-interested. Indeed, unless
the number of individuals in a group is quite small, or unless there is coercion
or some other special device to make individuals act in their common interest,
*rational, self-interested individuals will not act to achieve their common or
group interests.* In other words, even if all of the individuals in a large group
are rational and self-interested, and would gain if, as a group, they acted to
achieve their common interest or objective, they will still not voluntarily act
to achieve that common or group interest. The notion that groups of
individuals will act to achieve their common or group interests, far from being
a logical implication of the assumption that the individuals in a group will
rationally further their individual interests, is in fact inconsistent with that
assumption. This inconsistency will be explained [shortly].

If the members of a large group rationally seek to maximize their personal
welfare, they will *not* act to advance their common or group objectives unless
there is coercion to force them to do so, or unless some separate incentive,
distinct from the achievement of the common or group interest, is offered to
the members of the group individually on the condition that they help bear
the costs or burdens involved in the achievement of the group objectives. Nor
will such large groups form organizations to further their common goals in
the absence of the coercion or the separate incentives just mentioned. These
points hold true even when there is unanimous agreement in a group about
the common good and the methods of achieving it.

The widespread view, common throughout the social sciences, that groups
tend to further their interests, is accordingly unjustified, at least when it is
based, as it usually is, on the (sometimes implicit) assumption that groups act
in their self-interest because individuals do. There is paradoxically the logical
possibility that groups composed of either altruistic individuals or irrational
individuals may sometimes act in their common or group interests. But, as

later, empirical parts of this study will attempt to show, this logical possibility is usually of no practical importance. Thus the customary view that groups of individuals with common interests tend to further those common interests appears to have little if any merit.

None of the statements made above fully applies to small groups, for the situation in small groups is much more complicated. In small groups there may very well be some voluntary action in support of the common purposes of the individuals in the group, but in most cases this action will cease before it reaches the optimal level for the members of the group as a whole. In the sharing of the costs of efforts to achieve a common goal in small groups, there is however a surprising tendency for the "exploitation" of the *great* by the *small.*

II. PUBLIC GOODS AND LARGE GROUPS

The combination of individual interests and common interests in an organization suggests an analogy with a competitive market. The firms in a perfectly competitive industry, for example, have a common interest in a higher price for the industry's product. Since a uniform price must prevail in such a market, a firm cannot expect a higher price for itself unless all of the other firms in the industry also have this higher price. But a firm in a competitive market also has an interest in selling as much as it can, until the cost of producing another unit exceeds the price of that unit. In this there is no common interest; each firm's interest is directly opposed to that of every other firm, for the more other firms sell, the lower the price and income for any given firm. In short, while all firms have a common interest in a higher price, they have antagonistic interests where output is concerned. This can be illustrated with a simple supply-and-demand model. For the sake of a simple argument, assume that a perfectly competitive industry is momentarily in a disequilibrium position, with price exceeding marginal cost for all firms at their present output. Suppose, too, that all of the adjustments will be made by the firms already in the industry rather than by new entrants, and that the industry is on an inelastic portion of its demand curve. Since price exceeds marginal cost for all firms, output will increase. But as all firms increase production, the price falls; indeed, since the industry demand curve is by assumption inelastic, the total revenue of the industry will decline. Apparently each firm finds that with price exceeding marginal cost, it pays to increase its output, but the result is that each firm gets a smaller profit. Some economists in an earlier day may have questioned this result,[1] but the fact that profit-maximizing firms in a perfectly competitive industry can act contrary to their interests as a group is now widely understood and accepted.[2] A group of profit-maximizing firms can act to reduce their aggregate profits because in perfect competition each firm is, by definition, so small that it can ignore the effect of its output on price. Each firm finds it to its advantage to increase output to the point where marginal cost equals price and to ignore the effects of its extra output on the position of the industry. It is true that the net result is that all firms are worse off, but this does not mean that every firm has not maximized its profits. If a firm, foreseeing the fall in price resulting from the increase in industry output, were to restrict its own output, it would lose more than ever, for its price would fall quite as much in any case and it would have a smaller output as well. A firm in a perfectly competitive market gets only a small part of the benefit (or a small share of the industry's extra revenue) resulting from a reduction in that firm's output.

For these reasons it is now generally understood that if the firms in an industry are maximizing profits, the profits for the industry as a whole will be less than they might otherwise be.[3] And almost everyone would agree that this theoretical conclusion fits the facts for markets characterized by pure competition. The important point is that this is true because, though all the firms have a common interest in a higher price for the industry's product, it is in the interest of each firm that the other firms pay the cost—in terms of the necessary reduction in output—needed to obtain a higher price.

About the only thing that keeps prices from falling in accordance with the process just described in perfectly competitive markets is outside intervention. Government price supports, tariffs, cartel agreements, and the like may keep the firms in a competitive market from acting contrary to their interests. Such aid or intervention is quite common. It is then important to ask how it comes about. How does a competitive industry obtain government assistance in maintaining the price of its product?

Consider a hypothetical, competitive industry, and suppose that most of the producers in that industry desire a tariff, a price-support program, or some other government intervention to increase the price for their product. To obtain any such assistance from the government, the producers in this industry will presumably have to organize a lobbying organization; they will have to become an active pressure group.[4] This lobbying organization may have to conduct a considerable campaign. If significant resistance is encountered, a great amount of money will be required.[5] Public relations experts will be needed to influence the newspapers, and some advertising may be necessary. Professional organizers will probably be needed to organize "spontaneous grass roots" meetings among the distressed producers in the industry, and to get those in the industry to write letters to their congressmen.[6] The campaign for the government assistance will take the time of some of the producers in the industry, as well as their money.

There is a striking parallel between the problem the perfectly competitive industry faces as it strives to obtain government assistance, and the problem it faces in the marketplace when the firms increase output and bring about a fall in price. *Just as it was not rational for a particular producer to restrict his output in order that there might be a higher price for the product of his industry, so it would not be rational for him to sacrifice his time and money to support a lobbying organization to obtain government assistance for the industry. In neither case would it be in the interest of the individual producer to assume any of the costs himself. A lobbying organization, or indeed a labor union or any other organization, working in the interest of a large group of firms or workers in some industry, would get no assistance from the rational, self-interested individuals in that industry.* This would be true even if everyone in the industry were absolutely convinced that the proposed program was in their interest (though in fact some might think otherwise and make the organization's task yet more difficult).

Although the lobbying organization is only one example of the logical analogy between the organization and the market, it is of some practical importance. There are many powerful and well-financed lobbies with mass support in existence now, but these lobbying organizations do not get that support because of their legislative achievements. The most powerful lobbying organizations now obtain their funds and their following for other reasons, as later parts of this study will show.

Some critics may argue that the rational person will, indeed, support a large organization, like a lobbying organization, that works in his interest, because he knows that if he does not, others will not do so either, and then the organization will fail, and he will be without the benefit that the organization could have provided. This argument shows the need for the analogy with the perfectly competitive market. For it would be quite as reasonable to argue that prices will never fall below the levels a monopoly would have charged in a perfectly competitive market, because if one firm increased its output, other firms would also, and the price would fall; but each firm could foresee this, so it would not start a chain of price-destroying increases in output. In fact, it does not work out this way in a competitive market; nor in a large organization. When the number of firms involved is large, no one will notice the effect on price if one firm increases its output, and so no one will change his plans because of it. Similarly, in a large organization, the loss of one dues payer will not noticeably increase the burden for any other one dues payer, and so a rational person would not believe that if he were to withdraw from an organization he would drive others to do so.

The foregoing argument must at the least have some relevance to economic organizations that are mainly means through which individuals attempt to obtain the same things they obtain through their activities in the market. Labor unions, for example, are organizations through which workers strive to get the same things they get with their individual efforts in the market—higher wages, better working conditions, and the like. It would be strange indeed if the workers did not confront some of the same problems in the union that they meet in the market, since their efforts in both places have some of the same purposes.

However similar the purposes may be, critics may object that attitudes in organizations are not at all like those in markets. In organizations, an emotional or ideological element is often also involved. Does this make the argument offered here practically irrelevant?

A most important type of organization—the national state—will serve to test this objection. Patriotism is probably the strongest noneconomic motive for organizational allegiance in modern times. This age is sometimes called the age of nationalism. Many nations draw additional strength and unity from some powerful ideology, such as democracy or communism, as well as from a common religion, language, or cultural inheritance. The state not only has many such powerful sources of support; it also is very important economically. Almost any government is economically beneficial to its citizens, in that the law and order it provides is a prerequisite of all civilized economic activity. But despite the force of patriotism, the appeal of the national ideology, the bond of a common culture, and the indispensability of the system of law and order, no major state in modern history has been able to support itself through voluntary dues or contributions. Philanthropic contributions are not even a significant source of revenue for most countries. Taxes, *compulsory* payments by definition, are needed. Indeed, as the old saying indicates, their necessity is as certain as death itself.

If the state, with all of the emotional resources at its command, cannot finance its most basic and vital activities without resort to compulsion, it would seem that large private organizations might also have difficulty in getting the individuals in the groups whose interests they attempt to advance to make the necessary contributions voluntarily.[7]

The reason the state cannot survive on voluntary dues or payments, but must rely on taxation, is that the most fundamental services a nation-state provides are, in one important respect, like the higher price in a competitive market: they must be available to everyone if they are available to anyone. The basic and most elementary goods or services provided by government, like defense and police protection, and the system of law and order generally, are such that they go to everyone or practically everyone in the nation. It would obviously not be feasible, if indeed it were possible, to deny the protection provided by the military services, the police, and the courts to those who did not voluntarily pay their share of the costs of government, and taxation is accordingly necessary. The common or collective benefits provided by governments are usually called "public goods" by economists, and the concept of public goods is one of the oldest and most important ideas in the study of public finance. A common, collective, or public good is here defined as any good such that, if any person X_i in a group $X_1, \ldots, X_i, \ldots, X_n$ consumes it, it cannot feasibly be withheld from the others in that group. In other words, those who do not purchase or pay for any of the public or collective good cannot be excluded or kept from sharing in the consumption of the good, as they can where noncollective goods are concerned.

Students of public finance have, however, neglected the fact that *the achievement of any common goal or the satisfaction of any common interest means that a public or collective good has been provided for that group.*[8] The very fact that a goal or purpose is *common* to a group means that no one in the group is excluded from the benefit or satisfaction brought about by its achievement. As the opening paragraphs of this chapter indicated, almost all groups and organizations have the purpose of serving the common interests of their members. As R. M. MacIver puts it, "Persons . . . have common interests in the degree to which they participate in a cause . . . which indivisibly embraces them all."[9] It is of the essence of an organization that it provides an inseparable, generalized benefit. It follows that the provision of public or collective goods is the fundamental function of organizations generally. A state is first of all an organization that provides public goods for its members, the citizens; and other types of organizations similarly provide collective goods for their members.

And just as a state cannot support itself by voluntary contributions, or by selling its basic services on the market, neither can other large organizations support themselves without providing some sanction, or some attraction distinct from the public good itself, that will lead individuals to help bear the burdens of maintaining the organization. The individual member of the typical large organization is in a position analogous to that of the firm in a perfectly competitive market, or the taxpayer in the state: his own efforts will not have a noticeable effect on the situation of his organization, and he can enjoy any improvements brought about by others whether or not he has worked in support of his organization.

There is no suggestion here that states or other organizations provide *only* public or collective goods. Governments often provide noncollective goods like electric power, for example, and they usually sell such goods on the market much as private firms would do. Moreover, as later parts of this study will argue, large organizations that are not able to make membership compulsory *must also* provide some noncollective goods in order to give potential members an incentive to join. Still, collective goods are the characteristic organizational goods, for ordinary noncollective goods can always be provided by individual action, and only where common purposes or collective goods are concerned is organization or group action ever indispensable.

NOTES

1. See J. M. Clark, *The Economics of Overhead Costs* (Chicago: University of Chicago Press, 1923), p. 417, and Frank H. Knight, *Risk, Uncertainty and Profit* (Boston: Houghton Mifflin, 1921), p. 193.

2. Edward H. Chamberlin, *Monopolistic Competition,* 6th ed. (Cambridge, Mass.: Harvard University Press, 1950), p. 4.

3. For a fuller discussion of this question see Mancur Olson, Jr., and David McFarland, "The Restoration of Pure Monopoly and the Concept of the Industry," *Quarterly Journal of Economics,* LXXVI (November 1962), 613-631.

4. Robert Michels contends in his classic study that "democracy is inconceivable without organization," and that "the principle of organization is an absolutely essential condition for the political struggle of the masses." See his *Political Parties,* trans. Eden and Cedar Paul (New York: Dover Publications, 1959), pp. 21-22. See also Robert A. Brady, *Business as a System of Power* (New York: Columbia University Press, 1943), p. 193.

5. Alexander Heard, *The Costs of Democracy* (Chapel Hill: University of North Carolina Press, 1960), especially note 1, pp. 95-96. For example, in 1947 the National Association of Manufacturers spent over $4.6 million, and over a somewhat longer period the American Medical Association spent as much on a campaign against compulsory health insurance.

6. "If the full truth were ever known . . . lobbying, in all its ramifications, would prove to be a billion dollar industry." U.S. Congress, House, Select Committee on Lobbying Activities, *Report,* 81st Cong., 2nd Sess. (1950), as quoted in the *Congressional Quarterly Almanac,* 81st Cong., 2nd Sess., VI, 764-765.

7. Sociologists as well as economists have observed that ideological motives alone are not sufficient to bring forth the continuing effort of large masses of people. Max Weber provides a notable example. "All economic activity in a market economy is undertaken and carried through by individuals for their own ideal or material interests. This is naturally just as true when economic activity is oriented to the patterns of order of corporate groups. . . . Even if an economic system were organized on a socialistic basis, there would be no fundamental difference in this respect. . . . The structure of interests and the relevant situation might change; there would be other means of pursuing interests, but this fundamental factor would remain just as relevant as before. It is of course true that economic action which is oriented on purely ideological grounds to the interest of others does exist. But it is even more certain that the mass of men do not act in this way, and it is an induction from experience that they cannot do so and never will. . . . In a market economy the interest in the maximization of income is necessarily the driving force of all economic activity." (Weber [1947], pp. 319-320.) Talcott Parsons and Neil Smelser go even further in postulating that "performance" throughout society is proportional to the "rewards" and "sanctions" involved. See their *Economy and Society* (Glencoe, Ill.: Free Press, 1956), pp. 50-69.

8. There is no necessity that a public good to one group in a society is necessarily in the interest of the society as a whole. Just as a tariff could be a public good to the industry that sought it, so the removal of the tariff could be a public good to those who consumed the industry's product. This is equally true when the public-good concept is applied only to governments; for a military expenditure, or a tariff, or an immigration restriction that is a public good to one country could be a "public bad" to another country, and harmful to world society as a whole.

9. R. M. MacIver [1932], in *Encyclopaedia of the Social Sciences,* VII, 147.

2 • Introduction

The following selection is most of the second chapter of Brian Barry's *Sociologists, Economists and Democracy*. That book is a critical survey of economic and sociological theories of democracy. In the selection here Barry presents the central arguments of Anthony Downs's "economic theory of democracy" (1957) and of Mancur Olson's "logic of collective action" (1965). As he makes clear, part of Downs's argument—his analysis of the voter's decision whether to vote—is a special case of Olson's problem of voluntary contribution to a collective action. In both, the central calculation is of the benefits to the contributor (or voter) *from the contributor's own contribution alone* minus the cost of making that contribution. If the result of this subtraction is negative, one should not contribute if one is narrowly self-interested. When the number of other contributors or voters is large, the chance that my contribution or vote will make enough difference for the overall outcome to matter to me may be vanishingly small. Hence, if the cost of my contribution or the burden of my going to vote is at all significant, I am better off if I do not contribute or vote. This logic is relatively easy to grasp in the case of national elections in which one cannot expect one's vote to have more than a minuscule probability of affecting the outcome. It may be less obvious in the context of other kinds of collective action that interest various groups. That the logic of such situations is general, however, becomes clearer the more carefully one considers them, as Barry's carefully explicated examples help to show.

In addition to explaining the logic of Downs's and Olson's arguments, Barry goes on to criticize the fit of the theories with the facts of actual behavior in various contexts. One of the most glaring of the facts is that, contrary to the Downs-Olson logic, millions of people vote in national elections in many nations in which voting appears to be strictly voluntary. On the other hand, of course, other millions do not vote. Downs's theory perhaps explains the behavior of the millions who do not vote, but it leaves an uncomfortably large residual of unexplained behavior. Similarly, Olson's more general theory seems not to fit all the facts although he can argue, consistently with that theory, that much of the residual of cooperative behavior is motivated not by what individuals expect to gain from their groups' collective goods, but by what they get in individually targeted selective benefits in return for their cooperation. Even granting the role of selective incentives, actual behavior often appears inconsistent with the assumptions of the economic theory of participation, as Barry's examples amply suggest. Nevertheless, as Barry concludes, Olson's theory fits the gross pattern of effective political organization over the long run.

Finally, Barry criticizes a peculiar misuse to which economic explanations of behavior are often subject. Motivations of altruism, guilt, fairness, and so forth, are simply added into the black and red columns of benefits and costs to yield a supposedly "economic" analysis of behavior. One of the weaknesses of such analyses is that they are generally framed entirely at a speculative level without any credible measures of the additional motivations (e.g., Riker and Ordeshook 1968; Mitchell 1979; Moe 1980). It is a strength of Olson's analysis that the principal costs of participating in a group action and the principal benefits from provision of the group's good are often specifiable with substantial accuracy. This is less true of Olson's selective benefits but even for these, we often have a clear sense of their relative weight. Unfortunately, whenever various costs and benefits are in different units (of money, time, cleaner air, psychological well-being), the simple additive calculus of Olson's logic ceases to represent the nature of choice. I can subtract your dollar of cost (e.g., in union dues) from your expected dollar gains (in increased wages), discounting the latter by the (generally low) probability that it depends on *your* costs, with relative ease and confidence. I cannot subtract your dollars plus your time in costs from your psychological well-being from doing good plus your increment of cleaner air in benefits with any confidence. Indeed, such a subtraction is likely to be wrong-headed because these costs and benefits cannot be traded off in linearly additive fashion. This is not to say that these other considerations cannot enter into normal decisions—clearly they can and do. But qualitative accounts of their roles are likely to be more informative than any supposed addition and subtraction of some ill-defined units of them. Many proponents of theoretical extensions of Downs and Olson argue from common sense that these other considerations matter; they then violate common sense by simplistically joining them additively together, and conclude from their speculative equations that they have shown that behavior is after all economically rational, even narrowly self-interested.

This selection should present no technical difficulties for the reader.

2

POLITICAL PARTICIPATION
AS RATIONAL ACTION

Brian Barry

I. THE DECISION TO VOTE: DOWNS AND RIKER

[In his *An Economic Theory of Democracy* (1957) Anthony] Downs con-
structs a theory of politics in which there are, basically, only two kinds of
actor. There are the parties, and there are the voters. The internal processes of
the parties are abstracted from by the assumption that they consist of
single-minded teams, and a further assumption is that they are dedicated to
only one object, namely winning elections. 'The politicians in our model
never seek office as a means of carrying out particular policies; their only goal
is to reap the rewards of holding office *per se*' (Downs 1957, p. 28). There is
a clear analogy with the conception of the profit-maximising entrepreneur of
classical economic theory. The voters correspond to the consumers. But,
whereas there is not much point in asking why consumers do *anything* with
their money (as against throwing it away), it is a perfectly serious question
why voters should use their vote. For one has to make some effort in order to
cast a vote, yet what is the benefit to be derived from so doing? If we wish to
apply an 'economic' analysis, an obvious line to take is that with which
Downs begins: the value of voting is the value of the expected effect it would
have in changing what would otherwise happen.

But what are the components of this calculation? When there are only two parties, the matter is fairly simple. The citizen faced with the question whether it is worth voting or not first computes his 'party differential', that is, how much better off he would be (not necessarily in purely financial terms) if his preferred party won the election, and he then multiplies it by the probability that his vote for that party will change the result of the election so that his party wins instead of losing. Obviously, this means that he has to reckon the probability of the election's turning on a single vote, and in an electorate of millions this probability is so small that the value of voting will be infinitesimal, even for someone who has a large party differential. Thus, it seems to follow that rational citizens would not vote if there are costs involved—and it always takes time and energy to cast a vote. But in fact it is notorious that many people do vote. Even low turnouts of, say, 25% are, on this analysis, clearly inconsistent with rationality.

In a recent article, Riker has criticised Downs as if this were his last word on the subject. He says that 'it is certainly no explanation to assign a sizeable part of politics to the mysterious and inexplicable world of the irrational' (Riker and Ordeshook 1968, p. 25). And he then proposes an amendment to the theory. But the 'amendment' is in essence the same as one put forward by Downs himself, though Downs describes it as a factor increasing the reward of voting and Riker counts it as a reduction of the cost. Riker says that this reward consists of satisfactions such as 'compliance with the ethic of voting', 'affirming allegiance to the political system', 'affirming a partisan preference', 'deciding, going to the polls etc.', and 'affirming one's efficacy in the political system' (Riker and Ordeshook 1968, p. 28).

Now it may well be true that much voting can be accounted for in this way, and one can of course formally fit it into an 'economic' framework by saying that people get certain 'rewards' from voting. But this *is* purely formal. And it forces us to ask what really is the point and value of the whole 'economic' approach. It is no trick to restate all behaviour in terms of 'rewards' and 'costs'; it may for some purposes be a useful conceptual device, but it does not in itself provide anything more than a set of empty boxes waiting to be filled. The power of the 'economic' method is that, in appropriate kinds of situation, it enables us, operating with simple premises concerning rational behaviour, to deduce by logic and mathematics interesting conclusions about what will happen. Whether a situation is 'appropriate' or not depends on the extent to which other factors can safely be ignored.

Thus, the classical model of 'competitive equilibrium' in a market does approximate what happens in various 'real world' situations especially where profit-maximising traders make a living by dealing in some homogeneous commodity. But in a situation where, for example, all the participants believe in a 'just price' which is independent of supply and demand, the 'competitive equilibrium' model of price-determination will have no application. Again, we can bring this formally within the 'economic' framework by saying that the people get 'satisfaction' from keeping to the 'just price', or we can simply say that they are maximising subject to a constraint'. (Government controls are often dealt with in this way in economic analysis.) But neither of these devices helps very much. The point is that explanatory attention must shift to the question how people came to believe in a 'just price', how the belief is transmitted and maintained, and what determines the level of price which is believed right for each commodity. In other words, there are no interesting deductions to be drawn from the interaction of given 'tastes' in a market; the price can simply be read off from the universal 'taste' for a certain price. The question is how that taste arises, and this is a question that cannot be answered within the 'economic' framework.

II. THE BASIC LOGIC OF OLSON'S THEORY

We have examined a two-sector model (political entrepreneurs and ordinary citizens) in connection with a specific form of political activity, voting. We shall now move to an assumption of one sector, in other words an undifferentiated population. [...] We shall also leave for the present the relatively trivial action (from the point of view of the ordinary citizen's psychic economy) of casting a vote in an election and consider more costly activities, in time and money, such as contributing money or energy to an organization devoted to altering the state policy on some matters. We shall take this up by following the argument of *The Logic of Collective Action* by Mancur Olson, Jr. (1965). This is the only book fit to rank with Downs' *Economic Theory of Democracy*, as an exemplar of the virtues of the 'economic' approach to political analysis. Both books, as may be expected in pioneering works, suffer from obscurities and ambiguities which become apparent on close examination. But it is greatly to their advantage that, unlike so many books on political and sociological theory, they stimulate and repay this degree of careful attention.

The discussion so far will enable us to present Olson's central point very quickly, for it is essentially a generalization of the idea that the reward of voting (in rational 'economic' terms) is the party differential times the probability that one vote will alter the outcome of the election. Olson's argument is intended to apply wherever what is at stake is a 'public good', that is, a benefit which cannot be deliberately restricted to certain people, such as those who helped bring it into existence. A potential beneficiary's calculation, when deciding whether to contribute to the provision of such a benefit, must take the form of seeing what the benefit would be to him and discounting it by the probability that his contribution would make the difference between the provision and the non-provision of the benefit. Where there are large numbers of potential beneficiaries, and especially when none of them stands to gain a lot, Olson argues that the total contribution made to the provision of the benefit will be much less than it would be if the beneficiaries were all rolled into one person who did the best possible for himself. In many cases, he suggests, there will simply be no contributions at all.

An excellent example of a 'public good' is a state policy—for instance, a particular piece of legislation on tariffs or the labelling of consumer goods. Someone who stands to be benefited by this legislation will not automatically be advantaged by paying to support a lobby in its favour. He has to ask not whether an extra pound spent on campaigning will bring in more than a pound's worth of benefit to the potential beneficiaries taken all together, but whether an extra pound contributed by him will bring in more than a pound's worth of benefit to him. And on this basis he often will not contribute. He will not reason: 'If everyone fails to contribute, we'll all be worse off than if we all contribute, so I'll contribute'. For whether all, some or none of the others contribute will not be affected by whether or not he does, and it is therefore irrelevant to ask what would happen if they all acted on the same principle as himself.

Of course, where the beneficiaries form a small group in close contact with one another, the assumption that the decisions are independent of one another cannot be upheld. The members of the group can say to one another 'I won't contribute unless everyone else does', and, by making mutual threats of this kind, get the rate of contributions above what it would otherwise be. Even in quite small groups, however, this round of threats may be pretty hollow if some of the potential beneficiaries obviously could not afford *not* to contribute because they stand to gain so much. So the basic logic of self-interest may still show through. Thus, Olson has argued (Olson and Zeckhauser 1966) that, insofar as N.A.T.O. can be regarded as providing a 'public good' to the member countries—defence against 'Communist aggression'—one would expect from the theory that the bigger countries (especially the U.S.A.) would contribute more than in proportion to their G.N.P., and the smallest countries less than in proportion, and this is in fact the case.

There are, then, two general results if people apply an individually rational calculation to the decision whether to contribute to the provision of a public good. First, the total contribution will be 'too low'; and, second, the contribution of the greatest beneficiaries will be disproportionately high. The latter will tend to come about in conditions of independent decision as well as in the interdependent case discussed. Suppose the total benefit is £1,000, and that one potential beneficiary stands to gain £ 100 while 90 others stand to gain £ 10 each. The first man should think it worth spending £ 25 on promoting the benefit even if nobody else co-operates, provided he thinks that this expenditure has a better than one in four chance of bringing about the benefit. But it would not pay any of the others to contribute £ 2.50 unless he thought that £ 2.50 had one chance in four of bringing the benefit about.

III. APPLICATION OF OLSON'S THEORY

The bulk of Olson's short book consists of applications of the basic ideas to various kinds of social organization. His analysis has a destructive and a constructive side. The destructive part consists of pointing out that a common explanation of organizations providing 'public goods' to the members is fallacious. This is the explanation that it pays them to belong because by contributing to it they help it to succeed and thus increase the benefits to themselves. The question is whether the contribution that the individual makes increases the benefit *he* gets enough to make it worth while, and where there are many beneficiaries the discounted pay-off from the organisation's success is unlikely to be significant. The fallacy arises from treating 'the beneficiaries' as if they were a single individual deciding how to allocate his resources to the best advantage. Thus one must reject all conventional explanations of the existence of trade unions or pressure groups in terms of the self-interest of members stemming directly from the collective benefits provided. Similarly, if Marx's theory of class was intended to move from an assumption of individual self-interest to the 'rationality' of pursuing one's *class* interests once one realises what they are, then, Olson argues, it breaks down in precisely the same way.

The constructive side of Olson's work lies in his insistence that wherever we do find an organisation providing a public good and supported by the beneficiaries we must look for, and will normally find, motives other than the provision of the public good keeping people contributing to the organisation. Olson calls these 'selective incentives': that is to say, they are benefits which (unlike the public good) can be provided for members and effectively withheld from nonmembers, thus providing a particular gain to offset the cost of belonging. Olson suggests that trade unions do not gain members by preaching their advantages to the working class as a whole, or even to all the workers in a particular industry, but by providing selective incentives. These may in the earlier stages be such things as sickness and death benefits but, once established, the union may succeed in getting a 'closed shop' (i.e., make union membership a condition of employment enforced by the firm) or bring about the same result by informal social pressures. Another possibility is that the function of representing individual workers who have grievances against management may be to some degree a selective incentive offered by the union to its members. Again, Olson argues that pressure groups do not rely for membership on showing that they are doing a good job in promoting measures to benefit all members (since these would equally well benefit potential members who do not join) but, as predicted by his theory, their staffs tend to devote a great deal of energy to providing specific benefits—information and other services—on an individual basis to members.

How convincing are these applications of the basic idea? Let us divide this into two questions, one involving its application to the arguments of other writers, and the other involving its use in explaining actual social phenomena. It seems to me quite clear that Olson has succeeded in finding arguments in various writers which make sense only if one supplies the premise that it is in an individual's interest to support collective action that would be to his interests. Thus, D. B. Truman, in his influential book *The Governmental Process* (Truman 1951), really does seem to claim that wherever there is a common interest among people similar in some respect we have what he calls a latent group, and this group will be transformed from latency to actuality if its common interests are infringed. This is, of course, a very comforting notion for one who supports a group-dominated polity (as does Truman) because it suggests that if there are interests with no organisation this must show that they are being adequately catered for already. Olson is surely right to argue against this that 'latent groups' are latent not because there is no collective action that would advance the interest but because conditions are unpropitious for getting it organised.

The difficulty which a highly intelligent man can have in extricating himself from the fallacy attacked by Olson—moving from collective interest to individual interest without specifying selective sanctions—may be illustrated by referring to a recent lecture by the German sociologist, Ralf Dahrendorf (1967). In this, he repudiates what he claims to have been his earlier assumption that quasi-groups (defined as a category of person with a shared interest in something's happening) have a natural tendency to become actual, organised groups. I am not at all sure that his earlier theory (in Dahrendorf 1959) was definite enough to have committed him to this (or to anything else) but that is not the present point. What I wish to show is that Dahrendorf fails, in the lecture, to free himself from the fallacy exposed by Olson.

The idea he puts forward is that, starting from an axiom of self-interest, we can deduce the circumstances under which energy will be put into collective action, namely that it will be at a maximum when there is little scope for advancement by individual action. Collective action among the working class has declined, Dahrendorf asserts, and the explanation is that it is now possible to find self-fulfilment by, say, taking a holiday in Italy. But, on Olson's analysis, it is doubtful whether joining in collective action aimed at the benefit of the working class as a whole would ever be in the interests of an individual, if we are thinking (as Dahrendorf apparently is) of the benefit as simply the value to the individual of the result of the collective action. Dahrendorf would probably have been on a better tack had he argued that the *selective* incentives offered by being a prominent member of an organisation have declined in value because other sources of gratification have become available and also because the status gained in a local community from being, say, a Chapel Elder or a Labour Party officer, has less currency in a more mobile society with a more centralised status-hierarchy.

Turning to Olson's examples of successful and unsuccessful organisations, I think one has to say that he tends to pick the cases which support his thesis rather than start by sampling the universe of organisations of a certain type within certain spatio-temporal boundaries. This is especially significant in the matter of explaining the levels of success of different organisations. Olson seems on fairly safe ground when he suggests (with examples) that an organisation which starts offering selective incentives at a certain point in its history will find that recruitment increases. But can we hope to explain the generally higher levels of unionism in Britain than in the U.S.A. by saying that there are more selective incentives? Can we explain the variations in union membership between industries by selective incentives? And can we explain the rise of mass unionism in Britain in the 1880s and the decline in union membership after 1926 by this means? On the face of it, these seem more related to such things as the perceived prospects for the success of collective action: the 'new unionism' was reinforced by successful industrial action, while the fiasco of the General Strike led to disillusionment. Likewise, the more similar the positions of a large number of workers are, the more they are likely to see a chance for collective betterment by unionism (Lockwood 1958). Yet these are precisely the kinds of consideration that are ruled out by Olson, on the grounds that it is not rational for anyone to incur a cost where the increased amount of a public good that will thereby come to him personally is negligible.

IV. PARTICIPATION IN COLLECTIVE ACTION: SOME EXPLANATIONS

We thus arrive at a somewhat curious position. Downs tries to argue for the discounted value of the additional collective benefit (in this case the prospect of averting the collapse of the system) as an adequate explanation of voting. Olson, on the other hand, in accounting for membership of trade unions and pressure groups, dismisses the extra bit of collective benefit as an inadequate motive and insists on 'selective incentives'. The actual situation seems to be the same in both cases. In neither case would the marginal bit of collective benefit normally be sufficient to motivate an economically 'rational' person. Here Downs is wrong and Olson right. But, equally, in both cases a belief in the efficacy of the process does look as if it is related to participation, though not necessarily via an ill-calculated judgment of private self-interest. Whatever the reason why a person may attach himself to a cause, more enthusiasm for its pursuit is likely to be elicited if it looks as if it has a chance of succeeding than if it appears to be a forlorn hope. Nobody likes to feel that he is wasting his time, and that feeling may be induced by contributing to a campaign which never looks as if it has a chance. Thus, it has been suggested that extreme right-wing political groups flourish in California and certain other states not so much because the sentiments are so much commoner as because the political structure (especially the weakness of party organisations) makes it more likely that intervention will produce results (Wolfinger et al. 1964). In a similar vein, Banfield has argued that the fragmented decision-making structure in Chicago makes it easier for citizen groups to modify policy and thus encourages their activity (Banfield 1961).

Finally, a 'sense of duty' appears to be an important factor in voting, and perhaps it is in some voluntary associations too. To take a pure case, it is difficult to see what 'selective incentive' or personal benefit comes about from sending a cheque to Oxfam. It is, of course, true and important that organisations providing selective incentives (e.g. shops) and those raising money coercively to provide public goods (e.g. the government) succeed in getting hold of a lot more of our incomes. But the example shows that other factors must be allowed for somewhere.

Now, as we have already seen, we can fit anything into a loosely 'economic' framework, if we are sufficiently hospitable to different kinds of 'reward' and 'cost'. Thus, we could say that the sense of guilt at not contributing to some altruistic organisation provides a 'selective incentive', since the guilt is obviously not incurred if one contributes. Or, where an organisation is expected to provide collective benefits for its members (but, by definition, not exclusively to its members), a man might be said to feel the pangs of conscience if he shares in the benefits without contributing time or money to the organisation himself. It is interesting to notice that this is a moral position, in that it does not reflect pure self-interest, though at the same time it depends on the belief that one will benefit personally from the activities of the organisation.[1] A difficulty here is that sentiments of reciprocity are probably most likely to arise in face-to-face groups, and it is in these that social sanctions (a straightforward selective incentive) are most likely to be applied and to be effective. This implies that behaviour alone will often not enable us to infer the actor's motivation. But there are still two kinds of evidence. One is what people say, and the other is how they act when the non-co-operative move would remove them from the reach of the group's available sanctions. Examples, from armies in the Second World War, may be found for both. Thus, survey data on soldiers' attitudes for the U.S.A. and information on desertion rates in the closing stages of the war for Germany both bear out the point. (See Stouffer et al. 1949, and Shils and Janowitz 1948.) In both cases it can be concluded that unwillingness to let down 'buddies' seems to be a large component of 'morale', that is to say preparedness for fighting.

An alternative 'moral' position which might lead to participation in collective action would be a simple utilitarian one. On this basis someone might argue in a certain instance that the increment of benefits (or incremental probability of benefit) produced by his contribution would be greater than the cost incurred by himself, so there would be a net benefit (not to himself, of course, but to the human race as a whole) if he contributed. Olson himself argues, contrary to this, that even if a man's intentions were wholly altruistic it would not be rational to join an organisation producing collective benefits. 'Even if the member of a large group were to neglect his own interests entirely, he still would not rationally contribute toward the provision of any collective or public good, since his own contribution would not be perceptible' (Olson 1965, p. 64). This is surely absurd. If each contribution is literally 'imperceptible' how can all the contributions together add up to anything? Conversely, if a hundred thousand members count for something, then each one contributes on the average a hundred-thousandth. If it is rational for workers in an industry to wish for a closed shop, thus coercing everyone to join the union, this must mean that the total benefits brought by the union are greater than its total costs. (Otherwise it would be better not to have the union.) But if this is so, it must mean that anyone who wished purely to maximise the gains of workers in the industry would join the union voluntarily.

It should be clear that this is not inconsistent with the basic point of Olson's that we have accepted. Suppose, for example, that (up to some point) for every pound spent on a public good a thousand people will derive ten pounds'-worth of benefit [in total]. An altruist (who might or might not be one of the potential beneficiaries) would clearly find a good use for his funds here. But it would not *pay* one of the potential beneficiaries to contribute, because the benefit *to him* from giving a pound would be only one penny (ten pounds divided by a thousand).[2]

V. SELECTIVE INCENTIVES AS EXPLANATIONS

Obviously, the constant danger of 'economic' theories is that they can come to 'explain' everything merely by redescribing it. They then fail to be any use in predicting that one thing will happen rather than another. Thus, if an organisation maintains itself, we say 'It must have provided selective incentives'; and this is bound to be true since whatever motives people had for supporting it are called 'selective incentives'. Olson himself recognises that a 'selective incentive' can be *anything* that constitutes a benefit contingent on contributing to the organisation: 'In addition to monetary and social incentives [social status and social acceptance], there are also erotic incentives, psychological incentives, moral incentives, and so on' (Olson 1965, p. 61, fn. 17). He adds: 'The adherence to a moral code that demands the sacrifices needed to obtain a collective good therefore need not contradict any of the analyses of this study; indeed, this analysis shows the need for such a moral code or for some other selective incentive.' Nevertheless, he says that he does not intend to make use of such incentives because they are untestable, unnecessary, and unlikely to be of importance in the kinds of organised pressure group to be discussed. It is this restriction on the 'selective incentives' to be acknowledged that gives Olson's theory some real predictive bite, but in this form it does not seem capable of giving an explanation of all the relevant phenomena.

Suppose, however, that we fall back on making the theory a tautology. It is still a quite potent tautology, because it can be combined with empirical assertions to produce significant implications. Thus, it is possible to say, as Olson does, that many 'latent groups' (people with common interests in a certain kind of collective good) will not turn into organised groups because of the difficulty of getting selective incentives to operate. Consumer protection by law is to everyone's benefit, but organisations pressing for such legislation cannot count on economic rewards and sanctions, social pressure or moral principle to attract members in the millions. The most successful organisation is, as we would expect, one which is able to offer a selective incentive for membership, namely the Consumers' Association, with its reports on marketed goods. Similarly, churches (especially if they claim that attendance and obedience are necessary and sufficient conditions of salvation) are obviously in a better position to act as pressure groups, because of their command over selective incentives, than humanist or secular groups which have little to offer except the 'cause' itself.

Again, it is an important fact that, in the absence of economic or social 'selective incentives' which might make it 'pay' to join an organisation providing a public good, the reason for joining *has* to be altruistic. This surely throws light on the notorious difficulty of organising the poor and generally socially disadvantaged to press for improvements in their lot. Sometimes this is described as 'apathy' and regarded as something irrational, which might be expected to disappear with more information and more self-confidence. But since it is not rational from a self-interested point of view to contribute to a widespread collective improvement, one way of looking at this 'apathy' would be to say that the poor cannot afford the *luxury* of collective action.

It is not my intention to deny that malnutrition and debilitating diseases, which are often associated with poverty, must play a part; nor that lack of leisure, unfamiliarity with the routines of organisation and, in many societies, illiteracy are important factors inhibiting collective action. But I think it makes a difference to the way we look at collective action if we recognise that the collective betterment which might result from action cannot, at the individual level, be offset as a material benefit against the material cost of taking the action.

To put essentially the same point another way, we would expect to find a fairly direct relation between the costs of collective action for a category of people and the probability of collective action among them. (These costs might indeed be negative for the leisured and gregarious people who form a large element in the American and to some degree the British upper middle class.) But we would not by the same token expect to find any close connection between the potential collective benefits to be gained from political action and its probability, since it is (from the point of view of the individual) altruistic anyway. In fact, a good deal of upper middle class collective action is not directed towards the material benefit of the upper middle class, but towards such objects as the poor, people in other countries (once mainly their spiritual welfare, now more their material welfare), or, especially in Britain, animals.

Among the poor, the question to be asked is what can provide the incentives sufficient to overbalance the costs of collective action. One possibility is to arrange selective incentives. Thus, it is highly illuminating in this context to contrast the political 'machine' in American cities, with its relatively low-status clientele and provision of individual benefits (jobs, money, 'fixing' things) and the new style politics of the upper middle class, who 'come to party work not so much in search of a patronage job or some other form of political preference, but out of a combination of ideological and social purposes.'

In the absence of selective incentives, such as the old-style American city 'machine' dispensed (not, it should be said, in order to build support for collective benefits), what remains? An important answer that has been given is 'class consciousness', and Olson devotes a chapter to refuting Marx's theory of class. He argues (pp. 105-10) that Marx's theory falls into the fallacy he has exposed, for Marx believes that the self-interest of the workers will lead them to join in political action once they understand their common interest with other members of the working class in bringing about socialism.

Now, if 'class consciousness' is purely an intellectual recognition of a *class* interest, and in capitalist society everyone pursues his *individual* interest,

Olson is right and the theory is inconsistent. But does 'class consciousness' mean something more subtle than this, for example a feeling of 'solidarity' with a class, such that one actually identifies with its fortunes? This would fill the bill better, if we are looking for adequate motivation, though it needs to be supplemented by the proposition that one feels one ought to join in advancing the interests of the class. 'Identification' by itself would not be sufficient to provide motivation, unless it amounted to a dedication so absolute that one's private interests were virtually eliminated as a force. Otherwise it would still run into a variant of Olson's basic argument. For, suppose we allow that the success of the movement is worth more to someone if his sympathies or identifications are broad enough to make him value it for more than the prospective change in his own circumstances. We still have to recognise that the movement's success is unlikely to be worth so much to him *when discounted by the difference his own efforts would make* as to outweigh the cost to him of advancing the cause. Thus, some sort of anti-free-rider sentiment is still needed.

It is not clear whether Marx himself believed that 'class consciousness' could provide an adequate motivation for revolutionary action if it were simply an intellectual appreciation that one had interests in common with those in a similar class situation. Although, as Olson points out, Marx regarded self-interest as a dominant motive in capitalist society, he may have thought that the members of the working class were less exposed to its corrosive effects than were the capitalists. And his emphasis on close communications and other ties between the members of a class as a condition for the development of class-consciousness suggests that he may have had in mind something more like solidarity.

VI. CONDITIONS OF ECONOMIC RATIONALITY

Is it possible to carry any further forward the question raised earlier in the chapter: when is the 'economic' approach likely to work and when isn't it? The best lead in still seems to be the one mooted then, that the size of the cost is crucial. Olson himself suggests that 'there is a "threshold" above which costs and returns influence a person's action and below which they do not' (p. 164). But he apparently places the threshold very low: he contrasts voting for a union shop (below) with paying dues to a trade union (above). Where the threshold comes, if indeed there is one, must, of course, be an empirical matter.

Perhaps, rather than saying there is a threshold below which calculation has no place, we might suggest that where the cost is low it will take little to overcome it. Due to the opportunities for idiosyncrasy to operate, this may make it more difficult to predict whether action will be taken or not. But we can at least make the prediction that inertia will be a powerful force. Thus, when a positive effort is needed to join–sending off money, for example– organisations offering collective benefits may be expected to enjoy little success. But as soon as action is required to avoid joining, inertia will tend to work the other way. An excellent example of this is the 'political levy' which many trade unionists pay unless they contract out. The big increase in the numbers paying this levy when the basis was changed in 1946 from contract- ing in to contracting out is a vivid illustration of the fact that inertia is itself a powerful factor.

It might be argued that asking to contract out invites social sanctions from fellow-workers, and this may sometimes be so; but failure to contract in might equally do so. In any case, this argument merely invites us to push the question further back, for a work-group is itself too small a unit to benefit *collectively* from the increased probability of union control over the Labour party and/or electoral success of the Labour party. In other words, we cannot say that it would pay the work-group to institute a tax on itself, and that social sanctions are a substitute. (This might be true at the level of the union as a whole, if it is a large union, but it is not the union as a whole that exercises social sanctions.)

We might suggest that the main relevance of 'economic' reasoning here is to explain why it should matter so little to a Conservative trade unionist that he is paying a political levy to support the Labour party, as many apparently do. Just as it is not worth contributing if it involves a cost, neither is it worth not contributing if that involves a cost.[3] Another slightly less obvious example is the lack of protests by shareholders against proposals by the directors to pay sums of money to the Conservative party or satellites of it, or to engage directly in political advertising. This is in effect a charge on the shareholders from which there can be no contracting out (except by selling the shares) but the cost to each is negligible. This is not, of course, a pure 'Olson' situation, in that it might be rational to vote as a shareholder for a compulsory political levy on all shareholders while it would not be rational to contribute to a political campaign as an individual. But the chance of a single company's efforts making a difference is still too low to make it worthwhile from the shareholders' collective viewpoint to try.[4] And there is the thought- provoking case of the steel companies in the 1966 election: the shareholders of many companies stood to gain if renationalisation took place on the terms proposed by the Labour government.[5]

Individual membership of a political party, as against inertial contribution to one, requires that one should take the initiative in joining or at least allow oneself to be recruited. Thus, in Britain, individual membership of both major parties is much lower than the 'affiliated' membership of the Labour party; and the one with more 'selective incentives' (Conservative clubs and business contacts, and, of course, the heavily social emphasis of the Young Conservatives) has many more members (Blondel 1963). But we cannot avoid the recognition that many individual members cannot be explained in terms of 'selective incentives' unless we stretch the concept so as to lose any distinctive meaning and include sentiments ranging from fairly unreflective party loyalty to an elaborated set of political beliefs. And, if this point is weakened by the existence of face-to-face contacts in a local party, let us consider the phenomenon of Americans sending money through the post to the 'party of their choice'. (See Heard 1960, pp. 41-7.) Although this is a minority practice, it involves many millions of U.S. voters and seems to fall as far outside the 'economic' model as the contributions to famine relief or other charities mentioned earlier.

When the cost is small, it does appear that, though the economic model can account for some variations, its prediction of total failure for an organisation can be falsified rather easily either by 'selective incentives' (such as inertia) which are rather dubious, or by the 'moral' considerations which, in order to give the theory any teeth at all, we have decided to exclude. But can we say that, when the cost is great, the economic approach comes into its own? There is a certain amount of truth in this, in that the role of selective incentives tends to be much clearer in inducing participation.

Thus membership of a union may in some cases be pretty automatic; but attending meetings is rather more demanding than paying a subscription and, in the absence of selective incentives, few members go.[6] Strikes, finally, may well involve a substantial sacrifice by the worker and his family. But here 'selective incentives' come fully into play: ostracism and violence, verbal or even physical, may well be inflicted on the blackleg. It is easy to see that these are essential to overcome the fact that it would otherwise pay any individual employee to continue work, even though he stands to gain if the strike is successful.

Nationalist movements which are banned by the government concerned provide an interesting parallel: the government often argues that if the movement finds it necessary to use 'terrorism' on those whom it claims to represent, this shows that they do not really support it. Governments who employ this line of reasoning should reflect that exactly the same case could be made against them insofar as they find it necessary to resort to penal sanctions in order to raise taxes, enforce laws and conscript an army. In fact, the argument is equally fallacious in both instances. As Baumol pointed out, in a book which in some ways anticipates Olson (Baumol 1952), it is rational to support the coercion of ourselves along with others to finance the state, even if we would not contribute the same amount voluntarily. In exactly the same way, a man might welcome 'terrorism' aimed at providing a counter-sanction to those in the hands of the forces of 'law and order', just because he is aware that he and many others would not otherwise have an adequate incentive for supporting the opposition organisation.

These examples, however, raise in an acute form the question whether it is really true that where the costs are high the 'economic' mode of analysis comes into its own. Are not nation states and nationalist movements precisely the sorts of thing that are capable of eliciting action which incurs a substantial risk of very high cost without the presence of 'selective incentives'? I think the answer is that this is so, but that the qualifications already made apply here too. First, selective incentives still make a difference, though their absence (or at least their apparent inadequacy to offset the costs involved) does not reduce activity to zero. In Britain during the First World War the number of eligible men who volunteered to join the army was quite large; and, even if one recognises that many of the volunteers (especially in the earliest stages) did not expect to be killed and that there were social sanctions at work, we probably need to bring in other motives. However, it is significant that conscription was introduced later and that the selective incentives of penal sanctions did produce more men. Similarly with revolutionary movements: the amount of voluntary joining is above that explicable in terms of selective incentives, but tends to be only a minority of those who could participate. Again, coercion is often used to aid recruitment.

The second point is that not all ways of serving a state or movement are equally far outside the 'economic' calculus. Fighting, hardly surprisingly, is the furthest away, but at the other end economic dealings (in the ordinary sense of the word) are apparently difficult to dislodge from it. Even in wartime, states continue to rely on taxation rather than voluntary contributions for fiscal support, even if they can do without conscription for their armed forces; revolutionaries too seem to find food more difficult to obtain than men.

An attempt has been made (Coleman 1966) to get the sense of national identification into the 'economic' style of analysis, by showing that it can be expressed in terms of self-interest, but I do not think the attempt is successful. National identification does, in my view, lead to certain kinds of action outside the 'economic' framework, and the most useful thing is to work out the circumstances and areas in which it does. Coleman's attempt is, however, interesting in that it falls down on the same confusion between individual and collective benefit that undermined Downs's demonstration of the economic rationality of voting. Just as Downs suggested that a democratic form of political system might be regarded as an investment, yielding a steady stream of utility but needing to be kept going by [periodic] acts of voting, so Coleman suggests that one might regard the whole country as something in which one has a certain investment, again requiring sacrifices (money at least, and perhaps more) from the investors to keep it going. The fallacy is the same in both cases (and Downs inconsistently admits the point), namely that the condition of the investment is so little affected by the actions of one ordinary person that it would not pay to contribute anything to its upkeep.

Coleman's idea of an individual's 'optimum' division of resources between public and private use, based on self-interest but taking into account his 'investment' in the nation, is useless because the 'optimum' level of public contribution would be zero, exactly as deduced by Olson. And the analogy that Coleman draws between a citizen's 'investing' in the nation and one firm's investing liquid funds in another firm breaks down at the crucial point, for the profits of the company invested in are *not* a public good but go to the shareholders. If the state, like the firm, simply provided services in proportion to the taxes paid, the analogy would hold; but on that assumption the distinctive feature of the state, that it provides collective goods (including policies such as income redistribution), would be lost and with it the whole problem.

In this chapter I have tended to emphasise the things Olson's theory cannot explain. When a theory is so simple and the claims advanced for it are so sweeping this may be unavoidable. But it should not be allowed to conceal the fact that, for such a simple theory, Olson's does explain a great deal. Although not all variations in strength between organisations can be accounted for by the theory (including the fact that certain organisations exist at all), much of the pattern of effective organisation over the long term in a society does seem broadly to correspond with the predictions we would draw from Olson. This is no mean achievement for the 'economic' approach.

NOTES

1. Goldthorpe *et al.* seem to me to neglect this point in their discussion of the motives for joining a trade union. They contrast 'moral conviction' with a belief that 'union membership pays', but the latter belief needs to be broken down into conceptions of individual and collective benefit (Goldthorpe *et al.* 1968, p. 98; Table 39 on p. 97). Notice that this is not just a matter of finding out more exactly what people think, but of having, as an observer, a clear idea of the structure of the situation and its implications for distinguishing between self-interested behaviour and 'principled' or altruistic behaviour. The informant might not think of his behaviour explicitly as altruistic, though objectively it is.

2. It may be noted that the same analysis can be applied to Downs's calculus of voting. If someone adopts a utilitarian position he may well think it worth voting, either to increase the chance of one party winning or to protect the system. (Cf. Barry 1965, pp. 328-30.)

3. We can strike a further Downsian note here by adding that, in view of the small sums involved, it is not even worth making an effort to find out about the political levy. The realism of this conclusion is confirmed in a study of Luton workers: 'it would appear that in all groups except the craftsmen from a third to a half are making their contribution without realising this; that is to say, either they do not think they pay the levy but have not contracted out or they admit to having no knowledge of the levy at all' (Goldthorpe *et. al.* 1968, p. 111; see also Table 48 on p. 110).

4. Rose compares the prospective loss to the 'steel industry' which might arise in being nationalised as a result of the 1964 election, with the amount that 'the industry' spent in propaganda. He concludes that, since the prospective loss might have been expected to be £ 600 million, while the amount spent on campaigning was £ 1.3 million, this 'was reasonable if the chance of such propaganda decisively and positively influencing the result was at least about 1 in 450' (Rose 1967, p. 146). This as it stands obviously commits the fallacy of treating 'the industry' as a collectivity: on the face of it the relevant calculation is the cost and prospective benefit to *each company*. Perhaps steel companies are a small enough group to overcome this 'Olson problem' at least to the extent of, say, N.A.T.O.; but Rose's own account does not suggest much in the way of mutual coercion—or even co-ordination.

5. See Rose (1967) p. 280. It was, of course, still rational for the *directors* to spend (mainly) other people's money in an attempt to retain their own very desirable jobs.

6. Those that do are disproportionately made up of those motivated by ideological zeal, who thus fall outside the model. This again illustrates that it may be possible to give an 'economic' explanation of a *difference* in numbers (why x has a smaller membership than y) by adducing selective incentives, even though these cannot account for every feature of the situation (why x has any members at all).

3 • Introduction

The next selection is by Anatol Rapoport, one of the pioneers in the study of the prisoner's dilemma. It consists mainly of an account, interwoven with personal reminiscences, of the research carried on up to the date of the article (1974). In addition, it contains Rapoport's own reflections on the significance of the prisoner's dilemma. Rapoport, as will be seen, regards the structure of payoffs characterizing the prisoner's dilemma as presenting the actors with a genuine dilemma: a choice, as he calls it, between "individual" and "collective" rationality. What makes it a real dilemma is, he claims, the fact that each player does better by following individual rationality (confessing), but both do better if both follow collective rationality (not confessing). Thus there are, he maintains, two competing conceptions of rationality at work here.

This argument raises complex issues about the nature of rationality. Having drawn attention to it here, we refer readers to section V of the Epilogue, where it is discussed extensively in the context of a general analysis of the problem of rationality in society.

3

PRISONER'S DILEMMA— RECOLLECTIONS AND OBSERVATIONS

Anatol Rapoport

The dilemma in Prisoner's Dilemma arises from the circumstance that the question 'What is the rational choice?' is ambivalent unless 'rationality' is strictly defined. It turns out that in the context of non-constant-sum games like Prisoner's Dilemma actually two concepts of 'rationality' compete for attention, namely *individual* rationality, which prescribes to each player the course of action most advantageous to him under the circumstances, and *collective* rationality, which prescribes a course of action to both players simultaneously. It turns out that if both act in accordance with collective rationality, then *each* player is better off than he would have been had each acted in accordance with individual rationality. The situation has been, of course, known and intuitively appreciated throughout man's history as a social animal. Prescriptions of conduct in accordance with collective rationality are embodied in every ethical system. Such a prescription is spelled out in Kant's categorical imperative. It is incorporated in every disciplined social act, for instance in an orderly evacuation of a burning theater, where acting in accordance with 'individual rationality' (trying to get out as quickly as possible) can result in disaster for all, that is, for each 'individually rational' actor.

Nevertheless the formal presentation of the Prisoner's Dilemma game still evokes surprise in people confronted with the analysis for the first time. Perhaps this is because acting in collective interest is still associated in most

---

Reprinted by permission of D. Reidel Publishing Company and the editor from *Game Theory as a Theory of Conflict Resolution,* ed., A. Rapoport (Dordrecht: D. Reidel Publishing Company, 1974), pp. 18-34.

people's minds with moral rather than logical concepts. Doing what is for the common good evokes the idea of 'sacrificing' one's individual interest. On the other hand, calculation of what is best for oneself is felt to be unambivalently 'rational' (although perhaps on occasions not praiseworthy). There is a reluctance to question the very meaning of 'rationality', as one must when one becomes aware of the implications of purely logical analysis when applied to games like Prisoner's Dilemma.

Accordingly, a controversy is still carried on here and there about whether the one or the other choice in that game is 'really' rational. What is 'really' rational is, of course, a matter of definition and so not something that deserves a serious controversy. Much more interesting is the question of what people actually do when confronted with a Prisoner's Dilemma situation. In fact, if we could get an independent assessment of what constitutes a 'rational actor', the question of which choice is rational in Prisoner's Dilemma could be put to an experimental test. Then what a 'rational actor' does will provide the answer to the question.

Unfortunately, it is manifestly impossible to agree on criteria that designate a 'rational actor' to apply to real flesh and blood actors. However the question 'What will people (any people) do in a Prisoner's Dilemma situation?' remains an interesting one, as is attested by several hundreds of experiments that have been performed with this game in the past twenty years or so. This research is part of the 'history' of Prisoner's Dilemma. Another part is the penetration of the 'model' into discussions of international relations and of other situations where the psychology of conflict resolution seems to be potentially appropriate. For Prisoner's Dilemma is not only a model of a peculiar sort of conflict, involving 'partner-opponents', whose interests partly clash and partly coincide but also an inner conflict within each player: 'Shall I cooperate (act the way I want the other to act) or compete (look after my own interest)?' It is therefore not surprising that the game acquired a strong appeal for experimenting psychologists.

To my knowledge, the earliest experiments with Prisoner's Dilemma were performed by Flood in 1952. They were reported in a Rand Corporation research memorandum (Flood 1952) and do not seem to have attracted much attention at the time. The 'paradox' was discussed by several of the Fellows at the Center for Advanced Study in the Behavioral Sciences in Palo Alto during the first year of its operation (1954-1955). I believe it was introduced by Luce, and the first detailed analysis appeared subsequently in his and Raiffa's *Games and Decisions* (1957). For reasons I will mention below, those discussions made a very deep impression on me, and I carried the 'infection' with me to the Mental Health Research Institute at the University of Michigan, where I worked from 1955 to 1970. However, my own systematic experiments with Prisoner's Dilemma did not begin until 1962.

Possibly a decisive impetus to experimental work was given by a paper by Schelling (1958). At any rate, it seems that the first experiment since Flood's was performed by Deutsch (1958). Thereafter the number of experimental papers on Prisoner's Dilemma increased very rapidly.

The growth of interest in that game can be estimated from the time course of papers on experimental games and related subjects of which there are several comprehensive bibliographies (Guyer and Perkel 1972; Wrightsman, O'Connor, and Baker 1972; Shubik, Brewer, and Savage 1972). [...] In trying to account for this minor explosion, I shall resort to a bit of personal history.

[...]

I incorporated a three-person version of the [Prisoner's Dilemma] game in some experiments on the effects of sleeplessness [reported in Rapoport 1962]. A three-person version of the game was included as one of four tests administered during 32 hours of sleep deprivation, each test lasting eight hours. By changing the order of the tests administered to different groups of subjects, differences, if any, attributable to different periods of sleeplessness could be assessed. All tests involved three-person groups of subjects. In this way, the format of the experiment dictated the use of the three-person game.

The question asked was whether prolonged sleeplessness would have an effect on the ability of the three players to arrive at a 'tacit collusion' which leads to the cooperative solution of Prisoner's Dilemma. Since the game was played for almost eight hours (1200 trials), one might expect that at least in some cases such tacit collusion would be established. Our inexperience, however, introduced another factor. For humanitarian reasons, the subjects were allowed to take a coffee break after four hours of pushing buttons (to indicate their choices in the three-way game). To avoid *explicit* agreement on the cooperative solution, they were not allowed to discuss the game during the break, and they were monitored to insure compliance. Nevertheless, the change of performance across the break was dramatic. In the first four hour session hardly any collusions were achieved, which in retrospect seems hardly surprising. In variants of the three-person Prisoner's Dilemma where the *single* defector gets the largest payoff and the single cooperator suffers the most severe punishment, it is all but impossible for all three to 'balance' themselves on the precarious cooperative solution. Following the coffee break, however, collusion was achieved by a large majority of the groups. Evidently just taking coffee was enough to establish cooperation (by telepathy?). It did not occur to us to give the subjects coffee at separate tables in a control experiment.

In the article cited above, Schelling called attention to the importance of 'tacit cooperation between opponents'. The thrust of his argument was the recognition that the most important human conflicts are modeled more properly by non-zero-sum rather than by zero-sum games, inasmuch as the interests of the parties are seldom diametrically opposed. Even in war, the enemies are often forced by circumstances to 'cooperate' in the sense of exercising certain self-imposed constraints in order to avoid escalation harmful to both. Schelling went on to spell out the nature of these constraints and the role of (often tacit) communication in strategic conflict. None of these ideas has any relevance to the theory of the zero-sum game, because in that context 'cooperation' between the players makes no sense: there is no outcome that is preferred by *both* to another outcome. Next, opportunity to communicate has no bearing on the theory of the zero-sum game. The outcome of a game with a saddle point, played by rational players is determined; hence it is neither advantageous nor disadvantageous to reveal one's strategy to the opponent (if he is rational). In a zero-sum game without saddle points, where mixed strategies are optimal, it is always a disadvantage to communicate to the opponent the particular strategy one intends to use on a given play of the game. In contrast, in non-zero-sum games, it is sometimes of great advantage to communicate one's strategy choice to the other (provided the communication is credible); for this information may force the other to use a strategy that confers an advantage on the first player. The game of Chicken is a famous example of such a situation. If one player can make the other believe that he is irrevocably committed to the 'daring strategy', the other has no choice but to 'chicken out' if he wants to avoid disaster.

Subsequently, Schelling and those who followed his lead, notably Jervis (1970) made these aspects of 'strategic communication' central in the analysis of international relations. While global politics was definitely recognized as a 'non-constant-sum game', the central problem in the analysis remained implicitly that of finding 'optimal strategies', 'optimal policies', or the like. The object of the analysis was to provide insights into the dynamics of bargaining (threats, promises, commitments, bluffs) in the light of which the designers of policies and decision makers could achieve a degree of 'virtuousity' that would put them ahead in the game.

In reading Schelling's article, I too was impressed with the sterility of the zero-sum game model of serious human conflicts. However, I saw in his discussion of non-zero-sum models an attempt to introduce new techniques for the attainment of the same goals that are inherent in the zero-sum model: maximization of one's own utility. To be sure, the non-zero-sum model reveals that attempts to maximize one's own utility need not be identical with attempts to minimize the other's utility (as in zero-sum-games). But the focus of attention was still on the problem of finding 'optimal strategies' from the point of view of individual rationality. In my opinion, this stance obscures the principal lesson to be drawn from the analysis of non-constant-sum games, namely that in those games individual and collective rationality are often at cross purposes and that the beneficial effects of the latter can be attained in only two ways: (1) by changing non-cooperative games to cooperative ones where explicit agreements can always be enforced or (2) by abandoning individual rationality in favor of collective rationality. Prisoner's Dilemma became for me the paradigm illustrating either of these imperatives. I began to write profusely on the subject (1959, 1960) and in 1962, together with Chammah undertook systematic experimental investigations of the game, which were published in book form in 1965 (Rapoport and Chammah 1965).

As pointed out, other investigations began still earlier but the method really 'took off' in 1965 or thereabouts. Statistics collected by Guyer and Perkel 1972, suggest that the peak may have been reached around 1967, and it remains to be seen whether the 'explosion' peters out or becomes stabilized at some level determined by the availability of publication outlets.

Doubtless it is the 'conflict-cooperation' or 'cooperation-competition' dichotomy of Prisoner's Dilemma that attracts the experimenting social scientist, who sees in this simple 2 x 2 game an ideal experimental instrument. It offers the opportunity to gather large masses of data at small cost in time and money. The data are naturally quantifiable without resort to scaling techniques. Moreover, behavior in Prisoner's Dilemma can be spontaneous (in rapid repitition) thus revealing the underlying motivational structure, which may often be masked in attempts to elicit it by verbal responses. The question remains, to be sure, to what extent the laboratory findings shed light on the dynamics of 'real life' conflicts. This question is at the center of lively controversies, and we shall return to it. For the moment let us see what has been done in the last six or seven years of massive experimentation with Prisoner's Dilemma and closely related games.

The traditional laboratory experiment is designed to answer specific questions posed as hypotheses. These involve some relations among two sets of variables: independent variables, manipulated by the experimenter, and dependent variables, whose variations in consequence of changing the independent variables answer the questions posed. The values of the dependent variables are read off from processed data. The most frequently examined dependent variable in Prisoner's Dilemma experiments is the relative frequency of cooperative choices (usually designated by C) in a group of subjects. This frequency provides a natural measure of the 'amount of cooperation'. There are other dependent variables of equal, perhaps greater interest, for instance the relative frequencies of all the four outcomes and the conditional frequencies of C choices following each of these four outcomes. These conditional frequencies suggest intriguing psychological interpretations. For instance the frequency with which a subject chooses C (i.e., 'cooperates') just after a double cooperative outcome (CC) has occurred suggests a measure of 'trustworthiness': he does not take advantage of the other's willingness to cooperate by switching to the immediately rewarding D strategy. On the other hand, the tendency to repeat C after one has just cooperated *without* reciprocation suggests a determination to 'teach by example', to try to induce the other to cooperate even at the cost of receiving the worst of the four payoffs. Other conditional frequencies can be interpreted accordingly. Clearly, these conditional tendencies to choose C are refinements of the over-all crude tendency, hence are all 'measures of cooperation'.

The independent variables used most frequently in Prisoner's Dilemma experiments fall roughly into four categories.

(1) *Payoffs.* The crux of the dilemma is that D (the 'defecting choice') dominates C, hence is dictated by individual rationality. The outcome CC, however, jointly dominates DD, hence is prescribed by collective rationality. The dominance of D over C has two components, namely 'greed'—the hope to get the largest payoff if the other tries to cooperate, and 'fear'—the tendency to avoid the unilateral cooperator's 'sucker's payoff'. By changing the relative magnitudes of the eight payoffs of the game, the relative importance of the cross pressures (to cooperate and to 'defect') can be assessed.

(2) *The Strategy of the Other.* One of the players can be a confederate of the experimenter, playing a pre-programmed strategy in iterated plays of the game. By comparing the real subject's behavior in response to various programmed strategies, the experimenter may hope to learn which strategies elicit the 'most cooperation', for example, the best 'mix' of C and D choices or the best mix of rewarding the subject's cooperative responses and punishing the defecting ones.

(3) *Information and Communication.* The game-theoretic paradigm assumes complete information about the structure of the game. On the other hand, the paradigm of the non-cooperative game precludes any communication between the players except through their choices revealed after they are made in iterated play. In the experimental setting, however, both information and communication conditions can be varied. Information about the structure of the game (for example about the other's payoffs) can be partly withheld; limited communication (e.g., occasional standard messages) can be allowed.

(4) *The Subjects Themselves.* These can be assessed on 'personality scales' or chosen from different population, characterized by sex, age, background, nationality, etc.

Besides relating behavior to these manipulable variables, performance can be also examined in the time dimension. The question here is what, if anything, the subjects 'learn' in the course of iterated play.

The same question can be asked, of course, of the experimental community: what, if anything, has been learned from Prisoner's Dilemma experiments? It stands to reason that in any experiment on human behavior strikingly consistent results are not to be expected. Still some over-all impressions arise. With regard to payoffs, the results are the most straightforward. Increasing the payoff in any of the cells of the game matrix leads to an increase in the frequency with which the strategy containing that cell is chosen. In itself, the result is devoid of interest, being expected on common sense grounds. However it is instructive to see that 'in the mass', human behavior, at least in the laboratory, is predictable. Besides, it is of interest to assess the quantitative changes in choice frequencies brought about by changes in payoffs and through them the relative importance of the cross pressures. Thus it appears that 'greed' is a more effective instigator of defections than 'fear' and that the rewards associated with the double cooperative outcome are somewhat more effective in eliciting cooperation than punishments associated with the double defective outcome. With regard to information and communication, the results are again in the expected direction. In general, both information and communication are conducive to the establishment of cooperation. Again, however, it is the quantitative rather than qualitative results that are of interest: how effective are different kinds of information or communication? It has been established, for example, that information irrelevant from the game-theoretic point of view is nevertheless of psychological relevance, such as a preliminary meeting, even though entirely cursory, with the co-player.

The effects of the strategy of other are almost as clear cut as those of the payoffs. By and large, the 'amount of cooperation' in the programmed player's strategy has little or no effect on the subject's behavior if the strategy is non-contingent; that is, if the other's responses are prescribed without reference to the subject's responses. Notable exceptions are the 'pure' cooperative or non-cooperative strategies. The totally non-cooperative strategy elicits, as expected, very low levels of cooperation. The totally cooperative strategy, on the other hand, typically elicits either high cooperation or, on the contrary, 'exploitation', thus apparently separating subjects into 'cooperators' or 'exploiters'. As for the contingent strategies, the most effective one in eliciting the subject's cooperation appears to be Tit-for-tat, where the programmed player matches the subject's previous choice. Perhaps it is the most effective because it is the easiest of the contingent strategies to discern. The best strategy against Tit-for-tat is the choice of C throughout except on the last play, after which no retaliation can follow.

The personality of the subjects is the least satisfactory of the independent variables in that it is most difficult to quantify and in that it yields the most ambivalent results. It is however the variable of greatest interest to those psychologists who view behavior in Prisoner's Dilemma as a sort of projective test and hope to find significant correlations between it and the motivations supposedly induced by the personality profiles of the players. Some positive results have been reported in this area, for instance by Terhune (1970) who noted quite distinct patterns of behavior in three groups of subjects characterized respectively by high 'achievement need', high 'affiliation need' and high 'power need'. Also subjects recruited from different overtly recognizable populations (sex, background) behave differently at least in very long iterated runs of Prisoner's Dilemma.

Turning to the time courses of choices in iterated plays, we find an interesting typical pattern. On the whole, initial choices of C and D are about equally frequent. In the early phases of a long protracted run, the frequency of C choices tends to decrease, as if the subjects were learning that 'cooperation' does not pay in this game, learning, that is, to choose in accordance with 'individual rationality'. Eventually, however, the frequency of cooperative choices and especially of double cooperative choices increases, as if the subjects were finally learning to act in accordance with collective rationality. This increase, however, reflects only the 'average behavior' in massed protocols. Examination of separate protocols reveals that while some subject pairs learn to cooperate, others become entrapped in the DD outcome. The finding is a rough corroboration of the fundamental instability of the situation. It reminds strongly of Lewis F. Richardson's model of the unstable arms race, where an equilibrium is theoretically possible but where, in effect, the arms race can only either escalate indefinitely or, be reversed, leading to disarmament and steadily increasing cooperation.

Having examined the over-all results of extensive experiments with Prisoner's Dilemma as a laboratory simulation of typically ambivalent human conflict, we can try to answer the question of what has been learned and, implicitly, what is the value of experiments of this sort. In particular, do the results teach us anything about the dynamics of conflicts or techniques of conflict resolution? If the demand is for concrete practical 'know-how', the answer is clearly no. It is not merely a matter of rejecting foolhardy generalizations from laboratory to life. (Who would care to infer from the effectiveness of Tit-for-tat the advisability of guiding one's life by the eye-for-an-eye principle?) The difficulty is to find agencies both willing and able to learn from the one important lesson inherent in the Prisoner's Dilemma model, namely that 'individual rationality' can in many conflict situations be a trap. This lesson emerges from the logical analysis of the game. Whatever is observed in the laboratory simply calls our attention to the different conditions under which players fall or do not fall into that trap and how they sometimes get out of it when they do. These demonstrations are of no consequence to some one who by virtue of his position as policy maker or decision maker must orient himself to the problem of finding 'optimal strategies'. On the other hand some one who wants to guide his life by collective rationality as a matter of principle (the Kantian imperative), will interpret the results of the experiments as simply confirmations of his view. He may be encouraged by the finding that among the individuals called upon to play Prisoner's Dilemma just once (when the cooperative choice cannot be rationalized by individual rationality), about 40% choose C; or he may be discouraged by the finding that about 60% choose D. But a commitment to collective rationality is not likely to be affected by this finding, because the commitment is one of principle, not one based on 'maximizing expected payoff'.

Thus, the value of the experimentation is to be sought not in specific findings but in the arousal and dissemination of interest in the idea. So far, the Prisoner's Dilemma 'fad' has had two consequences in research circles, both being technical developments in the theory of the non-cooperative game. Recall that the 'paradox' of the game calls in question the significance of the equilibrium outcome as a 'solution' of all such games. The identification of the 'solution' with an equilibrium is a straightforward generalization of the 'solution' of the constant-sum game. There the rationality of the equilibrium cannot be challenged. However, the compelling nature of this solution rests on deeper grounds. It is shown that if a two-person constant-sum game has several equilibria, they are all 'equivalent' and 'interchangeable'. They are equivalent in the sense that the payoffs to each of the two players' are equal at all the equilibrium outcomes. They are interchangeable in the sense that if each player chooses *any* of the strategies containing an equilibrium, the outcome is an equilibrium. Therefore in the context of the two-person constant-sum game it is possible to make an unambiguous prescription to each player: Choose a strategy that contains an equilibrium. The result will be a defensible 'solution' of the game.

In analyzing the general (non-constant-sum) non-cooperative game, it has been shown that every such game contains at least one equilibrium. However, if there are several equilibria, they need be neither equivalent nor interchangeable. This makes it impossible to prescribe an optimal strategy to the individual players even if one assumes that any equilibrium outcome is a defensible 'solution' of the game. This is because, if the equilibria are not interchangeable, such a prescription, if followed may result in an outcome that is not an equilibrium, hence not defensible as a solution.

Harsanyi (1962) holds it as axiomatic that 'rationality' of both (or all) players implies a unique defensible solution of a non-cooperative game. (Recall that the concept of rationality includes a conviction that both or all players are rational like oneself.) Accordingly, Harsanyi undertook to remove the ambiguity introduced by non-equivalent and non-interchangeable equilibria of the general non-constant-sum game. To do this he, in effect, introduces the notion of 'tacit bargaining', a bargaining that would take place if communication were allowed. If also enforceable agreements were possible, communication, whether explicit or tacit, would turn the non-cooperative game into a cooperative game. This is, however, where Harsanyi draws the line. He distinguishes the non-cooperative game not by the circumstance that communication is excluded from it (since it is replaced by 'tacit' communication) but by the exclusion of *enforceable* agreements. In the absence of such agreements only equilibria can be considered as possible solutions. However Harsanyi's bargaining procedure enables him to remove from considerations all equilibria but one (or a set of equivalent ones).

Now Prisoner's Dilemma has a single equilibrium (DD), which is trivially equivalent to and interchangeable with itself. Therefore in Harsanyi's scheme it is *the* solution of the game. Had game theory remained on the formal level, there would be nothing further to say about this game. However, because the game aroused so much controversy, the 'solution' that violates collective rationality has to be defended. Harsanyi's defense is most interesting. It does not issue as a defense of 'toughmindedness' versus 'idealism' of the sort one often encounters among the adherents of the so called 'realist' school of international relations. Rather it is an argument about the *inevitability* of the 'bad' solution in the absence of enforceable agreements and can thus be construed as an argument in favor of enforceable agreements if the 'bad' equilibrium is to be avoided. The argument does not specify the nature of the 'enforcements'. One can, therefore if one wishes, (at least this is my interpretation) invoke 'internal' enforcements based on self-imposed (conscience determined) sanctions for breaking the agreement. From the moral point of view, therefore, Harsanyi's defense of the non-cooperative 'solution' of Prisoner's Dilemma is by no means reprehensible. It need not be construed as an 'advice' to players to play noncooperatively, but on the contrary, as an advice to seek ways of effecting enforceable agreements so as to turn the uncooperative game into a cooperative one. If my interpretation is correct, then Harsanyi's view does not differ essentially from my own.

Another development along similar lines was undertaken by Howard (1971). Howard introduces the notion of 'meta-strategies'. A meta-strategy is to an ordinary strategy what a move is to a strategy in an ordinary game. Thus one player's meta-strategy in Prisoner's Dilemma would be a decision of which of the two strategies to choose contingent on the other's choice, *if that choice were known*. Thus in Prisoner's Dilemma each player has four meta-strategies of the first order (four mappings of one's own two strategies upon the two strategies of the other). However a choice of a meta-strategy of the first order by each player may not determine the game. Another step is required to meta-strategies of the second order, of which each player has sixteen (the mappings of the four meta-strategies of the first order on the other's two simple strategies). The meta-games examined are those in which one of the players has four first order meta-strategies and the other sixteen meta-strategies of the second order. In general, outcomes that are not equilibria in the original game may turn out to be equilibria in the meta-game. Moreover, further extensions to higher order meta-games yield no new equilibria in two-person games. The interesting result is that in the meta-game derived from Prisoner's Dilemma, the cooperative (*CC*) outcome turns out to be an equilibrium (in addition to the original equilibrium) and so a defensible solution of the game in terms of 'meta-rationality', which in this case coincides with collective rationality. Howard's procedure like Harsanyi's also introduces 'tacit bargaining'. However the results transcend Harsanyi's in the sense that Pareto-optimal outcomes that may not have been equilibria in the original game turn out to be equilibria. Thus the 'paradox' of Prisoner's Dilemma can be resolved by invoking a 'higher' strategy space. Such resolutions have been observed in the history of mathematics when apparent 'paradoxes' (e.g., incommensurability of well defined quantities) were resolved by extending the conceptual repertoire (e.g., extending the concept of number from rationals to reals).

Finally, preoccupation with Prisoner's Dilemma as 'the' standard representative of the non-constant-sum non-cooperative game led to examination of other such games. In 1966, Guyer and I published a list of 78 types of 2 x 2 games (involving two players with two strategies each; see Rapoport and Guyer 1966). The discrete classification was made possible by restricting the payoffs to an ordinal scale so that only the ordinal magnitudes of each player's four payoffs, as they are placed in the game matrix, determines the 'species' of the game. These 'species' were then grouped into 'genera', 'orders', and 'classes' depending on the pressures operating on one or both players to choose one strategy in preference to the other. The richness of the variety revealed the formidable complexity of even the simplest of strategic conflicts, once one considers not only the 'rational solution', whichever way one chooses to define 'rationality', but also all the cross pressures that introduce ambivalence into most of these situations. The majority of these games turn out to be asymmetric. That is, the strategic positions of the two players are unequal in them. They thus provide the opportunity of studying the behavior of the 'underdog' vis-à-vis the 'top-dog' in situations with a skewed distribution of 'power'. Subsequently several investigators undertook experimental work on other than Prisoner's Dilemma games.

This latter development may perhaps save the current interest in experimental games from extinction. If Prisoner's Dilemma has not yet been mined dry experimentally, there is probably sufficient payoff in the form of interesting, possibly surprising findings to be extracted from the other 77 varieties (or at least a dozen or so distinctive categories) of 2 x 2 games to keep a generation of investigators busy.

In summary, the impact of Tucker's anecdote about the two prisoners has been on the perception of human conflict as something different from a problem of finding a 'utility maximizing course of action', which is the principal theme of classical decision theory. The value of this change of perception depends on how pervasive it becomes. In circles where policies and far-reaching decisions affecting the entire human race are made, 'rationality' is still predominantly identified with strategic calculations be they 'cost benefit analyses' or 'image building' with the view of gaining for one self or for one's client the most advantageous attainable position in competition for resources, influence or power. This is at best 'zero-sum mentality'—at best if it takes into account the countervailing efforts of opponents and attributes rationality to them. Usually calculations of this sort are not even cast in the form of zero-sum games but rather implicitly as games against nature, where nature is modeled as a stochastic environment and the only 'active' decisions are made by the actor whose interests are to be promoted.

The zero-sum model is one step removed from the game against nature: it takes into account the countervailing efforts of an opponent and attributes rationality to him.

Both the game against nature model and the two-person zero-sum game model are extremely seductive, because the problems posed by them can in principle be solved unambiguously and moreover often challenge the inge-nuity of the analyst. Consider the complexity of a 'game' between an ICBM, programed with evasive strategies and an ABM programmed with pursuit strategies calculated to frustrate the evasive strategies. Solution of such problems brings understandable satisfaction to the scientific entourage of military establishments. A perusal of the literature on applications of game theory to logistic and military problems reveals that *all* of them are cast in the form of two-person zero-sum games. But 'optimal' solutions of such games are obviously available to both sides and the net result of the expenditure of intellectual effort (not to speak of resources) is simply a growing sophistica-tion of the 'art of war'. Benefits of this development accrue at most to the practitioners of the profession. They are a threat to the rest of humanity. For this reason, deflection of attention at least in intellectual circles away from the 'classical' problems of decision theory, especially from its augmentation by the theory of the zero-sum game, and the consequent raising of searching questions about the meaning of 'rationality' in situations other than games against nature and conflicts with diametrically opposed interests is to be welcomed.

4 • Introduction

David Gauthier is a philosopher who has, over the course of the last fifteen years, produced a series of important articles on the relations between rational self-interest and morality (Gauthier 1974a, 1974b, and 1977). We present here the last two thirds of his "Reason and Maximization." In the first third, omitted here, Gauthier begins by stating the problem to be addressed. This is immediately recognizable as the one posed by Rapoport, by means of his distinction between individual and collective rationality. As Gauthier puts the point: "It is rational to maximize one's utilities, but it is not rational to do this by a straightforward policy of individual utility-maximization. In examining the connection of rational activity and maximizing activity, this paradox must be elucidated" (Gauthier 1975, p. 412).

The rest of the introductory part of the paper is devoted to developing an analysis of the concept of rationality. For the present purpose, we need attend only to the conclusion of this analysis, which is stated as follows: "A person acts rationally only if the expected outcome of his action affords him a utility at least as great as that of the expected outcome of any action possible for him in the situation" (Gauthier 1975, p. 418). This formula presupposes, as Gauthier points out, that all outcomes can be compared in terms of preferability and (to take account of choices under conditions of uncertainty) that the strengths of preferences can be given numerical values by defining them over lotteries. This procedure is discussed by Kenneth Arrow in the article by him appearing in Part II of this book. The curious reader may wish to consult it, but nothing crucial turns on the details of it in the balance of Gauthier's discussion.

We may now take up the part of the article reprinted here and outline the course of the argument. In the first section, Gauthier asks how individual utility maximization is supposed to be carried out in different kinds of situation. The simplest is one in which the choice is between alternatives known with certainty, and here one obviously chooses the outcome with the highest utility. More complicated but raising no problems of principle is the kind of case in which the choice is between actions that are connected to alternative outcomes only by probability relations. Here the solution is to maximize expected utility. If this sounds too simple to be plausible, one must bear in mind that most of the real complexities have already been subsumed in the assignment of numerical utilities to outcomes.

The third case, and the one of interest here, is that of strategic interaction. In this kind of case, what action will maximize A's utility depends on what B chooses to do, and vice versa. An example of a payoff matrix representing such a state of affairs is given in section I of the part we reprint. In fact, the easiest such cases to analyze are zero-sum games: there are two mountain passes, for example, and the traders want to take the one where the bandits are not, while the bandits want to lie in wait above the one that the traders take. The fundamental theorem of game theory (Luce and Raiffa 1957, pp. 71-73) holds that in all zero-sum games there is a mixed strategy (i.e., one in which the choice of an actual strategy is made by associating a probability with each alternative) such that each player can guarantee himself a certain expected payoff whatever the other does.

There seems to be something strange about making a life or death decision by rolling dice, but the rationale is hard to fault. Suppose, for example, that one mountain pass gives the attackers a much better chance of intercepting the traders than the other, if both go to it. Then the immediate thought is that the traders would be crazy not to take the pass that gives them a greater chance of survival whenever the bandits are there too. But assuming the bandits agree about the relative safety of the passes, they will expect the traders to choose the safer one, and will certainly go there to lie in wait. But if they will certainly be at the safer pass, the traders should obviously take the more dangerous pass, since the bandits certainly won't be there. But if we say that the traders should definitely take the more dangerous pass, we contradict the assumption on which the recommendation was based, namely that they will (and will be expected by the bandits) to take the safer one . . .

The upshot of all this to-ing and fro-ing is that most of the time the traders should take the safer pass and most of the time the bandits should lie in wait for them at the safer pass, but that occasionally each should choose the more dangerous one. If the traders make the journey regularly, we can give this a straightforward interpretation in terms of frequency; if only once, we have to define it in terms of a priori probabilities. Either way, it is hard to deny that it is better for each party to refuse to commit itself to an invariable strategy. (In the one-shot case, variable versus invariable could be interpreted counterfactually: "If we were to take this journey sixty times we would take the safer pass fifty times and the more dangerous one ten times.") Of course, every now and then the traders will pick the more dangerous pass and the bandits will simultaneously have picked the same pass—with disastrous results for the traders. But it is still true that *ex ante* that was the right thing to do, just as an outsider at a horse race may be a better bet than the favorite, even if you think the favorite is more likely to win.

As an aside here, it may be worth observing that the rationale for playing a mixed strategy in a zero-sum game depends on the idea that your opponent is capable of carrying on the "if he thinks that I think that he thinks" process of reasoning just as well as you are. If you think he will stop at the first move (e.g., that the traders will always take the safer pass), or the second move (that they will expect the bandits to think that, so they will always take the more dangerous pass), or the third move (which gets them back to the safer pass), or at any finite number of steps, you should adapt to that and choose the pure strategy that is best against that. Similarly, if you expect him to deviate from the optimal mixed strategy you should depart from the standard game theoretical prescription to take advantage. Suppose, for example, that the bandits are four times more likely to succeed in intercepting the traders when both are at the more dangerous pass than when both are at the safer one, but the traders are known to roll a die and take the more dangerous pass one time in six. Then the bandits should always wait at the safer one, for the optimal (minimax) mixed strategy for the traders would have been to take the more dangerous pass one time in five.

Does this idea of assuming the other player to reason like yourself carry over to the prisoner's dilemma? Could we argue as follows: if I cooperate then I can assume that the other player will reason as I will and cooperate too? (see Howard 1971). This kind of reasoning is considered critically in section V of the Epilogue to this book. But it may be said now that it is not lent support by the case of zero-sum games. The analog that each player draws between his own mental processes and those of the other player is simply that each is equally smart. Since it is a zero-sum game there is no room for any other consideration since by definition the players' interests are strictly opposed. The extension to saying "If I think like a Kantian he will think like a Kantian" is a large one and nothing in the analysis of zero-sum games warrants it.

Let us now return to Gauthier. The example that he gives in the payoff matrix in section I of his article is a much less clear case for the analysis of strategic interaction than is the kind of zero-sum game just discussed. It is true, as he says, that what is best for A depends on what B does and vice versa. But the mixed strategy that he proposes, in which each plays each of his strategies with equal probability, is dominated by outcome 0_{12}. (It yields 1 1/2 units each, while 0_{12} gives 3 to A and 2 to B.) Moreover, 0_{21} is dominated by both 0_{22} and 0_{12}, and 0_{22} is dominated by 0_{12}. The outcomes arising from A's second strategy are thus both inside the Pareto-optimal frontier. In a series of plays it ought to be very easy for A and B to settle on 0_{12}. Moreover, if B could make his move before A, it would be possible in a noncooperative game for 0_{12} to be arrived at even if the game were played only once. All that B has to do is play his second strategy. A, following his own interest, will then pick his first strategy, producing the outcome 0_{12}.

In another way, the example is quite useful, though Gauthier does not exploit this use. In the next section, he points out that the equilibrium brought about by players maximizing against one another may not be Pareto-optimal. The example he gives of this phenomenon is the prisoner's dilemma. (Here, as we know, the equilibrium is not a pair of mixed strategies but simply consists in both confessing.) But, as we have seen, his example in section I has already illustrated the point, since the noncooperative solution that Gauthier endorses clearly fails to be Pareto-optimal.

The rest of the article does not introduce any new technical ideas and the argument may therefore be summarized briefly. That does not mean that it is unproblematic, but we hope that readers will be able to see the problems without requiring any further explanation or background material. In section III, Gauthier points out that, since the equilibrium that comes about as the result of each party maximizing against the other is sometimes not Pareto-optimal, there must in such cases be some alternative outcome that they would agree upon as preferable to each. He assumes, as the next stage in the argument, that the Pareto-optimal outcome in such cases will not be a self-enforcing outcome, that is to say that each player has an interest in deserting it so as to take advantage of the cooperation of the other. Then, an agreement to cooperate would not solve the problem among self-interested players unless it could be enforced. This is true of prisoner's dilemmas and some other games that are not exactly prisoner's dilemmas in their ordering of payoffs but have this one characteristic in common. (Harsanyi [1977, pp. 278-280] extended the concept of a prisoner's dilemma to cover all such cases. This seems an unfortunate usage.) Thus, in the first matrix Gauthier presented, if we suppose an agreement between A and B to play their first and second strategies respectively, B would have an incentive to defect to his first strategy in which case A in self-defense would have a reason for playing his second strategy. However, there are other games in which equilibria may be suboptimal but in which an optimum, once achieved, would be self-enforcing. In such cases, agreement would be enough and no enforcement would be required. (For a discussion of such cases, see the introduction to the selection by Schelling.) In any case, it may be conceded that there are cases, of which the prisoner's dilemma is paradigmatic, in which an agreement will not by itself get self-interested players out of a suboptimal equilibrium. This is all that Gauthier needs for the purposes of section III.

The final two sections of the article propose, in a way somewhat reminiscent of Rapoport, that morality may be equated with what Gauthier calls constrained maximization. What this means is, roughly speaking, that rational people should recognize the self-defeating nature of attempts all round at straightforward maximization and should instead be prepared to settle for a reasonable share in a Pareto-optimal outcome. (What is a reasonable share is not discussed in the article, but Gauthier has indicated elsewhere that he has in mind one that gives each party an, in some sense, equal gain over what he could get playing noncooperatively.)

Unfortunately, Gauthier does not (any more than did Rapoport) make it clear exactly what kinds of situation this conception of rationality is intended to apply to. Inasfar as he talks of interdependent decisions as the context they might appear to be cases in which what one person does on one occasion modifies (or has a chance to modify) what others do in future. In such cases (e.g., prisoner's dilemma games played an indefinite number of times) there is a persuasive case to be made for the view that, at least in favorable circumstances, things can be set up so that each player has an interest (from a purely selfish point of view) in cooperating so as to keep the cooperation going in future.

But it is not clear that Gauthier wishes to confine his argument to such cases, since he seems to use "independent" and "interdependent" as if they were equivalent to "straightforward maximizing" and "constrained maximizing." But the issue is of course precisely whether or not what Gauthier calls constrained maximizing (e.g., playing the cooperative move in a prisoner's dilemma) *is* rational maximizing of any sort in the absence of genuine interdependence between the choices of the parties, that is to say in the absence of a real possibility of one party's choice affecting another's. That cannot be settled by definition. It requires a careful analysis of the situation. It will be argued in the Epilogue that in a one-shot prisoner's dilemma case, there is an ineluctable choice between morality (construed as a recommendation to cooperate) and self-interest, which, in spite of anything suggested to the contrary by Rapoport and Gauthier, calls for noncooperation.

4

REASON AND MAXIMIZATION

David Gauthier

I

Is utility-maximization always possible? If rationality is identified with the aim of individual utility-maximization, and if there are situations in which it is not possible to maximize one's utilities, then there are situations in which it is not possible to act rationally. This is not a conclusion one would willingly accept. Hence a proof of the possibility of utility-maximization, in all situations, is required.

But this task is beyond the compass of this essay. Here, I can consider only three types of situations. The first, and simplest, is that in which the person knows the full circumstances in which he is to act, and the effects of his (intended) action on those circumstances; hence he is able to correlate a determinate outcome with each of his possible actions. This case is unproblematic. The utility of each outcome may be related to the corresponding action, and utility-maximization is achieved by selecting that action, or one of those actions, with greatest utility.

The second case is that in which the person is uncertain about the circumstances, or the effects of his action in those circumstances. To each of

Author's Note: I am grateful to the Canada Council for research support during part of the period in which the ideas in this paper were developed. Earlier versions were discussed in my graduate seminar, and at the Institute on Contractarian Philosophy of the Canadian Philosophical Association. I am grateful for comments received on those occasions; I am especially grateful to David Braybrooke, Steven de Haven, Aaron Sloman, and Howard Sobel for their ideas.

Reprinted by permission of the publishers and the author from *Canadian Journal of Philosophy,* Vol. 4, 1975, pp. 418-433, some footnotes omitted, © 1975 by Canadian Association for Publishing in Philosophy.

his possible actions he is able to correlate, not a determinate outcome, but only a determinate set, each member of which is the outcome resulting from a particular combination of circumstances and effects possible given the action. If we suppose, however, that he can make some estimate of the probabilities of these various possible circumstances and effects, then he can correlate a unique expected outcome with each possible action, the expected outcome being the appropriate probability-distribution over the set of outcomes. And the utility of this expected outcome (its expected utility) may be determined from the utilities of the outcomes belonging to the set; it is simply the sum of the products of the probabilities and utilities of all the members of the set. This expected utility may then be related to the corresponding action, and utility-maximization is achieved by selecting that action, or one from those actions, with greatest expected utility.

The third, most difficult case is that in which there is more than one person, each rational, and the outcome is the product of their actions in the circumstances. I shall not demonstrate that utility-maximization can be achieved, but only that one problem which arises from the interaction of the persons can be resolved. To illustrate the problem, consider the simplest possibility—two persons, A and B, each able to correlate a determinate outcome with each pair consisting of a possible action for A and a possible action for B. Suppose now that A expects B to perform some one of his actions—or, failing this, assigns a probability to each of B's possible actions, so that he expects, as it were, a probability distribution over B's possible actions. In either case, he can correlate an expected outcome with each of his possible actions, and proceed as before to maximize.

But A must take B's rationality into account. Since B is rational, A must suppose that the action he expects B to perform will maximize B's expected utility, given the action B expects A to perform. A's intended action, then, is utility-maximizing for A against that possible action of B which A expects B to perform, which in turn is conceived by A as utility-maximizing for B against that possible action of A which A expects that B expects A to perform. Now let us make one further, crucial, simplifying assumption. Let us suppose that A assumes that B's expectation is correct. That is, the possible action of A, which A expects that B expects A to perform, is A's intended action. Hence A's action is utility-maximizing for A given that action of B which A expects B to perform, which in turn is utility-maximizing for B given A's action. Hence from A's point of view (and also, of course, from B's, which is assumed to be exactly parallel), each action must be utility-maximizing for the agent given the other's action.

It is not obvious that this requirement can always be satisfied. Indeed, it can not be, unless each person is able to select, not only from his possible actions, but also from all probability-distributions over his possible actions, in deciding what to do. To show this, let us consider a simple example. Suppose that A and B find themselves in a situation in which each has but two alternative possible actions. Let these be a_1 and a_2 for A, b_1 and b_2 for B. There are four outcomes, one for each pair of possible actions, which we represent as $0_{11} = a_1 \times b_1$, and similarly 0_{12}, 0_{21} and 0_{22}. Now let there be a utility-function for each person such that the utilities of the outcomes are as shown in this matrix, A's utilities appearing first:

	b_1	b_2
a_1	0_{11} (0,3)	0_{12} (3,2)
a_2	0_{21} (1,0)	0_{22} (2,1)

It is evident by inspection that if A expects B to perform b_1, A should perform a_2, but if B expects A to perform a_2, B should perform b_2. On the other hand, if A expects B to perform b_2, he should perform a_1, but if B expects A to perform a_1, he should perform b_1. There is no pair of actions such that each is utility-maximizing against the other.

However, if we allow probability-distributions over actions, there is such a pair. For if A expects B to randomize on an equal basis between b_1 and b_2, then any of his possible actions is utility-maximizing, and if B expects A to randomize on an equal basis between a_1 and a_2, then any of his possible actions is utility-maximizing. Hence the probability-distributions ($\frac{1}{2}a_1 + \frac{1}{2}a_2$) and ($\frac{1}{2}b_1 + \frac{1}{2}b_2$) are utility-maximizing against each other.

I shall say that the members of an n-tuple of actions, one for each of the n agents in a situation, are in *mutual equilibrium* if and only if each member of the n-tuple maximizes the respective agent's utility, given the other members of the n-tuple. It has been shown by Nash that, if we include probability-distributions over possible actions as themselves possible actions, then in every situation with finitely many persons, each with a finite range of actions, there is at least one n-tuple of possible actions, such that its members are in mutual equilibrium.[1] Hence one condition which is necessary if each action is to be utility-maximizing can be satisfied.

This completes my argument here for the possibility of utility-maximization. The important conclusion for present purposes is that, in a situation involving several persons in which each assumes the correctness of the others' expectations, each must expect all of the actions to be in mutual equilibrium, if each is to maximize his utilities. If then we suppose that each person can determine correctly the actions of all persons, the identification of rationality with the aim of utility-maximization entails that for rational persons in situations of interaction, all actions must be in mutual equilibrium.

II

Moral philosophers have not been slow to challenge the identification of rationality with individual utility-maximization.[2] To maximize one's utilities is to act prudently, in that extended sense of the term which has become philosophically commonplace, or to act from self-interest, where self-interest is taken to embrace all one's aims, and not only one's self-directed aims. To identify rationality with the aim of utility-maximization is then to identify it with prudence, and in so far as morality is distinct from prudence, to distinguish it from morality. The moral man is not always rational, and the rational man not always moral. To many persons these consequences are unacceptable. Moral philosophers have responded in various ways; the most radical response has been to deny the rationality of utility-maximization.

Not all forms of this denial concern our present argument. But one of the principal objections to the rationality of utility-maximization rests on the insistence that reason and utility are indeed related, but in a way which is deeper than and incompatible with the relationship we have developed. And this type of objection we must consider.

Note first that it is in general not possible for every agent in a situation to achieve his maximum utility. Let us say that an outcome is best if and only if it affords each person in the situation at least as great a utility as that afforded him by any other outcome; then in general no outcome in a situation is best. Hence it would be futile to suppose that we should seek always to bring about best outcomes. However, in every situation there must be at least one outcome, and there may be many outcomes, which afford each person a *maximum compossible utility,* that is, the greatest utility each can receive, given the utilities received by the others. Such outcomes are termed *optimal* or *efficient;* an outcome is optimal if and only if there is no alternative possible outcome affording some person a greater utility and no person a lesser utility. It may seem evidently reasonable to require that in any situation, every person should act to bring about an optimal outcome. For if the outcome is not optimal, then some persons might do better, yet no person do worse.

With the conception of optimality established, the first step of the objection is to point out that individual utility-maximization may lead to a non-optimal outcome. The well-known Prisoner's Dilemma is sufficient so show this. The dilemma is found in any situation which can be represented by such a matrix as this:

	b_1	b_2
a_1	0_{11} (1,1)	0_{12} (10,0)
a_1	0_{21} (0,10)	0_{22} (9,9)

It is evident on inspection that whatever B does, A maximizes his utility by his action a_1. Similarly, whatever A does, B maximizes his utility by his action b_1. Hence if we identify rationality with utility-maximization, and assume A and B to be rational, they will achieve the outcome 0_{22}, with a utility of 1 to each. But 0_{22} would have afforded each a utility of 9. The actions a_1 and b_1 are in mutual equilibrium, and indeed are the only actions in mutual equilibrium in this situation, but their outcome is not optimal. Hence we have a situation in which the requirement that individual utility-maximizers act in mutual equilibrium is incompatible with the proposal that the outcome of interaction be optimal.

Only in some situations will individual utility-maximization lead to a non-optimal outcome. But since the possibility of these situations can not be ruled out, individual utility-maximizers can not reasonably suppose that in the long run they will do as well for themselves as possible. Whenever they find themselves in an interaction situation in which no equilibrium n-tuple of actions leads to an optimal outcome, they will act to bring about an outcome which denies at least some of them utilities which they might have attained without any utility cost to the others.

But do persons behave irrationally in bringing about a non-optimal state of affairs? This has not yet been argued, so that the objection is incomplete. Consider, then, the following argument, which purports to show that because the policy of individual utility-maximization leads, in some situations, to non-optimal outcomes, it is therefore not rational.

What is rational for one person is rational for every person. Hence what is correctly judged rational for one person must be judged rational for every person, on pain of error. And what one person correctly judges rational, every person must judge rational, on pain of error. Suppose then that some person, A, correctly judges himself rational to maximize his own utility. Then he must judge each person rational to maximize his (that person's) utility. And every person must judge each person rational to maximize his own utility.

What constraint does the identification of rationality with the aim of utility-maximization impose on this judgment? Since there is in general no best outcome, the constraint may not require that every person suppose his own utility maximized by that policy of action he judges rational for each to follow. But the constraint must surely require that every person expect for himself the maximum utility compossible with that received by each other person, from that policy of action he judges rational for each person. Thus, if every person correctly judges each person rational to maximize his own utility, then the policy of individual utility-maximization must afford every person maximum compossible utility, or in other words, individual utility-maximization must yield optimal outcomes, and only optimal outcomes. But we have shown that individual utility-maximization does not always yield optimal outcomes. Therefore every person does not correctly judge each person rational to maximize his own utility. Person A does not correctly judge each person rational to maximize his own utility. And so A does not correctly judge himself rational to maximize his own utility.

This argument captures a way of thinking about the universality of rational judgments which is supposed to rule out the rationality of prudence. But it is a bad argument. It will be recalled that I have presupposed that we ascribe rationality primarily to the individual person. Our concern is with practical reason, and so with the rational *agent*. On the instrumental conception of reason, the rationality of an agent is shown by the relation between the actions he takes himself to perform, and his ends, his basis of action. If we consider this basis of action to enter into his point of view, then we may say that the rationality of an agent is determined by assessing his intended actions in relation to his point of view.

This is not to say that what is rational from one point of view is not or may not be rational from another point of view. What is rational is rational *sans phrase*. But it is the point of view of the agent which determines, from every point of view, whether his actions, and he himself, are rational. If a person A is to assess the rationality of another person B, then it is the relation of B's actions to B's utility, and not the relation of B's actions to A's utility, which is relevant.

The fallacy in the argument just outlined is now easily detected. The fallacious step is the claim that every person must expect for himself the maximum utility compossible with that received by each other person, from that policy of action he judges rational for each person. A's maximum compossible utility is not the relevant criterion for assessing the rationality of the actions of persons other than himself, and hence not the relevant criterion for assessing the rationality of a policy of action in so far as it determines the actions of other persons.

In explicating practical rationality, the argument fails to take seriously the position of the *agent*. The question whether the aim of utility-maximization is rational is the question whether it is rational to *act* in a maximizing manner. It is not the question whether it is rational to act and to *be acted on* in this manner, for this question makes no sense. There is no way of being acted on which is as such either rational or irrational; there is no *rational patient* corresponding to the *rational agent*. There is, of course, the question whether utility-maximization is the most *desirable* way to act and be acted on, and this indeed is the question which is answered negatively by consideration of the Prisoner's Dilemma, for it is in part whether one's utility is maximized, given the utilities received by the other persons, if one acts and is acted on in accordance with the tenets of individual utility-maximization. But the answer to this question does not answer the question how it is rational to act, unless the way in which one acts determines the way in which others act. If in choosing how to act, one chooses how one is to be acted upon, then one's role as patient becomes relevant to one's role as agent. But this is to go beyond the argument we have considered.

III

Let us then turn to the supposition that the way in which one acts determines the way in which others act, and *vice versa.* So far we have considered only *independent* action, action in a manner which each person selects for himself. But we may contrast this with *interdependent* action, action in a manner on which all agree. Interdependent action is action in *civil society,* by which I understand a common framework of action. Independent action, then, may be termed action in a *state of nature.*

Since reason is the same for all, rational persons must adopt the same manner of action if they share the same condition. But this does not obliterate the distinction between independent and interdependent action. Independent rational persons will each *separately* adopt the same manner of action. Interdependent rational persons will *collectively* adopt a common manner of action. Interdependent persons will act in the same manner, *because* all have agreed so to act; if they are rational, they will act because all have rationally agreed so to act.

What is the rational manner of interdependent, or agreed, action? This question would seem to be equivalent to, on what manner of action is it rational to agree? The identification of rationality with the aim of utility-maximization provides at least a necessary condition for rational agreement.[3] It would not be rational to agree to a way of acting if, should that way of acting be adopted, one would expect a utility less than the maximum compossible in the situation with the utility afforded by the agreement to every other party. And so it is rational for all concerned to agree to a way of acting only if, should it be adopted, each person may expect the maximum utility compossible, in the situation, with that utility which each other person expects. Or in other words, an agreed way of acting is rational only if it leads to an outcome which is optimal so far as the parties to the agreement are concerned.

Individual utility-maximization does not guarantee an optimal outcome. Thus, although in a particular situation, an agreement that each person seek to maximize his own utilities may lead to an optimal outcome, such an agreement will not in general lead to an optimal outcome, and so it is not, in itself, rational. But if it is not rational to agree to individual utility-maximization as such, then individual utility-maximization can not be the rational manner of interdependent action. The argument against the identification of rationality with the aim of utility-maximization, misapplied to independent action, succeeds for interdependent action.

Indeed, it seems that the identification of rationality with the aim of individual utility-maximization leads to a contradiction. Consider any situation, such as that exemplified by the Prisoner's Dilemma, in which there is at least one outcome which affords greater utility to each person than the outcome of rational independent action. Then it is evidently possible to specify at least one agreement such that the outcome of acting on it affords each party to the agreement an expected utility greater than that which he can expect by independent action. Hence if each person in the situation is rational, each must be willing to enter into some agreement. But if one enters an agreement rationally, then one must act rationally in so far as one acts in accordance with the agreement, at least if the circumstances remain as one envisages them in entering the agreement. Hence it must be rational for each person in the situation to act in accordance with some agreement.

Since the outcome of any agreement which each enters rationally must be optimal, the agreed actions of the persons can not be in mutual equilibrium. Thus the agreement must require at least one party to it to act in such a way that the expected outcome does not afford him a utility at least as great as that of the outcome of some other action open to him. But then it can not be rational for him to act in accordance with the agreement. Therefore there is at least one party to the agreement for whom it is both rational and not rational to act in accordance with the agreement. This is a contradiction; therefore either it is rational for such a person not to enter the agreement, or it is rational for him to keep the agreement. But the condition established in III, that a person acts rationally only if the expected outcome affords him a utility at least as great as that of the expected outcome of any possible action, is violated in either case. Therefore rationality can not be identified with the aim of individual utility-maximization.

This last argument is again fallacious. A rational person must be willing to enter into an agreement only if entry would afford him a greater expected utility than any alternative action. But since in a situation of the type under consideration, any agreement leading to an optimal outcome would require some person to act irrationally, then, if every person is rational, the agreement must be violated. And so such an agreement must fail to secure its intended outcome. But then the actual expected outcome of entering the agreement need not afford each party a greater utility than the expected outcome of independent action. Since this can be known at the time of making the agreement, it is not the case that each person could rationally expect a greater utility from entry than from non-entry. And so it is not the case that it must be rational for each to enter an agreement. It would be rational for each to enter into an agreement, were it rational for each to keep it, but since it is not rational for each to keep it, it is not rational for each to enter it.

Our reply defends the consistency of identifying rationality with the aim of utility-maximization only at the cost of denying the possibility of rational interdependent action in any form which genuinely differs from rational independent action. A rational agreement can not require any person to perform an action which does not lead to an expected outcome with utility for him at least as great as the utility of the expected outcome of any action possible for him. Agreement, then, can not enable man to escape from Prisoner's Dilemma situations. In such situations any mutually beneficial agreement would require each person to act irrationally, and so no one has reason to make such an agreement.

We seem obliged to conclude, with Hobbes,[4] that man can not escape the state of nature by agreement alone. Of course, if by agreement actions can be made literally interdependent, so that what each party to the agreement does actually depends on what every other party does, then independent violation is impossible, and the agreement may prove effective. Or if by agreement the actions possible for each party may be altered, so that it is no longer possible for each to violate in a utility-maximizing manner, then the agreement may prove effective. Or again, if by agreement the utilities of some of the possible outcomes may be altered, so that the action which one would rationally perform in the absence of agreement no longer leads to an outcome with maximum possible utility, then also the agreement may prove effective. But in each of these cases the effectiveness of the agreement is secured by eliminating any conflict between the action required by the agreement, and the action which leads to an outcome with maximum expected utility for the agent. The agreement will then permit each person to seek to maximize his own utilities, but will impose constraints which ensure that this pursuit of individual utility-maximization will in fact lead to an optimal outcome.

But it would be a counsel of despair to conclude that rational interdependent action is impossible. The straightforward identification of rationality with the aim of individual utility-maximization, although not inconsistent, is nevertheless inadequate, because it denies the possibility of agreements which require one or more of the parties to refrain from the maximization of individual utility, yet secure to each of the parties greater utility than is possible without such agreement. This inadequacy does not, however, show that rationality is not connected with maximizing activity. For it is just because those persons who identify rationality with straightforward individual utility-maximization will not always achieve optimal outcomes, that their conception of rationality is inadequate. I shall, therefore, attempt to formulate more adequately the connection between rationality and maximizing activity, and then demonstrate that this more adequate conception can in fact be derived from an initial acceptance of the view that a person acts rationally only if the utility to him of the expected outcome of his action is as great as possible.

IV

Suppose that we restrict the rationality condition established in III to independent action. Thus it reads: a person acting independently acts rationally only if the expected outcome of his action affords him a utility at least as great as that of the expected outcome of any action possible for him in the situation. And suppose that we formulate a parallel condition for interdependent action, based on the claim that it is rational to agree to a way of acting only if, should that way of acting be adopted, one's expected utility would be the maximum compossible with the expected utility of each other party to the agreement. The condition would be: *a person acting interdependently acts rationally only if the expected outcome of his action affords each person with whom his action is interdependent a utility such that there is no combination of possible actions, one for each person acting interdependently, with an expected outcome which affords each person other than himself at least as great a utility, and himself a greater utility.*

Note that this latter condition in effect implies the former. For to act independently is to act interdependently with oneself alone. Hence by the condition for interdependent action, one acts rationally only if the expected outcome of one's action affords one (as the sole person with whom one is acting interdependently) a utility such that one has no possible action with an expected outcome affording one greater utility. And this is equivalent to the condition of independent action.

It is therefore possible to eliminate the phrase 'acting interdependently' from the formulation of the new condition. It is then a general alternative to the unrestricted condition established in III. This new condition requires each person to seek to maximize his utility, not given the *actions* of all other persons in the situation, but rather given the *utilities* of those with whom he acts interdependently, and the actions of any other persons—persons not party to the agreement. This condition does not represent a policy of utility-maximization, as ordinarily understood. Nevertheless, the policy following from this condition is clearly intended to maximize the agent's overall expected utility, by enabling him to participate in agreements intended to secure optimal outcomes, when maximizing actions performed in the absence of agreement would lead to non-optimal outcomes. Hence I propose to term this the condition of agreement-constrained utility-maximization, or for short, the *condition of constrained maximization*. And by constrained maximization, I shall mean that policy, or any policy, which requires individual utility-maximization in the state of nature, and agreed optimization in society.

Agreed optimization, I should note, is not a determinate policy of social action. In most situations there are infinitely many expected outcomes which are optimal; an agreement must single out one such outcome for each situation to which it applies, and require the actions which lead to that outcome. The condition of constrained maximization must be combined with a condition of agreement, to test the rationality of policies of action. We may assume that a rational condition of agreement will require that the expected outcome afford each party to the agreement greater utility than the expected outcome of independent action, for otherwise a rational person will not enter an agreement. But this generally allows considerable opportunity for negotiation, and no test has been provided for the rationality of such negotiation. To provide such a test is to determine the rational distribution of those utilities which are the product of agreement, or, in other words, to determine the rational manner of cooperative activity. This task, which may also be expressed as the task of developing a theory of distributive justice, I have attempted elsewhere.[5]

Leaving aside this question, then, how can we defend constrained maximization? If we identify rationality with the aim of individual utility-maximization, we are led, as I have shown, to the condition of III, which may be termed the *condition of straightforward maximization*. A policy of straightforward maximization requires individual utility-maximization under all circumstances, and thus destroys the real possibility of society as a condition in which men act differently than in the state of nature.

We resolve this problem by introducing a new consideration. Suppose a person is to choose his conception of rationality. In such a situation of choice, the several possible actions have, as their outcomes, different possible conceptions of rationality. Hence his action, in choosing, is open to rational assessment. What conception of rationality is it rational for him to choose?

This may seem an impossible question to answer. For, it may be urged, one can only assess the rationality of a choice given some conception of rationality. But if the choice is among such conceptions, by what conception can one make the assessment? It might be suggested that one should assess one's choice by the conception chosen; it is rational to choose a conception of rationality if, given that conception of rationality, it is rational to choose it. This condition, however, seems to be necessary rather than sufficient. If the choice of a certain conception of rationality is not rational, given that conception, then it is surely not a rational choice. But there may be several incompatible conceptions of rationality, each of which is self-supporting in the manner just considered.

Let us return to our point of departure—economic man. The traditional view of his rationality is expressed by the condition of straightforward maximization. We shall assume this condition, and ask what conception of rationality one should choose to afford one the expectation of maximum utility. Is it rational for economic man to choose to be a straightforward maximizer? Or is the form of rationality traditionally ascribed to him not self-supporting?

Our previous arguments make the answers to these questions evident. If we compare the effects of holding the condition of straightforward maximization, with the effects of holding the condition of constrained maximization, we find that in all those situations in which individual utility-maximization leads to an optimal outcome, the expected utility of each is the same, but in those situations in which individual utility-maximization does not lead to an optimal outcome, the expected utility of straightforward maximization is less. In these latter situations, a constrained maximizer, but not a straightforward maximizer, can enter rationally into an agreement to act to bring about an optimal outcome which affords each party to the agreement a utility greater than he would attain acting independently. Now it does not follow from this that such an agreement will come about, for at the very least the status of the other persons in the situation—whether they are straightforward or constrained maximizers, or neither—will be relevant to what happens. And even if an agreement is reached, a constrained maximizer is committed to carrying it out only in the context of mutual expectations on the part of all parties to the agreement that it will be carried out. It would not be rational to carry out an agreement if one supposed that, because of the defections of others, the expected outcome would afford one less utility than the outcome one would have expected had no agreement been made. Nevertheless, since the constrained maximizer has in some circumstances some probability of being able to enter into, and carry out, an agreement, whereas the straightforward maximizer has no such probability, the expected utility of the constrained maximizer is greater. Therefore straightforward maximization is not self-supporting; it is not rational for economic man to choose to be a straightforward maximizer.

Is it, then, rational for economic man to choose to be a constrained maximizer? Is there any other conception of rationality, adoption of which would afford him the expectation of greater utility? It is evident that in the context of independent action, either maximizing conception affords one the expectation of the greatest utility possible. In the context of interdependent action, one's expectation of utility will depend on the type of agreement one makes. We have noted that the condition of constrained maximization does not determine this. But the constrained maximizer is committed only to make and carry out agreements which afford him the expectation of greater utility than independent action.

Here then I can argue only that to choose to identify rationality with constrained optimization, in so far as it commits one to seek optimal outcomes, may well afford one an expectation of utility as great as is afforded by the choice of any other conception of rationality, and at least affords one the expectation of greater utility than to choose to identify rationality with straightforward maximization. Hence a rational person who begins by adopting the policy of individual utility-maximization, in accordance with the condition of straightforward maximization, will, following that policy, choose a different conception of rationality, and will prefer a policy which requires agreed optimization whenever possible, to his original policy, and possibly to any alternative policy.

V

The supposition that a person chooses, or can choose, his conception of rationality raises many problems which fall outside the scope of this essay. Some may argue that the supposition is unintelligible, insisting that, whatever the status of other norms, the norms of rationality are given and not chosen. Now there is a sense in which this is so from the standpoint of each individual, even on our position. For a person does not and can not begin by selecting a conception of rationality *in vacuo*. Rather, he begins and must begin with a conception which he does not choose, but which affords him the rational basis for a further choice, which may confirm the original conception or may set it aside in favour of a different conception. But the initial conception itself need be given only from the individual's standpoint. Conceptions of rationality are, I should suppose, not fixed in human nature, but rather the products of human socialization. There seems to me little doubt that the conception of rationality has undergone social change, that neither in classical nor in mediaeval society was rationality identified with maximizing activity. But I have claimed that in our society the received conception, which most persons do accept initially given their socialization, does identify rationality with maximizing activity. And this identification is usually expressed by the condition of straightforward maximization.

Far from supposing that the choice of a conception of rationality is unintelligible, I want to argue that the capacity to make such a choice is itself a necessary part of full rationality. A person who is unable to submit his conception of rationality to critical assessment, indeed to the critical assessment which must arise from the conception itself, is rational in only a restricted and mechanical sense. He is a conscious agent, but not fully a self-conscious agent, for he lacks the freedom to make, not only his situation, but himself in his situation, his practical object. Although we began by agreeing, with Hume, that reason is the slave of the passions, we must agree, with Kant, that in a deeper sense reason is freedom.

In philosophical literature, the classic example of the man who is bound by his conception of reason is Hobbesian man, the self-maintaining engine. The restricted rationality of Hobbesian man becomes evident in Hobbes' insistence that, although men recognize the rational necessity of interdependent action, the necessity, in other words, that each man should covenant with his fellows "to lay down [his] right to all things; and be contented with so much liberty against other men, as he would allow other men against himself,"[6] yet "the Validity of Covenants begins not," and so interdependent action is impossible, "but with the Constitution of a Civill Power, sufficient to compell men to keep them."[7] Men recognize the rationality of entering society, but force, not reason, is required to keep them there.

Hobbesian man is unable to internalize the social requirement that he subordinate his direct pursuit of survival and well-being to the agreed pursuit of optimal outcomes which best ensure the survival and well-being of each person. Thus in our terms Hobbesian man actually remains in the state of nature; the civil power, the Sovereign, can effect only the appearance of civil society, of interdependent action. The real difference between the state of nature and civil society must be a difference in man, and not merely in the external relations of men.

While acknowledging Hobbes' masterful portrayal of the straightforward maximizer, we must offer a different conception of rational man. To the received conception of economic man, we must add Rousseau's recognition that the "passage from the state of nature to civil society produces in man a very remarkable change, in substituting justice for instinct in his conduct, and giving his actions the morality which previously they lacked."[8] This passage introduces the last of the concepts we must relate to the identification of rational activity with maximizing activity, the concept of morality. We must conclude by giving economic man a moral dimension.

In our argument, two contexts of action have been distinguished: independent action, in which each person determines his own principle of action, which has been identified with the state of nature, and interdependent action, in which all act on a common principle, which has been identified with civil society. The rational policy of independent action is individual utility-maximization; the rational policy of interdependent action is, or rather involves, agreed optimization. Both of these policies satisfy the condition of constrained maximization, which I have argued best expresses the identification of rational activity with maximizing activity. Only the first of these policies satisfies the more usual condition of straightforward maximization, which I have argued is inadequate because it rules out rational interdependent action. Economic man is usually assumed to accept the condition of straightforward maximization; if we are to continue to identify him with rational man, we must suppose instead that he accepts the condition of constrained maximization.

The policy of individual utility-maximization may be identified with prudence, provided we think of the prudent man as characterized by an exclusive and direct concern with what *he* wants, whatever that may be, and not necessarily by a concern for himself as the object of his wants. The policy of agreed optimization may be identified with morality. For if it be agreed that morality must be rational, or at least not anti-rational, and that morality involves some restraint in the pursuit of one's wants and desires, then agreed optimization is the only candidate. For on the condition of constrained maximization, it is rational to restrain one's pursuit of one's own aims only to fulfill an agreement to seek an optimal outcome unattainable by independent utility-maximization.

Morality may thus be placed within the bounds of the maximizing activity of economic man, given our enlarged conception of economic man, and yet distinguished from prudence, from the direct pursuit of one's wants and desires. The moral man is no less concerned with his own well-being than is the prudent man, but he recognizes that an exclusive attention to that well-being would prevent him from participation in mutually beneficial agreements.

We might then express the relation between prudence and morality accurately, if apparently paradoxically, by saying that the prudent man considers it rational to *become* moral, but not rational to *be* moral. On prudential grounds he can justify the adoption of moral, rather than prudential, grounds of action, but only if he does adopt moral grounds, and so becomes a moral man, can he justify a moral, rather than a prudential, policy of action.

In this essay I have not attempted to develop an adequate theory of either prudential or moral action. In situations in which men interact independently, rational persons with full knowledge will perform actions in mutual equilibrium, but I have not considered the problem of coordination, which arises in those situations in which there is more than one set of possible actions in mutual equilibrium. In situations in which men interact interdependently, rational persons with full knowledge will perform actions leading to an optimal outcome, but as I have indicated previously, I have not considered the problem of cooperation, or distributive justice, which arises in selecting a particular optimum.

We must not expect that an account of morality, based on agreed optimization, will necessarily resemble our existing conception of morality. There is little reason to suppose that our present conception has developed to correspond to rationality, conceived as identified in any way with utility-maximization. In particular, it is evident that morality, as agreed optimization, can concern only the production and distribution of those benefits which men can secure for themselves only by agreement; it can not concern those benefits which men can or could secure for themselves independently. Our present conception of morality is by no means limited in this respect.

The implications of a rational morality, given the identification of practical rationality with any form of maximization, have not, I think, been adequately understood by our utilitarian and contractarian moral theorists.[9] But these implications are in fact quite straightforward consequences of the conception of man with which this essay began. The morality, and the rationality, with which we have been concerned, are the morality and rationality of economic man, and it is to the adequacy of economic man, as our conception of what it is to be human, that we must turn if rationality as constrained maximization, and morality as agreed optimization, should seem questionable doctrines.

NOTES

1. J. F. Nash, "Non-cooperative Games," *Annals of Mathematics,* LIV (1951), 286-295.

2. Cf. G. E. Moore, *Principia Ethica* (Cambridge, 1903), secs. 58-61; also Richard B. Brandt, *Ethical Theory* (Englewood Cliffs, N.J., 1959), pp. 369-375.

3. I shall not introduce a sufficient condition in this paper.

4. Cf. Hobbes, *Leviathan,* Chaps. 14, 15, 17.

5. "Rational Cooperation," *Nous,* VIII (1974), 53-65. Cf. also my paper, "Justice and Natural Endowment: Towards a Critique of Rawls' Ideological Framework" [1947a]. Also on this subject cf. R. B. Braithwaite, *Theory of Games as a Tool for the Moral Philosopher* (Cambridge, 1955).

6. Hobbes, *Leviathan*, Chap. 14.

7. *Ibid.*, Chap. 15.

8. J-J Rousseau, *Du contrat social*, I, viii. Translation mine. Cf. also Kurt Baier, *The Moral Point of View* [Ithaca, N.Y., 1958], pp. 311-315.

9. John Rawls and R. M. Hare are two leading examples. For Rawls the identification is quite explicit; cf. *A Theory of Justice* (Cambridge, Mass., 1971), pp. 142-143. For Hare it is more difficult to document, but it is surely implicit; cf. *Freedom and Reason* (Oxford, 1963), Chaps. 6, 7, esp. pp. 92-93, 122-123. My paper "Justice and Natural Endowment, Etc.," referred to in footnote [5] *supra,* attempts to show Rawls' failure to grasp the implications of rational morality. To show Hare's failure is certainly not the work of a footnote, but in a phrase, he goes astray because his universal prescriptivism conflates agent and patient; cf. [I] *supra.*

5 • Introduction

The next two selections, by Thomas C. Schelling and Russell Hardin respectively, make explicit the analytical connection between an n-person prisoner's dilemma and the problem of collective action set out by Olson. The discussion by Schelling shows how the ordinary two-person prisoner's dilemma can be generalized to any number of players and introduces an ingenious diagrammatic treatment of the payoffs facing a player in an n-person prisoner's dilemma (Figure 2). Even those who normally make it their practice to skip such diagrams, hoping to pick up what is going on from the prose, will find that Figure 2 repays the modest amount of effort required to understand its construction.

If we focus our attention on any one of the diagrams, we see that it consists of two solid lines marked L (left) and R (right). (The dotted line may be ignored for now.) L is the noncooperative move (the equivalent of confessing) and R is the cooperative move (the equivalent of nonconfessing). Positions along the horizontal axis represent various proportions of people (other than the person whose choice we are studying) who are playing the cooperative move: at the left-hand extreme, nobody else is cooperating, while at the right-hand extreme everybody else (all n of them) is cooperating. The vertical axis represents the payoffs of our actor; the further up, the higher the payoff to him. What the two solid lines do is relate the choice he makes (L or R) to those of all the others, and show how his own payoffs vary with both his own and their choices.

We can immediately see that our chooser (who makes the $n + 1^{th}$ person in the situation) gets a higher payoff by making the noncooperative move, whatever proportion of others are cooperating: at any point along the horizontal axis the L curve is above the R curve. At the same time, the more people other than our actor who make the cooperative move, the better off he is, whichever choice he makes: both the L and R curves slope upward to the right. These two characteristics define a prisoner's dilemma along with a third, namely that the payoff from cooperating when others cooperate is higher than the payoff from not cooperating when others do not. This is represented by the relation between the position on the vertical axis of L at the left hand side of the diagram and R at the right hand side: the payoff from cooperation when all others cooperate (R at the right extreme) is always higher than the payoff from noncooperation when all others do not cooperate (L at the left extreme). If this were not so, there would be no "dilemma," because universal noncooperation would be better than universal cooperation.

As Schelling points out, it makes a lot of difference what is the proportion (or number) of people who have to cooperate before the R curve rises above the level (marked with a horizontal line) of payoff received in a situation where nobody cooperates. At one extreme, cooperation is useless unless it is universal: one parked car makes a narrow street impassable to traffic; one power mower shatters the silence on a Sunday morning, and so on. At the other extreme, few people may be needed to cooperate to bring their payoffs above the noncooperative level—though of course below those of the free-riders who enjoy the benefits without cooperating themselves. This number Schelling calls k. It may be seen that where k is small we have the kind of case that Chamberlin considered to be favorable to the provision of public goods: that of "inclusive" goods. An inclusive good is one where the use by free-riders of what has been provided by others does not reduce the utility of the good to the providers. An example given by Schelling is that of a lighthouse: it will be provided if enough shipowners are willing to contribute to its cost to make each feel that the gain from having it outweighs the cost of the contribution, even if these cooperative shipowners are only a small proportion of all those whose ships will benefit from the existence of the lighthouse.

The selection from Schelling printed here is the first third of a chapter in his book *Micromotives and Macrobehavior* (1978). The whole book is devoted to a variety of explorations of the ways in which the individual choices of people may leave them all worse off than would some alternative set of choices. It is thus highly relevant to the overall theme of this collection and we recommend it with enthusiasm to anyone who wishes to go further. It is quite accessible and displays throughout the clarity, wit, and stylistic grace exhibited to good effect in our excerpt.

The remainder of the chapter from which we have drawn here deploys the graphical apparatus presented in Figure 2 in contexts where the payoffs do not take the form characteristic of a prisoner's dilemma. As Schelling points out, the prisoner's dilemma is not the only kind of case in which "there is one way that everybody can act so that everybody is doing what is in his own best interest given what everybody else is doing, yet *all* could be better off if they *all* made opposite choices" (Schelling 1978, pp. 224-225). As he says, "we should probably identify as the generic problem, not the inefficient equilibrium of prisoner's dilemma, but all the situations in which equilibria achieved by unconcerted or undisciplined action are inefficient—the situations in which everybody could be better off, or some collective total could be larger, by concerted or disciplined or organized or regulated or centralized decision" (Schelling 1978, p. 225).

Thus, the daylight saving mentioned in the title of the chapter, but not referred to in the part we reprint here, is (as represented by Schelling) an illustration of a quite different structure of payoffs from those that characterize a prisoner's dilemma. The most important thing about time is that we should all have the same idea about the way in which, say, 8 a.m. relates to sunrise on a given day in a given place. I would much prefer it if Chicago were on Eastern Standard Time, so that it would stay lighter in the evenings (I don't have too much use for the mornings), but I set my watch like everybody else. The essence of the game involving time is that it is a coordination game in which it is more important that we all have the same time than what time it is. But that does not mean it is a pure coordination game, if we understand by that one in which all equilibria are equally good. Without organization we will be locked into standard time all the year round, even if we would all prefer daylight saving time in the summer.

The prisoner's dilemma is nevertheless worth taking as a starting place—as, it may be noted, Schelling himself takes it—because it presents the most stark case of a conflict between what Rapoport called individual and collective rationality. This is because the three characteristics shared by all the diagrams in Figure 2 guarantee that, while everyone would be better off with universal cooperation than with universal noncooperation, each person is always better off not cooperating, given the actions of the others. Although, as Schelling observes, the prisoner's dilemma is not the only alternative to a coordination game in which "the superior choice is self-enforcing once arrived at" (1974, p. 225), it is the furthest distance from one. Thus, the payoff matrix presented in the first section of Gauthier's article would require enforcement to ensure an efficient outcome if the choices were made simultaneously, but would allow for the outcome O_{12} to be arrived at if B made his choice first. A prisoner's dilemma would not permit this easy a solution. We can thus take the prisoner's dilemma as representing the most intractable form of a situation in which the pursuit of individual self-interest leads to mutual frustration.

5

HOCKEY HELMETS, DAYLIGHT SAVING, AND OTHER BINARY CHOICES

Thomas C. Schelling

Shortly after Teddy Green of the Bruins took a hockey stick in his brain, *Newsweek* (October 6, 1969), commented:

> Players will not adopt helmets by individual choice for several reasons. Chicago star Bobby Hull cites the simplest factor: "Vanity." But many players honestly believe that helmets will cut their efficiency and put them at a disadvantage, and others fear the ridicule of opponents. The use of helmets will spread only through fear caused by injuries like Green's—or through a rule making them mandatory.... One player summed up the feelings of many: "It's foolish not to wear a helmet. But I don't—because the other guys don't. I know that's silly, but most of the players feel the same way. If the league made us do it, though, we'd all wear them and nobody would mind."

The *Newsweek* story went on to quote Don Awrey. "When I saw the way Teddy looked, it was an awful feeling.... I'm going to start wearing a helmet now, and I don't care what anybody says." But viewers of Channel 38 (Boston) know that Awrey did not.

This chapter is about binary choices with externalities. These are either-or situations. An "externality" occurs if you care about my choice or my choice

---

Selection is reprinted from *Micromotives and Macrobehavior* by Thomas C. Schelling, pp. 213-224, with permission of the author and publisher, W. W. Norton & Company, Inc. Copyright © 1978 by W. W. Norton & Company, Inc.

affects yours. You may not care but need to know: whether to pass on left or right when we meet. Or you may not need to know but care: you will drive whether or not I drive, but prefer that I keep off the road.[1]

Paying or not paying your share is an example, or wearing a helmet in a hockey game. So is keeping your dog leashed, voting yes on ERA, staying in the neighborhood or moving out, joining a boycott, signing a petition, getting vaccinated, carrying a gun, or liability insurance, or a tow cable; driving with headlights up or down, riding a bicycle to work, shoveling the sidewalks in front of your house, or going on daylight saving. The question is not how *much* anyone does but how *many* make the one choice or the other.

Joining a self-restraining coalition, or staying out and doing what's done naturally, is a binary choice. If we contemplate all the restraints that a coalition might impose, the problem is multifarious; but if the coalition is there, and its rules have been adopted, the choice to join or not to join is binary. Ratifying a nuclear treaty or confirming a Supreme Court justice is multifarious until the treaty is drafted or the justice nominated; there then remains, usually, a binary choice.[2]

In some cases the arrangement matters. If everybody needs 100 watts to read by and a neighbor's bulb is equivalent to half one's own, and everybody has a 60-watt bulb, everybody can read as long as he and both his neighbors have their lights on. Arranged in a circle, everybody will keep his light on if everybody else does (and nobody will if his neighbors do not); arranged in a line, the people at the ends cannot read anyway and turn their lights off, and the whole thing unravels. Here we'll consider only situations in which people are identically situated. Everybody's outcome, whichever way he makes his choice, depends only on the *number* of people who choose one way or the other.

KNOWLEDGE AND OBSERVATION

If people need to know how others are choosing, to make their own choices, it will matter whether or not they can find out what everybody is doing. I can tell how many people have snow tires if I look around; it is harder to know how many cars that pass me in an emergency have tow chains. I have no way of knowing who is vaccinated, unless I ask people to roll up their sleeves; but my doctor can find the statistics and tell me. I have a good idea how many people regularly wear ties and jackets to the faculty dining club hall; but going to a party it is hard to find out, until after I have made my choice and go, how many people are going black-tie, or in sneakers.

Continuous or repeated binary-choice activities, when they are easily visible and there are no costs in switching, may allow easy, continuous adjustment to what others are doing. Once-for-all choices are often taken in the dark. Some choices, like resigning in protest, are necessarily visible; some, like loaded guns and vaccination scars, can be revealed or concealed; some, like fouling or not fouling a public pond, may be not only invisible but unrevealable. For discipline and enforcement it will usually matter whether individual choices or only the aggregates or percentages can be monitored. Unless I say otherwise, I shall usually have in mind that people can see and adapt to the choices of others; but we should keep in mind that this is a special case, and often an especially easy one to deal with.

What people actually "see and adapt to" is sometimes not the number of choices one way or the other but the consequences. While the senator who considers voting against the President's nominee for the Supreme Court probably cares directly about the number of negative votes, the owner of the double-parked automobile is more interested in the safety in numbers than in the numbers themselves. Parents who decline vaccination for their children should be interested in how much safety the vaccination of others provides, not in the numbers themselves, although they may have a more reliable estimate of numbers than of risk. The distinction between numbers per se and their consequences—which it is that one cares about, and also which it is that one can observe—is a distinction that ought, in a particular case, to be explicit; but I shall usually speak as though it is the choices themselves that a person can see and that he cares about.

What we have, then, is a population of n individuals, each with a choice between L and R ("Left" and "Right") corresponding in our diagrammatic analysis to the two directions on a horizontal scale or, in an actual choice, to the two sides of a road, or two political parties. For any individual the payoff to a choice of L or R depends on how many others choose Left or Right.

PRISONER'S DILEMMA

A good place to begin is the situation known—in its two-person version—as "prisoner's dilemma." It involves a binary choice for each of two people and can be described as follows:

1. Each has an *unconditional preference:* the same choice is preferred, irrespective of which choice the other person makes.
2. Each has an *unconditional preference* with respect to the *other's choice:* this preference for the other person's action is unaffected by the choice one makes for oneself.
3. These two preferences go in *opposite* directions: the choice that each prefers to make is not the choice he prefers the other to make.

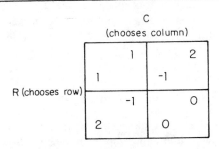

Figure 5.1

NOTE: Lower-left number in each cell denotes the payoff to R (choosing row), upper-right number the payoff to C (choosing column).

4. The strengths of these preferences are such that both are better off making their unpreferred choices than if both make their preferred choices.

An illustrative matrix is in Figure 1. One person, R for "Row," makes a choice that can be represented as a choice of upper or lower row; C ("Column") chooses left- or right-hand column. The lower-left number in a cell of the matrix denotes the payoff value to R, the upper-right number the payoff to C. R prefers the lower row irrespective of C's choice, and C the right-hand column whatever R chooses. That way both get zero. If both make "unpreferred" choices, they get the upper-left cell for 1 apiece; each could gain a point there, at a cost of two points to the other, by switching to the preferred row or column.

That situation is a fairly simple one to define. But when we turn to the multi-person version, the definition is ambiguous. "Other" is "all others" when there are only two; with more than two there are in-between possibilities. We have to elaborate the definition in a way that catches the spirit of prisoner's dilemma, and see whether we then have something distinctive enough to be assigned a proper name.

EXTENDING THE DEFINITION

There are two main definitional questions. (1) Is an individual always better off, the more there are among the others who choose their unpreferred alternative? (2) Does the individual's own preference remain constant no matter how many among the others choose one way or the other? Tentatively answering yes, for purposes of definition, to these two questions, and assuming that *only numbers matter* (not people's identities), and that all payoff rankings are the same for all players, a *uniform multi-person prisoner's dilemma*—henceforth MPD for short—can be defined as a situation in which:

1. There are n people, each with the same binary choice and the same payoffs.
2. Each has a preferred choice whatever the others do; and the same choice is preferred by everybody.
3. Whichever choice a person makes, he or she is better off, the more there are among the others who choose their unpreferred alternative.
4. There is some number, k, greater than 1, such that if individuals numbering k or more choose their unpreferred alternative and the rest do not, those who do are better off than if they had all chosen their preferred alternatives, but if they number less than k this is not true.

Taking the four numbered statements as a plausible extension of the prisoner's-dilemma idea, and as what I shall mean by MPD, we have at first glance an important parameter, k. It represents the minimum size of any coalition that can gain by abstaining from the preferred choice. It is the smallest disciplined group that, though resentful of the free riders, can be profitable for those who join (though more profitable for those who stay out).

On a horizontal axis measured from 0 to n, two payoff curves are drawn. (I switch, for convenience, to a population of $n + 1$, so that "n" is the number of "others" there are for any one person.) One curve corresponds to the preferred choice; its left end is arbitrarily taken as zero point, and it rises to the right, perhaps leveling off but not declining. Below it we draw the curve for the unpreferred choice. It begins below 0, rises and crosses the axis at some point denoted by k. We use L ("Left") to stand for the preferred alternative and R ("Right") for the unpreferred. The number choosing Right is denoted by the distance of any point rightward from the left end. At a horizontal value of $n/3$, one third of the way from left to right, the two curves show the value to a person of choosing L or R when one-third of the others choose R and two-thirds choose L.

Figure 2 shows several curves that meet the definition. The only constraints on these curves are that the four extremities of the two curves be in the vertical order shown and that the curves rise to the right and not cross. Matching the pictures in Figure 2 with actual situations is good exercise but I leave it to you. In A the disadvantage of a Right choice is constant; in B the cost of a Right choice grows with the number making that choice, L benefiting more than R from the externality.

The "values" accruing to Right and Left choices for different individuals may or may not be susceptible to some common measure. Reactions to

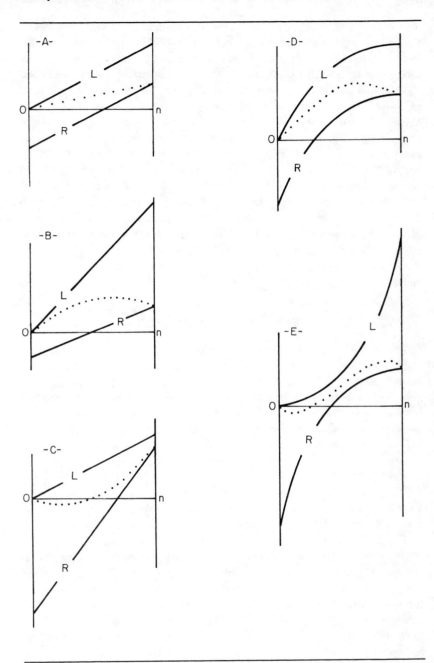

Figure 5.2

smells, noises, and other irritants cannot be summed over the population. Even if there is a common measure—frequency of illness, time lost in waiting in line, busy signals on the telephone—an indiscriminate summation may produce a total of little interest. But there are cases in which some measurable total is of interest. Even without supposing that my time is as valuable as yours, it can make sense to inquire about the total amount of lost time between us. And often a simple total can be taken to represent an appropriately weighted sum, if there is no expected correlation between the weights one would attach to different individuals and their likely choices of Left and Right. The dotted lines in Figure 2 show the total values (or average values) corresponding to the numbers choosing Right and Left. At the left end of the scale, everybody is choosing Left, and the total (or average) coincides with the Left curve. On the right-hand side, it coincides with the Right curve. Midway between left and right sides it is midway vertically between the curves, and at the one-third and two-thirds marks it is located at one-third of the vertical distance, or two-thirds of the vertical distance, from curve L to curve R.

THE SIGNIFICANT PARAMETERS

In the description of MPD a crucial parameter is k, the minimum size of a viable coalition. "Viable" means that on an either-or basis, assuming that nobody else cooperates, some group of cooperators can benefit from choosing the Right strategy if their number is up to k. This is the minimum-sized coalition that makes sense all by itself. Evidently it takes more than one parameter to describe one of these MPD situations: Figure 2 suggests how much they can differ even if k is held constant. But staying with k for the moment, we might ask whether we shouldn't focus on k/n, or, for that matter, $n-k$.

If n is fixed, they come to the same thing. But n can vary from situation to situation, so the question whether k, k/n, or $n-k$ is the controlling parameter is not a matter of definition. It depends on what the situation is.

If k is the number of whaling vessels that abide by an international ration on the capture of whales, the crucial thing will probably not be k but $n-k$. If enough people whale indiscriminately, there is no number of restrained whalers who will be better off by restraining themselves. If there is an infinitely elastic supply of cars for the turnpike, no matter how many among us restrict our driving we will not reduce congestion. And so forth.

On the other hand, if the whalers want a lighthouse and the problem is to cover its cost, they need only a coalition big enough to spread the cost thin enough to make the lighthouse beneficial to those who pay their shares. If the value of the lighthouse to each boat is independent of how many benefit, whalers numbering k or more can break even or better by sharing the costs, no matter how many enjoy the light free of charge.

And if it is proportions that matter—the fraction of vessels carrying some emergency equipment—k will vary proportionately with n. So we have a second characteristic of the uniform MPD: the relation between k and n.

A third is what happens to the difference in value between Left and Right. Does the incentive to choose Left—to stay out of the coalition—increase or decrease with the size of the coalition? The more the rest of you restrict your whaling, the more whales I catch by staying out of the self-restraining coalition if entry into the whaling industry is limited and I am already in the business. Alternatively, if joining a coalition means only paying my share of the lighthouse, it becomes cheaper as more join.

We can measure this by the change in the vertical distance between our two curves with the number who choose Right. In Figure 2 some of the curves open toward the right, showing an increasing difference, and some taper with a diminishing difference.

There is a fourth important parameter if we treat these payoff values as additive numbers. This is the number choosing Right that *maximizes the total value* (denoted, in Figure 2, by the highest point on the dotted curve). If the rationing scheme is too strict, whalers may collectively get more whales or make more profit if some choose Left, that is, some stay out. The optimum number to be vaccinated against smallpox will usually be less than the entire population, because the risk of infection is proportionate to the number vaccinated while the epidemiological benefits taper off before 100 percent.

In some cases, collective maximization ought to occur only when all choose Right if the terms of the coalition have been properly set. It would be silly to have a limit of one deer per season if the rangers then had to go out and hunt down the excess deer. It makes sense to set the limit so that deer hunters are best off when all abide, rather than relying on some free riders to cull the herd. But sometimes the thing cannot be arranged; it may be hard to devise a scheme that allows everybody one and one-third deer per season.

A conflict of interest intervenes then. Consider vaccination: if the optimal number is 90 percent of the population and nobody can be nine-tenths vaccinated, there has to be a system to determine who gets vaccinated. (Actually, people can be "fractionally" vaccinated, through longer intervals between revaccinations with some lapse of immunity.) With turnpikes and deer hunters one can search for a quantitative readjustment that makes optimum benefits coincide with universal membership, even if people have to be allowed four deer every three years to take care of the fractions.

There has not been a case of smallpox in the United States since 1949, and it is now believed to have disappeared in the rest of the world. Complications from the vaccine cause an occasional death and mild allergic reactions in about one vaccination out of a thousand. The Public Health Service no longer recommends routine vaccination of youngsters. Because immunity wanes, many adults who were once vaccinated may be unprotected now.

Suppose the Public Health Service announced that, considering together the disease and its contagion and the hazards of vaccination, optimally the United States population should be two-thirds vaccinated. What do you elect for your children? (Suppose it simultaneously mentions that if, as is *nationally* optimal, two-thirds of the population is vaccinated, it is *individually* better to be unvaccinated!)

There can be more conflict if the collective maximum occurs to the left of *k*. Unless a distributive problem can be solved, achievement of a collective maximum then entails net losses, not merely lesser gains, for those who choose Right. If choosing right is voluntary, all-or-none, and non-compensable, any viable coalition has to be inefficiently large.

It is worth noticing that a coalition—even an involuntary coalition—can change payoffs by its mere existence. In a recent article on high school proms the author described the reaction, when she tried to make tuxedos optional, of "the boys who wouldn't, on their own, go out and rent a tux, but who like the idea of being forced to wear one. . . . For many this would be the only time they'd have an excuse to dress up." Remember Bobby Hull's diagnosis of the aversion to helmets: vanity. A voluntary helmet may be seen as cowardly, but nobody thinks a baseball player timid when he dons the batting helmet that the league won't let him play without. Motorcycle helmets are not only worn regularly, but probably worn more gladly, in states that require them. I shall continue to assume in this chapter that payoffs depend only on the choices and not on the way the choices are brought about, but the reader is alerted to alternative possibilities.

I have used "coalition" to mean those who are induced to choose Right. They may do it through enforceable contract, or someone's coercing them, or in the belief that if they do others will but not if they don't, or by a golden rule.

But "coalition" often has an institutional definition. It is a subset of the population that has enough structure to arrive at a collective decision for its members, or for some among them, or for all of them with some probability, in this particular binary choice. They can be members of a union or a trade association or a faculty or a gun club or a veterans' organization, who elect to act as a unit in a political campaign, in abiding by some rule, in making a contribution, or in joining some larger confederation. And this could take either of two forms, disciplining *individual* choices of the members or making a *collective* choice on behalf of them.

NOTES

1. "Externality" is not the term I would coin for this book but it is fixed in economics and you will have to be familiar with it. It refers to the effects of a firm's actions, or an agency's or a person's, that are beyond and outside—"external to"—the firm's accounting or the agency's purview or the person's interests and concerns, but within the accounting, the purview, or the interest of somebody else.

2. An intriguing account of complex interdependencies with $n = 101$ and an almost-binary choice—absence and abstention being possible alternatives—with varying degrees of reversibility of choice, incomplete and sometimes manipulated information, small networks of special influence, and non-uniform preferences among the participants, is Richard Harris' story of the Senate's action on Judge Carswell, "Annals of Politics," *The New Yorker*, December 5 and 12, 1970, and *Decision*, Ballantine Books, Inc., 1971.

6 • Introduction

The article by Russell Hardin gives a formal analysis of the relation between Olson's treatment of collective action and the n-person prisoner's dilemma. There are three main points. The first is the demonstration that the collective action problem as described by Olson is structurally identical to that of an n-person prisoner's dilemma. This seems self-explanatory so no comment is required.

The second point exploits the structural identity so as to draw on findings from experimental studies of prisoner's dilemma games and apply them to the problem of the voluntary provision of public goods. It has been found, Hardin notes, that about half of the players in an experimental game will in fact cooperate with a persistently (i.e., noncontingently) cooperative partner. (This, of course, must refer to experiments in which the game is played more than once between the same subjects.) Hardin suggests that this finding has potential relevance to public good provision and may help to explain why small groups are more hopeful sites for collective provision to occur in.

Let us suppose that many people are willing to contribute to a public good so long as the benefit they derive from the provision of the good exceeds the cost to them of the contribution. This is an ethical rule that is appealed to, for example, by public television in the United States: "If you get thirty-dollars' worth of enjoyment from your PBS station each year, send us your subscription." If half the people who would benefit from a public good would be willing to obey this rule, and the other half would be inveterate free riders, taking the benefit but not contributing to the cost, then, Hardin suggests, the prospects for voluntary provision of a collective good are poor. (This, of course, raises the question how public television survives. Part of the answer is that it is so cost-effective that it can still raise a good deal of money from people who do follow the postulated ethical rule even if at least fifty percent of its regular watchers are free riders—as it would appear they are. Public television also raises money by commercial sponsorship, which is a form of low-key advertising aimed at high-status people by Mobil, Exxon, and other firms that would like to generate a capital stock of diffuse goodwill to offset the negative effects on public opinion of their much more lucrative depredations.)

Some small groups might, however, by a sheer statistical fluke, have a greater proportion of cooperative people in them than the average, and thus be more likely, other things being equal, to be able to get contributions to a public good off the ground. Other small groups will, by parity of reasoning, have fewer than their "fair share" of cooperative people, of course. But if a group with the average proportion of cooperative people (and the "law of large numbers" leads us to predict that the proportion in large groups will cluster round the average in the population) does not get the provision of a public good started, a group with fewer than its fair share does no worse. So the random fluctuation around the norm in small groups will either produce better results than those found in large groups or results that are no worse, from the point of view of prospects for voluntary collective provision.

The third point that is made by Hardin is as follows. Let us again exclude from consideration outcomes where anyone is paying more in contributions than he receives in benefit from a collective good. Among the remaining choices, he is able to show that, if everyone is symmetrically placed in relation to a certain public good, and if we treat contribution/ noncontribution as a binary choice, and if the ratio of total benefit to total cost where all contribute is greater than unity, a majority would prefer a situation in which all contribute to *any* other situation—not only to one in which nobody contributes. (The only exception is where the ratio is exactly 2:1 and where there is an even number of people involved.) Thus, contribution all round is the "agreeable" solution. But it is not a self-enforcing agreement, as we noted in the introduction to Schelling's piece. Everyone, therefore, has a good self-interested reason for supporting "mutual coercion mutually agreed on." This is, of course, Hobbes's solution to the calamities of the "state of nature" and the theme is picked up by William Baumol in his *Welfare Economics and the Theory of the State,* excerpts from which form our following selection.

6

COLLECTIVE ACTION
AS AN AGREEABLE
n-PRISONERS' DILEMMA

Russell Hardin

In *The Logic of Collective Action,* Mancur Olson (1965) has proposed a mathematical explanation for the notable failure of the memberships of large interest groups to work together to provide themselves with their mutually desired collective goods. He concludes that the success of a group in providing itself with a collective good depends on the logical structure of the group.

> In a small group in which a member gets such a large fraction of the total benefit that he would be better off if he paid the entire cost himself, rather than go without the good, there is some presumption that the collective good will be provided. In a group in which no member got such a large benefit from the collective good that he had an interest in providing it even if he had to pay all the cost, but in which the individual was still so important in terms of the whole group that his contribution or lack of contribution to the group objective had a noticeable effect on the costs or benefits of others in the group, the result is indeterminate. By contrast, in a large group in which no single individual's contribution makes a perceptible difference to the group as a whole ... it is certain that a collective good will *not* be provided unless there is coercion or some outside inducements [p. 44].

Author's Note: I am pleased to thank Hayward R. Alker, Jr., Joan Rothchild, and Jean-Roger Vergnaud for the help and advice they gave in the preparation of this paper.

Reprinted from *Behavioral Science,* Vol. 16, No. 5, 1971, pp. 472-479 by permission of James Grier Miller, M.D., Ph.D., Editor.

These three sorts of group can be distinguished as the privileged group (i.e., the group in which at least one member could justify his full payment for the provision of the good on the basis of his sufficiently great return), the intermediate group, and the latent group.

Common sense and experience seem to confirm Olson's conclusions, although they seem to suggest a logic counter to our expectations. They suggest that "rational, self-interested individuals will not act to achieve their common or group interests" (Olson 1965, p. 2). To clarify the logic of collective action, therefore, Olson gives a mathematical demonstration, which can be easily summarized.

The advantage (A_i) which accrues to an individual member (i) of a group as the result of his contribution to the purchase of the group collective good is given by:

$$A_i = V_i - C,$$

where V_i is the value to i of his share of the total collective good provided to the group at cost C to i. Clearly, if A_i is to be positive, then V_i must be greater than C. But this implies that i will contribute toward the purchase of the group collective good on his own rational incentive only if his share of that part of the good purchased at his cost is worth more to him than it cost him (Olson 1965, pp. 22-25). Hence, the collective good will be provided in a privileged group, where this condition is met, but not in a latent group, where it is not met.

COLLECTIVE ACTION AND PRISONERS' DILEMMA

As with the prisoners' dilemma, we have for the latent group a result that tells us that individual effort to achieve individual interests will preclude their achievement, because if the collective good is not provided, the individual member fails to receive a benefit that would have exceeded his cost in helping purchase that good for the whole group. It would be useful to perform a game theory analysis of collective action to demonstrate that the logic underlying it is the same as that of the prisoners' dilemma. First, however, since Olson's analysis was accomplished from the perspective of an individual in the group, let us consider a particular instance of collective action in the game of Individual vs. Collective.

Individual vs. Collective

Let us construct a game matrix in which the row entries will be the payoffs for Individual, and the column entries will be the per capita payoffs for Collective, where Collective will be the group less Individual. The payoffs will be calculated by the prescription for rational behavior: that is, the payoffs will be benefits less costs. The group will comprise ten members whose common interest is the provision of a collective good of value twice its cost. There are two possible results of having one member of the group decline to pay his share: either the total benefit will be proportionately reduced, or the costs to the members of the group will be proportionately increased. Let us assume the former, but either choice would yield the same analysis. For the sake of simplicity, assume also that there are no initial costs in providing the collective good and no differential costs as payments and resultant benefits rise, that is, assume exactly two units of the collective good will be provided for each unit paid by any member of the group.[1]

MATRIX 1
INDIVIDUAL VS. COLLECTIVE

		Collective	
		Pay	Not Pay
Individual	Pay	1, 1	−0.8, 0.2
	Not Pay	1.8, 0.8	0, 0

If all members of the group pay 1 unit (for a total cost of 10 units), the benefit to each member will be 2 units (for a collective good of 20). The individual payoffs will be benefit less cost, or 1 unit. In the matrix, the first row gives the payoffs to Individual if he contributes his share; the first column gives the per capita payoffs to the remaining members of the group, i.e., to Collective, if they pay. The second row gives the payoffs to Individual if he does not pay, and the second column gives those for Collective if it does not pay. The various payoffs are readily calculated, e.g., if Individual does not pay but Collective does, the total cost will be 9 units, the total benefit will be 18 units, and the per capita benefit will be 1.8 units (for Individual cannot be excluded from the provision of the collective good); consequently, Individual's payoff for this condition will be his benefit less his cost for a pleasant 1.8 units. From the payoffs for the game in Matrix 1, one can see that it is evidently in Individual's advantage to choose the strategy of not paying toward the purchase of the collective good.

Since it is individuals who decide on actions, and since each member of the group sees the game matrix from the vantage point of Individual, we can assume that Collective's strategy will finally be whatever Individual's strategy is, irrespective of what Collective's payoffs suggest. The dynamic under which Individual performs is clearly the same as that for the prisoners' dilemma: his strategy of not paying dominates his strategy of paying. For no matter what Collective does, Individual's payoff is greater if he does not pay. This can be seen more clearly perhaps in Matrix 1a, which displays only the payoffs to Individual for each of his choices. As in prisoners' dilemma, not paying is invariably more lucrative than paying.

The payoffs to the two players in a game of prisoners' dilemma are shown in Matrix 2, and Row's payoffs only are shown in Matrix 2a. In this classic game, the delight of game theoreticians, Row and Column will both profit (1 unit each) if both cooperate, and both will lose (1 unit each) if both defect. But as is clear in Matrix 2a, Row is wise to defect no matter what Column does. The Matrices 1a and 2a are strategically equivalent; the preference orderings of the payoffs to Individual and to Row are identical as shown by the arrows in Figure 1.

n-Prisoners' Dilemma

For the theorist of n-person games, a more cogent analysis of the problem of collective action defined by the game of individual vs. Collective would require a 10-dimensional matrix pitting the payoffs of each individual against all others.

MATRIX 1a
INDIVIDUAL'S PAYOFFS

Individual			
	Pay	1	-0.8
	Not Pay	1.8	0

MATRIX 2
PRISONERS' DILEMMA

		Column	
		Cooperate	Defect
Row	Cooperate	1, 1	$-2, 2$
	Defect	2, -2	$-1, -1$

MATRIX 2a
ROW'S PAYOFFS

Row			
	Cooperate	1	-2
	Defect	2	-1

The payoffs can easily be calculated. The cell defined by all players paying would be (1,1,1,1,1,1,1,1,1,1), and that defined by all players not paying would be (0, . . . , 0). Every other cell would have payoffs whose sum would be equal to the number (m) of players paying in that cell; each player would receive a payoff of $2m/10 - 1$ if he paid, or $2m/10$ if he did not pay. Anyone able to visualize a 10-dimensional matrix can readily see that each player's

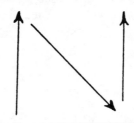

Figure 6.1   Preference ordering for row and individual

dominant strategy is not to pay, because it yields the best payoff for whatever the other players do. The rest of us can easily enough calculate that whereas the payoff to player i is $2m/10 - 1$ with m players including himself paying, the payoff to i with $m - 1$ players not including himself paying would be the preferred $2(m - 1)/10$ (in the latter case i's payoff is 0.8 units greater than in the former). Hence, for each player i, the strategy of not paying dominates the strategy of paying. But playing dominant strategies yields all players the poor payoff $(0, \ldots, 0)$, and this solution is the only equilibrium for the game.

The game now defined is simply the 10-prisoners' dilemma, to which any solution algorithm generalized from the 2-prisoners' dilemma can be applied. To generalize the game further, n prisoners can be substituted for 10, and a ratio r of benefits to costs (with cost being 1 unit to each player) for the ratio of 2 assumed in Individual vs. Collective. The result is analogous, with the choice of not paying always yielding a payoff $(n - r)/n$ units higher than the choice of paying (the bonus increases as n increases); and if all pay, all receive payoffs of $(r - 1)$. Olson's privileged group would be the case in which r is greater than n in some player's perception (if costs are a matter of binary choice between paying a fixed sum for all players who pay, or paying nothing).

In this game there is only one (strongly stable) equilibrium (at the payoff of zero to every player, i.e., all players not paying); but this equilibrium solution is not Pareto-optimal. Moving from the equilibrium to the payoff of r to every player (i.e., all players paying) would improve the payoff to every player. Among the 78 strategically nonequivalent 2×2 games in the scheme of Rapoport and Guyer (1966), prisoners' dilemma is unique in its class. It is the only game defined by the condition that it has a single strongly stable equilibrium which, however, is Pareto-nonoptimal. Hence, the generalized game of collective action defined above is logically similar to prisoners' dilemma. (It should be clear that the reason for the equivalence of prisoners' dilemma and the game of collective action for a large, i.e., latent, group is precisely the condition that in such a group a player's contribution to the purchase of the collective good is of only marginal utility to himself. Hence, his payoff is increased by almost the amount he does not pay when he does not pay.)

Empirical Consequences

The significance of this result is that any analysis which prescribes a solution for prisoners' dilemma must prescribe a similar solution for the game of collective action. That means that the vast body of experimental and theoretical work on prisoners' dilemma is relevant to the study of collective action in general (and conversely that the growing body of work on collective action can be applied to the study of the prisoners' dilemma). In particular, any analysis of prisoners' dilemma which yielded the conclusion that the mutual loss payoff was not rational would, by implication, contravene Olson's (1965, p. 44) claim that, for logical reasons, in a latent group "it is certain that a collective good will *not* be provided unless there is coercion or some outside inducements." Considering the fact that there are arguments that the rational solution to prisoners' dilemma is the payoff which results from mutual cooperation, before turning to the rationale of group success, we should perhaps reconsider why it might be that, empirically, latent groups do generally seem to fail. Let us view the 10-prisoners' dilemma defined above in the light of some 2-prisoners' dilemma experimental results.

Some experimental data suggest that about one-half of bona fide players cooperate with and one-half exploit a noncontingent, 100 percent cooperative adversary-partner in 2-prisoners' dilemma (Rapoport 1968). In the 10-prisoners' dilemma described above, let us assume that this result would mean that 5 of the players would not pay even if the other 5 did pay. In this circumstance, the benefit to each player would be 1 unit, and the cost to each of the 5 payers would be 1 unit: hence, the payoff to the payers would be zero. Consequently, even an analysis which prescribed cooperation, or paying, as the rational strategy under the assumption of all players rational would allow nonpayment as a rational strategy to players in a real world game in which habitual nonpayers drained off any positive payoff to the payers. Assuming the validity of the generalization from the prisoners' dilemma experimental data, in real world games in which the law of large numbers applies and in which the perceived benefits of the collective good are not more than twice the costs, one can expect no provision of the collective good for reasons different from Olson's logic. In the intermediate group (where the statistics of large numbers do not apply), even with benefits considerably less than twice the costs, there is some statistical chance that a collective good will be provided. In either case, the prospects for success decline as the ratio (or perceived ratio) of benefits to costs decreases, and as the differential perception of that ratio increases while the average perceived ratio remains constant.

As Olson (1965, p. 24) notes, the issue is not so much what an adversary-member's payoff will be, but rather whether anyone will choose to play the game at all. In the 10-prisoners' dilemma analysis here, by a different logic, it follows that one of the basic tenets of game theory is in one sense not useful in real world application. Ordinarily, in game theoretical analyses the actual values of payoffs are not important; the only consideration is the rank ordering of payoffs. But clearly, the normal inducement to play a real world game is the expectation of positive payoffs. Hence, a rational player in the game of collective action does not refuse to pay merely because his strategy of not paying is dominant and yields a higher payoff; rather he refuses to pay because enough others in the group do not pay that he would suffer a net cost if he did. Consequently, it would be irrational for him to play the game, and not playing means not paying. (However, this reasoning cannot be considered to give a proof that collective action will fail. That remains an empirical matter.)

THE CONDORCET CHOICE SOLUTION OF
THE GAME OF COLLECTIVE ACTION

The usual analysis of prisoners' dilemma prescribes a strategy: the dominating strategy which in the 10-person game of collective action discussed above would be not to pay. Because the general employment of that strategy produces an undesirable outcome, and because many (roughly half) of the subjects in some 2-prisoners' dilemma experiments have not employed that strategy, it would be useful to analyze the outcomes (as opposed to the strategies) of the larger game of collective action. The matrix for the 10-person binary choice game has 2^{10} or 1024 cells, each of which is a uniquely defined potential outcome of the game. Instead of considering the strategies of the players, let us view the game as though the 10 players were collectively choosing among the 1024 outcomes. With a simple notation these 1024 outcomes can be represented as 20 classes of outcomes. We can readily ascertain which among these classes are realizable outcomes, and can determine whether any among the realizable outcomes is a Condorcet choice. It will be a simple matter to demonstrate that in any game of collective action with n players and a ratio r, $r > 1$, of benefits to payments there is a Condorcet choice among the realizable outcomes, and it is the outcome defined by all players paying and all receiving payoffs of $r - 1$ units.

2*n* Classes of Outcomes

In the 10-person game of collective action, the possible outcomes in the view of an Individual in the game are as in Matrix 3. The entries in the top row are Individual's payoffs when all ten players pay, nine players including Individual pay, etc. Those in the bottom row are Individual's payoffs when he does not pay, ranging from the case in which all nine other players pay to the case in which no one pays. The upper left payoff results from only one outcome of the game: all pay. The upper row payoff of 0, however, results from 126 different outcomes of the game: all the possible combinations in which Individual and four other players pay while five players do not pay.

It will be useful to represent these classes of outcomes more generally. Let N_k represent any outcome in which exactly k players, including Individual, do not pay. And let P_k represent any outcome in which exactly k players, including Individual, pay. Matrix 3 can be rewritten as Matrix 3a. It is now a simple matter to rank order the outcomes according to Individual's preference; the position of an outcome P or N is determined by the payoff to Individual associated with it.

MATRIX 3
Payoff to i in 10-Prisoner's Dilemma, r = 2

Number besides *i* who pay		9	8	7	6	5	4	3	2	1	0
Payoff to *i* if *i*	pays	1.0	0.8	0.6	0.4	0.2	0	-0.2	-0.4	-0.6	-0.8
	does not pay	1.8	1.6	1.4	1.2	1.0	0.8	0.6	0.4	0.2	0

MATRIX 3a

Pay	P_{10}	P_9	P_8	P_7	P_6	P_5	P_4	P_3	P_2	P_1
Not Pay	N_1	N_2	N_3	N_4	N_5	N_6	N_7	N_8	N_9	N_{10}

Table 1 presents Individual's preference ordering and gives the total number of outcomes in the full 10-dimensional game matrix associated with each payoff class.

Clearly, Individual can guarantee himself his minimax payoff (N_{10} at the lower right in Matrix 3a). Those outcomes P_4, P_3, P_2, and P_1 which fall below the minimax line in Table 1, therefore, are outcomes which he can unilaterally prevent by not paying. Similarly, however, every other player in the game can prevent his own P_4, P_3, P_2, and P_1 outcomes, so that the

TABLE 1

Payoff Class	Number of Outcomes in this Class
N_1	1
N_2	9
N_3	36
N_4	84
P_{10}, N_5	1,126
P_9, N_6	9,126
P_8, N_7	36,84
P_7, N_8	84,36
P_6, N_9	126,9
P_5, N_{10}	126,1
P_4	84
P_3	36
P_2	9
P_1	1
	Total 1024

complementary outcomes N_6, N_7, N_8, and N_9 of opposing players will be prevented (for instance, an N_9 can occur only if some player is willing to pay when no one else does, thus putting himself into a P_1 outcome). Hence, none of these outcomes is realizable, i.e., they would require that some player willingly decline below his minimax, as few of us are wont to do.[2] The only outcomes which can obtain in a play of the game are those of Table 2. It is from this set of realizable outcomes that the players must seek an agreeable outcome. If one of these outcomes is a Condorcet choice for the set, it is the prominently rational outcome of the game.

Condorcet Choice

We can define strong and weak Condorcet choices.[3] Let C be the collective (i.e., the group) of n members choosing among outcomes in the matrix of an n-person collective action game, and let j and k be outcomes from the set M of realizable outcomes in the game matrix (in the 10-prisoners' dilemma matrix there are 1024 cells, of which 639 are realizable outcomes). Let c_{jk} be the number of those in C who prefer outcome j to outcome k, and let c'_{jk} be the number of those in C who are indifferent to whether outcome j or outcome k obtains. Clearly, $c_{jk} + c_{kj} + c'_{jk} = n$.

TABLE 2

N_1	
N_2	
N_3	
N_4	
P_{10}, N_5	
P_9	
P_8	
P_7	
P_6	
P_5, N_{10}	

Definition: j is a strong Condorcet choice if it is preferred by a majority in C to every k ($\neq j$) in M. Reduced to symbolic brevity, this condition is

$$c_{jk} > n/2 \text{ for all } k \neq j.$$

Definition: j is a weak Condorcet choice if it is not a strong Condorcet choice but if, for each $k \neq j$, more of those in C prefer j to k than k to j. This condition is simply

$$c_{jk} > c_{kj} \text{ for all } k \neq j.$$

It should be clear that there can be at most one Condorcet choice.

From the definition of the game of collective action for n players the following theorem for the existence of a Condorcet choice among the set of realizable outcomes can be derived.

Theorem: For an n-person game of collective action, P_n is a Condorcet choice from the set of realizable outcomes for the game; it is a strong Condorcet choice except in a game in which n is even and $r = 2$, in which case P_n is a weak Condorcet choice from the set of realizable outcomes.

The proof of this theorem, which is not difficult but is tedious, is left to the appendix. However, it will be instructive to see that it holds for the case of 10-prisoners' dilemma. We need only to compare the outcome P_{10} to each of the other realizable outcomes listed in Table 2 to show that P_{10} is preferred to each of these others. Given an outcome of the class N_1, nine players will prefer P_{10}. Similarly, given an outcome of the class N_2, N_3, or N_4, eight, seven, or six players, respectively, will prefer P_{10}. And nine, eight, seven, or six players will prefer P_{10} to any outcome of the class P_9, P_8, P_7, or P_6, respectively. Finally, given an outcome of the class N_5, the five players whose outcomes are of the class P_5 will prefer outcome P_{10}; and the five players whose outcomes are of the class N_5 will be indifferent to the choice between N_5 and P_{10}. Consequently, a clear majority of the players will prefer P_{10} to any outcome except N_5, in which case all of those with a preference will prefer P_{10}. It follows that P_{10} is a weak Condorcet choice. It is weak because the game has an even number of players and a ratio of benefits to contributions of 2.[4]

Degeneracy—Back to the Prisoners' Dilemma

At the limits of the preceding analysis there occur several classes of degenerate games of collective action. These result when $r = 1$ or $n = 2$.

In the degenerate case of $r = 1$, the realizable outcomes are P_n and N_n, and all players are indifferent as to which of these obtains. For all cases of $r < 1$, the only realizable outcome is N_n. The game will not be played.

In the degenerate case of $n = 2$ there are five possibilities: $r < 1$, $r = 1$, $1 < r < 2$, $r = 2$, $r > 2$. The first two of these are degenerate in r. In the case of $r = 2$, all outcomes are realizable and the outcome of both pay is a weak Condorcet choice. If $r > 2$, each player's return from his own contribution is greater than his contribution, so presumably both will pay and reap appropriate benefits (recall that in general $r > n$ implies that the group is a privileged group in Olson's terms). The interesting cases remain. They are those for $1 < r < 2$. They are represented in Matrix 4.

The payoffs in the games of Matrix 4 are related according to the preference ordering (if $1 < r < 2$):

$$r/2 > (r - 1) > 0 > (r/2 - 1).$$

This condition meets the definition of the symmetric 2-prisoners' dilemma game. For example, Rapoport and Chammah (1965, pp. 33-34) define the symmetric prisoners' dilemma by the condition that the payoffs (as given in Matrix 5) satisfy the relation:

$$T > R > P > S,$$

in which the letters didactically stand for Temptation (to defect), Reward (for cooperating), Punishment (for defecting), and Sucker's payoff (for cooperating). Note that the preference ordering for row is as in Figure 1.

MATRIX 4

$r - 1, r - 1$	$(r/2 - 1), r/2$
$r/2, (r/2 - 1)$	$0, 0$

MATRIX 5

R, R	*S, T*
T, S	*P, P*

From the preference ordering and Matrix 4, it can be seen that only the outcomes $(r-1, r-1)$ and $(0, 0)$ are realizable, and that of these $(r-1, r-1)$ is a strong Condorcet choice.

CONCLUSION

It has been shown that the problem of collective action can be represented as a game with a strategic structure similar to that of prisoners' dilemma. The logic which prescribes that a member of a group should not contribute toward the purchase of his group collective interest is the same as that which prescribes that a player in a game of prisoners' dilemma should defect (i.e., should not cooperate). However, from the set of all realizable outcomes in a game of collective action in which the ratio of benefits to contributions exceeds 1, the outcome in which all contribute is a Condorcet choice. The existence of a Condorcet choice, which is by definition unique, implies that a real world group could decide in favor of the Condorcet choice over every other realizable outcome. Consequently, it is rational in a world in which distrust seems endemic to use sanctions to enforce all members of an interest group to contribute toward the purchase of the group interest (Olson, 1965, p. 51). In a world not quite Hobbesian a threat of all against all might, ironically, help overcome distrust.

However, the threat of all against all is not a logical necessity; rather, it is only a potentially useful device, given human psychology. For, there is debate in the literature on the prisoners' dilemma as to whether the cooperative or the noncooperative outcome is rational or logically determinate. Therefore, it can hardly be granted that, as Olson contends, in the absence of sanctions in a latent group "it is certain that a collective good will *not* be provided," whereas in an intermediate group the result is merely indeterminate. The clarity of the analogy between the logic of collective action and the strategic structure of the prisoners' dilemma game makes it seem likely (as suggested above) that the differences in the statistics of success for the intermediate and latent groups is a function of statistics on, for example, the social distribution of distrust; but in any case it is not a derivation from the logic inherent in the group interactions.

NOTES

1. Within a broad range, this assumption entails only that the payoffs in the upper right and lower left cells in Matrix 1 will contain payoffs only slightly higher or lower than might have been the case for a real world problem. Consequently, the logical dynamics of the game are unaffected by the assumption.

2. The use of this term conforms with Howard [1971] in whose metagame theory an outcome is metarational for all players if every player's payoff in that outcome is at least equal to his minimax payoff. Hence, the only realizable outcomes are those which are metarational for all players.

3. Named for the eighteenth century French economist and intellectual in general, the Marquis de Condorcet, who studied the problem of electoral majorities, believed in man's capacity for unlimited progress, and chose to poison himself rather than meet the guillotine during the Terror.

4. It was noted above that prisoners' dilemma is the only one of the Rapoport-Guyer games with a strongly stable equilibrium that is not Pareto-optimal. This statement can be made stronger. Every outcome in the 2-prisoners' dilemma is Pareto-optimal except the outcome of mutual loss. In a game of collective action this stronger statement also usually holds. However, if r divides n, then any outcome defined by $N_{n/r}$ for n/r of the players is not Pareto-optimal. (This is because $n - n/r$ of the players would benefit in a shift from this outcome to P_n, and the other n/r players would be indifferent to the shift.) All other outcomes in any game of collective action are Pareto-optimal except the single dismal solution N_n.

7 • Introduction

W. J. Baumol's *Welfare Economics and the Theory of the State* was first published in 1952. Although it antedated Mancur Olson's treatment of the problem of collective action, it never seems to have made a similar impact on those outside the field of economics, and is at present regrettably out of print. We have chosen two complete chapters to reprint here, which bear particularly closely on the subject of the collection. But the whole book may be strongly recommended, even to those with no training in economics. The exposition is very clear and straightforward, and relatively nontechnical.

Baumol's theme is well captured by his title, *Welfare Economics and the Theory of the State*. Starting from the premises of neoclassical welfare economics, Baumol focuses attention on the role of externalities in providing a justification, on those premises, for a society-wide coercive agency, in other words a state. In these introductory remarks, we shall endeavor to explain two of the terms just used, "neoclassical welfare economics" and "externalities," and then, armed with these, return to Baumol's argument.

"Neoclassical economics" is not a term with a completely precise meaning, but may be said to include what most people simply think of as "economics," and to encompass the best known figures in the recent history of the subject such as J. R. Hicks, Paul Samuelson, and Kenneth Arrow. Two of the key ideas in neoclassical economics that underlie Baumol's discussion are those of equilibrium and marginal analysis, and these are worth a few words for the benefit of those unfamiliar with this kind of economic analysis. The central concern of neoclassical economics is the way in which production and consumption are determined in an (idealized) market, and that concern is considered to be satisfied when an equilibrium has been established to exist. Roughly speaking, an equilibrium exists in an economy when none of the actors in that economy (producers or consumers) can improve its situation by unilaterally changing its behavior, given the behavior of all the others; and a given actor may be said to be in equilibrium when that actor, taking the behavior of all others as given, cannot improve its own position by changing its behavior. Thus, to take the most elementary case, supply and demand for some commodity are in equilibrium in a market when the price is such that there are no unsatisfied buyers (i.e., people who at that price would like to buy more than is available) or frustrated sellers (i.e., people who at that price would like to sell more than they can find buyers for).

Baumol does not confine his analysis to idealized markets, and he does not, in the selections given here, make explicit use of the concept of equilibrium. But central to his whole discussion is the question posed in equilibrium analysis: under what circumstances can we identify situations in which nobody has any incentive to change his behavior after all the other actors have made their moves?

The other basic idea in neoclassical economics that needs a few words is that of marginal analysis. This concept permeates Baumol's book, though it becomes explicit in our selections only in section II, where he mentions the standard prescriptions of welfare economics for an optimum (a term to be explained below). The underlying assumption of marginal analysis is the slogan used as an epigraph by Alfred Marshall in his *Principles of Economics* (1920) *natura non facit salta*—nature does not make leaps. This assumption makes possible the application of the calculus in economics, and it would scarcely be an exaggeration to say that neoclassical economics is built on the calculus. Now, in the calculus, the conditions for a maximum are given when the first derivative is zero. Marginal analysis is the translation into economic terms of that mathematical notion.

Thus, we left our consumers and producers, in the discussion of equilibrium, trying to "improve their position," given the actions of others. Let us first give this more precision. A mere desire for improvement is not enough to yield determinate results in economic analysis. We therefore postulate no less than that any rational actor must be taken to be attempting to maximize something. In the case of firms (producers) this is normally taken to be profit; in the case of households (consumers) it is said to be utility.

We can now ask what are the conditions for maximizing profit or utility and these turn out to be most clearly expressed in marginalist terms. Thus, if we suppose that the only question facing a firm is how much to produce of some commodity, we can, in principle, construct a schedule connecting the marginal profit (marginal revenue minus marginal cost) of each additional unit of production. This may be expected to be negative for the first units (because of fixed costs), then to become positive and eventually to turn negative at some point. Profit is maximized where the marginal profit accruing from a further unit of production is zero, or, to put it another way, when marginal cost equals marginal revenue. The same kind of analysis can be applied to other decisions by a firm.

For a consumer, utility is maximized when the marginal utility derived from each commodity purchased is equal; in other words, when the last unit of any one kind of thing bought yields the same utility as the last unit of any other. Equilibrium, then, is to be defined against a background of maximization by all economic agents, construed in this manner.

Welfare economics is the branch of economics that is concerned with evaluation and prescription. Clearly, in order to function it requires evaluative premises. That is to say, welfare economics is a branch of applied ethics or it is nothing. Some would conclude that in that case it is nothing, but the dominant line has been to posit what are claimed to be very weak evaluative principles. We shall be pursuing one development of this in the second part of the collection, when we follow Arrow's proof of the impossibility of combining several such principles, and the work to which that proof has given rise. For the present, however, we may concentrate on just one of Arrow's principles, Pareto optimality. This, as will be seen, plays a central role in the first selection (section I) from Baumol and was, indeed, taken as the crucial element in the welfare economics of that period. (Little [1950] is a philosophically acute discussion of the "state of the art" at about the same time as Baumol's book was written.)

To explain the position of this principle, we should begin by noting that the dominant evaluative view in classical economics was utilitarianism. The workings of the economy were, like everything else, to be judged in accordance with their tendency (or nontendency) to maximize the sum total of human happiness (or, perhaps, happiness within the society in question). For a variety of reasons, some better than others, economists in the twentieth century have shied away from the utilitarian criterion, and have sought to replace it with something weaker. As Baier points out in the essay we reprint in Part II of this collection, it is precisely the retreat to weak principles that has set the stage for the crisis precipitated by Arrow. Let us, however, for now follow through the way in which Pareto optimality came to seem a logical candidate to replace the utilitarian criterion.

Vilfredo Pareto, who gives his name to the principle, is best known as a sociologist on the grand scale. But he was originally an economist and his *Cours d'economie politique* (1896-1897) was a respected text in its day. Pareto was in fact a good deal more subtle in his analysis than almost any subsequent economists. He distinguished between "utility" as something that an individual maximizes by most effectively pursuing the satisfaction of his entire set of drives ("residues" for Pareto) and "ophelimity" (from Greek ōphelimon: beneficial or profitable), which is maximized when an individual gets the maximum of satisfaction from his purchases in a market. Without explaining his reasoning, Pareto said that the "utility of a society" made sense, in that, for example, a government had to trade off the loss to a criminal of punishing him against the gain to the security of the rest of the community. But the notion of the "ophelimity of a society" was nonsense, because different people's ophelimities were noncomparable. However, one could define an alternative concept, which could be used by economists in their scientific work. This was "ophelimity *for* a society" and could be said to be maximized under certain conditions. Pareto first defined two kinds of moves that might be made from a given situation.

> Movements of a first type, P, are such that, beneficial to certain individuals, they are necessarily harmful to others. Movements of the second type, Q, are such that they are to the advantage, or to the detriment, of all individuals without exception (Pareto 1980, §871 = 1935 §2128).

Movements of the second type, Q, are now called Pareto-superior moves. Pareto then went on to formulate the notion of "the maximum ophelimity for a community" and thus gave birth to what is now called Pareto optimality:

> When the community stands at a point Q, it is obvious that from the economic standpoint it is advisable not to stop at that point, but to move on from it as far as the movement away from it is advantageous to all. When, then, the point P, where that is no longer possible, is reached, it is necessary, as regards the advisability of stopping there or going on, to resort to other considerations foreign to economics—to decide on grounds of ethics, social utility, or something else, which individuals it is advisable to benefit, which to sacrifice. That point plays in the situation a role analogous to the role of the point where the maximum of individual ophelimity is obtained and at which, accordingly, the individual stops. Because of that analogy it has been called *point of maximum ophelimity FOR the community* (Pareto 1980, §872 = 1935, §2129).

Subsequent economists have given up Pareto's careful distinction between ophelimity and utility, and have run into a good deal of gratuitous trouble as a result. Thus, that a perfectly competitive market equilibrium is a Pareto optimum has been an article of faith since Adam Smith (even if not formulated precisely in those terms) though it was proved rigorously only in 1951 (Arrow 1951, Debreu 1951; see also Arrow and Debreu 1954; Debreu 1959; Arrow and Hahn 1971). This proposition holds only for ophelimity, whereas economists also take up notions such as Pareto-optimal distribution arising from interdependent utility functions (where my utility depends partly on yours), and this makes sense only if the subject is utility rather than ophelimity. (Pareto specified that one could define "utility for a society" on the same lines as "ophelimity for a society.") As we shall see in Part II, the difficulties in social choice theory arise to a large extent from the heterogeneous nature of the "preferences" admitted into the aggregation process. The boundary that Pareto drew between welfare economics, as the sphere of ophelimity, and other modes of evaluation that deal in utilities has been breached.

In modern welfare economics, Pareto superiority and Pareto optimality are defined in a slightly weaker form than they were defined (in different words) by Pareto. According to Pareto, we are to say that society is better off in state x than state y if and only if everyone is better off in state x than in state y. In the less strong formulation, we are to say that state x is Pareto-superior to state y if nobody is worse off in state x than in state y and at least one person is better off. Pareto optimality may now be defined in a correspondingly weak form as follows: a state of society is Pareto-optimal if there is no state of society that is Pareto-superior to it, that is, no state of society such that in moving to it, nobody would be made worse off and at least one person would be made better off. Pareto optimality is thus a sort of efficiency: to say that some situation is suboptimal is to say that there is some other situation available as a feasible alternative in the transition to which nobody would lose and some would gain.

We should, however, be careful not to overstate the case. There will be many—in principle, infinitely many—Pareto-optimal alternatives open to a society at any given time. However inequitable some situation may be, it is Pareto-optimal if there is no way of making at least one person better off without making at least one person (Caligula, the Shah of Iran, Idi Amin, Hitler, Somoza) worse off. And there is, as Pareto acknowledged, no criterion internal to the principle for comparing alternative Pareto-optimal states of affairs with one another, even if one has only a single well-off person slightly worse off than the other, and everybody else much better off. In the 1940s, economists toyed with the idea that one situation might be said to be better than another if it were *potentially* Pareto-superior, that is to say, if the gainers could, even if they in fact did not, compensate the losers from the change. But this ran into problems of internal consistency and was soon abandoned.

It should also be noted that it would be a complete fallacy to say, as one may easily be tempted to slip into doing, that any Pareto-optimal situation is better than any suboptimal one. In fact, between most suboptimal situations and most optimal ones, no comparison can be made, in terms of the Pareto criterion. Only that subset of Pareto optima that dominate (i.e., are Pareto-superior to) a given suboptimal situation can properly be said to be better than it.

Thus, the scope of the Pareto principle is very narrow. It makes only very selective comparisons. Even here, it is a value judgment that a Pareto-optimal situation is superior to a suboptimal one that it dominates. But it is thought by many economists to be an uncontroversial, obvious, or rational one.

The link with rationality can be made stronger if a further step towards
individualism (or, better, subjectivism) is taken. "Better off" leaves it open as
to whose judgment is to be taken as decisive: I may think, for example, that
you would be better off without something that you happen (unwisely, in my
opinion) to want. If so, the fact that you would be, in my view, better off in
situation x than situation y, does not give you a reason for agreeing, if you
think that situation y is preferable to situation x. This complication can be
eliminated by stipulating that the expression "A is better off in x than in y"
is to be taken as equivalent to "A prefers x to y." And this step has been
endorsed as a part of orthodox welfare economics. Thus, having first taken
the line that we will refuse ever to judge that it is worth making A worse off
in order to make B better off, we now further abdicate from making
potentially controversial judgments, this time about whether or not people
are better off in one situation than another. Instead, we take their own
(stated or inferred) preferences as the final arbiter of that.

The Pareto principle, now formulated in terms of preferences, reads as
follows: x is Pareto-superior to y if and only if everyone weakly prefers x to
y; and x is Pareto-optimal if and only if there does not exist some y that is
Pareto-superior to it. "Weak preference" as used here is a term of art. To say
that A weakly prefers x to y means that A either prefers x to y or is
indifferent about the choice between x and y. In other words, the only
preference relation ruled out is that of preferring y to x. (This has the
linguistically curious implication that A could weakly prefer x to y and at the
same time y to x—if he is indifferent about the choice between them.)

So stated, the Pareto principle edges closer toward being obvious,
uncontroversial, and a deduction from the concept of rationality. We can,
indeed, begin to see how it is sometimes referred to as a condition of
collective rationality. For the central element of individual rationality (as the
term is used by economists, social choice theorists and game theorists) is that
of people getting more, rather than less, of what they want—getting further
up their preference schedules. (See further on this notion section II of the
Epilogue to this book.) But if a Pareto-superior move is one in which some
get higher up their preference schedules and the rest get no lower, it is hard to
see why the same concept of rationality should not indicate that it is
collectively rational to make the change.

However, the very triviality of the conclusion should alert us to the
suspicion that not much is now being said. We are left with near-tautology
that if everyone in some society prefers one state of affairs to another, it is
better for that society if the preferred state of affairs is brought about. (Of
course, if others outside the society are adversely affected, the state of affairs
preferred by all the members of the society may still be judged worse by an
"impartial spectator," so the qualification "better for the society" is needed.)

It is not a strict tautology because, although *ex hypothesi* nobody in the society has any objection to the change, it is still open for anyone else to believe that some people in the society are mistaken about their interests and would be better off without the change. This person can still therefore say that the move does not make everyone better off. And he can indeed say that it is not rational to make the change. But this line of challenge is, of course, open only to those who do not equate rationality with moving up one's preference schedule.

The price paid in return for the simplification achieved by eliminating everything save preferences as the raw materials for an evaluation is an extremely heavy one. For it has the consequence that it is almost impossible to say when one situation is Pareto-superior to another, and certainly impossible to state any robust general conditions for Pareto superiority. Thus, consider a case in which you get something you prefer but I think you will really be worse off, and in which nobody (including myself) is in the ordinary sense of the term affected one way or the other. Then, if I have a disinterested concern for your welfare, I will prefer that the change not be made. Since there is now one person who prefers the status quo to the alternative, namely me, the change is no longer a Pareto-superior move. Or suppose that you are genuinely made better off, in my opinion (as well as yours), and, again that nobody else is, in the ordinary sense, affected one way or the other; but now suppose that I simply don't like the idea of your being better off. Then, again, we cannot say that the change would constitute a Pareto-superior move.

We have, at last, arrived, as promised long ago, at the concept of an externality. And we have, at the same time, arrived with enough intellectual baggage to be able to see how externalities precipitate what Baumol calls "the wreck of welfare economics." First, the concept of externality. The term has been variously defined, in accordance with different economists' theoretical interests and political predilections (see Buchanan and Stubblebine 1962). But for our purposes the rough definition given by Schelling in the first footnote of the selection from him will suffice. The term "externality," he says, "refers to the effects of a firm's actions, or an agency's or a person's, that are beyond and outside—'external to'—the firm's accounting or the agency's purview or the person's interests and concerns, but within the accounting, the purview, or the interest of somebody else." For the case in hand, the particular application of the general idea of externality that is relevant is its application to the market: an externality is an effect (desired or undesired) on someone that is not reflected in the market. Thus, if I envy your prosperity or dislike the sound of your new recording of *Goetterdaemmerung* through the walls of my apartment, that is an externality of consumption. (So also if I rejoice in your prosperity and enjoy muffled Wagner.) An externality of production occurs when the cost to the firm of producing something that enters into its accounts does not include all the actual effects. The stock case is air pollution from a factory chimney, which is a cost to those downwind (and possibly a benefit to those upwind if they like lurid sunsets), but is not included in the firm's accounting.

The connection with "the wreck of welfare economics" is as follows. Economists, having come up with the Pareto criterion, naturally wished to apply it to the evaluation of economic institutions. The main effort of neoclassical economists has been directed to trying to show that, under certain ideal conditions, a perfect market would give rise to a Pareto optimum. This is, as we have seen, an inherently weak claim, given that there are infinitely many potential Pareto optima, and one may well prefer (on distributive grounds) another optimum or even a suboptimum if that is all that can in practice be realized. But an equally serious limitation is the conditions required for a market to produce a Pareto optimum. Among these is lack of externalities. As soon as externalities exist, the claim that a perfect market (even with all the other conditions) produces an optimum collapses. That is to say, each person's preferences should extend strictly to his own consumption alone, and nobody should have any preferences for the conduct (or existence) of productive operations that are not captured by the market. (For example, the unpleasantness of the working conditions in a certain factory should be compensated for in a perfectly functioning labor market by higher wages than would be paid elsewhere for the same work.) Clearly, however, externalities are rife, so the fundamental theorem of welfare economics is left high and dry. This is set out and discussed clearly in the second selection from Baumol so there is no need to go into it further here. The only additional comment that seems called for is to point out that the conjecture stated by Baumol that departure from one of the conditions for an optimum may require departure from the others in order to arrive at a second best has been proved by Lipsey and Lancaster (1956).

A final word may be useful, however, on a few of the specifics in section I, which corresponds to the first of the two chapters selected for reprinting here. "The ideal on Pareto's criterion" is the condition of Pareto optimality. As we have seen, the whole idea of Pareto optimality is that for a suboptimal ("nonideal") situation there is some other situation that is weakly preferred by all. Therefore, it ought in principle to be possible to agree on a move from any suboptimal situation to a Pareto-optimal one that dominates it. But, as Baumol points out, there are difficulties in actually achieving such a shift. These are discussed in subsections 1 and 2 of section I, and will be familiar in general terms from Olson's treatment of the problem of collective action. Then in section 3, Baumol discusses conditions under which "ideal" conditions may nevertheless be achieved. The particular way in which he poses the problem is to imagine that a society has a choice between the alternatives of cartelization all round and no cartelization. He assumes (though this clearly need not be the case) that everybody loses with cartelization all round in comparison with no cartelization. How then, could one achieve the "ideal" of noncartelization?

The first answer is at the core of Olson's "small group" phenomenon. Each person watches the others and, as soon as any cartelization occurs, the others are expected to cartelize too. This can be conceptualized as an iterated n-person prisoner's dilemma in which defection by any party meets immediate and universal retaliation by the rest. Baumol illustrates this from the experience of cartels, and one must be alert to the change of reference here. From the point of view of a cartel, the "ideal" *is* restriction of production to push prices above their market equilibrium level, and, as Baumol points out, the fear that a price cut (advantageous to each firm if the others do not follow suit, but disadvantageous if they do) will be followed by all other firms may keep potential defectors in line. The "kinked demand curve" referred to here is a graphical expression of the idea: the demand curve, instead of sloping smoothly down to the right (when quantity is plotted on the horizontal axis and price on the vertical axis), is almost horizontal to the left of the currently prevailing price and almost vertical to the right of it, making a "kink" at the point representing the status quo. This reflects the idea that if a firm raises its price above the prevailing level, it loses a lot of sales (because other firms don't follow suit), but that if it lowers it, it doesn't gain sales (because the others do follow suit). If this is so, then the firm loses by departing from the status quo in either direction.

The second solution offered by Baumol is that the problem may not arise if cartelization is too difficult to carry out. This is obviously true, though not very interesting from the present point of view. Again, however, one should keep in mind a dual perspective. From the point of view of the whole society, perfect competition is the cooperative solution to a prisoner's dilemma, since all benefit (it is supposed) from competition all round rather than cartelization all round. But from the point of view of would-be colluders (say, farmers who wish they could get an agreement to restrict production) the free market *is* a prisoner's dilemma. The same point may, of course, be made of the prisoners in the original story: from the point of view of the rest of the society, their dilemma is a good thing if it produces two (true) confessions.

The third solution is that of state intervention, in this case presumably through antitrust activity. As Baumol has emphasized earlier in the book, this is the classic formula of social contract theory. Mutually destructive behavior is escaped from by mutual coercion mutually agreed on. Within liberal social and political theory (of which economics may be regarded as a branch), the justification for the state thus lies in its providing a solution to the problems posed by externalities and public goods.

7

WELFARE ECONOMICS AND THE THEORY OF THE STATE

William J. Baumol

THE STABILITY OF IDEAL AND NON-IDEAL SITUATIONS

I

When there is a deviation from the ideal on Pareto's criterion it is always possible to improve the situation by inducing each individual whose activity is deleterious to the best interests of the group to modify his ways. What is in effect involved is an increase in the productive capacity of the group. This means that every member of the group can obtain exactly as much as before the change and in addition there will be something left over. If this residue is divided in such a manner as to use part of it for a bonus to those who must modify their activity in order for this surplus to occur at all, then it will be rational for a voluntary switchover to ideal activity to take place.

Since *ex hypothesi* the possibility of such a rearrangement does in fact exist with each deviation from the ideal, it may seem paradoxical to suppose that such a deviation will ever fail to disappear where people are rational and the cost of administration of a compensatory arrangement is not prohibitive.

When a large number of individuals is involved there are several means whereby a deviation from the ideal may be eliminated without government intervention (but it should be noted that each of these is a departure from purely individualistic behaviour).[1] First, some person or set of persons may

Reprinted by permission of the publishers and the author from *Welfare Economics and the Theory of the State*, Second Edition, by William J. Baumol, Cambridge, Mass.: Harvard University Press, pp. 173-179, 204-207, Copyright © 1965 by William J. Baumol.

deliberately set about to organize the change; but for several reasons such direct action may not always be undertaken. It involves initiative which may not in all cases be forthcoming, especially where the number of people concerned is so large that few consider themselves sufficiently influential for the task. It involves a risk of miscalculation which may result in at least an opportunity loss to the organizers. Finally, it may encounter recalcitrance on the part of some persons which may arise out of mistrust of motives, lack of confidence in the outcome, or because, should others be induced to act ideally, they may then be able to gain by acting individualistically.

When there is established no such specific co-ordinating system, the elimination of the non-ideal situation becomes considerably more difficult. Each individual is now necessarily operating by himself, and his ability to modify the circumstances in which he finds himself is limited.

Let us consider the extreme but not necessarily unrealistic case of a large group of individuals many of whom are not acting ideally, and assume that the activities of each of these adversely affect the welfare of many other members of the group. What alternatives are open to any one such person to improve his situation? If he switches to an ideal course of activity by himself he will, on the balance, only worsen his own position. He may seek to arrange with other individuals that they act ideally in return for which he would compensate them for any disadvantage accruing to them from the change, but since he is an isolated individual this course, too, is likely to prove unprofitable to him, the ill effects from the activities of the other persons of the group which he suffers being only a small proportion of the total ill effects created.

Let us call our individual A, and let B be some member of the group whose activity affects A adversely. Since the undesirable consequences of B's activity are assumed to be spread over many members of the group, A, as has been stated, may be subjected to only a small proportion of these. While the sum total of the ill effects of B's untoward activity is taken to exceed in value what he gains from deviating from the ideal, it is by no means necessarily true that A's loss exceeds the gain of B. If B's gain does exceed A's loss, then A will not be able profitably to induce him to switch to an ideal course of activity. We must conclude that the only way to eliminate a generally disadvantageous situation of the sort contemplated is by concerted action of all the individuals involved.

We have now come to the root of the paradox: we have seen how an economy composed of rational individuals may involve a situation in which some modification is possible which would improve everyone's lot. So long as complete co-ordination of the activities of the individuals composing the economy cannot be readily effected, situations such as we have just described are likely to arise. Their essential characteristic is that the individual members of the economy will find it distinctly to their disadvantage to act alone in a manner calculated to eliminate the presumably undesirable circumstance. This sort of situation is especially likely to occur where none of the individuals involved plays a dominant role in the economy. The minimum formal condition necessary for such a departure from the ideal to persist is very easily satisfied—it requires merely that among the individuals who are not behaving ideally there be one the adverse effects of whose activities be so widely diffused through the community that no *one* person can profitably bribe him to change his ways.

II

The standard example of the smoke nuisance in cities is a particularly convenient illustration, and may be briefly recapitulated to show how it fits in with the analysis. The besmirching of city air by industrial enterprises can often be mitigated by various devices, and it may be to the net advantage of the community to install these. It is noteworthy that, should the entrepreneurs in control of the smoke-producing firms live in this community, each will suffer some ill effects of his own activities along with everybody else, and so each of them may be contributing to his own discomfort.[2] But if one entrepreneur introduces smoke-reducing devices into his own firm he will not necessarily cause other entrepreneurs to emulate his example. If the contribution of his one firm to the total smoke content of the atmosphere is small the effect may be unnoticeable. If the individual offered to compensate each of the offending firms for the installation of smoke-eliminating devices it would amount to his offering to bear the entire cost of the smoke-reducing equipment by himself. It is thus that the minimization of smoke nuisance in a community, even where those who create the smoke are at the same time inhabitants, cannot always be left to the independent action of the individuals comprising that community. If it is judged that there exist opportunities for the reduction of smoke whose cost is justified from the point of view of the community as a whole, then government action may be justified.

III

It is not legitimate to argue that once the ideal is attained no individual can improve his circumstances by any means and so there will be no inducement for anyone to inaugurate any change. It is true that it cannot be profitable for *everyone* to enter into an alternative arrangement, for since the arrangement was initially ideal there can be no net gain to all from such a change. However, this does not imply that the situation will not tend to break down at all, although we can easily picture a stable, ideal situation, for example, if the cost of arranging any deviation is prohibitive.

By hypothesis total welfare is in an ideal situation in some sense at a maximum. This implies, generally, that if the welfare of any one individual is to increase, it must do so at someone else's expense, i.e. by means of a redistribution of existing want-satisfying items. This means that where activity designed to alter the distributive arrangements can be undertaken successfully, an ideal situation may be departed from in pursuit of self-interest.

Consider, for example, a money economy in which welfare is automatically distributed in proportion with money wealth. Assume that the elasticity of demand for every commodity taken by itself is less than unity, and that the producers (or sellers) of each commodity can, by a *ceteris paribus* restriction of the output of that commodity, increase their wealth. In that case it will pay any individual to organize a restriction in output of the commodity which he produces or sells provided this is done in no other line of endeavour. Now it is true that he runs the risk of actually losing in the process if his commodity fails to be the only one whose output is restricted, because if that happens the end situation will be one where the total amount of every good available for distribution is less than before and the relative claims of different members of the group to these goods is unaltered. But the risk of incurring this loss will not necessarily deter a member of the group from deviating from the initial arrangement. If the output of his commodity is not restricted at all, this does not preclude restriction of the quantity of other commodities. Should this occur not only will there be a smaller amount available of most commodities but this particular person will also obtain a smaller share than previously, at least until a restriction of the output of his own commodity can also be arranged. In this case anyone may obtain a temporary gain and set some sort of minimum to any ultimate loss by immediately involving himself in a deviation from the ideal situation.

It is true that any deviation from the ideal, once it is realized, may be unstable in turn, for it will be possible for every member of the group to gain by returning to an ideal with possibly some redistributive modifications in the original arrangements. But the arrangement is again liable to be an uneasy one, continually subject to breakdown.[3]

While it may be true that a return is possible from every non-ideal arrangement to an ideal one with a net gain to every member of the group, it may not be possible thereby even to equal the position that would obtain for *each* member of the group if he by himself attained the best conceivable arrangements from his own point of view. If every member of the group hopes that he will, through his own actions, be able to achieve the best possible results from the point of view of his own interests, he will seek to do so, and under the terms of the last hypothesis this would mean a deviation from the requirements of the ideal arrangements for at least some members of the group.

We have seen, then, that an ideal arrangement is conceivable which is imperfectly stable. It is also possible, however, to construct examples of stable ideal situations. I shall consider two of these (of particular interest) obtained by simple modification of the last example.

First let us consider the case where every member of the group has the following expectations: if the production of his particular commodity remains unrestricted so will that of every other commodity. However, if the production of his commodity is restricted, then that of every other commodity will be restricted almost immediately and in such proportion as to maintain the initial division of money incomes. Clearly then it is not in the interest of any individual to restrict his output, for the effect upon him will be simply that he obtains the same proportion as before of a reduced quantity of commodities. Since we assume in our simplified example that restriction of output is the only way the existing arrangement can be changed, it is clear that it will tend to be stable.

It is noteworthy that the stability of the situation is related to the nature of expectations. An individual's expectation that the decisions of the other members of the economy are largely unaffected by his own will tend to be destabilizing. On the other hand the expectation of a definite reaction on the part of other members of the group of such a nature as to amount to retaliation or the imposition of economic sanctions will be stabilizing. Moreover, all emulatory deviation from the ideal on the part of other members of the group in an attempt to protect themselves from the predatory activities of one of their number is likely to serve effectively (and automatically) in the imposition of such sanctions, for the only way an individual can gain by a deviation from the ideal is by successfully affecting a redistribution of welfare in his own favour. If others follow suit and successfully prevent a reapportionment of welfare, thereby departing from the ideal, the individual whose action initiated the deviation will necessarily be one of those who suffer.

A second example of a stable ideal can be obtained by another slight modification of our instability example. Suppose the production of every commodity were so thoroughly diffused among the members of the group that it was, for practical purposes, impossible to arrange a restriction of output. Then every individual might well find himself with no practical alternative but to act ideally. A generalization of this is that a co-operative arrangement will tend to be stabilized if every individual taken by himself plays so insignificant a part in affecting distributive arrangements that an effective deviation on favourable terms would be difficult to organize.

Actual instances of both the stability and instability of ideal arrangements can be found in practice. We recall that a collusive arrangement of monopolistic or quasi-monopolistic nature is a co-operative arrangement which is likely to be ideal (in the sense of total profit maximization) from the point of view of the entrepreneurs entering the agreement, so that the instability of pools and other cartelization arrangements provides an example of an unstable ideal situation—a theme which runs through the literature of the subject.[4] Where cartel arrangements are stable, the reason tends to be the threat of economic sanctions typified by the price leadership case with the kinked demand curve for the output of the firm.

One may be led to suspect, on the other hand, that where an entire community operates its economy co-operatively, any element of stability is more likely to result from the relative impotence of the individual as an influence on the distributive arrangements than from the automatic imposition of sanctions.[5] The latter, in a large group, seems likely to succeed only when they are applied as a conscious instrument of government policy. My reason for doubting the efficacy of automatically applied sanctions in a large group is that sanctions must by definition be applied when and only when the individual deviates from the course required of him. If the individual plays only an insignificant role, however, it is difficult to conceive of a slight change in the nature of his activities setting up significant reactions except as the result of consciously directed policy.[6]

II. THE WRECK OF WELFARE ECONOMICS?

So long as we confined our discussion to generalities we could make some statements which were not purely destructive. However, we were thereby largely avoiding the field of welfare economics. We have attempted to distinguish the cases in which rationality on the part of the citizens may lead them to desire the intervention of government. Having done this, are we now in a position to tender objective, unambiguous advice on specific problems? Can we say, in any given case, that the government should, or should not, intervene? Further, if we could give a verdict in favour of intervention, are we able to recommend the type and extent of the intervention? Here, [...] I have serious doubts.[7]

We can obviously make recommendations about certain types of business practice such as those involving the use of physical violence as an instrument of monopolization, stock market manipulation, or even the problem of unemployment, for there are here involved patent misuses of resources which are frowned upon under the system of value judgments usually accepted by the economist. But if we ask ourselves, once our resources are all in some sense usefully employed, whether they are, or how they can be, *best* employed (the problem of ideal output), or whether anything should be done about their existing employment, then the answer is much more difficult.

Here welfare economics seems to have produced its most widely cited results, and it is here that the bulk of the analysis has been directed; but how much confidence can we have in the results? We are given rules, often guardedly and with many provisos. In a completely nationalized economy, subject to the usual reservations, firms should sell their wares at prices equal to marginal costs. But if the costs of production of firms are interrelated so that marginal costs to the firm and to society differ, why should these goods be offered at their marginal cost to the firm producing them? And if in addition there are external economies of consumption, why should we take the purchase price of an article as a measure of its marginal social utility? Surely the use of the marginal cost equal to price rule for maximizing social welfare implies that we take marginal cost to be marginal social cost and price to be equal to marginal social utility, thus giving marginal social utility equal to marginal social cost which, by the usual argument, is a necessary condition for maximization of net social welfare.[8]

Indeed, in the presence of external economies many peculiar things become possible: monopoly outputs may be too great and competitive outputs too small. We cannot assume because we know nothing about how external economies and diseconomies affect the usual conclusions in the various fields concerned, that on the average the deviations will cancel out, for that is the fallacy of assuming the equiprobability of the unknown. Unless we can in any given case estimate the magnitude and effects of the external economies, or unless we can in particular cases show that they are negligible, as positivist economists we are entitled to say nothing at all.[9] In a world where external economies exist, are we entitled to maintain on theoretical grounds alone that rationing is apt to aggravate deviations from ideal output, or that income taxes are less desirable than direct taxes from this point of view,[10] or that the sale of ration coupons should be permitted? Most of the conclusions which seem to represent the achievement of welfare economies thus seem to be open to question, and some of them appear completely untenable.

The problem in sum is this: so long as we recognize the existence of particular types of interdependence in the results of the activities of our economic units, our analysis is likely to break down completely. We know, moreover, that the simplifying premise that these types of interdependence are negligible or non-existent is misleading. Such an assumption is not neutral; rather it leads inexorably to the acceptance of *laissez-faire*. Nor must we be deceived into believing that we have found a meaningful conclusion if that conclusion is in the form: such and such is the case unless there are present important external economies or diseconomies. This tells us merely that we have still not begun to investigate what may be the most significant part of our problem. We have merely chosen to give to our ignorance a local habitation and a name.

Can it be argued in general that external economies of production and consumption are unimportant? I doubt this very much.[11] We need merely consider how the costs of production of two factories with identical personnel and equipment would vary were one placed in an isolated and uninhabited region and the other in an industrial community, though the geographical and climatic conditions were the same. Indeed, by assuming identical personnel we lose some of the force of the illustration, for the training and skill of employees is an example of the benefits derived from geographical proximity of firms.[12]

Similarly we may perhaps see the force of external economies of consumption by imagining how our consumption demands and expenditure pattern would change (though our opportunities were unchanged) if we were placed in another community and completely absorbed its culture as though we had been born there.

On the other hand, it may be argued that the effects of a small change in one person's purchases, or in one firm's output, will have very little effect on the economic *milieu,* and so these effects can in any case be ignored. But it is, I think, the role of government to concern itself with the aggregate results of these small effects which may reach such importance as to appear among the main objects of regulatory activity. Indeed, it is even plausible that our consumption desires are so indefinite and flexible that most of the problems dealt with in the discussions of consumers' sovereignty are trivial and unimportant so long as what is done follows consumers' demands in a somewhat rough and ready way. Does it really profoundly affect the welfare of the body of consumers if purchases are influenced by price manipulation? It is possible that the answer may be in the affirmative, but can we be sure of this?

Two points should here be made clear. First, I do not mean to imply that we must throw up our hands altogether and take no action of any sort on the practical questions concerned because our analytic structure is in too highly imperfect a state to enable us to give categorical answers in our role as economic theorists. Such a council [sic] of paralysis through despair is not my intent. I believe that the politician is, in many cases, justified in taking, and indeed forced to take action on many such questions, perfect analysis or no. Indeed, I cannot deny that some reliance on common sense and experience will be of the utmost value any more than I can reject the desirability of good intentions. Nor do I suggest that the politician cannot receive useful assistance in these matters from the judgment and observation of the "practical" economist.

Secondly, I sincerely believe that welfare theory even as it stands has an important contribution to make; for it can be most useful in rejecting shoddy arguments and easy fallacies, a role where help should always be welcome. As

Professor Pigou once pointed out, abstract arguments, if they only construct empty boxes, cannot show what is (empirically) right, but can often (by demonstrating contradiction) indicate what is wrong and, perhaps even more often, what is unproved. There can be little doubt that such service has proved invaluable in the past. Indeed, this possibility provides the main *raison d'être* for this book.

Nevertheless the fact that categories like "external economies" and "external diseconomies" remain largely empty economic boxes prevents any further application of welfare theory as it now stands.

Is there any hope of further progress based on empirical investigation[13] and analysis of the problem of the interdependence of activities of economic units? I cannot pretend to offer even tentative answers. It seems to me, however, that if the subject is to achieve primary importance for practical men, this question must be faced and answered.

NOTES

1. Cf. Trygve Haavelmo, "The Notion of Involuntary Economic Decisions," *Econometrica,* January 1950.

2. Thus it seems to me somewhat too facile to suggest that social and economic difficulties arise merely because of conflict of the interests of the members of society. The view that "nothing which hurts them will hurt me" will not do. Individuals generally live as members of a society, and there are many things which affect the welfare of that society as a whole and thereby that of each of its constituents. [...] Many of the difficulties besetting a society may well arise as a result of this.

3. Note the peculiarity of the position—one from which deviations may tend to be eliminated, but which continually tends to break down and is hence unstable, and about which there may thus be perpetual oscillation amply illustrated by the history of the repeated formation and breakdown of loosely organized trusts. Cf. R. A. Musgrave, "The Voluntary Exchange Theory of Public Economy," *Quarterly Journal of Economics,* February 1939, p. 219, footnote 5.

4. Cf., for example, W. Z. Ripley [1916], *Trusts, Pools and Corporations,* and also David Lynch [1946], *The Concentration of Economic Power.* The theme recurs frequently throughout the T.N.E.C. *Hearings.*

5. The stability of the economic arrangements in some primitive communities may be attributed to tradition whose influence may be interpreted either as an irrational element or as rational pursuit of conservative predilections. For some interesting examples of primitive economies cf. *Cooperation and Competition Among Primitive Peoples* (editor, Margaret Mead [1937]).

6. Note that the term stability is employed throughout in the old-fashioned undynamic sense—cf. Samuelson [1947], *Foundations of Economic Analysis,* Chapter IX. In the present analysis the dynamic approach is clearly inappropriate since we are not primarily interested here in whether, once a given situation is departed from, it will

tend to be re-established (it is clearly to this problem which the dynamic analysis applies). Rather, we want to know whether there will be any motive or tendency for a departure from the situation once it is somehow attained.

7. [. . .] Cf. I.M.D. Little, "The Foundations of Welfare Economics," *Oxford Economic Papers,* 1949, especially p. 238. Cf. also Little's *Critique of Welfare Economics* [1950], especially Chapters XI and XIV.

8. This is not to deny that a satisfactory formal analysis is possible giving rules of more general validity. Cf., for example, Gerhard Tintner, "A Note on Welfare Economics," *Econometrica,* 1946. I do, however, doubt the utility of such rules as a guide for action. On the whole subject, cf. J. E. Meade, "Mr. Lerner on 'The Economics of Control,' " *Economic Journal,* April 1945.

9. For a contrary approach to this sort of problem see Jacob Viner [1937], *Studies in the Theory of International Trade,* pp. 324-5.

10. For the argument, cf. A. Henderson, "The Case for Indirect Taxation," *Economic Journal,* December 1948, but cf. I.M.D. Little, "Direct versus Indirect Taxes," *Economic Journal,* September 1951.

11. But cf. Ellis and Fellner, "External Economies and Diseconomies," *American Economic Review,* 1943, especially pp. 509, 511.

12. Dr. Rosenstein-Rodan has suggested to me that this may largely account for the failure of many "backward areas" to be industrialized. It may be particularly relevant in the case of India, where, for a long period, investments were secure and wages continued low.

13. A promising first attempt has been made since this was written. See K. William Kapp [1950], *The Social Costs of Private Enterprise.*

8 • Introduction

Social Limits to Growth by Fred Hirsch is a highly readable book which will be found quite accessible by anyone who works through Part I of this collection. Much of the interest in the book lies in the detailed working out of its themes, with many ingenious and apposite illustrations. We were for this reason drawn toward excerpting one of the substantive chapters here, but in the end, we decided that it would be most useful to present the first chapter, which provides an overview of the argument as a whole. We hope that this will whet the reader's appetite for the rest of the book.

The selection from Hirsch follows on naturally from the one from Baumol, because Hirsch's theme is precisely the importance—and increasing importance—of externalities in the economies of the advanced industrial countries. As an eminent sociologist remarked in the 1950s, when the debate on the "embourgeoisement" of the working class was at its height, a washing machine is a washing machine is a washing machine. It may lose its social cachet once everyone else has one but it still washes clothes just as well as before. The same cannot, however, be said of a cottage on the lake, on the assumption that what attracted one originally was the absence of other cottages. Hirsch argues that, as material prosperity increases, goods of the second kind become relatively more important, with the result that welfare (roughly speaking, satisfaction with one's purchases) does not rise commensurately with income. People become obscurely frustrated because they expect to enjoy what was once the privilege of a few, but find that, try as they may, they do not succeed.

Clearly, the problem is, in formal terms, that of externalities of consumption. And Hirsch, like Baumol, points out that the phenomenon of externalities plays havoc with the standard economic indicators of welfare. Thus, as Hirsch observes, an increase in the per capita national income becomes less and less reliable as an index of real satisfaction derived from consumption. In principle, it should be possible, Hirsch suggests, to avoid by appropriate collective action wasteful competition for fixed resources. This would presumably require widespread recognition of the problem in the terms posed by Hirsch, and then imaginative and creative political leadership to propose attractive solutions. So far one must, it seems, be rather pessimistic.

8

SOCIAL LIMITS
TO GROWTH

Fred Hirsch

This book tries to give an economist's answer to three questions.

(1) Why has economic advance become and remained so compelling a goal to all of us as individuals, even though it yields disappointing fruits when most, if not all of us, achieve it?

(2) Why has modern society become so concerned with distribution—with the division of the pie—when it is clear that the great majority of people can raise their living standards only through production of a larger pie?

(3) Why has the twentieth century seen a universal predominant trend toward collective provision and state regulation in economic areas at a time when individual freedom of action is especially extolled and is given unprecedented rein in noneconomic areas such as aesthetic and sexual standards?

Let us call these three issues (1) the paradox of affluence, (2) the distributional compulsion, and (3) the reluctant collectivism.

My major thesis is that these three issues are interrelated, and stem from a common source. This source is to be found in the nature of economic growth in advanced societies. The heart of the problem lies in the complexity and partial ambiguity of the concept of economic growth once the mass of the population has satisfied its main biological needs for life-sustaining food, shelter, and clothing. The traditional economic distinction between how much is produced, on what basis, and who gets it then becomes blurred. The issues of production, of individual versus collective provision, and of distribution then become intertwined.

Reprinted by permission of the publishers from *Social Limits to Growth* by Fred Hirsch, Cambridge, Mass.: Harvard University Press and London: Routledge and Kegan Paul Ltd. (A Twentieth Century Fund Study), pp. 1-12, Copyright © 1976 by the Twentieth Century Fund.

This development marks a profound change. It is a change that economists in particular find difficult to accept because it has the appearance of scientific retrogression. Traditionally, the contribution of the economist to charting a way to economic progress has consisted largely of unscrambling the aspects of economic activity just mentioned—distinguishing between the share of the pie and its size, between the motivation of individual actions and their collective result. It was on these distinctions that the science of economics was launched by Adam Smith two centuries ago. Smith showed that pursuit by individuals in an uncoordinated way of their own interests could yet serve the interests of all and that the poor man in the rich community could live better than native kings.

The progress of economics has been devoted largely to developing and refining these insights, which has resulted in enormous advances in the quantification of economic phenomena. This quantification in turn supports not merely the claim of economics to primacy in the ranking of the social sciences but also its established primacy in the agenda of public policy. In the past generation, electoral politics throughout the industrial world, and beyond it, has been increasingly dominated by the big economic numbers—gross national product, personal disposable income, and the rate at which these indicators of material prosperity grow.

Yet in advanced societies, those in which the mass of the population has risen above merely life-sustaining consumption, the stage may now have been reached where the analytical framework that the economist has come to take for granted—but that the sociologist has long disputed—has become a hindrance in understanding some key contemporary problems. Confronting these problems in the framework of the traditional analytical separation leaves the answers in the air. The three broad questions listed at the outset—the paradox of affluence, the distributional compulsion, the reluctant collectivism—are puzzles or paradoxes when viewed in isolation. A clue to their resolution is to approach them as interconnected products of a neglected structural characteristic of modern economic growth. That is what this book tries to do.

I

The structural characteristic in question is that as the level of average consumption rises, an increasing portion of consumption takes on a social as well as an individual aspect. That is to say, the satisfaction that individuals derive from goods and services depends in increasing measure not only on their own consumption but on consumption by others as well.

To a hungry man, the satisfaction derived from a square meal is unaffected by the meals other people eat or, if he is hungry enough, by anything else they do. His meal is an entirely individual affair. In technical terms it is a pure private good. At the other extreme, the quality of the air that the modern citizen breathes in the center of a city depends almost entirely on what his fellow citizens contribute toward countering pollution, whether directly by public expenditure or indirectly through public regulation. Clean air in a metropolis is a social product. In technical terms, it is close to a pure public good.

These polar cases, however, are relatively few in number. It has recently become recognized by economists who specialize in these matters that the major part of consumption is neither purely private nor purely public. What is generally referred to as private or personal consumption is nonetheless affected in its essence—that is, in the satisfaction or utility it yields—by consumption of the same goods or services by others; and in that specific sense it can be said to contain a social element. Correspondingly, what is generally referred to as public consumption contains some of the characteristics of private goods, in the sense that its costs and benefits are or can be confined to a limited group.

The range of private consumption that contains a social element in the sense described is much wider than is generally recognized. In textbooks on economics, public goods are discussed in the context of goods and facilities that can be provided only, or most economically, on a collective basis, open to all and financed by all. City parks and streets and national defense are prominent examples. In addition, elements of public goods are recognized in side effects of private transactions such as pollution and congestion occurring in particular identifiable situations. But a more general public goods element can be attributed to a wide range of private expenditures. Thus the utility of expenditure on a given level of education as a means of access to the most sought after jobs will decline as more people attain that level of education. The value to me of my education depends not only on how much I have but also on how much the man ahead of me in the job line has. The satisfaction derived from an auto or a country cottage depends on the conditions in which they can be used, which will be strongly influenced by how many other people are using them. This factor, which is social in origin, may be a more important influence on my satisfaction than the characteristics of these items as "private" goods (on the speed of the auto, the spaciousness of the cottage, and so forth). Beyond some point that has long been surpassed in crowded industrial societies, conditions of use tend to deteriorate as use becomes more widespread.

Congestion is most apparent in its physical manifestation, in traffic jams. But traffic congestion can be seen as only a special case of the wider phenomenon of social congestion, which in turn is a major facet of social scarcity. Social scarcity is a central concept in this analysis. It expresses the idea that the good things of life are restricted not only by physical limitations of producing more of them but also by absorptive limits on their use. Where the social environment has a restricted capacity for extending use without quality deterioration, it imposes social limits to consumption. More specifically, the limit is imposed on satisfactions that depend not on the product or facility in isolation but on the surrounding conditions of use.

What precisely is *new* about this situation? The limits have always been there at some point, but they have not until recent times become obtrusive. That is the product, essentially, of past achievements in material growth not subject to social limits. In this sense, the concern with the limits to growth that has been voiced by and through the Club of Rome[1] is strikingly misplaced. It focuses on distant and uncertain physical limits and overlooks the immediate if less apocalyptic presence of social limits to growth.

So long as material privation is widespread, conquest of material scarcity is the dominant concern. As demands for purely private goods are increasingly satisfied, demands for goods and facilities with a public (social) character became increasingly active. These public demands make themselves felt through individual demands on the political system or through the market mechanism in the same way as do the demands for purely private goods. Individuals acquire both sets of goods without distinction, except where public goods are provided by public or collective action; even there, individuals may seek to increase their own share by private purchases.

These demands in themselves appear both legitimate and attainable. Why should the individual not spend his money on additional education as a means to a higher placed job, or on a second home in the country, if he prefers these pleasures to spending on a mink coat or whiskey or to a life of greater leisure? That question was being loudly voiced in the mid-1970s as part of a middle-class backlash in both Britain and the United States. It can be answered satisfactorily only by reference to the public goods or social content of the expenditures involved.

Considered in isolation, the individual's demand for education as a job entree, for an auto, for a country cottage, can be taken as genuinely individual wants, stemming from the individual's own preferences in the situation that confronts him. Acting alone, each individual seeks to make the best of his or her position. But satisfaction of these individual preferences itself alters the situation that faces others seeking to satisfy similar wants. A round of transactions to act out personal wants of this kind therefore leaves each individual with a worse bargain than was reckoned with when the transaction was undertaken, because the sum of such acts does not correspondingly improve the position of all individuals taken together. There is an "adding-up" problem. Opportunities for economic advance, as they present themselves serially to one person after another, do not constitute equivalent opportunities for economic advance by all. What each of us can achieve, all cannot.

A break between individual and social opportunities may occur for a number of reasons; excessive pollution and congestion are the most commonly recognized results. A neglected general condition that produces this break is competition by people for place, rather than competition for performance. Advance in society is possible only by moving to a higher place among one's fellows, that is, by improving one's performance in relation to other people's performances. If everyone stands on tiptoe, no one sees better. Where social interaction of this kind is present, individual action is no longer a sure means of fulfilling individual choice: the preferred outcome may be attainable only through collective action. (We all agree explicitly or implicitly not to stand on tiptoe.) The familiar dichotomy between individual choice and collective provision or regulation then dissolves. Competition among isolated individuals in the free market entails hidden costs for others and ultimately for themselves. These costs are a deadweight cost for all and involve social waste, unless no preferable alternative method of allocation is available. But the same distortion may result from public provision where this responds to individual demands formulated without taking account of subsequent interactions.

A conspicuous example is provided in certain aspects of education. People possessing relatively high educational qualifications are seen to enjoy attractive professional and social opportunities. This situation induces a strong latent demand for access to such qualifications. Such demand may flow through the market, in the willingness of individuals to pay higher fees for educational services supplied by private institutions without public support. In our own times, the demand more often is directed to the state, to broaden access to the higher strata of the educational pyramid. The state is expected to foster equality of educational opportunity and perhaps also equality of educational outcome. But these concepts present a number of difficulties, some well known and some less so.

The concept of equal opportunity, or equality at the starting gate, is not much less question-begging when applied to education than when applied to life chances in general, the central ambiguity being which starting handicaps are to be removed. At the limit, the criterion of an equal start is an equal finish. Worse, equal outcome in education would be impeded not only by differences in individual talent and inclination; the concept also fails to allow for an important function education performs in a modern society, that is, sorting or screening. In its own way education is a device for controlling social scarcity.

To the extent that education in fact functions so as to sort out those who can best survive and master an educational obstacle course, improved performance by some worsens the position of those who would otherwise be ahead. The "quality" of schooling, in effect, exists in two dimensions. There is an *absolute* dimension, in which quality is added by receptive students, good teachers, good facilities, and so on; but there is also a *relative* dimension, in which quality consists of the differential over the educational level attained by others. The enormous resistance induced in both the United States and Britain by public attempts to integrate previously inferior schools with previously superior schools cannot be fully understood without reference to both these aspects of educational quality. Even if complete assurance could be given that absolute quality would be fully preserved, the previous incumbents of the superior schools would still lose their edge. This loss in turn can be expected to induce them to demonstrate their proficiency in a tougher or longer course of study. To the extent that education is a screening device (a qualification that must be kept firmly in mind), then the possibility of general advance is an illusion.

What is possible for the single individual is not possible for all individuals—and would not be possible even if they all possessed equal talent. Individuals, whether shopping for educational advance in the market place or pushing for educational advance through political demands, do not see the break between individual and social opportunity; that is, they do not see that opportunities open to each person separately are not open to all. It follows that response to individual demands of this kind, whether in market processes or in public provision, cannot deliver the order.

Consumers, taken together, get a product they did not order; collectively, this result involves potential social waste. Consumers individually find that their access to socially scarce goods and facilities, where these are attainable even in part through market processes, is determined in accord not with absolute but with relative real income. The determining factor is the individual's position in the distribution of purchasing power. Frustration of individual expectations then results from both these characteristics: from social waste, which cuts into the level of welfare[2] available to all; and from an imposed hierarchy that confines socially scarce goods to those on the highest rungs of the distributional ladder, disappointing the expectations of those whose position is raised through a lift in the ladder as a whole.

So the distributional struggle returns, heightened rather than relieved by the dynamic process of growth. It is an exact reversal of what economists and present-day politicians have come to expect growth to deliver.

The compelling attraction of economic growth in its institutionalized modern form has been as a superior substitute for redistribution. Whereas the masses today could never get close to what the well-to-do have today, even by expropriating all of it, they can, in the conventional view, get most if not all the way there with patience in a not too distant tomorrow, through the magic of compound growth. But, as outlined above, once this growth brings mass consumption to the point where it causes problems of congestion in the widest sense—bluntly, where consumption or jobholding by others tends to crowd you out—then the key to personal welfare is again the ability to stay ahead of the crowd. Generalized growth then increases the crush.

Thus the frustration in affluence results from its very success in satisfying previously dominant material needs. This frustration is usually thought of as essentially a psychological phenomenon, a matter of our subjective internal assessment. What we previously had to struggle for now comes easily, so we appreciate it less. The analysis of this book fastens on a separate consequence of generalized material growth that is independent of any such psychological revaluation; it affects what individuals get as well as the satisfaction it brings them. What they get, in the growing sphere of social scarcity, depends to an increasing extent on their relative position in the economic hierarchy. Hence, the paradox of affluence. It embodies a distributional compulsion, which in turn leads to our reluctant collectivism.

These sources of frustration with the fruits of economic growth are concealed in the economist's standard categorization. Strictly speaking, our existing concept of economic output is appropriate only for truly private goods, having no element of interdependence between consumption by different individuals. The bedrock is valuation by individuals of goods and opportunities in the situation in which they find themselves. At any moment of time and for any one person, standing on tiptoe gives a better view, or at least prevents a worse one. Equally, getting ahead of the crowd is an effective and feasible means of improving one's welfare, a means available to any one individual. It yields a benefit, in this sense, and the measure of the benefit is what individuals pay to secure it. The individual benefit from the isolated action is clear-cut. The sum of benefits of all the actions taken together is nonetheless zero.

This reckoning, it should be emphasized, is still made on the measure of the individual's own valuation, the same valuation that imputes a positive benefit to the individual action. Since individual benefits of this kind simply do not add up, the connection between individual and aggregate advance is broken. Yet the modern concepts of economic output, and of growth in that output, are grounded on individual valuations and their addition. Individual preference is assumed to be revealed implicitly in market behavior—in the consumer's choice between products at their given market prices, in the worker's choice between jobs and between different opportunities of job training at the going rates of pay and conditions. If individual valuations do not add up, then the aggregated valuations based upon them become biased measures.

Unfortunately no better quantitative measure of economic output has yet been found. The need for a flanking set of social indicators is now widely accepted, at least in principle. The end product of such a system would be an integrated system of numbers comparable with the national income accounts. This objective is far from being realized. There is no social performance indicator that can be systematically calculated and easily understood.

The national accounts have been developed into an elaborate ground plan of the economy that is used for a large variety of purposes. The gross national product and its components are the best indicators of personal and national prosperity we have, if only because they are the only such indicators. They thereby maintain a strong hold on public attention. Inevitably, this attention has given its own validity to the analytical categorization which lies at the base of national accounting, as well as of the older, related economic concepts from which it grew. The products of the economics numbers factory enjoy a brisk demand; and the economic inducement to cater to effective demand is not suspended for economics itself. Nor are economists immune from the instinct of trade unionists; they too judge the social worth of their performance by the prosperity and prestige it brings to their craft.

The ambiguity in the concept of economic output pointed out here is of secondary or even negligible significance in making use of the conventional measures of national accounts for the formulation of official policy designed to regulate or stabilize the short-term performance of the economy. For comparisons of welfare over extended periods of time, in estimates of long-term economic growth, and in league tables of living standards among countries in different situations at a given period of time, national accounting measures are notoriously less suitable.

What is stressed here is a different limitation, one almost wholly neglected by economists: the problem of translating individual economic improvement into overall improvement. In the standard model of thinking, if the fruits of aggregate advance appear inadequate or disappointing, the deficiency merely reflects inadequate economic effort or excessive demands by individuals, or poor organization or inadequate capital equipment currently available to them. Too much has been expected too soon. This conceptual framework adopted by economists concerned with policy has penetrated the thinking, expectations, and performance criteria of politicians and electorates of all western countries. As a consequence, conventional wisdom thinks in terms of "excessive expectations." The populace wants it now. It cannot have it now. It is too impatient. The implication is that the gathering of the fruit must await exercise of the necessary virtues—essentially, effort and restraint. Yet for those aspects of individual welfare where the connection between individual and aggregate advancement does not exist, or is broken under the stress of widening access to limited availabilities, the established conceptual framework is invalid. Its application to ultimate consumer satisfaction in this sector operates as a frustration machine.

Thus to see total economic advance as individual advance writ large is to set up expectations that cannot be fulfilled, ever. It is not just a matter of scaling down demand and expectations that are extravagant in relation to effort by workers or to the availability of technology or the use made of it. This view has become the conventional one on problems of excess demand and inflation. The appropriate solution to the problem so conceived is simple, at least in principle: to adjust expectations down and/or performance up. The necessary adjustment is purely quantitative. If all put a little more into the pool and take a little less out for a while, then present expectations can in time be fulfilled. So runs the predominant message of politico-economic managers in the postwar generation. Only hold back a little, and the good things you rightly crave will come to you or, at least, to your children. The inflationary explosion of the early 1970s and the severe world recession that followed attempts to contain it have been widely interpreted in this vein—as a painful interruption in a progressive improvement in living standards that could be restored and sustained once the public was prevailed upon to exercise the necessary restraint.

It follows from this line of thought that the chief culprits responsible for derailing the train of technological advance are those institutions that inflate economic demands beyond the steady but limited growth in capacity to fulfill them. Trade unions exercising the bargaining power of their collective strength stand out as such culprits. It is the collective element in their activities—the mobilization of economic strength greater than the sum of the individual parts—that is seen to intrude on the balance and viability of an individualistic economy. The unquestioned premise of this approach is that competitive individualistic advance can ultimately deliver the goods. If it cannot, which participants in collective activity may instinctively feel and as the present analysis explicitly argues, then defensive collective expedients must be looked at in a new light.

To the extent that the mismatch between current expectations and resources is qualitative rather than quantitative, the restraint necessary would be not patience but stoicism, acceptance, and social cooperation—qualities that are out of key with our culture of individualistic advance. Yet without such qualities, the traditional response by the public to the prospect of satisfaction as reward for extra effort or temporary abstinence will worsen the problem. For addition to the material goods that can be expanded for all will, in itself, increase the scramble for those goods and facilities that cannot be so expanded. Taking part in the scramble is fully rational for any individual in his own actions, since in these actions he never confronts the distinction between what is available as a result of getting ahead of others and what is available from a general advance shared by all. The individual who wants to see better has to stand on tiptoe. In the game of beggar your neighbor, that is what each individual must try to do, even though not all can. The only way of avoiding the competition in frustration is for the people concerned to coordinate their objectives in some explicit way, departing from the principle of isolated individual striving in this sphere. That is to say, only a collective approach to the problem can offer individuals the guidance necessary to achieve a solution they themselves would prefer. The principle is acknowledged in the standard liberal analysis, but confined to the exceptional case.

How a satisfactory collective view is to be arrived at, and then implemented, remains a large and mostly unresolved problem of its own. Collective action can involve familiar distortions and inefficiencies. The means to a collective solution may be inadequate. To the extent that this is so, the analysis put forward here carries no clear-cut implications for immediate policy. The distortions and frustrations entailed in uncoordinated individual actions may still appear as the lesser evil. However, a change in the nature of a problem is not undone by deficiencies in the tools available for tackling it. Correct diagnosis is likely to yield some implications for policy, if only to stop banging into the wall.

By collapsing individual and total opportunities for economic advance into a single process grounded on individual valuations, the standard view has obscured a significant change in the nature of the economic problem. It has thereby overstated the promise of economic growth. It has understated the limitations of consumer demand as a guide to an efficient pattern of economic activity. It has obscured the extent of the modern conflict between individualistic actions and satisfaction of individualistic preferences. Getting what one wants is increasingly divorced from doing as one likes.

II

Together, these limitations imply a substantial modification in the menu offered by economic liberalism, including that embodied in programs of liberal socialism. The preponderant implication is that choices are more restricted and price tags are higher, in the form of costlier tradeoffs, than the traditional menu has suggested. The traditional liberal opportunities, which are still held out as a prospect attainable by all who are prepared to adopt the requisite liberal values, appear instead to have the marks, in certain key respects, of minority status. Offered to the majority, they are available only to a minority. Tensions and frustrations have inevitably resulted.

That is one major undercurrent of the modern crisis in the liberal system. Positional goods, in the language introduced in the next chapter, become an increasing brake on the expansion and extension of economic welfare. Social scarcity tightens its grip. Economic liberalism is in this sense a victim of its own propaganda: offered to all, it has evoked demands and pressures that cannot be contained.

In a further sense, economic liberalism has been the victim of its own success. Its singular efficiency has resided in its capacity for decentralization of knowledge and of decision-making. This decentralization is achieved essentially by harnessing the ancient individual instinct of maximization of personal advantage (more strictly, of pursuit of individual interests, however self-oriented or otherwise they may be: "self-interest" should be understood as a shorthand way of expressing the wider concept of privately oriented behavior). Socially beneficial results have thereby been obtained without the necessity of socially oriented motivation. Good has been done by stealth. Adam Smith's invisible hand has linked individual self-interest with social need. But the conditions in which this link has been achieved over a wide area can now be seen not as stable conditions that can be relied on to persist or to be readily maintainable by deliberate action. Rather, they can be seen in important respects to have been special conditions associated with a transition phase from an earlier socioeconomic system. The generally benign invisible hand was a favorable inaugural condition of liberal capitalism.

There are two ways in which the novelty of the liberal capitalist order was associated with what can now be seen as transient inaugural conditions. First, full participation was confined to a minority—the minority that had reached material affluence before liberal capitalism had set the masses on the path of material growth. Second, the system operated on social foundations laid under a different order of society.

The successful operation of economic liberalism undermines both these supports. It spreads demand for participation to all. At the same time, it erodes the social foundations that underlie a benign and efficient implementation of the self-interest principle operating through market transactions.

Those who have understood the rationale of the free market as an organizing device have always recognized key areas of public life in which the maxim of laissez-faire—or nonintervention through public policy—was inappropriate. In these selective areas, public policies would be applied essentially as a supplement to market behavior directed to maximization of individual advantage. The idea has been either to constrain such behavior by law, for example, through the income tax law, or to influence behavior by deliberately adjusting market opportunities, for example, through indirect taxes or subsidies or conditional grants. In both instances, reliance is still placed on the self-interest principle for compliance. A critical omission from this approach is the role played by the supporting ethos of social obligation both in the formulation of the relevant public policies and in their efficient transmission to market opportunities. Why expect the controllers, alone, to abstain from maximizing their individual advantage?

In brief, the principle of self-interest is incomplete as a social organizing device. It operates effectively only in tandem with some supporting social principle. This fundamental characteristic of economic liberalism, which was largely taken for granted by Adam Smith and by John Stuart Mill in their different ways, has been lost sight of by its modern protagonists. While the need for modifications in laissez-faire in public policies has been increasingly accepted, the need for qualifications to self-interested behavior by individuals has been increasingly neglected. Yet correctives to laissez-faire increase rather than decrease reliance on some degree of social orientation and social responsibility in individual behavior. The attempt has been made to erect an increasingly explicit social organization without a supporting social morality. The result has been a structural strain on both the market mechanism and the political mechanism designed to regulate and supplement it.

In this way, the foundations of the market system have been weakened, while its general behavioral norm of acting on the criterion of self-interest has won ever-widening acceptance. As the foundations weaken, the structure rises ever higher. The deeper irony—which can also be seen as a fortunate legacy—resides in the success of the market system in its initial phase, on the shoulders of a premarket social ethos.

A system that depends for its success on a heritage that it undermines cannot be sustained on the record of its bountiful fruits. These fruits themselves, real as they are, are yet a false promise. Offered in the shop window, they outshine the competition. But delivery is limited to select customers—the minority offering; worse, it is limited to early customers—the transient offering. It is possible that even an inferior selection of goods offered by the same store would still outshine any available alternative. But that is another matter. What is seen to be on offer is the selection in the window. If this offering is not what it looks, it is important to show how and why. Only in that way can expectations and performance be adapted to what can feasibly be provided.

NOTES

1. The Club of Rome is an informal international association, styling itself as an invisible college, which is best known for its "world model" representing the interconnections of resources, population, and environment in the mode of systems dynamics. The message, which received worldwide popular acclaim and widespread professional criticism, was contained in Donella H. Meadows, Dennis L. Meadows, Jorgen Randers, and William W. Behrens III, *The Limits to Growth,* A Report for the Club of Rome's Project on the Predicament of Mankind (London: Earth Island Limited, 1972).

2. In the sense of some concept of ultimate consumer satisfaction [. . .].

9 • Introduction

Paul Samuelson's original, mathematical explication of the theory of public goods has become one of the most cited and reprinted articles in all of economics. It was severely criticized upon publication as unnecessarily mathematical (Enke 1955) and readers of this volume may find Samuelson's explication obscures as much as it clarifies. Fortunately, most of the difficulty of the article is on related issues of public finance rather than on the central points of the distinction between public and private goods.

Samuelson's larger concern is with public finance, with optimal levels of public expenditure. To address that problem he supposes it is necessary to understand the demand for two classes of goods: private-consumption and collective-consumption goods. First, consider private goods. I buy as much of any given private good as I want given that I have limited resources and that I want other goods as well. Under the usual assumptions of market analysis, the production and consumption of private goods will attain optimal levels (recall the discussion of Pareto optimality in the introduction to the selection from Baumol). When I consume a unit of a private good (such as a hamburger), it is unavailable for anyone else to consume. Optimal provision of private goods is straightforward. Given our various constraints, I want 1 hamburger at the prevailing price, you want 2, and so forth, for a total, say, of 35 billion according to one sign. (This is what Samuelson calls "horizontal addition" of our marginal-rate-of-substitution schedules.)

Public goods are remarkably different: in Samuelson's words, they are goods "which all enjoy in common in the sense that each individual's consumption of such a good leads to no subtraction from any other individual's consumption of that good." Hume once supposed that fresh water was such a good. Optimal provision of a public good is not so simple as that for private goods. Once a public good is provided at some level, everyone gets it at that level. To discover what level of provision is optimal, however, requires a collective or centralized determination. We would have to know how much every individual would be willing to pay to have the good supplied at each level. Then we would have to sum how much all would be willing to pay at any given level (Samuelson's vertical addition), and compare the sums at all levels. If the marginal increase in the sum as we move from one level to a slightly higher level exceeds the marginal increase in the costs of supplying the public good at the higher level, then we should supply the good at least to that higher level. The optimal level will be that at which the marginal increase in the sum of individual valuations of the good equals the marginal increase in the cost of supplying the good.

Why does this difference between the two classes of goods matter? If all goods were purely private, a market would achieve optimal levels of production and consumption without any centralized knowledge. Each good would be provided at its price and I would buy as many units as I desired within the limits of my limited resources and my desire for other goods. The market would be an analog computer determining an optimal outcome, and no one would need to know very much of what went on within that computer. What of public goods? There is no analog computer equivalent to the market for private goods. If a public good is to be supplied at an optimal level, there must be some device for eliciting all of the information about individual preferences needed to construct the sums discussed above. What is at issue is strictly these aggregate societal valuations, and not the individual contributions to them. As Samuelson says, "no decentralized pricing system can serve to determine optimally these levels of collective consumption." To see why, let us follow his presentation.

In section II Samuelson spells out optimality conditions for a world of s individuals, n private goods, and m public goods. The first of these conditions (1) specifies that the set of private goods must be in optimal supply, which is to say that no mutual gains could be made from exchanging private goods. This condition defines the set of Pareto frontiers for the private good economy given any fixed level of supply of the m collective goods. In the welfare economics of Bergson, Samuelson, and others, a social welfare function determines which of the large number of frontier points "should" obtain (Samuelson speaks of an "ethical observer"). Any such function, U, which is a function of the utility functions of all s individuals in the society, must meet condition 3. Condition 2 specifies the optimality conditions for the supply of the public goods given their marginal production functions, F_{n+j}, relative to the marginal production functions, F, of the private goods. Under this condition, if should not be possible to make anyone better off without making someone else worse off by reducing the level of production of any of the public goods in order to produce more of *any* other good. In the optimality condition 1 for the production and distribution of private goods, each individual's relative rates of change in utility for any two goods are independently equated to relative changes in production of the goods. In the optimality condition 2 for the production of public goods (there is no issue of distribution since there is a unique level available to everyone), it is the *sum* of all individuals' marginal utilities from each public good relative to their marginal utilities from each private good which must equal relative changes in production of the goods.

To make easier intuitive sense of all this, assume for a moment that there are only two goods, one private and one public, and that an individual's utility for each is separable from that for the other. Now condition 2 reduces simply to the claim that, at the optimal level of provision, the *sum* of all individuals' marginal utilities for the public good should equal the marginal cost of producing it, where the marginal cost is measured in units of the private good. (In a graphical presentation of his theory, Samuelson [1955] uses a two-good market.)

In section III, Samuelson takes up the implications of public goods for what is sometimes called the second fundamental theorem of welfare economics. According to this theorem, any desired optimal outcome of the market (any point on the Pareto frontier for private goods) can be achieved through normal operation of the competitive market—to achieve it requires only an appropriate set of cash transfers (Samuelson's "lump-sum" taxes, L^i). Clearly, this theorem is generally of no practical import despite Samuelson's assertion that it could be achieved by political decision-making "of a computationally minimum type." (For further comment on this point, see closing paragraphs of this introduction.)

Now if we have worked out all the equations in conditions 1-3 to set the production of public goods at optimal levels, we can then (in theory, of course) determine the lump-sum transfers that will produce whatever overall outcome we desire and let the market, with all its strong incentive mechanisms, work to achieve that outcome (we may have to use some of the transfers to provide the collective consumption goods). Unfortunately, however, we can work out all these equations only if we know everyone's utility functions. How could a government discover these? It might poll the populace. Alas, when we are asked what our interests are, it may not be in our interest to say. For example, if each individual's taxes to pay for collective goods are levied according to that individual's benefits received from them, one would not have incentive to state honestly what benefits one received. Even if taxes are not individually related to benefits, one might assert a very strong interest in some only mildly desirable collective provision in order to appear to outweigh those who do not care for the provision. Various devices for evoking honest statements (true "revelation of preferences") have been proposed (Clarke 1971; Groves and Ledyard 1977a), but they all have serious flaws (Groves and Ledyard 1977b; Feldman 1980, pp. 114-134).

Remarkably, in this last discussion, Samuelson's paper already suggests how our two problems—collective action and the Arrow problem—are related.

Samuelson notes that optimal allocation of collective goods must be done centrally, that a decentralized spontaneous achievement of an optimal allocation is impossible. But even a well-intentioned government might find it hard to allocate collective goods optimally because it might find it hard to determine the optimal levels of provision. Optimal levels are defined, of course, by the interests of all affected parties and a government would have to discover these interests and somehow aggregate them. Any system for doing so will be subject to manipulation as discussed by Gibbard in the selection in the second part of these readings. (For a relatively accessible treatment of the issues discussed here, see Feldman 1980, ch. 6.)

One should not be misled by Samuelson's apparent implication that achieving a particular optimal outcome in a market for private goods only is any easier (even in theory) than achieving one in a market for both private and public goods. The kind of information required to compute lump-sum transfers in advance of letting the market run is extensive information on individual utility functions. This is no more available to a government than is adequate information on trade-off functions for public goods. Moreover, the incentives to misrepresent one's trade-off functions may be as great for private as for public goods: all of us would presumably prefer to have the largest possible premarket transfers. The result of manipulation in the private goods case, however, will not be suboptimality. Rather it will only move the society to a different optimal outcome. In the effort centrally to control public good provisions, manipulation may actually lead to suboptimality.

The whole notion of doing the computations required to solve Samuelson's conditions 1-3 for a particular outcome has an absurd ring to it—the earlier Wittgenstein would have called it metaphysical. When near the end of section III Samuelson speaks of the "truth" that the solution to these conditions "exists," he is speaking nonsense. Economists too readily indulge such nonsense.

9

THE PURE THEORY OF PUBLIC EXPENDITURE

Paul A. Samuelson

I. ASSUMPTIONS

Except for Sax, Wicksell, Lindahl, Musgrave, and Bowen, economists have rather neglected the theory of optimal public expenditure, spending most of their energy on the theory of taxation. Therefore, I explicitly assume two categories of goods: ordinary *private consumption goods* $(X_1, \ldots, X_n)$, which can be parcelled out among different individuals $(1, 2, \ldots, i, \ldots, s)$ according to the relations

$$\bar{X}_j = \sum_{i=1}^{s} X_j^i;$$

and *collective consumption goods* $(X_{n+1}, \ldots, X_{n+m})$, which all enjoy in common in the sense that each individual's consumption of such a good leads to no subtraction from any other individual's consumption of that good, so $X_{n+j} = X_{n+j}^i$ simultaneously for each and every ith individual and each collective consumption good. I assume no mystical collective mind that enjoys collective consumption goods; instead I assume each individual has a consistent set of *ordinal preferences* with respect to his consumption of all goods (collective as well as private), which can be summarized by a regularly smooth and convex utility index $u^i = u^i (X_1^i, \ldots, X_{n+m}^i)$ (any monotonic

Reprinted from *Review of Economics and Statistics,* Vol. 36, 1954, pp. 387-389 by permission of the author and North-Holland Publishing Company, © 1954 by North-Holland Publishing Company.

stretching of the utility index is of course also an admissible cardinal index of preference). I shall throughout follow the convention of writing the partial derivative of any function with respect to its jth argument by a j subscript, so $u_j^i = \partial u^i / \partial X_j^i$, etc. Provided economic quantities can be divided into two groups, (1) *output* or goods which everyone always wants to maximize and (2) inputs or factors which everyone always wants to minimize, we are free to change the algebraic signs of the latter category and from then on to work only with "goods," knowing that the case of factor inputs is covered as well. Hence by this convention we are sure that $u_j^i > 0$ always.

To keep production assumptions at the minimum level of simplicity, I assume a regularly convex and smooth production-possibility schedule relating totals of all outputs, private and collective; or $F(X_1, \ldots, X_{n+m}) = 0$, with $F_j > 0$ and ratios F_j / F_n determinate and subject to the generalized laws of diminishing returns.

Feasibility considerations disregarded, there is a *maximal* (ordinal) *utility frontier* representing the Pareto-optimal points—of which there are an (s − 1)-fold infinity—with the property that from such a frontier point you can make one person better off only by making some other person worse off. If we wish to make normative judgments concerning the relative ethical desirability of different configurations involving some individuals being on a higher level of indifference and some on a lower, we must be presented with a set of ordinal interpersonal norms or with a *social welfare function* representing a consistent set of ethical preferences among all the possible states of the system. It is not a "scientific" task of the economist to "deduce" the form of this function; this can have as many forms as there are possible ethical views; for the present purpose, the only restriction placed on the social welfare function is that it shall always increase or decrease when any one person's ordinal preference increases or decreases, all others staying on their same indifference levels: mathematically, we narrow it to the class that any one of its indexes can be written $U = U(u^1, \ldots, u^s)$ with $U_j > 0$.

II. OPTIMAL CONDITIONS

In terms of these norms, there is a "best state of the world" which is defined mathematically in simple regular cases by the marginal conditions

$$\frac{u_j^i}{u_r^i} = \frac{F_j}{F_r} \qquad \begin{array}{l} (i = 1, 2, \ldots, s; r, j = 1, \ldots, n) \text{ or} \\ (i = 1, 2, \ldots, s; r = 1; j = 2, \ldots, n), \end{array} \tag{1}$$

$$\sum_{i=1}^{s} \frac{u_{n+j}^i}{u_r^i} = \frac{F_{n+j}}{F_r} \qquad \begin{array}{l} (j = 1, \ldots, m; r = 1, \ldots, n) \text{ or} \\ (j = 1, \ldots, m; r = 1), \end{array} \tag{2}$$

$$\frac{U_i u_k^i}{U_q u_k^q} = 1 \qquad \begin{array}{l} (i, q = 1, \ldots, s; k = 1, \ldots, n) \text{ or} \\ (q = 1; i = 2, \ldots, s; k = 1). \end{array} \qquad (3)$$

Equations (1) and (3) are essentially those given in the chapter on welfare economics in my *Foundations of Economic Analysis* [1947]. They constitute my version of the "new welfare economics." Alone (1) represents that subset of relations which defines the Pareto-optimal utility frontier and which by itself represents what I regard as the unnecessarily narrow version of what once was called the "new welfare economics."

The new element added here is the set (2), which constitutes a pure theory of government expenditure on collective consumption goods. By themselves (1) and (2) define the $(s - 1)$ fold infinity of utility frontier points; only when a set of interpersonal normative conditions equivalent to (3) is supplied are we able to define an unambiguously "best" state.

Since formulating the conditions (2) some years ago, I have learned from the published and unpublished writings of Richard Musgrave that their essential logic is contained in the "voluntary-exchange" theories of public finance of the Sax-Wicksell-Lindahl-Musgrave type, and I have also noted Howard Bowen's independent discovery of them in Bowen's writings of a decade ago. A graphical interpretation of these conditions in terms of *vertical* rather than *horizontal* addition of different individuals' marginal-rate-of-substitution schedules can be given; but what I must emphasize is that there is a different such schedule for each individual at each of the $(s - 1)$ fold infinity of different distributions of relative welfare along the utility frontier.

III. IMPOSSIBILITY OF DECENTRALIZED SPONTANEOUS SOLUTION

So much for the involved optimizing equations that an omniscient calculating machine could theoretically solve if fed the postulated functions. No such machine now exists. But it is well known that an "analogue calculating machine" can be provided by competitive market pricing, (*a*) so long as the production functions satisfy the neoclassical assumptions of constant returns to scale and generalized diminishing returns and (*b*) so long as the individuals' indifference contours have regular convexity and, we may add, (*c*) so long as all goods are private. We can then insert between the right- and left-hand sides of (1) the equality with uniform market prices p_j/p_r and adjoin the budget equations for each individual

$$p_1 X_1^i + p_2 X_2^i + \ldots + p_n X_n^i = L^i \quad (i = 1, 2, \ldots, s), \qquad (1')$$

where L^i is a lump-sum tax for each individual so selected in algebraic value as to lead to the "best" state of the world. Now note, if there were no collective consumption goods, then (1) and (1') can have their solution enormously simplified. Why? Because on the one hand perfect competition among productive enterprises would ensure that goods are produced at minimum costs and are sold at proper marginal costs, with all factors receiving their proper marginal productivities; and on the other hand, each individual, in seeking as a competitive buyer to get to the highest level of indifference subject to given prices and tax, would be led as if by an Invisible Hand to the grand solution of the social maximum position. Of course the institutional framework of competition would have to be maintained, and political decision making would still be necessary, but of a computationally minimum type: namely, algebraic taxes and transfers $(L^1, \ldots, L^s)$ would have to be varied until society is swung to the ethical observer's optimum. The servant of the ethical observer would not have to make explicit decisions about each person's detailed consumption and work; he need only decide about generalized purchasing power, knowing that each person can be counted on to allocate it optimally. In terms of communication theory and game terminology, each person is motivated to do the signalling of his tastes needed to define and reach the attainable-bliss point.

Now all of the above remains valid even if collective consumption is not zero but is instead *explicitly set* at its optimum values as determined by (1), (2), and (3). *However no decentralized pricing system can serve to determine optimally these levels of collective consumption.* Other kinds of "voting" or "signalling" would have to be tried. But, and this is the point sensed by Wicksell but perhaps not fully appreciated by Lindahl, now it is in the selfish interest of each person to give *false* signals, to pretend to have less interest in a given collective consumption activity than he really has, etc. I must emphasize this: taxing according to a benefit theory of taxation can not at all solve the computational problem in the decentralized manner possible for the first category of "private" goods to which the ordinary market pricing applies and which do not have the "external effects" basic to the very notion of collective consumption goods. Of course, utopian voting and signalling schemes can be imagined. (Scandinavian consensus," Kant's "categorical imperative," and other devices meaningful only under conditions of "symmetry," etc.) The failure of market catallactics in no way denies the following truth: given sufficient knowledge the optimal decisions can always be found by scanning over all the attainable states of the world and selecting the one which according to the postulated ethical welfare function is best. The solution "exists"; the problem is how to "find" it.

One could imagine every person in the community being indoctrinated to behave like a "parametric decentralized bureaucrat" who *reveals* his preferences by signalling in response to price parameters or Lagrangean multipliers, to questionnaires, or to other devices. But there is still this fundamental technical difference going to the heart of the whole problem of *social* economy: by departing from his indoctrinated rules, any one person can hope to snatch some selfish benefit in a way not possible under the self-policing competitive pricing of private goods; and the "external economies" or "jointness of demand" intrinsic to the very concept of collective goods and governmental activities makes it impossible for the grand ensemble of optimizing equations to have that special pattern of zeros which makes *laissez-faire* competition even *theoretically* possible as an analogue computer.

IV. CONCLUSION

To explore further the problem raised by public expenditure would take us into the mathematical domain of "sociology" or "welfare politics," which Arrow, Duncan Black, and others have just begun to investigate. Political economy can be regarded as one special sector of this general domain, and it may turn out to be pure luck that within the general domain there happened to be a subsector with the "simple" properties of traditional economics.

10 • Introduction

One of the sharpest reactions to the preceding paper was against the very notion of a public good in Samuelson's sense. For example, Margolis (1955) argued that very little of what governments provide can meaningfully be called public goods. Oddly, both sides have prevailed. Almost no one asserts that there are very many "pure" public goods. But it is also true that Samuelson's category has gone on to be widely used in analysis and to be refined in many ways. In the following selection, John G. Head discusses the "polar" case of public goods. He takes it as an ideal type from which to draw insights even about actual cases which are less than pure.

In sections which are not reprinted here, Head opens his paper with a quick account of the history of developments in the theory of public goods from nineteenth-century continental economists to recent commentaries on them, to Samuelson and others, such as Musgrave (1959). Head then puts forth three characteristics of goods that he thinks are analytically distinct, all of which might be associated with public goods. These are jointness of supply, impossibility of exclusion, and impossibility of rejection.

Jointness of supply (also called *nonrivalness of consumption* and many other things) characterizes those goods which, in Samuelson's words, "all enjoy in common in the sense that each individual's consumption of such a good leads to no subtraction from any other individual's consumption of that good." There are few examples of goods that enjoy pure jointness. At some level of consumption physical goods seem to suffer crowding effects, as highways, parades, and even the aurora borealis must. Many goods that are commonly cited as public goods are in fact merely in abundant natural supply and are "free goods." Hence, provision of these goods may not be a problem since they already exist, as fresh air still does in many places. Examples of goods that are strictly joint in supply over *any* range of demand—in the sense that the quantities of them available are literally not diminished by use—are not physical commodities but such "things" as ideas and information, and even these are likely to involve (marginal) costs of transmission to additional users. Hence, the notion of jointness is perhaps *only* that of an ideal type. (The notion of purely private consumption is similarly an ideal type.) Nevertheless, it can usefully be said to approximate the conditions of enough interesting cases of real goods to make it an indispensable ideal type for analysis.

The significance of jointness of supply may be guessed from the fact that Samuelson, in the preceding paper, made it the defining characteristic of public goods. Samuelson was interested in the "pure theory" of public finance. The public should finance any good whose (marginal) cost of supply to an additional user is zero. Hence, presumably, he called such goods "public" goods. This is not the same as to say that the marginal cost of production of these goods is zero—it may not be. For example, one might produce a parade with 100 marching bands or with 101. If the bands have to be paid, the larger parade will cost a bit more. But if 101,000 instead of 100,000 people watch the parade by standing along the ample sidewalks, there need be no additional cost involved in accommodating the extra 1000 spectators.

Now it happens that very many goods share with this parade the characteristic that they are joint in supply *over typical levels of demand.* For example, on a large percentage of all airline flights, the planes are not at all full. Each of these planes could accommodate more passengers at no cost (unless the flight offers dinner, say). Samuelson would not argue that the airlines should therefore be run by the state at no charge to passengers as he probably would argue that most highways should be. The difference between airline flights and most highways must turn on something other than jointness. It turns on Head's second characteristic of public goods, or at least on an approximation of it: the *impossibility of exclusion.* Although he does not address the issue in the foregoing paper, Samuelson perhaps had some sense of the significance of exclusion when he stipulated by equation that each individual's consumption of each collective consumption good is equal to every other individual's. Clearly, a significant difference between airlines and highways is that passengers can easily be excluded from the former at a relatively low cost, whereas cars can be excluded from many highways only at a relatively high cost. Indeed, some tollroads are said to spend almost as much collecting tolls as the tolls are worth. For many roads, "price exclusion" (I am excluded from driving a Rolls Royce Corniche by its price) hardly makes sense because of its gross inefficiency. For the airlines, price exclusion makes eminently good sense.

What of literal *impossibility of exclusion*? Since we are dealing with the vocabulary of economists, we may safely assume that this, too, is only an ideal type. Indeed, this particular term has the ring of politics so that one may safely conclude, on a paraphrase of Mao, that, if necessary, exclusion comes at the end of a gun. There is surely no good produced external to my self from which I could not be excluded by sufficient force. Hence, we can practically be interested only in the cost of exclusion. If the American nuclear deterrent were to be funded by voluntary subscriptions—as American public television partly is—I could not cheaply be excluded from the benefits

of the colllective effort. Given the prices to be charged, however, we can
expect to see considerable advances in the technology of exclusion for many
goods for which exclusion is now costly. For example, the spread of cable
technology may soon make public television marketable with easy price
exclusion—and therefore, no longer a public good.

There has been debate over the relative significance of these two
characteristics. Samuelson considers jointness more important; Musgrave and
Olson consider nonexcludability more important. The argument for the
importance of jointness is roughly as follows. Efficiency in the production of
market goods is achieved only if their prices equal their marginal costs of
production. For public goods, the notion of marginal cost is ambiguous. It
could mean the marginal cost of producing an additional unit of the good (as
by making a bridge of three lanes rather than two). Or it could mean the cost
of extending supply of the present level of supply to another consumer. The
second meaning is clearly crucial for the market provision of public goods.
For a good that is perfectly joint in supply, the marginal cost in this second
sense is zero. The efficient price for such a good would therefore be zero. But
this would produce the inefficient result that the good would not be
produced by any firm. One escape from this reductio ad absurdum is to
remove the good from the market and to let it be publicly provided.

What of exclusion? Suppose the joint good above were subject to very easy
exclusion. Now a firm might produce it and sell access to it at a price that was
more than zero. The result might be inefficient, of course, but then
Samuelson has demonstrated for us that optimal (i.e., efficient) provision *by
the state* is effectively impossible. Hence, we are reduced to informed
guessing about whether market or public provision is farther from optimality.
The biggest element in that guess might often be the cost of exclusion relative
to the cost of producing the good, and the cost of exclusion is a function of
present technology. Now suppose exclusion from the good were very costly.
Then no firm could make a profit by producing the good since a firm could
not exclude anyone from enjoying the good even after refusing to pay for it.
Unless better technologies for exclusion are invented, we should therefore
expect the market not to produce the good at all, even though nonprovision
might be severely suboptimal. For such a good it is at least possible that the
state could come much closer to optimality. Hence, as Head concludes at the
ends of sections I.2 and I.3, impossibility of exclusion seems to be the more
significant characteristic of public goods.

There is also a question of the logical relationship between the ideal
typical characteristics of jointness and nonexcludability. Analytically,
jointness clearly does not imply impossibility of exclusion. You may have a
wonderfully good idea or tune but you may easily be able to keep it away
from me. The literal impossibility of exclusion, however, does imply jointness

because if no one can be excluded then everyone can enjoy the good at no cost.[1] (For an excellent, lucid discussion of jointness and nonexcludability, see Snidal 1979.)

Finally let us consider Head's third characteristic: *impossibility of rejection*. When the aurora borealis is on display I can easily refuse to look. When the steel mills of Gary belch, I may not easily refuse to breathe their stench. The former good can be rejected, but the latter cannot. The impossibility or high cost of rejection may sensibly be seen as the essential characteristic of *collective bads* such as air pollution or our neighbor's stereo. This is not to say that anything that cannot be rejected is a bad, but only that anything that is a collective bad is so only if it cannot very easily be rejected. If I could costlessly filter out the good from the bad gases in those breezes from Gary, Gary's pollution might not be a bad. Again, although he grew up in Gary, Samuelson does not raise this issue in his definition of public goods. Nevertheless, we may reasonably consider nonrejectability the defining characteristic of public bads just as nonexcludability is the defining characteristic of public goods. The two categories are not quite symmetric, however, since any bad from which exclusion is costless can, by implication, easily be kept out of joint supply. For example, if U.S. Steel could costlessly exclude me from breathing its vapors, presumably it would—and on a warm day I would still be able to see Gary. For something which we all consider a good, however, whether or not we can reject it will not likely be of concern to us.

The part of Head's paper reprinted here should be relatively easy reading without further commentary. As is Samuelson in the preceding paper, Head is concerned primarily with the issues that public goods raise for public finance. His discussion should make many of these clear. The most important general conclusion of his paper is that the factor that makes for difficulties in public finance is not jointness but nonexcludability. This is also, of course, Olson's conclusion for the problem of voluntary collective action as we have emphasized in our introductory essay for this section of readings. To the extent this conclusion is correct then, again, it does not matter for the analysis of collective action whether the goods that groups seek are goods that can be put into joint supply.

But we have also said that there is no good external to oneself from which one's exclusion is impossible. Then what is at issue? What is possible is that exclusion of some people will be politically inexpedient or too costly to bother with. The purely technical analysis of the technology of provision of a good or of the technology of exclusion from it can therefore at best be suggestive for the analysis of collective action. In politics virtually any good can become the object of collective action—all that matters is whether noncontributors de facto will be excluded, not whether in theory they could be. Hence, although the analysis of public goods has surely enhanced our understanding of the nature of the problem of collective action, it does not finally play a major role in determining what will or will not be realms for collective action or when collective action will fail or succeed. The politics of collective action can be directed at the provision of virtually any good, no matter how "private" or "public" the good. It is the nature of politics, not the nature of the goods, that determines the logic of collective action.

NOTE

1. In the part of his paper not reprinted here, Head argues the contrary. But his argument is by a muddled example that involves a particular set of people who cannot be excluded from the benefits of local police protection. Since to spread that protection to a larger population would cost more money, the good is not in joint supply. But that means that the larger population is excluded from the good. If one wishes, however, to assert that at least no one in the local population can be excluded, as Head asserts, then one must also grant that for *this population* the good is in joint supply.

10

PUBLIC GOODS: THE POLAR CASE

John G. Head

I. PROVISION OF PUBLIC GOODS

As in the early Continental literature, it is clear from the original discussions by Samuelson and Musgrave that the pure public good is taken as an extreme case to illustrate the need for public provision. For Samuelson it is a 'strong polar case' which the student of public expenditure can set against the equally extreme Walrasian model of a purely private economy (1955, p. 350). For Musgrave it is a case '... where the market mechanism fails altogether ... Social wants must be satisfied through the budget if they are to be satisfied at all' (1959, pp. 8-9). It is clearly recognized by both Samuelson and Musgrave that political provision for public goods must pose difficult problems. There is, however, a clear implication that the market failure problem is such that the political mechanism could hardly prove inferior.

1. The Benchmark of Optimal Provision

The first step in Samuelson's analysis, and perhaps his major positive contribution, is the rigorous statement and derivation of the optimum conditions for public goods supply. As in modern welfare analysis of a private goods economy, these conditions provide a benchmark for the assessment of market performance and political provision.

Samuelson's central finding is that the conditions for *efficient resource allocation* in a world with a public good differ radically from the more

Reprinted from *Modern Fiscal Issues: Essays in Honour of Carl S. Shoup,* edited by Richard M. Bird and John G. Head, by permission of the author and the University of Toronto Press, pp. 7-16, © University of Toronto Press, 1972.

familiar conditions for a private goods world. In the simple two-person, two-good case of his 1955 paper, he shows that, where one of the two goods is public, the marginal rate of transformation must equal the summed marginal rates of substitution, i.e., $MRS^1 + MRS^2 = MT$. This contrasts with the corresponding private goods case in which we require $MRS^1 = MRS^2 = MT$.

In accordance with his 'social welfare function' approach to welfare economics Samuelson then goes on to determine the conditions for a welfare maximum where ' . . . the social welfare significance of a unit of any private good allocated to private individuals must at the margin be the same for each and every person' (p. 353). This further distributional requirement is, however, no different from that for an all-private-goods world.

Samuelson's treatment of the distributional aspects has been the cause of considerable confusion and dispute. Buchanan in particular has argued strongly that the normative theory of public goods should not go beyond the conditions for efficient resource allocation (1968, pp. 193-197). This is a basic question of welfare methodology which continues essentially unresolved.[1]

2. Problems of Market Provision

In view of its fundamental importance, it is surprising to find that Samuelson and Musgrave devote relatively little space to the analysis of market performance in public goods supply. This has proved particularly confusing as it appears that each is focusing on the market failure problems caused by only one of the two basic public goods characteristics. Though some aspects remain controversial, the position has been considerably clarified by subsequent discussion in which the market failure problems caused by the joint supply and non-exclusion characteristics have been analysed separately. In the following review we shall focus on questions of allocative efficiency and ignore distributional considerations. This is appropriate whether we follow Samuelson or Buchanan on welfare methodology. In the Samuelson framework the market mechanism is generally incapable of handling the distribution problem with or without the presence of public goods; the central question at issue is whether it is capable of handling the allocation problem.

Joint Goods

Abstracting completely from the existence of price-exclusion problems, the possibility of market supply of 'purely joint goods' can be considered.

The first point to note is that Samuelson's derivation of the conditions for allocatively efficient supply of pure public goods holds without essential modification for purely joint goods. This is easily seen once it is recognized that the equal consumption condition on which it is based is *necessary for*

Pareto-effiency even where it does not hold *by definition.* (We abstract from the possibility of negative marginal evaluation.) The basic allocative requirement, $\Sigma MRS = MT$, therefore derives from the joint supply characteristic and is unaffected by the presence or absence of nonexcludability. The question is, therefore, whether a market mechanism can be expected to satisfy this requirement. Two main types of market structure have been considered, perfect competition and monopoly. [We consider them in order.] (a) *Perfect competition.* In his first paper Samuelson appears to argue that *even if we could abstract from the fundamental problem of preference concealment* a competitive market mechanism would still be incapable of ensuring an allocatively efficient supply of purely joint goods [this volume]. This question has been examined in detail recently by Thompson (1968), who reaches the surprising conclusion that purely joint goods will be *over-supplied* by a competitive market.

Thompson explicitly assumes that both producers and consumers have perfect knowledge of all preference functions. Under these conditions he argues that perfect competition will produce a system of rational price discrimination such that each consumer is charged a unit price equal to his marginal valuation. (It is clear from Thompson's discussion that this unit price is to be interpreted as the all-or-nothing price per unit in terms of private good at which the consumer would just be willing to purchase a given quantity of service; it is therefore equal to *average* valuation rather than 'marginal' valuation.) No consumer would be willing to pay more; and no seller would be willing to accept less, since a concession to any one customer would force the seller to grant a similar concession to all his other customers. Free entry and exit from the industry ensures that in equilibrium summed unit prices, and hence summed average valuations, just equal marginal cost (the minimum average cost of the marginal firm). If average valuation were equal to marginal valuation (or marginal rate of substitution) for each consumer, the allocative requirement $\Sigma MRS = MT$ would therefore be satisfied. In fact, of course, average valuation necessarily exceeds marginal valuation for each consumer, and $\Sigma MRS < MT$. Purely joint goods are therefore over-supplied under perfect competition. To illustrate the possible degree of misallocation involved, Thompson notes that in the special case of constant costs the community would be just as well off with a zero output of the joint good (Thompson 1968).

The analysis of this special case is still controversial. If, however, we provisionally accept Thompson's analysis as correct, the basic objection remains that the perfect knowledge assumption is hopelessly unrealistic. According to both Samuelson and Musgrave, the central problem of public goods supply is that consumers will not reveal their preferences for public goods. Even in the Thompson model of perfectly competitive provision, this problem duly emerges when the perfect knowledge assumption is relaxed. Assuming that the seller still attempts to set discriminatory prices equal to average valuation, each consumer now has an incentive to mask his true preferences in an attempt to attract a lower price. As a result it is likely that the whole attempt to discriminate would be abandoned. With non-discriminatory pricing the problem of strategic concealment of true preferences disappears in the competitive model. Output is not Pareto-efficient, however, since a uniform price must exclude some individuals who could otherwise enjoy additional units of service at the existing level of output at no extra cost. Others, moreover, would be willing to pay more for the existing level of output which tends as a result to be too low.

(b) *Monopoly.* The problems of competitive market provision do not, of course, exclude the possibility that some other marketing technique may prove superior. The effects of conferring a legal monopoly on a single producer have been much discussed in the recent literature. [. . .]

Abstracting from preference-concealment problems, a profit-maximizing monopolist would clearly choose, if possible, to discriminate perfectly, in order to cream off the full amount of consumer surplus. Since the services of a joint good cannot generally be retraded, price discrimination is feasible and the resulting output should be Pareto optimal. This is easy to see if we imagine the monopolist to sell units of the service incrementally to each consumer. For a particular consumer he will therefore charge a very high price for the first units, and the incremental price charged will fall steadily for additional units. For the marginal unit the price charged must equal marginal valuation or marginal rate of substitution. Profit will clearly be maximized by pushing output to the point where summed marginal prices just equal marginal cost, i.e., where $\Sigma \text{MRS} = \text{MT}$. At this point each consumer is in effect paying the all-or-nothing price per unit at which he would just be willing to purchase the total output, and these summed all-or-nothing prices exceed marginal cost. In contrast to the case of perfect competition, however, this excess is not competed away by the entry of new firms attracted by the monopoly profit, and output remains Pareto optimal.

As Samuelson has particularly emphasized (1967, p. 201), the knowledge assumptions underlying this analysis are once again hopelessly unrealistic. No monopolist could possibly possess such detailed information on consumer preference functions. The monopolist is effectively in a bilateral monopoly relationship with each consumer. He is therefore faced with a whole host of small-number preference-revelation problems, as each consumer has every incentive to misrepresent his preferences in an attempt to obtain a better bargain. At most, only a very crude approximation to perfect discrimination is conceivable and some under-expansion of the service seems likely. If, on account of information problems or because of franchise requirements, uniform pricing is adopted, inefficiency and under-expansion are once again inevitable. This is true even if the monopolist is price-regulated to ensure price-marginal cost equality.

Public Goods

The above discussion clearly demonstrates that marketing techniques are not generally capable of ensuring an allocatively efficient supply of purely joint goods. There is no sign, however, of the traditional conclusion that, in the case of public goods, little or nothing can be provided through the market. Although the amount supplied may well be suboptimal, substantial quantities can nevertheless be marketed, and in very special cases a grossly excessive output is conceivable.

The traditional conclusion is, however, to be found in Musgrave's original contribution to the modern discussion (1959, pp. 8-9). Musgrave specifically attributes the complete failure of the market to impossibility of exclusion: 'People who do not pay for the services cannot be excluded from the benefits that result; and since they cannot be excluded from the benefits, they will not engage in voluntary payments. Hence the market cannot satisfy such wants. Budgetary provision is needed if they are to be satisfied at all' (p. 8). In the analysis of purely joint goods this second major public goods character- istic is completely ignored. It is therefore interesting to reconsider the market failure problem when the further characteristic of impossibility of exclusion is superimposed on joint supply.

If price exclusion is impossible it might appear that even the suboptimal quantities which might be expected under uniform pricing of a purely joint good will no longer be forthcoming. Nothing can be charged and nothing will therefore be provided. Even the artificial device of an omniscient monopolist would seem to fail, since although he may be able to design a set of Pareto-efficient differential prices, this price set is now completely unenforce- able. Market failure is again complete.

This conclusion, however, requires modification when it is recognized that, even if price-exclusion is impossible, some individuals may nevertheless be willing to contribute voluntarily. Particularly where the number of consumers is small, substantial amounts may be purchased, even under completely independent adjustment. Moreover, in small-number cases, consumers may be able to reach a voluntary agreement among themselves to purchase a more nearly Pareto-optimal quantity. This possibility has been stressed particularly in the modern externality literature stemming from the pioneering paper by Coase (1960). However, small-number preference-revelation problems arise, analogous to those we have just considered in the joint supply context, as each consumer has an incentive to misrepresent his preferences in an attempt to obtain a better bargain. Pareto-optimal supply could not therefore in general be expected.

As Musgrave explicitly recognizes (1959, pp. 9-10), the dramatic market failure implications of non-excludability emerge only where large numbers of potential consumers are involved. This seems the appropriate case to consider in connection with a pure public good since the efficient size of the sharing group is literally infinite. In this situation ' . . . the satisfaction derived by any individual consumer is independent of his own contribution' (p. 9). According to Musgrave, nothing will therefore be contributed voluntarily; non-revelation of preferences is complete. Even here some modification is necessary to take account of the fact that small quantities may well be purchased even under independent behavior. Complete market failure strictly requires not merely large numbers of consumers but also that summed marginal evaluations fall short of marginal cost over all ranges of output for any subgroup of consumers of critically small size. Even in the more general large-number case, however, the traditional conclusion still holds in the sense that output will be enormously suboptimal.

As Buchanan has particularly emphasized (1968), there is in this case no strategic concealment of true preferences in an attempt to achieve a better bargain. Behaviour is strictly independent; other consumers are treated as part of the natural environment. These large-number preference-revelation problems associated with non-excludability should therefore be clearly distinguished from the small-number preference-revelation problems encountered in the joint supply context, and from small-number preference-revelation problems in general. These distinctions have been the subject of considerable confusion and debate in the modern literature, but the major differences seem now to have been resolved.

Conclusion. The above analysis shows that both joint supply and impossibility of exclusion pose significant market failure problems. For the standard large-number case of a pure public good it seems reasonable to conclude that impossibility of exclusion is the *more potent* cause of market failure. (We abstract from the somewhat artificial analysis of competitive oversupply.) From this point of view the current emphasis on joint supply as the *essential* public goods characteristic seems rather misleading.

3. Problems of Political Provision

The demonstration of significant market failure problems in public goods supply provides, of course, no guarantee that government can do better. In their original contributions both Samuelson and Musgrave explicitly recognize that political provision for public goods must pose difficult problems. The problem of determining individual preferences is particularly stressed by both.

Voluntary Exchange Models

The modern discussion of political provision has been very strongly influenced by the early Continental literature, especially the benefit theories of

Wicksell and Lindahl. As a result, there has been a general tendency to regard a pseudo-market solution as some sort of a model or ideal for collective provision. This is true, for example, of Musgrave (1959, 1969) and Buchanan (1967, 1968), though Samuelson (1955) provides a notable exception. In this solution, following Lindahl, each person is to be charged a price per unit of public good equal to his marginal evaluation or marginal rate of substitution in terms of numeraire private good, and output is pushed to the point where the sum of these tax-prices just equals marginal cost of the public good. At such a point, Σ MRS = MT, and output is Pareto optimal.

If we assume that the political planner has full knowledge of all preference functions, it is clearly true that efficient allocation *can* be achieved in this way. Marginal evaluations are known and tax-prices per unit can be charged which just equal marginal evaluation at a Pareto optimal level of output. However, as Samuelson has particularly emphasized in recent contributions (1967, 1969), efficient allocation can equally well be achieved in other ways. For example, a more Wicksellian solution would be to require that tax prices be set equal to marginal evaluation *only for the marginal unit of public good*; different prices might be charged for infra-marginal units. More generally there is no necessity to establish *any* market-type or 'voluntary exchange' relationship between tax-price and marginal evaluation. If individual preferences are known, tax-prices have no conceivable allocative function to perform.

The central problem of public goods supply is, however, that true preferences are unknown. The crucial question is therefore whether the political consensus model with simultaneous determination of public goods quantity and tax-price provides an efficient preference-revelation mechanism. The allocative performance of these voluntary exchange models has been analysed in detail in the modern literature. In general, however, it seems clear that preference-revelation problems arise which are precisely analogous to those which we have already discussed in a market context.

In small-number models of the sort analysed by Lindahl each party has an obvious incentive to conceal true preferences in an attempt to obtain a more advantageous agreement in terms of public goods quantity and tax-price. Some approach to an allocatively efficient solution should, however, be possible. There is still some dispute on this issue with some writers, such as Buchanan (1968) stressing the incentive to Pareto-optimal agreements, while others, such as Samuelson (1969, p. 107) and Musgrave (1959, pp. 79-80), emphasize the bargaining difficulties.

In large-number models the basic Wicksellian dilemma arises that each person may refuse to contribute voluntarily since public goods quantity is seen to be virtually independent of his own tax contribution. Genuine bargaining may therefore prove impossible. In spite of Buchanan's ingenious argument to the contrary (1968, pp. 92-94) it seems very doubtful whether possession of the veto in the Wicksellian model could significantly improve performance as compared with the corresponding large-number market situation.

Majority-Voting Models

The problems of political provision have also been explored in the more realistic setting of majority voting. Thus, for example, Anthony Downs (1957) has analysed the problems of public goods supply in a majority-voting model characterized by competition for political power between two vote-maximizing political parties. If both parties have full knowledge of all preference functions, competition for votes will tend to force the adoption of a Pareto-optimal program. This is in contrast to the corresponding case of market provision where the introduction of competition between omniscient profit-maximizing firms produces over-expansion of public goods supply. Since the rational voter's choice should depend only upon his total net utility, there is no obvious reason why the program chosen by either party should be presented in voluntary exchange form with an explicit tax-price (marginal or average) for the public good equal to marginal evaluation. The same Pareto-optimal program (with any accompanying redistributive measures) could be presented in infinitely many different ways, all of equivalent vote-catching potential.

When we relax the unrealistic assumption that the parties have full knowledge of voter preference maps, we encounter preference-revelation problems. If it is believed that, for distributional or other reasons, tax shares will be related to revealed preferences, voters will have an obvious incentive to behave strategically. In its attempt to design a vote-maximizing Pareto-optimal program, each party finds itself in a bilateral monopoly relationship with the voters, each of whom has every incentive to misrepresent his true preferences in an attempt to obtain a lower tax burden. Evidently no close approach to Pareto optimality could reasonably be expected in large-number cases. It is interesting to notice that this problem is closely analogous to that of the profit-maximizing monopolist attempting to supply a purely joint good through the market. In contrast to this latter case, however, where under-supply seemed likely, there is no obvious reason to suppose that output will be too small rather than too large.

Analysis of the Downs model serves to bring out very clearly the possible advantages of the political mechanism in public goods supply. Although the preference-revelation problems owing to the joint supply characteristic remain, there is no sign of the fundamental non-exclusion problem that, since nothing can be charged, nothing will be provided. Possession of the tax power (or printing press) effectively transforms the public good into a joint good for purposes of political provision. By contrast, the political mechanism has no obvious advantage over the market system in relation to the joint supply characteristic. Here again it seems that the current emphasis on joint supply as the essential public goods characteristic is very misleading.

Finally the log-rolling models of Buchanan and Tullock (1962) serve to warn us of 'political externalities' which may impair political performance further. Under majority voting, interest groups may combine to support projects yielding special benefits, the cost of which is borne by the community at large. As a result some of the advantages of public provision in relation to the non-excludability characteristic may be dissipated by the emergence of analogous problems in the political process. Under realistic assumptions of imperfect knowledge, a similar inefficiency can be predicted in the Downs model. Contrary to Buchanan and Tullock, however, there is nothing in the logic of this argument to suggest the necessity of over-expansion rather than under-expansion.

II. INTERPRETATION OF THE PARABLE

Over the past fifteen years, since it was first discussed in the modern literature, the Musgrave-Samuelson polar case has been repeatedly criticized on the grounds that few if any public services fit the original definition. In reply, Samuelson has argued that consideration of the polar case may nevertheless yield insights for public expenditure theory comparable to those of the equally extreme Walrasian model of private expenditures (1955, p. 350). The theory of a pure public good therefore provides a parable of public expenditure problems.

Although the modern debate has undoubtedly served to clarify a number of obscurities in the original Musgrave-Samuelson formulation, the central policy implication of the parable has not been clearly brought out. In particular, our analysis suggests that the current emphasis on jointness as the essential characteristic of the public goods concept is dangerously misleading. The political mechanism has an obvious comparative advantage over the market in dealing with problems of non-excludability. It has no such advantage in relation to the jointness characteristic.

Although the pure public goods concept is of little direct practical importance, it can readily be generalized to cover the wide range of goods exhibiting elements of either or both the joint supply and non-excludability characteristic. Our analysis suggests that here again any significant advantages from public intervention will be found to derive fundamentally from the non-excludability elements rather than from generalized joint supply problems.

NOTE

1. For a recent discussion, see Head (1968).

11 • Introduction

Against the general conclusion of Olson's analysis, John Chamberlin argues from a Cournot analysis that group size should not so clearly be a correlate of the likelihood of group failure. The argument is one put forward simultaneously by McGuire (1974). In the usual Cournot analysis of duopoly it is supposed that only two firms are in competition in a given market. Theirs is a small group collective action problem because if they concert their pricing decisions they can expect jointly to obtain monopoly profits, which would substantially exceed competitive profits. Despite their joint interest, however, each has a private interest in undercutting the other in order to obtain a larger share of total sales and profits. If they cannot successfully collude to maintain a joint pricing strategy (perhaps because collusion is illegal), they may nevertheless be able tacitly to achieve an equilibrium price from which it would not benefit either firm to change. Under the usual static assumptions of market economics there will be an equilibrium. The Cournot model describes how firms acting under Cournot behavioral assumptions reach the equilibrium price if they are not already there. The Cournot assumptions are essentially the pregame theory assumptions that players in a market are relatively stupid: they are short-sighted and they assume that all other players are unstrategic while they are strategic. They react to their environment, which includes the actions of others, while assuming that no other will take their actions into account.

Suppose that a firm in a duopoly, seeing that it can increase its profit by increasing or decreasing its level of production, does so. As a result, price is likely to decrease or increase. Hence, the profits of the second firm will be affected and it will react by changing its level of production, thereby again affecting the price of the common product. Now the profits of the first firm will be affected in turn and it will react. For a duopoly under relevant conditions this series of reactions (which will define the two "reaction curves" for the firms) will lead eventually to the equilibrium price, from which point there will be no further reactions. This behavior fits the Cournot assumption because each firm in turn reacts to the current situation by changing to a level of production that would be optimal only if the other firm did not subsequently react, as it will do.

Chamberlin extends this analysis by generalizing it from two to *n* participants and by applying it to any producers (whether firms or individuals) of any collective good (whether price level or other beneficial effect). He then derives the level of production as a function of n to show that under many logical conditions the level rises as n increases (some of his results are presented in an appendix not reprinted here). This conclusion runs contrary to Olson's claim that for a very large group "it is certain that a collective good will *not* be provided unless there is coercion or some outside inducements" (Olson 1965, p. 44). However, Chamberlin's contradiction of Olson on this point is not categorical since there are two assumptions in Chamberlin's analysis that severely limit the applicability of his conclusions to typical instances of collective action.

The first of these has to do with a property of public goods that we have already mentioned and that was more fully discussed in the preceding two papers of this section and in the introductions to them. Chamberlin notes that collective goods may be divided into "inclusive" and "exclusive" public goods. These terms, which are Olson's, are somewhat confusing since they are not equivalent to the distinction between goods from which people can and cannot be excluded. An "inclusive" good is in purely joint supply—once it is available to anyone at a given level it can be made available to everyone at that level at no additional cost. As we discussed in the introduction to Head's paper, the purely joint good may be an ideal type of which there are few if any extant examples. An "exclusive" good is one that suffers crowding as more people use it, as beaches, highways, and public parks eventually do, so that either the level or quality of it available to each user falls. Such a good is therefore not in purely joint supply. It is probably reasonable to claim that most collectively provided goods are to some degree exclusive in this sense. Olson's size argument (that large groups are more likely to fail than are small groups) applies to exclusive goods but not to inclusive goods—this is essentially Chamberlin's conclusion.

The second limiting assumption in Chamberlin's analysis is more telling and it is one that he does not appear to acknowledge. For the Cournot series of reactions to begin, some individual must decide to purchase *some* of the collective good. Given their cost functions, this is an egregious assumption for many collective goods. For example, if cleaner air is a public good for residents in some metropolitan area, the Cournot analysis, if its other conditions are met, implies that adding more residents may lead to more expenditure on the public good, but *only if* we can assume that there was *already* some voluntary individualistic expenditure. Chamberlin assumes that the quantity of the collective good that an individual would buy even if no one else had bought any is a positive quantity, x_i^0. One might reasonably assume no such thing and might expect voluntary expenditures to continue at their original level of nothing after new residents arrive. Hence, one might suppose that Olson's argument is about whether size affects x_i^0. If $x_i^0 = 0$ for every member of the group, there will be no provision even under the Cournot analysis.

11

PROVISION OF COLLECTIVE GOODS AS A FUNCTION OF GROUP SIZE

John Chamberlin

INTRODUCTION

Interest in the theory of collective goods has been increasing among political scientists since the publication of Mancur Olson's *The Logic of Collective Action.*[1] Drawing on developments in the theory of public goods by Samuelson and others,[2] Olson shows how this theory can be used to analyze the formation of voluntary associations including, among others, such important political groups as international alliances and special interest groups. Among Olson's major conclusions are the following:

(1) "unless the number of individuals in a group is quite small, or unless there is coercion or some other special device to make individuals act in their common interest, *rational, self-interested individuals will not act to achieve their common or group interests.*"[3]

(2) "The larger a group is, the farther it will fall short of providing an optimal supply of any collective good, and the less likely that it will act to obtain even a minimal amount of such a good. In short, the larger the group, the less it will further its common interests."[4]

Author's Note: The author wishes to thank Philip Gregg and Mancur Olson for many helpful comments on earlier drafts of this paper. Research support was provided by the Institute of Public Policy Studies, The University of Michigan.

Reprinted from *American Political Science Review*, Vol. 68, 1974, pp. 707-713 and 715, by permission of the American Political Science Association and the author, © 1974 by The American Political Science Association.

Two separate questions are addressed in the conclusions cited above. The first question concerns the amounts of a collective good that will actually be provided by groups whose only difference is in size. The second question is a relative one, involving a comparison between the amount of the collective good actually provided and that amount which would be provided if the optimality conditions of the economic theory were satisfied. The conclusions cited above assert that everything else being equal, small groups will fare better than large groups in both actual and relative performance in providing collective goods. The analysis that follows is concerned with the first of these questions—the relationship between group size and the amount of the collective good actually provided by the group. The closest that Olson comes to specifying the form of this relationship is the following paragraph:

> In a small group in which a member gets such a large fraction of the total benefit that he would be better off if he paid the entire cost himself, rather than go without the good, there is some presumption that the collective good will be provided. In a group in which no one member got such a large benefit from the collective good that he had an interest in providing it even if he had to pay all of the cost, but in which the individual was still so important in terms of the whole group that his contribution or lack of contribution to the group objective had a noticeable effect on the costs or benefits of others in the group, the result is indeterminate. By contrast, in a large group in which no single individual's contribution makes a perceptible difference to the group as a whole, or the burden or benefit of any single member of the group, it is certain that a collective good will *not* be provided unless there is coercion or some outside inducements that will lead the members of the large group to act in their common interest.[5]

While this paragraph is not explicit about the form of the relationship in question, it seems not unreasonable to infer from it and the second of Olson's conclusions cited above that he considers the relationship to be a decreasing one. It remains open to question whether the relationship is a gradually decreasing one, or a step function, with the step (down) occurring at the point where any one individual's actions become imperceptible to others. It is shown below that the relationship between group size and the provision of a collective good is more complex than Olson asserts and that, in many cases, it is the opposite of that suggested by Olson.

The next section discusses collective goods and the framework in which group activity will be analyzed. The paper then analyzes the relationship between group size and the provision of collective benefits. The last section discusses the results, compares them with those of Olson, and comments on some additional factors which influence a group's ability to provide its members with collective benefits.

DERIVATION OF THE MODEL

A collective good is generally characterized by one or both of the following two properties.[6]

(1) Consumption of the good by one individual does not subtract from
    others' consumption of the good. This property is often referred to as
    nonrivalness of consumption.[7]
(2) Individuals who do not share in paying for the good cannot be
    excluded from enjoying the benefits of the good. The benefits accrue
    automatically to all individuals. This is referred to as the nonexclusion
    property.

These two properties result in individuals having incentives to misrepresent
their preferences for collective goods and to engage in strategic behavior to
avoid paying for the benefits of these goods. The ensuing problems make the
provision of an optimal amount of a collective good via a market or the
political process extremely unlikely. Of primary interest in this analysis are
those goods for which the nonexclusion property holds. The activities of
interest groups clearly fulfill this condition, for if political action is undertaken by others and an individual benefits from government policy as a result
of this action, the individual cannot be excluded from these benefits. The
nonrivalness property plays an important part in the analysis as well. Using
this property, Olson classifies groups as "inclusive" or "exclusive" according
to the type of collective benefits their members receive.[8] These categories
correspond to the endpoints of the continuum measuring the degree to which
the nonrivalness of consumption property is met. A pure collective good,
which exhibits perfect nonrivalness, is an "inclusive" good, and the group
which receives the benefits of the good may also be labeled "inclusive." An
individual's evaluation of an "inclusive" collective good is not affected by the
number of persons in the group who receive the benefits. On the other hand,
an "exclusive" good exhibits the same rivalness of consumption as does a
private good but the nonexclusion property still holds. In this case, the
benefit any single individual receives from a unit of the good decreases as the
size of the group increases. An instance of such a good is Olson's example of a
price increase brought about in an industry through output restriction. The
benefits of this price increase (increased profits) are available to any producer
(or potential producer) who supplies some of the demand for the industry's
product. The total amount of increased profit is limited, however, and the
consumption of these profits is subject to perfect rivalness. In contrast, an
"inclusive" good, such as a decrease in the corporate income tax, is not
subject to rivalness at all. An unlimited number of firms can receive the
benefits of the lower tax without detracting from the benefits received by the
other firms.

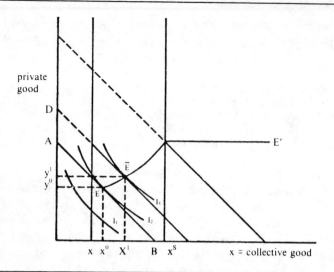

Figure 11.1 Income consumption curve

In arriving at the conclusions cited earlier, Olson assumes that there is no cooperation among the parties involved, that is, no cost sharing arrangements are permitted, and each individual must bear the entire cost of any increase in the amount of the collective good which he initiates. The amount of the collective good provided is thus determined through a process in which the individual reacts independently to the behavior of others in deciding how much of the collective good to provide by himself. The noncooperative nature of this process is also crucial to Olson's "exploitation" hypothesis, for this hypothesis is based upon an examination of the properties of the equilibrium of this noncooperative process.[9] This process may be illustrated as follows. Consider an individual faced with a choice of allocating his income to purchases of two goods, one a private good (y) and the other a collective good (x). His preferences for these goods are shown in Figure 1 by a set of indifference curves. His budget constraint is given by the line AB, and he maximizes his satisfaction by purchasing a commodity bundle on the highest indifference curve consistent with the budget constraint. In Figure 1, his optimum allocation is at point E (with amounts x^0 and y^0 of the two goods), the point of tangency between indifference curve I_2 and the budget line AB. Suppose another individual provides an amount $\bar{x}$ of the collective good. Because of the non-exclusion property, this amount of the collective good is automatically available to the first individual. This has the effect of shifting the vertical axis in Figure 1 to the right by the amount $\bar{x}$. The individual's

θ

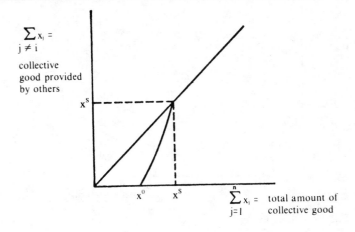

Figure 11.2   Locus of equilibria

budget line is also shifted to the right by the amount $\bar{x}$, since he now consumes this amount of the collective good without having to pay anything for it. If the private good has a price of one, this action by the other individual has the effect of increasing the first individual's income by an amount AD, and he is free to spend his income as he chooses so long as he consumes at least an amount $\bar{x}$ of the collective good. The individual now finds his equilibrium at $\bar{E}$, and he pays for an amount $(x^1 - \bar{x})$ of the collective good. If all possible amounts of the collective good provided by others were considered, the locus of the equilibria of the individual would be the line EE', known as the "income-consumption" curve. Note that if others provide an amount x^s of the collective good, the individual will devote his entire budget to the purchase of the private good. The locus of equilibria is shown in a slightly different manner in Figure 2, where the vertical axis now indicates the amount of the collective good provided by other individuals and the horizontal axis measures the total amount of the collective good provided. A reaction curve for the individual can be derived by considering the horizontal difference between the 45° line and the locus of equilibria in Figure 2. The reaction curve is shown below in Figure 3, indicating that the individual will provide an amount x^0 of the good if no one else provides any, and that he will provide none if the amount provided by others exceeds an amount x^s. The form of the reaction curve depends upon the individual's income elasticity of demand for the collective good. Goods may be placed in three classes on the basis of their income elasticities—inferior goods, normal goods, and superior goods.[10] In the case of an inferior good, an extra unit of

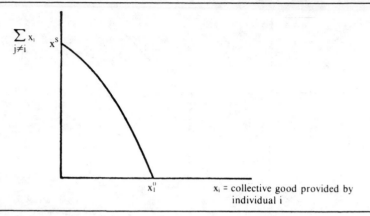

Figure 11.3   Reaction curve

the collective good provided by others induces the individual to cut back his own provision of the good by at least one unit. For a normal good, an extra unit provided by others induces a reduction in the provision by the individual of less than one unit, and for a superior good, an extra unit provided by others induces no reduction, and perhaps an increase, in the amount provided by the individual. These categories of goods have corresponding reaction curves with the following slopes:

type of good	*slope of reaction curve*
inferior	negative and $\geqslant -1$
normal	< -1, but finite
superior	infinite or positive

Three representative reaction curves are shown in Figure 4.[11] It is to be expected that most collective goods will have normal income elasticities.[12]

The case in which two such individuals are independently reacting to one another is shown in Figure 5. The independent adjustment process will reach an equilibrium E where the reaction curves intersect.[13] The equilibrium results in A purchasing x_A^E of the good and B purchasing x_B^E of the good. Both individuals consume an amount of the collective good equal to the sum of these two purchases.

ANALYSIS

Attention may now be turned to examining the relationship between group size and the amount of a collective good provided by the uncoordi-

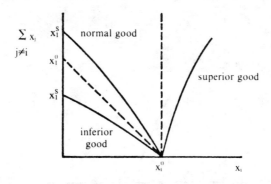

Figure 11.4 Types of reaction curves

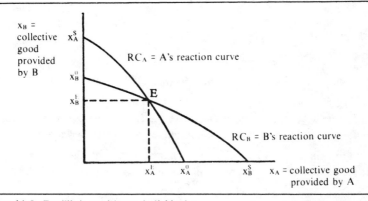

Figure 11.5 Equilibrium with two individuals

nated activities of the group members. For any group, this amount is found by determining the equilibrium of the process described above. One further assumption will be made at this point. In order to facilitate the analysis, it will be assumed that all individuals in a group are identical in terms of preferences and resources.[14]

Consider first the case of an inclusive collective good. The reaction curve for the ith individual is shown in Figure 6. Since the good is "inclusive," the reaction curve is unaffected by group size and thus this one curve will serve as a basis to analyze groups of different sizes. The assumption that all individuals are identical makes solution for the equilibrium quite easy, for if the individuals are identical, each will provide the same amount of the collective good at the equilibrium. In Figure 6, if x_i^E is the amount of the good

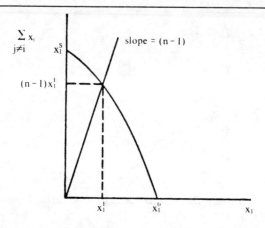

Figure 11.6 Equilibrium for an inclusive good

provided by the ith individual at the equilibrium for a group of size n, then the amount provided by others must be $(n-1)x_i^E$. Thus the equilibrium for a group of size n is found where a straight line through the origin with slope $(n-1)$ intersects the reaction curve. As the size of the group increases, the equilibrium moves along the reaction curve from x_i^0 (when $n=1$) to x_i^s (as $n \to \infty$), as shown in Figure 7. Two characteristics of the provision of an "inclusive" collective good are evident at this point:

(a) $x_i^E \to 0$ as $n \to \infty$

(b) $n x_i^E$ (the total amount provided) $\to x_i^s$ as $n \to \infty$

The relationship between $n x_i^E$ and n may now be established. The total amount of the good provided is equal to the sum of the horizontal and vertical components of the equilibrium ($n x_i^E = x_i^E + (n-1)x_i^E$). If the reaction curve is stated as a function of x_i, say $f(x_i)$, then $n x_i^E = x_i^E + f(x_i^E)$. The relationship between $n x_i^E$ and n is established by examining the derivative of $(x_i^E + f(x_i^E))$ with respect to x_i^E,

$$\frac{d}{dx_i^E}(x_i^E + f(x_i^E)) = 1 + f'(x_i^E),$$

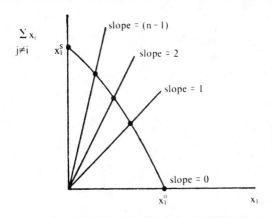

Figure 11.7 Locus of equilibria for an inclusive good

where $f'(x_i^E)$ is the slope of the reaction curve at $x_i = x_i^E$. If $f'(x_i^E) > -1$, nx_i^E increases as x_i^E increases, meaning that nx^E decreases as n increases. If $f'(x_i^E) = -1$, then nx_i^E is unaffected by group size, and if $f'(x_i^E) < -1$, nx_i^E increases as n increases. This result indicates that if the collective good is not an inferior good (i.e., the slope of the reaction curve is less than -1), then the amount of the good actually provided by a group increases with group size (approaching x_i^s as n becomes infinite). Note that while nx_i^E is increasing with n, x_i^E is decreasing. The decrease in the contribution of each individual (x_i^E) is more than offset by the increase in group size. Thus, in the case of "inclusive" collective goods which are not inferior goods, the relationship between group size and the amount of the good actually provided is the opposite of that asserted by Olson.

The case of an "exclusive" collective good may be analyzed in the same way, with one exception. If the good is "exclusive," the reaction curve for an individual changes as group size changes. A possible set of reaction curves for an individual are shown in Figure 8, where RC_n is the individual's reaction curve for a group of size n. This set of curves indicates that as group size becomes infinite, the reaction curves converge to the origin. This is an extreme case of an "exclusive" good, and it is possible that the reaction curves, although shifting toward the origin, will not converge to the origin. This case will be considered later. The equilibrium for a group of size n is found in this case where a straight line through the origin with slope $(n-1)$ intersects the reaction curve for that size group. The path of these equilibria

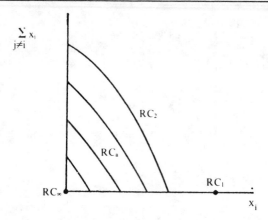

Figure 11.8   Reaction curves for an exclusive good

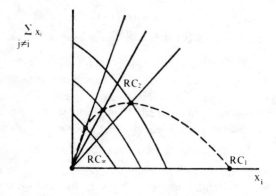

Figure 11.9   Locus of equilibria for an exclusive good

is shown by the broken line in Figure 9. From the figure it is clear that, for an "exclusive" collective good:

(a) $x_i^E \to 0$ as $n \to \infty$

(b) $n x_i^E \to 0$ as $n \to \infty$

(c) $n x_i^E$ decreases as $n \to \infty$.

These conclusions correspond to those of Olson.

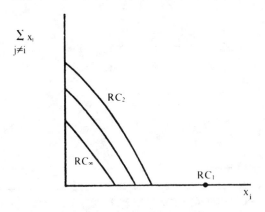

Figure 11.10   Reaction curves for an intermediate good

For a good in the interior of the "inclusive-exclusive" continuum, the reaction curves bear some similarity to those for an "exclusive" collective good. For these "intermediate" goods the reaction curve shifts toward the origin as group size increases, but the set of curves converges to some curve above the origin, an indication of the fact that, even as the group becomes infinitely large, the nonrivalness property still holds to a certain degree. Such a set of curves is shown in Figure 10. The path of equilibria is found in the same manner as that of an "exclusive" good. Two possible cases arise, however, as shown in Figure 11. In both cases:

(a) $x_i^E \to 0$ as $n \to \infty$
(b) $nx_i^E \to x_i^s > 0$ as $n \to \infty$.

But nx_i^E may increase *or* decrease as n increases, as indicated by Figures 11a and 11b respectively. In the first case, nx_i^E increases with group size, indicating that the income effect outweighs the crowding effect, while in the second case the opposite is true. Based on this finding, it would seem that any collective good can be placed into one of two broad categories, "inclusive" and "exclusive," depending upon whether the amount of the good actually provided (nx_i^E) increases or decreases as group size increases.

DISCUSSION

Olson recognizes the possibility of members of a large group providing some amount of a collective good, but the tone of the following remarks

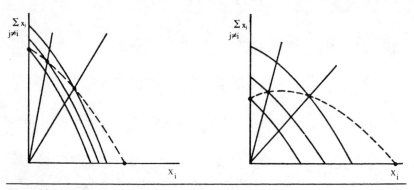

Figure 11.11   Loci of equilibria for two intermediate goods

indicate that he considers this possibility of little general interest or of little empirical significance or both:

> There is one logically conceivable, but surely empirically trivial, case in which a large group could be provided with a very small amount of a collective good without coercion or outside incentives.[15]

> Moreover, apart from a special case . . . , it can be demonstrated that even the provision of a minimal amount of a collective good is less likely in large groups than in small ones when behavior is rational and self-interested.[16]

Nothing in the above analysis would seem to support Olson's statement that the result obtained for "inclusive" goods applies only to a "special case." Only three major assumptions were necessary for the analysis, and none of these is, in theory, less valid for large groups than small groups. The behavioral assumption that an individual will act as if his actions will not affect the actions of others is, if anything, more likely to be valid for large groups than for small groups. The assumptions implicit in the use of a budget line—i.e., that there exist no fixed costs in the provision of the collective good and that the price faced by an individual is unaffected by the actions of others—affect all groups similarly, since they present the same barrier to action to all individuals.[17] Finally, the assumption that each individual has perfect information about the actions of others and the effects of his own actions applies equally, in theory, to all groups regardless of size. In reality, these information conditions no doubt represent a greater obstacle to large groups than to small groups, but differences in group performance reflecting this fact cannot be derived from a model based on certainty, such as Olson's or the one provided in the previous section. Olson's lack of clarity regarding the relationship under consideration may stem partly from his use of the concept of "the fraction of the group gain" (benefit) received by the individual.[18] For an "exclusive" good, the fraction of the group benefit received by an individual plays an important part of the individual's decision, and its consideration leads to the inverse relationship between group size and amount of the good provided that was found for an "exclusive" good in the previous section. For an "inclusive" good, however, the fraction of the total benefit received by a single individual is not so important, since there exists no rivalness of consumption. The addition of an individual to a group does not decrease the benefit any individual receives from a unit of the collective good, although it does decrease the fraction of the total benefit the individual receives. This decrease in the fraction of the total benefit results in the enlarged group's providing a more suboptimal amount of the collective good, but not necessarily a lesser absolute amount, as was shown. Olson's failure to differentiate in his formal analysis between "inclusive" and "exclusive" collective goods, and the important difference this distinction makes in the use of the "fraction of total benefit" concept may partially explain his conclusions regarding the possibility of action by large groups.

Another reason for Olson's conclusions may be his emphasis on the degree of suboptimality of group performance rather than on the amount of the collective good actually provided. It is with respect to the former criterion that large groups fare so poorly. Since in Olson's analysis smaller groups appear to fare better under both criteria, the choice of which criterion to use does not appear to be particularly important. In light of the analysis presented above, however, this choice takes on greater importance. With respect to the second criterion, all groups are constrained by a rather low upper bound on the amount of the good actually provided (x_i^s). The fact that this is the amount at which an individual will provide none of the good himself makes the upper bound seem particularly low. But there seems to be no reason to suggest a priori, as Olson seems to, that the actual amount provided by a large group will have little empirical importance, while the amount provided by a small group will be empirically important. Such a conclusion must be the result of a fuller consideration of the appropriateness of the two measures of group performance.[19] The political process may be a sphere in which the amount actually provided is the appropriate criterion, particularly if several groups are involved and are in opposition to one another. The outcome in such a case is likely to be a function of the relative *actual* strengths of the groups' efforts. For one interested in understanding and predicting the outcomes of such conflicts, the actual amount of the collective good provided (in this case, political action, defense, etc.) will be more useful than measures of suboptimal performance. This is particularly true since in such a case the optimal amounts are themselves relative, being a function of the behavior of the opposing group. Most of the work making use of the theory of collective goods has thus far dealt with the actions of a single group. In light of this emphasis, an important next step in applying this theory to the study of political phenomena would be the consideration of the behavior of several groups in competition. Such a consideration may yield a better understanding of the relative powers of competing groups and of the appropriate criteria by which group action should be judged.

NOTES

1. Mancur Olson, Jr., *The Logic of Collective Action: Public Goods and the Theory of Groups* (Cambridge, Mass.: Harvard University Press, 1965). A somewhat different and more general formulation of Olson's analysis subsequently appeared in an article co-authored by Olson and Richard Zeckhauser, "An Economic Theory of Alliances," *Review of Economics and Statistics,* 48 (November, 1966), 266-279.

2. See Paul Samuelson, [this volume]; "Diagrammatic Exposition of a Theory of Public Expenditure," *Review of Economics and Statistics,* 37 (November, 1955), 350-356; and John Head, "Public Goods and Public Policy," *Public Finance,* 17 (November 3, 1962), 197-219.

3. Olson, p. 2., [reprinted in this volume].

4. *Ibid.,* p. 36.

5. *Ibid.,* p. 44.

6. See Head, "Public Goods and Public Policy," for a full discussion of the characteristics of collective goods.

7. Samuelson makes the following distinction between the polar cases of private and pure collective goods. For a private good,

$$\sum_{i=1}^{n} x^i = X,$$

while for a pure collective good $x^1 = x^2 = \ldots = x^i = \ldots = x^n = X$, where x^i is the consumption of individual i, and X is the amount of the good produced. See Samuelson, [this volume].

8. Olson, pp. 36-42.

9. It is important that the nature of this process be understood. In particular, it is important to note how the "imperceptibility" of an individual's actions is treated. The process is one of dynamic adjustment, in which each individual reacts to the behavior of others on the assumption that they will not perceive his action (more correctly, will not change their behavior as a result of his action), even though in reality this is not the case. The model is equivalent to a Cournot duopoly model. See Kalman Cohen and Richard Cyert, *Theory of the Firm: Resource Allocation in a Market Economy* (Englewood Cliffs, New Jersey: Prentice-Hall, Inc., 1965), chapter 12, for one discussion of this

model. It is important to distinguish this treatment of "imperceptible" actions from the cases in which the effects of an individual's actions are either imperceptible to himself because of uncertainty, lack of information, etc., or are imperceptible to others for the same reasons. The analysis in Olson's book and in the article by Olson and Zeckhauser assumes that each individual has perfect knowledge of the (past) actions of all individuals and of the production function for the good in question. For an examination of the problem of an actor's behavior under uncertainty, see Norman Frohlich and Joe Oppenheimer, "I Get By With a Little Help From My Friends," *World Politics,* 23 (October, 1970), 104-120. For a discussion of Olson's "exploitation" hypothesis (that the small exploit the great), see Olson, p. 35.

10. For a discussion of this classification, see Cohen and Cyert, pp. 75-76 as well as Olson and Zeckhauser, p. 270, footnote 15.

11. In Figure 4, the curves are drawn in such a way that it appears that a good is always inferior (or normal, or superior). This is generally not the case. The good may fall in different classes for different individuals, and as the level of consumption of the good rises for an individual, the good may move from one class to another.

12. In *The Logic of Collective Action,* Olson ignores income effects, considering only the case in which the slope of the reaction curve is -1 (the case of no income effects). Olson and Zeckhauser consider income effects more fully, particularly on p. 270, footnote 15. If collective good is a superior good in the framework under consideration, groups will be led either to invest all of their resources in the provision of the good (if the slope of the reaction curve is positive) or to provide an amount of the good in direct proportion to group size (if the slope of the reaction curve is infinite). Since such behavior is highly unlikely, superior goods will be ignored in the analysis to follow.

13. Under the assumptions of the model, an individual will change his behavior if the point (x_A, x_B) corresponding to the amounts of the collective good provided by the individuals does not lie on the individual's reaction curve. Since the intersection of the two reaction curves is the only point at which neither individual will change his behavior, this is the only possible equilibrium. If both reaction curves are continuous, an equilibrium will exist. Sufficient assumptions for a continuous reaction curve are that the individual have a continuous utility function and that the indifference curves derived from this function obey the condition of strong convexity (i.e., if two possible allocations are indifferent, then their weighted average with positive weights is preferred to them). The particular configuration shown in Figure 5 is not guaranteed, but is the most likely case. Other possibilities are shown and discussed in the Appendix. It should be noted that this equilibrium also results if the problem is viewed as a noncooperative game rather than as a Cournot duopoly problem.

14. This assumption greatly simplifies the analysis to follow without affecting the substance of the results.

15. Olson, p. 48, footnote 68.

16. Mancur Olson, "Increasing the Incentives for International Cooperation," *International Organization,* 25 (Autumn, 1971), 866-874, at p. 866, footnote 1.

17. Olson, (*The Logic of Collective Action* [p. 22]) points out the importance of fixed costs as a barrier to collective action. He suggests that cooperative action may be necessary to overcome this barrier. In making use of a budget line, the present analysis ignores fixed costs. It should be emphasized that the inability of a group to overcome these costs via noncooperative action will not be a function of group size.

18. *Ibid.,* p. 23.

19. It may well be true, although no empirical evidence is available, that there are differences between the types of collective goods desired by small and large groups, and that these differences are such that an amount x^s_i of one good may be an "adequate" amount for the small group but an amount x^s_i of another good may be "inadequate" for its group, a large one. Such a possibility seems of sufficient interest to merit further thought.

II

INDIVIDUAL PREFERENCES AND COLLECTIVE DECISIONS

I. THE SETTING OF ARROW'S THEOREM

The readings in this section are representative of much of the vast literature which has grown up largely in response to Kenneth Arrow's general possibility theorem (now commonly known as Arrow's impossibility theorem). There are many variants on the theorem itself as well as variant proofs of it, and there are also numerous theorems which are cousins to it, theorems for both possibilities and impossibilities. As explained briefly by Vickrey and at greater length by Arrow in their selections here, the impetus for the original proof was the twentieth-century remaking of utility theory in economics. Cardinal utility in the Benthamite sense led to an apparently easy specification of what is the best social arrangement: that one of all possible arrangements which implies the greatest good for the greatest number. To calculate the good or utility of an arrangement one need only add up the utilities to all people.

But the notion of cardinal utility fell on hard times when it was found to be unnecessary for price theory, equilibrium analysis, and other theoretical economic concerns. And the notion of comparing my utility directly to yours with such accuracy as to permit social addition had long been suspect. Hence, in economics, cardinal utility theory was replaced by ordinal utility theory. In ordinal theory, I need not be able to specify how much utility I attach to x and to y; I need merely know how x and y are ordered in my preferences. Unfortunately, while much of economic theory could easily do without cardinal utility, the analysis of "social welfare" seemed to be left without an obvious goal if individuals' utility schedules were only ordinal and were therefore not additive. The "new welfare economics" is a reconstruction of the economic analysis of social welfare on ordinal utility bases.

Arrow's concern is to discover the limits on what we can say about comparisons of the social welfare of alternative states of affairs when the welfare is somehow determined by aggregation out of individuals' ordinal preference schedules over alternative states rather than by addition of all individuals' utilities in each state of affairs. For the latter, of course, although it is absurd to think it could actually be done, one need only compare sums and take the largest. For the former, one must first define a rule by which to perform the aggregation. Arrow assumes that "society" should have a preference ordering over states of affairs just as individuals presumably do. He then supposes that any aggregation rule that would be acceptable must meet a small number of conditions such as that the rule should not allow dictatorship. He proposes a set of supposedly innocuous conditions and then goes on to prove that *no* aggregation rule can meet these conditions.

Arrow (1963, p. 24) defines a *social welfare function* (hereafter SWF) as "a process or rule which, for each set of individual orderings $R_1, \ldots, R_n$ for alternative social states (one ordering for each individual), states a corresponding social ordering of alternative social states, R." This is perhaps not worded with sufficient care since he clearly means his SWF to turn a given set of individual orderings into a *unique* social ordering. Note that additive utilitarianism cannot be a process defining an SWF. To see this, consider a very simple example, indeed an example of the simplest possible class of social choice problem: a two-person (A and B) society choosing between two outcomes (x and y). Suppose each person weights the outcomes to yield a social sum S as follows:

	A	B	S
x	70	20	90
y	30	80	110
ordering	$x > y$	$y > x$	$y > x$

Suppose now that B reconsiders (perhaps because of new information) so that we have:

	A	B'	S'
x	70	40	110
y	30	60	90
ordering	$x > y$	$y > x$	$x > y$

The social *ordering* has been reversed although the individual orderings have remained as before. Hence, the single set of individual orderings $A(x > y)$, $B(y > x)$ yields two different possible social orderings so that additive utilitarianism cannot be an SWF. This is not surprising since the point of Arrow's endeavor is to found social choice on orderings only, and not on cardinal utility measures.

II. THE THEOREM AND ITS CONDITIONS

Arrow's theorem is that no SWF can meet the four conditions U, P, D, and I, which will be spelled out and briefly discussed in this section. He could as well have made the definition of an SWF one of his conditions, which we could call condition O for the fact that an SWF is a unique *O*rdering based only on individual orderings. Then Arrow's theorem would be: *No social choice procedure can meet the five conditions O, U, P, D, and I.*

At this point, social choice theory becomes complicated because the conditions of Arrow's theorem have been stated in many forms. Since, as Blau (1957) pointed out, Arrow's original proof was flawed and Arrow presented his own variants of the theorem, subsequent authors have been licensed to do it their own ways. Naturally, many authors have thought that Arrow's conditions could be modified to advantage (often to make the conditions seem less demanding so that the theorem would seem even more impressive). Several variant statements of the conditions are given in the papers reprinted here, and if we had included more statements of the theorem we would most likely have included other variants of the conditions. We will present the conditions not in order to present yet another variant, but in order to clarify their meanings and the roles they play in the theorem.

> Condition U (unrestricted domain): The social choice rule must work for all logically possible combinations of individual orderings of the alternatives in the set of all alternatives, X.

This condition may often be factually irrelevant for the obvious reason that not all logically possible combinations of individual orderings will be displayed in a given society. However, much less than this condition is generally required to block the aggregation of individual orderings into a social ordering that meets the other conditions. For example, consider a maximally contentious group, say, a political science department, facing a typical collective choice problem, the selection of a new chairperson. If there are five plausible candidates, there are 120 distinct possible orderings even ruling out indifference and the likelihood that someone thinks there are other plausible candidates. Since, fortunately, there are seldom 120 political scientists involved in making any decision let alone housed in a single department, the members of our department would not display most of these orderings. But if about one-third of the members rank the candidates in each of the following three orders, there can be no social ordering generated by majority voting:

$$
\begin{array}{ccc}
x & y & z \\
y & z & x \\
z & x & y \\
v & v & v \\
w & w & w
\end{array}
$$

Condition P (Pareto optimality): For any pair of alternatives x, y in X, if everyone prefers x to y, the society prefers x to y.

This is a very weak principle in the sense that, at first glance, it is hard to imagine anyone's objecting to it and perhaps also in the sense that we commonly think of collective choice problems as sufficiently contested that no leading candidate is likely to be unanimously preferred to another. On the other hand, the import of many constitutional safeguards is to prevent societies from choosing certain outcomes over others even when there is unanimous or near-unanimous preference for the former.

Condition D (nondictatorship): There is no one whose individual preference for x over y (for any x and y in X) is the social preference regardless of the preferences of others.

This condition presumably requires no justification. But note that one cannot establish that someone is a dictator merely by inspection, that is, by showing that that individual's ordering is identical to society's under the given choice rule. To show that A is a dictator one must invoke condition U and show that A's preferences prevail no matter what the preferences of others are.

Condition I (independence of irrelevant alternatives): Let S be any subset of alternatives in the full set, X, which individuals and the society are to order. If a set of individual orderings over X is modified in such a way that each individuals' paired comparisons among the alternatives in S are left invariant, the social orderings resulting from the original and modified sets of individual orderings should be identical for the alternatives in S.

This final condition is not only the most controversial of Arrow's conditions, it is also the least understood. This may largely be due to the fact that Arrow's original statement of the condition is not perspicuous, but quite apart from that, its definition is complex. (The definition here is taken from Luce and Raiffa [1957, p. 338].) Let us break it into two parts.

The definition of an SWF says that for a given set of individual orderings there is a unique social ordering. Condition I says that, if individual orderings over some subset of all outcomes are fixed while the orderings of other outcomes vary, the internal ordering of that subset remains fixed in the overall social ordering. Since the set of all outcomes is also a subset to which condition I applies, condition I replicates the unique ordering condition in the definition of an SWF (hence in condition O) and is therefore partly redundant. Like the definition of an SWF, it says that no matter what else changes, so long as the individual orderings do not change, neither can the social ordering change.

At the other extreme, condition I also implies that the social ordering of any two-element subset is determined exclusively by the individual orderings of those two elements. This implies that we can determine the relative ordering of any pair within the general social ordering by applying our choice rule exclusively to that pair. This is the significance of condition I for Arrow's theorem: it allows us to make deductions about society's ordering of x and y from individual orderings of x and y independently of other considerations. In proofs of the theorem, condition I is generally invoked (often only implicitly) whenever society's ranking of two outcomes out of the larger set is established or assumed. For example, when it is said that someone is decisive in society's ranking of x over y, license is being drawn from condition I to rank x ahead of y in the social ordering independently of the rankings of other alternatives. Just as (by the transitivity property of an ordering) we could construct an individual's complete ordering from a knowledge of all the individual's pairwise orderings, so (by condition I) we must be able to construct the social ordering by letting our choice rule work on pairs of outcomes.

Because of the redundancy in condition I, it is sometimes said that this condition knocks out social choice rules that take account of cardinal rather than merely ordinal preferences, for example, by giving weight to intensities of preference. In fact, these are already ruled out by stipulation in the definition of an SWF as noted above. Hence, much of the criticism of condition I is largely off-target and should rather be directed at the notion that there should be a social ordering based only on individual orderings. Nevertheless, one must agree with Luce and Raiffa (1957, p. 338) that "this condition is extremely powerful." Part of its power is that one cannot easily intuit what it means or why it matters. All of the other conditions, including condition O, are more transparent in their meanings and implications.

Perhaps because of its subtlety, condition I is apparently the condition that is most readily taken for granted in proofs of Arrow's and related theorems. One might invoke it without being consciously aware of doing so, and some extant proofs do not explicitly acknowledge that certain of their steps are licensed only by it. Once discussion is cast in terms of binary preference relations such as R, it is easy for us to fall into the presumption that we can establish the social order of x and y by reference only to individual preferences between x and y.

III. SOME DECISION PROCEDURES

We have already discussed additive utilitarianism as a procedure and have noted that it runs afoul of condition O (that is, it does not generate a unique social ordering from any given set of individual orderings). It must therefore also violate condition I. What other properties does additive utilitarianism as a decision procedure have? Despite violating the uniqueness requirements of conditions O and I, it does meet the transitivity requirement of condition O since "greater than or equal to" is a transitive relation over the natural numbers. This system will work over any domain (and therefore meets condition U): I may assign any utility I please to any outcome. It clearly meets the Pareto condition, since if everyone prefers x to y, x will receive a larger sum and be ranked ahead of y in the social choice. Alas, the simplest form of additive utilitarianism might be dictatorial. For example, Stalin might have claimed that his utility for each outcome was so large as to swamp the sum of all others' utilities for any outcome. With his sensitive soul, the Great Gardener may have experienced $10^{100^{100}}$ utiles of pleasure from his reign in particular—and who are we to balk at a world so filled with pleasure.

Extraordinary capacity for experiencing utility (or pleasure) is an obvious weakness of this form of utilitarianism not so much, perhaps, because it is a credible possibility, as because it opens the whole system to easy manipulation. The obvious response—at least in theory—to a super-sensitive Stalin is that I, too, am super-sensitive. Every five-year-old seems to understand how to manipulate outcomes by staking the happiness of the world on an ice cream cone this minute. Hence, one does not require Arrow's logical paraphernalia to reject this form of utilitarianism as a *practical* decision procedure, although it might be a quite plausible procedure for an administrator or legislator to apply in making choices for the larger society.

There is another procedure that superficially seems to be a version of additive utilitarianism: so-called *point* or *Borda systems*. Under such systems, in a three-candidate election, we might each be required to allot three points to our first choice, two to our second, and one to our last. The social ranking would then be in order of the sum of these points. Because of the numerical additions involved in it, one might think this to be a cardinal measure. In fact, however, this system is strictly ordinal in the sense that I cannot make anything more than my ordinal preferences known through the assignment of points to candidates. Not surprisingly, therefore, it does not violate condition O since it will turn any given set of individual orderings into a unique social ordering. But it does violate condition I. For example, suppose A and B are choosing among three alternatives and they have the following preferences:

A	B	Social Choice
y	z	y (5 points)
x	y	z (4 points)
z	x	x (3 points)

Now A and B change the relative positions of x but do not change their individual orderings over z and y. We now have:

A	B	Social Choice
y	z	z (5 points)
z	x	y (4 points)
x	y	x (3 points)

The social ordering of y and z has been reversed despite the fact that their ordering was not changed within any individual's ordering.[1]

We have already discussed majority rule as a decision procedure in the example of the contentious political science department. That example should be familiar as a variation on the voter's paradox. The problem in the voter's paradox is that there are cyclic majorities in the sense that x is preferred to y, y to z, and z to x in majority votes. By the transitivity requirement of an SWF, these first two relations imply that x is preferred to z. But, by condition I, we must also have z preferred to x from the last of these relations. Majority voting therefore fails Arrow's test.

The problem of cyclic preferences in the voter's paradox is a function of not only simple majority voting, but of any majority voting short of unanimity. Cycles can occur with, say, 90 percent majority voting if there are at least 10 issues or candidates, and with 99 percent majority voting if there are at least 100 issues or candidates (there also have to be at least 10 or 100 voters, respectively). However, greater-than-simple-majority voting will not meet Arrow's conditions for the further reason that it will not convert all plausible sets of individual preferences into social preferences unless we extend the definition of the procedure to include rules for handling cases for which there is an insufficient majority to be decisive.

If majority decision is subject to cyclic majorities, one may ask, why is that not a problem in the vast number of majority decision systems in practical use? A large part of the answer is that, because preferences are not randomly distributed, cycles often do not occur. A larger part of the answer may be that our institutions for majority voting are designed so as to "overcome" the problem of cyclic preferences by assuring the selection of a unique first choice. For example, there are very few pure majority systems actually in use. A pure system would require comparisons between all pairs. We avoid any such elaborate (and potentially revealing) test by using plurality voting, runoffs, preliminary narrowing of the field, *Robert's Rules of Order,* committee chairperson's power to order the agenda, and so forth, to balk certain comparisons. Some athletic competitions are conducted by round-robin matching of all pairs, some by one-on-one elimination. Social decisions are almost never accomplished by full round-robin matching of all pairs. They are commonly made by one-on-one or plurality elimination. For example, consider the following choice among x, y, and z by a three-person society.

A	B	C
x	y	z
y	z	x
z	x	y

A full round-robin test would yield the social choice $x > y$, $y > z$, $z > x$. But if A chairs the committee, A can have us vote first between y and z (z loses), and then between the winner and x. That way x wins.

Are our majoritarian institutions therefore defective? Several of the following papers try to answer that question in various ways. One important answer is that often *which* alternative is chosen is less important in the long run than that *one* of the alternatives is definitively chosen, if only to let our committee go home. Furthermore, majority decision as a procedure has too much to recommend it in certain circumstances for us to forgo it merely out of logical scruples.

We could endlessly canvass other social choice procedures to show how they fall afoul of Arrow's conditions. With each it would be possible to show that it directly violates one or more of the conditions other than condition U for some set of individual orderings. Such an exercise might increasingly give us some sense of the power of Arrow's theorem. We might gain more, however, from a survey of the proof of the theorem, to which we should turn.

IV. PROOF OF THE THEOREM

The proof of Arrow's theorem may seem formidable. However, the actual proof is not itself particularly hard to follow. That Vickrey can do it more or less verbally in little more than a page should be reassuring. What is harder than to follow it stepwise is to grasp it whole—or even in substantial parts. To facilitate understanding of the whole, we will discuss the general strategy of the proof and point out the principal tricks involved in it.

To discuss the proof we need one new definition. To say that A is *decisive* for the social ranking of x over y means that, if A prefers x to y and everyone else prefers y to x, society prefers x to y—that is, A prevails over the unanimous opposition of all others. The proof then proceeds in two parts, in both of which conditions O, U, P, and I are assumed. In one it is shown that if A is decisive over some pair x, y then A is a dictator, that is, whenever A prefers any alternative, u, to another, v, society does likewise no matter what the preferences of other members of the society. We can call this the dictatorship lemma. On its face it is implausible and startling—but it is remarkably easy to prove. The other part of the proof is to show that under any social choice rule there must be someone who is decisive over some pair of alternatives. If we couple this result with the dictatorship lemma, we see that there must be a dictator—but this is contrary to condition D. Hence, Arrow's theorem is proved because no social choice rule is compatible with all of the conditions O, U, P, I, and D.

Let us first consider the dictatorship lemma. Again, this lemma says that if there is someone, A, who is decisive over some pair of alternatives under a given choice rule, then A must be decisive over every pair. The proof of this is accomplished by invoking conditions I and U with a vengeance. First, U is invoked to show that decisiveness for x against y implies decisiveness for x against any other element, z, in the set of alternatives, if only A prefers x to z. Then, I is invoked to say that if A is decisive over x and z in that case (that is, for that set of orderings) then, even if all other parts of the individual orderings change while the orderings over x and z do not, A's preference over x and z must still prevail. By continuing in this manner one can show that if A prefers any v to any w, so must society—just because A is decisive in the choice over x and y. The only challenge in this part of the proof once this trick is mastered is to determine what small set of A's binary preferences would generate the complete set of A's possible preference orderings. Each piece of the proof involves seeking out a case in which there is a relevant unanimous preference so that one can use condition P to specify the relationship between, say, x and z. Each piece is accomplished on analogy with the following demonstration that, if A is decisive for x over y and A prefers x to z, then the society prefers x to z.

Suppose A prefers x to z and that *everyone* prefers y to z. Since everyone prefers y to z, then (by condition P) society must prefer y to z. But since A is decisive in preferring x to y so that society prefers x to y, then by the transitivity requirement of condition O, society must prefer x to y to z, hence x to z. Furthermore, since we have stipulated nothing about the order of x and z in the orderings of anyone except A, we have shown that society prefers x to z if A does, *no matter what anyone else's ranking of x and z is.*

Where does condition I come into this? We have shown that society prefers x to z in the event that everyone prefers y to z. But, by condition I, the only things that matter for the social ordering of x and z are the individual orderings for x and z. It is irrelevant that we found the social ordering of x over z by tricking up the case in which everyone prefers y to z because, if society ever prefers x to z for a given set of individual orderings of x and z, then it must always prefer x to z for that set of individual orderings of x and z.

The trick used above is applied to show that for any pair, v, w, if A prefers v to w, then so does society. Note that in the piece above we have had to invoke O, U, P, and I. Hence, having a dictator is compatible with these four conditions. The remaining part of the proof of Arrow's theorem is to show that these four conditions taken together are compatible *only* with a dictatorial social decision rule. Let us follow it.

If anyone is a dictator, the conditions of Arrow's theorem are violated; for the theorem to be false, therefore, it is necessary that there never be a dictator. Assume a society and a social choice rule for which there is no dictator. From the dictatorship lemma it follows that no individual is decisive for any pair of alternatives under consideration by the society. But for any pair of alternatives, say x and y, some set of individuals must be decisive under a given choice rule since, if everyone prefers x to y, then by condition P the society must prefer x to y, so that at the very least the set of everyone in the society is decisive. Consider the set of all decisive sets of individuals. If the society has a finite number of members, this set must have a smallest decisive set.[2] Call it V. (There may be more than one smallest set, in which case, call one of these V.) Assume V is decisive for x against y, which means that if all the members of V prefer x to y when all others prefer y to x, then society prefers x to y.

Since by assumption no individual is decisive for any pair, V must have more than one member. Therefore we can divide V into V_1, which includes only one member, and V_2, which includes all other members of V. Let V_3 be the set of all members not in V (V_3 might be empty). Add to the society's consideration now a third alternative, z. Suppose the preference order of V_1 is x, y, z; that of all members of V_2 is z, x, y; and that of all members of V_3 is y, z, x. (We are licensed to do so by condition U.) By assumption, V is decisive for x against y, and the society prefers x to y, that is, $x P y$. But where does society rank z? Society cannot prefer z to y, since then V_2 would be decisive for z against y (the members of V_2 prefer z to y while all others prefer y to z), but V_2 has one less member than V, which was assumed to be the smallest decisive set. Therefore, society either prefers y to z or is indifferent between them, that is, $y R z$. Since condition O requires social orderings to be transitive over both preference and indifference, $x P y$ and $y R z$ implies $x P z$. But this means that V_1, a single individual, is decisive for x against z. Again, this is contrary to the assumption that V is the smallest decisive subset. Hence, we cannot simultaneously meet the conditions O, U, P, I, and D.

This part of the proof is accomplished by a neat reductio ad absurdum: the smallest decisive subset of the members of society must have more than one member or there is a dictator (by the preceding lemma). Hence, the smallest decisive subset can be divided into two distinct subsets at least one of which must itself be decisive over some pair of alternatives for some set of individual preference orderings. But this contradicts the assumption of the original subset that it was the smallest decisive subset. If from an assumption one can prove its contrary, something is clearly wrong. Incidentally, as a glance back at the preference orders for V_1, V_2, and V_3 over the alternatives x, y, and z will show, this part of the proof uses a variation on the voter's paradox to achieve its result.

As already noted, there have been many other proofs of some version of Arrow's theorem. Plott cites a version by Wilson (1972). By assuming cyclic preferences over a very large set of alternatives, MacKay (1980) proves a more restricted version of the theorem (see Hardin 1980). Most extant proofs follow a strategy and format much like those used here, by Arrow (1963), and by Vickrey in the paper reprinted here. Fishburn (1970) uses a different format to prove by induction on n, the number of members of the society, that if all of our conditions are met, then n cannot be finite. Hence, in an infinite population there would be no Arrow problem—but then one might sooner have a finite population with its Arrow problems.

V. CAVEATS AND CRITIQUES

It is probably fair to say that the most important aspects of Arrow's theorem are two which were established independently beforehand: that various versions of additive utilitarianism are not workable and that majority voting can be subject to cyclic majorities. Arrow's endeavor was largely a response to the first of these and his proof takes crucial advantage of the second. Little, in his paper here, rejects the claim that Arrow's result is significant for welfare economics. Oddly, then, the economist Arrow may have contributed more with his theorem to the study of political decision-making, and especially to democratic theory, than to economics. Indeed, when the theorem is conceived in the context of the problem of welfare economics, it is apparent that it has a metaphysical sound rather like that of Samuelson's notion of the lump-sum transfers that would move our society to any preferred state of affairs (see the introduction to Samuelson's paper in the previous section of readings). Arrow demands that we as individuals be able to rank all feasible states of affairs for the whole society. I have no idea how to set about such a task nor presumably does Arrow. What is often easy to do, however, is to rank all available candidates or issue-positions in a formal election. It happens that Arrow's peculiar results follow even for the latter kind of choice problem—although their significance for that realm must be severely qualified, as a brief consideration of the actual practice of majority rule suggests.

Majority rule is distinguished in a fundamental way from the problem that Arrow sets himself. Arrow and much, though not all, of the so-called Arrow literature are concerned with general social welfare, with choosing whole states of affairs for the society. Hence, the alternatives from which the choice is made are mutually exclusive. Since only one of them can be selected, there can be no interaction between it and any of the other alternatives. Majority rule is so radically different in its concern as to seem almost unrelated. In systems of majority rule, we commonly choose bits and pieces of whole states of affairs, and we choose sequentially. If the notion of a whole state of affairs is meaningful at all in normal choice contexts, it can only be said to be what happens rather than what is chosen. Furthermore, the various choices we make—each by more or less independent majority vote—often so thoroughly interact with each other as to make us try to package our choices over many of the sets of alternatives that separately (as sets) come before us. Any effort at packaging, however, involves strategic considerations that only compound the problems of misrepresentation and manipulation discussed by Vickrey and Gibbard.

Yet, despite technical differences in the nature of the majority rule and social welfare problems, Arrow's theorem clearly applies to typical problems of actual social choice. If we simply recast Arrow's formulations to refer to candidates in an election, we get the result that there is no election procedure that meets the conditions O, U, P, I, and D. But in this context, the demand that there be one universally workable procedure no longer makes sense so that we may no longer need to be concerned with meeting condition U. For example, the collective goods of our previous section of readings are often provided through collective choice procedures. But it is axiomatic for a collective good that all those who would benefit from its provision under some cost-sharing scheme would prefer that the good be provided under that scheme than not be provided at all. Hence, condition U can be partly ignored.

Whether it is violated to such an extent as to prevent the occurrence of cyclic majorities depends on the range of plausible cost-sharing schemes that could go into the set of alternatives from which to choose. Under certain circumstances there will be Condorcet winners—that is, choices that defeat all alternatives by majority vote—and in other circumstances there will not be (see Hardin's paper reprinted in the first section of readings here, and Hardin 1976).

U is not the only condition that we might question in actual choice contexts. Condition O is not only too stringent; it is fundamentally wrong-headed in many piecemeal decision contexts. We often *can* make acceptable interpersonal comparisons of utility—that is often why we help others. But there is an even more pervasive and fundamental objection to condition O in actual contexts. If we are choosing not whole states of affairs but only small pieces of the whole state of affairs, condition O and, with it, condition I collapse before the implications of the complementarity between various pieces. Two goods are *complementary* if in combination each somehow enhances the value of the other or, in traditional language, if the whole is greater than the sum of its parts. One of the great successes of the ordinal revolution in utility theory is the elegant ease with which the ordinal theory handles complementarity (for a survey of the issues and the history of complementarity, see Samuelson 1974). The problem of complementarity arises in the present context when, for example, we think that our orderings in *this* election should in part turn on what *other* elections have been or are going to be held.

Condition O requires that the social ordering of a set of alternatives be based only on individual orderings of those alternatives. Just what this could mean if the alternatives are not whole states of affairs, but only variations on a piece of the whole state of affairs, is perhaps unclear. Arrow himself blurs this distinction in his defenses of condition I. He speaks then of real-world types of elections over candidates, not of social choices over whole states of affairs (Arrow 1963, pp. 26-27). Unfortunately, whereas it is not logically objectionable to speak of individual orderings of whole states of affairs in the abstract, it may be objectionable to speak of individual orderings of variations on some piece of the whole state of affairs in the abstract, i.e., independently of specifying which variations on the other pieces are to be chosen. Do you prefer Lincoln or Roosevelt? ham or cheese? The only plausible answer to such questions is some variant of "that depends." It is not meaningful to assert that such choices are independent of other considerations (the very phrase "irrelevant alternatives" sounds like a deliberately persuasive definition in this context). When would it ever be meaningful? When the alternatives are different amounts of money or utility, when they are relatively definitive of whole states of affairs, or when enough of the remainder of the whole state of affairs can be taken for granted. Since significant social choices commonly fit into none of these categories, conditions O and I not only are, but often should be, violated in majority rule and in other actual social choice procedures.

This latter point perhaps merits some elaboration. That my individual preferences over piecemeal choices should violate individual equivalents of conditions O and I should be clear. Indeed, this is largely the insight that undercuts the most simplistic notion of some versions of classical additive utilitarianism: that the total utility to me of a state of affairs is the sum of the utilities to me of all the components of that state of affairs. Ordinal utility theory for individual preferences as developed since Hicks and Allen (1934) takes account of complementarity effects: I may like pretzels in general, but I may also especially like them with beer (I may even not like them at all unless they are with beer). Hence, in individual preference orderings, our preference for pretzels over, say, watercress sandwiches may turn on whether we are being served beer or English tea. Can we now jump from the violation of conditions O and I in piecemeal choices at the individual level to their violation in piecemeal choices at the societal level? Might we not want society to have orderings that are independent of irrelevant alternatives even though individuals do not? The answer depends largely on the extent to which condition U is actually violated. If everyone prefers pretzels with beer and sandwiches with tea it would be perverse collectively to serve pretzels with tea. Indeed, we may go further to claim, in an argument similar to that of Rae, Straffin, and Barry in their selections reprinted here, that if we were choosing the collective decision rule that would optimize our individual expectations in such a matter, we might readily prefer a rule that violated conditions O and I whenever individual preferences did on the simple ground that on the average, over a large number of such decisions, we would expect to come out better under such a rule.

What then is the significance of Arrow's theorem? It is not that social choice is impossible. As we know, it happens all the time—indeed, even political science departments are often able to select their chairpersons through reasonable procedures. The theorem says not that no procedure will ever work, but that no procedure will always work. But given that actual social choice procedures are invariably concerned with piecemeal choices, two of the conditions of the theorem are in principle not met, so that one cannot be sure of any generalization beyond the voter's paradox. Hence, the theorem may not have advanced our understanding of political decision-making much beyond what was well if not widely understood before this century. Let us therefore briefly return to Little's claim that the theorem is irrelevant to welfare economics.

The term "social welfare function" was introduced by Bergson (1938) in his effort to deal with the obvious problem of a welfare economics based on ordinal rather than cardinal utility. Bergson's social welfare function is unspecified—it is whatever one might think is the "best" outcome for the society (recall Samuelson's "ethical observer" in his paper reprinted here). Suppose we turned Bergson's social welfare function into a social choice rule. Arrow's conditions O and P block its use as an SWF. Against condition O, Bergson's function selects only a "best" state of affairs and need not order all states (although one might suppose that one could iteratively apply the function to the subset that remained after the best was selected and so forth to order the whole set). The more serious violation, however, is of condition P since Bergson's function might select a state to which some other is unanimously preferred. It is a traditional joke that God created people with desires that are hopelessly sinful, but then holds us to account by divine standards. Arrow's conditions in principle rule out divine ordering of our alternatives. They similarly rule out Bergson's social welfare function. (Bergson's own discussion of Arrow's theorem is well worth reading [Bergson 1954].)

VI. A GUIDE TO THE READINGS

The readings in this section fall into three major groups. First are several papers on Arrow's theorem and general criticisms of its significance. Plott gives a survey of major implications for democratic theory; Little comments more extensively on the relevance of Arrow's result for welfare economics; Arrow surveys the field stimulated by his original work at a distance of nearly three decades; and Baier, a philosopher to these three economists, puzzles over the significance of Arrow's conditions and theorem. The second group of papers addresses what is probably the most important class of complex social choice procedures, majority rule. In the spirit of Arrow's theorem, May sets out the logical defining conditions for majority rule; Rae argues that of all voting systems, bare majority rule maximizes one's chance of getting the result one prefers; Straffin generalizes and proves Rae's conjecture and discusses other criteria that one might want a voting system to meet; and Barry discusses the implications of this sort of self-interest justification for the majority principle, as well as the conditions under which self-interest argues against that principle. Finally, the third group of papers takes up the issue of strategic manipulation of the social choice by sophisticated members of the society, an issue raised in a different context in Samuelson's paper in the first section of this book. Vickrey conjectures that any system that violates condition I is likely to be subject to manipulation by misrepresentation of preferences and Gibbard discusses his proof of that conjecture. Vickrey's paper could as well have been placed with the first group of readings here, because it presents a solid survey of the central issues in the Arrow literature as well as a concise proof of Arrow's theorem.

One might wonder why the readings divide in this way and why these particular readings were included. The choice of several papers on Arrow's theorem and conditions is obvious enough and we think the four papers here are generally models of exegesis from varied perspectives. Anyone who reads them with care must come to appreciate much of the subtlety of the Arrow problem. That there should be substantial space given over to majority rule should not be surprising inasmuch as it is so important in actual societies and as it is the realm in which the voters's paradox—the forerunner of the Arrow problem—arises. The final two selections are perhaps less obvious. They represent what is probably the most important recent new development in the Arrow literature, although the problem of strategic manipulation may be one of the oldest issues raised here (recall the problem faced by Pliny as discussed in the introductory essay to this volume). It was elegantly (and in three-color diagrams) put forward by Farquharson (1969) and has been discussed by many perceptive students of social choice problems. It was then shown to be an inescapable problem in virtually all social choice mechanisms in simultaneous publications by Gibbard (reprinted here) and Satterthwaite (1975). One can claim fairly that the strategic manipulation of collective outcomes is the underlying concern of game theory and the motivation for its invention. Hence, this issue brings together three of the most important social science insights of the twentieth century: game theory, the Arrow problem, and the logic of collective action or the prisoner's dilemma.

NOTES

1. In his paper here, Plott (fn. 2) says that the Borda count, *contra* Arrow, does not violate condition I. This is because Arrow's condition of Independence of Irrelevant Alternatives is not well stated and Plott has restated it in his conditions III and VI. If it is stated in a form equivalent to that stated previously, it includes Plott's condition III, which is violated by the Borda count.

2. Arrow, p. 100, implicitly assumes the number of members is finite when he supposes that, if one is removed from the set, the remainder set is therefore necessarily smaller than the original set. (For infinite sets, this conclusion does not follow.)

12 • Introduction

We begin our readings in Part II with a beguiling introduction to the basic ideas of social choice theory by one of its contemporary masters, Charles Plott. Although informal statements of the Arrow result abound, Plott's is particularly valuable because it was originally designed for an audience of political scientists and political theorists. It therefore highlights the potential significance of the subject for wider issues of social theory and practice.

The exposition in the first section is quite easy to follow, and sets out some of the puzzles about the aggregation of preferences that underlie results such as Arrow's. The second section (of which we have space to print only the opening part) requires careful reading, but provides as clear an explanation and rationale as can be hoped for of the general requirements for preference aggregation that Arrow showed to be incompatible. We have omitted altogether an extensive third section that discusses the application of the results in social choice theory to the evaluation of processes for making social decisions. We hope, however, that the extract printed here, which amounts to little more than a fifth of the whole article, will whet some readers' appetites for the rest. We believe that the effort will be found to be well repaid.

It would perhaps be as well to repeat here a couple of points that Plott makes at the end of the original paper (pp. 587-588). The first is that there are alternative ways of setting out the general nature of the problem of preference aggregation.

> Some, following Arrow, formulate the problem as a mapping from individual preferences into a social preference. Others start with a choice function and make no explicit reference to a social preference. We implicitly started with a social preference existence axiom (an implicit Principle 0). From this and other axioms we could *deduce* the Arrow formulation [p. 587].

The other point is that there are a variety of alternative ways of setting out the axioms. Plott's do not exactly correspond with those of Arrow or with those that can be found elsewhere in the literature. But they all come to much the same thing.

The only point that we should like to make on our own account at this stage is the following: Plott maintains that the Arrow results, and others like it in the theory of social choice, undermine the whole tradition of liberal or individualistic political theory that has been developed in the last few centuries. We would suggest that the reader may find it worth asking on what understanding of the essential content of such political theory that statement would be correct.

12

AXIOMATIC SOCIAL CHOICE THEORY: AN OVERVIEW AND INTERPRETATION

Charles R. Plott

Why should a political scientist be interested in something like social choice theory? At this early stage of the subject's development, studying it will be of little help to those who want to understand broad questions about the evolution of institutions. It might be of limited help to those who study narrow questions about behavior, but only because of a close relationship between social choice theory and theories of strategic behavior. Political scientists interested in the normative aspects of systems are the potential customers, for it is out of concern for their problem, at least their problem as seen through the eyes of two economists, K. J. Arrow and Duncan Black, in the 1940s, that the field seems to have been born.

The subject began with what seemed to be a minor problem with majority rule. "It is just a mathematical curiosity," said some (Dahl and Lindblom 1953, p. 422). But intrigued and curious about this little hole, researchers, not deterred by the possibly irrelevant, began digging in the ground nearby as

Author's Note: Financial support supplied by the National Science Foundation is gratefully acknowledged. An early draft of this paper was presented at an MSSB conference on Democratic Theory and Social Choice Theory, Key Biscayne, 1975. The comments by participants have led to several changes. W. T. Jones and Paul Thomas provided many helpful editorial comments, and I have enjoyed the benefit of many discussions on this subject with colleagues John Ferejohn, Mike Levine, and Steven Matthews.

Reprinted from *American Journal of Political Science*, Vol. 20, No. 3, 1976, pp. 511-527 by permission of the University of Texas Press and the author, © 1976 by The University of Texas Press.

described below in the first section. What they now appear to have been uncovering is a gigantic cavern into which fall almost all of our ideas about social actions. Almost anything we say and/or anyone has ever said about what society wants or should get is threatened with internal inconsistency. It is as though people have been talking for years about a thing that cannot, in *principle,* exist, and a major effort now is needed to see what objectively remains from the conversations. The second section of the paper [first quarter only included here] is an attempt to survey this problem.

Are these exaggerated claims? If this essay serves its purpose we will find out. The theory has not been translated into the frameworks of political and social philosophy with which political scientists are most familiar, so its full implications are yet to be assessed. Perhaps by outlining what seem to be the major results and arguments within a single integrated theme which makes them accessible to such a broad professional audience, new modes of thought can be brought to bear on the problems and we can successfully demonstrate what social choice theorists have been unable to demonstrate—that such claims are in fact exaggerated. If the results go the other way, if the claims are not exaggerated, then perhaps the paper will supply the reader with some new tools and perspectives with which to attack old, but very important problems.

The central result is broad, sweeping, and negative. Paul Samuelson rates it as one of the significant intellectual achievements of this century (Samuelson 1967). It certainly weighed heavily in the decision to award K. J. Arrow the Nobel prize in economics. Most of the remaining work can be interpreted as attempts to discredit this central discovery. An outline of these attempts following a development of the theorem forms the second section of the paper. The first section is devoted to providing several examples of the types of problems that the major result claims are pervasive. Care must be taken, however, not to confuse the examples with the meaning of the result. They should be taken as symptoms of something much more serious and as examples which bring a little closer to home what is otherwise a very abstract argument. [. . .]

I. PARADOXES OF VOTING

As an introduction to axiomatic social choice theory, let's examine a few paradoxes about voting processes. "Paradoxes" might be the wrong word. In fact one of the real paradoxes is why we regard the following examples as paradoxes. Nevertheless, paradox or not, everyone usually agrees that there is definitely something unintuitive and peculiar going on.

The standard example is the following majority rule cycle. Suppose there are three people [1,2,3] and three alternatives [x,y,z] . The first person feels x is best, y is second, and z is third. The second person thinks y is best and it is followed in order by z and then x. The third person prefers z most with x in second place and y last.

In order to save printing costs, let's adopt the shorthand way of representing such situations used by students of these problems. The notation "P" will mean "preferred" and the notation "I" means "indifferent" and any subscript on the letters simply denotes the name of the person to whom the attitude is ascribed. For example, P_i is the preference of individual i. So we have:

first person	xP_1yP_1z,	(x is preferred to y is preferred to z)
second person	yP_2zP_2x,	(y is preferred to z is preferred to x)
third person	zP_3xP_3y,	(z is preferred to x is preferred to y)

Now which alternative should this society get? Naturally, it should get what it wants. Which alternative does it want? Naturally, it wants what the majority prefers. But then the social preference, P_s, looks like this:

$$xP_syP_szP_sx$$

since 2 and 3 prefer z to x, 1 and 2 prefer y to z, and 1 and 3 prefer x to y. This result is called a *majority rule cycle* or *majority preference cycle*.

There are four standard responses to this. The first is "ugh!" which requires no elaboration. The second response amounts to throwing out the implied definition of social preference. "This cycle doesn't mean anything; the group will choose the best thing when they meet—just let them vote and things will be OK as long as they come to *some* agreement." The trouble is that the outcome depends only upon the voting sequence. The outcome is y, x, or z, depending only upon whether the agenda sequence A, B, or C, respectively is adopted. This is true in theory and in fact (Plott and Levine, 1975). Now, what kind of social philosophy should depend upon that?

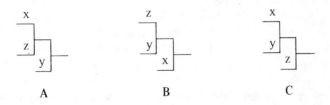

A   B   C

The third reaction amounts to a denial that the phenomenon exists. "Well, you pulled that one out of a hat, but how often will such a crazy case occur?" If everything is random, the answer is not what the asker expected to hear. In this case the answer is simply "*almost* always." The probability of this event approaches *one* as the number of alternatives approaches infinity and it approaches it *very* rapidly. In this sense the cycle is *the* case and *not* the exception.

But, one might argue, everything is not random—people have similarities in preferences. How does that affect the probabilities? A considerable amount of work has been exerted in an effort to characterize the types of individual preference configurations for which the majority rule process does not have this cyclical property. What has been learned will be outlined below, but in general, the results have not been encouraging. This line of questioning, if anything, has supported the view that the phenomenon is pervasive.

The fourth reaction is a claim that there is no paradox at all. "When the majority rule cycle occurs, then society is simply indifferent—any of the alternatives in the cycle is as good as any other." Now this is a rather clever position but there are still problems. Consider the following example, this time with three people and four options.

first person	$yP_1xP_1wP_1z,$
second person	$xP_2wP_2zP_2y,$
third person	$wP_3zP_3yP_3x.$

Now suppose first, that w is the status quo—the alternative which involves "doing Nothing"—and second, that the following sequence of votes occurs.

As the reader can see if he traces out the process, the ultimate choice is z. But *everyone* prefers w, the status quo, to z, the option finally chosen. So, here we have a majority rule cycle that contains two options, one of which is unanimously preferred to the other. That means that proponents of this idea would have society be indifferent between two alternatives even though one was unanimously preferred to the other. Process behavior like this would violate even a minimal concept of efficiency. An economist would ask: "Why should a society accept one alternative when another alternative exists which would make *everyone* better off?" Almost all social philosophers would agree that all concepts of sovereignty require that a people *unanimous* should not be refused.

"Well," says the skeptic, "that's easy to cope with. Simply find some way to first eliminate the Pareto dominated options, those which are unanimously beaten by some other option, and then apply majority rule to what remains." For lack of a better term call this "modified majority rule."

The problem with this line of argument is that it does not sit well with the concept of a social preference. To see this, suppose people have the preferences as listed in the example immediately above and that z and y are the only options open. By majority rule, z will be chosen, and we would conclude that society prefers z to y, or more strongly, we would conclude that z is better than y. Now suppose the options are expanded to the set {w,x,y,z}. Using the process proposed above we eliminate z from consideration, since everyone prefers w to z, and declare w, x, and y all "equally good" or all "equally preferred." They are all in the majority rule cycle, and all are better than z. But notice this is in flat contradiction to the conclusion above, that z was socially preferred to y. Even though we have not formally defined a concept of social preference, most people would intuitively object to this type of inconsistency. We must abandon either this skeptic's idea, and thus majority rule, or our intuitive ideas about social preference.

Let's try the former. After all, there are lots of processes other than majority rule and many of them are successfully used. A prime example is the Borda count, or point voting system, described as follows. Each person ranks the options under consideration and assigns each a number in accord with its level in the ranking. That is, the least preferred gets 1 point, the next least gets 2 points, etc. Points are all totaled and the option which receives the greatest number of points is chosen. Consider the four-option, seven-person example, first discovered by Fishburn (1974), given in Table 1. The point totals are shown in the box. Clearly y is best, and it is followed in ranking by x, w, and z in order. But, suppose z was eliminated from early consideration (if not by some natural cause) since it gets the least points, and besides it is Pareto-dominated by y. With z gone there are only three options, so points are assigned to {w,x,y} in magnitude from 1 to 3 rather than 1 to 4 as before. With this done, the result on the right is discovered. Now the social ordering w, x, and then y. This is exactly the *inverse* of what it was in the first set of circumstances.

The social preference, as defined through the Borda count, certainly goes against intuitive ideas about how a concept like social preference should behave. So, we are back to a junction we have visited before. Either we must abandon our intuitive ideas about social preference—and perhaps, as will be considered below, with this goes much of our heritage, centuries of work and reasoning in the field of social philosophy—or we must examine additional processes.

We will take the latter route first, since the former route would be presumptuous, at best, and perhaps grossly wasteful of perfectly good ideas. Having taken it, however, we will be forced to return to this junction again and begin to slowly and painfully seek where the first route leads. That is the

TABLE 1   Borda Count: A Four-Option, Seven-Person Example

Individual Rankings

Mr. 1	Mr. 2	Mr. 3	Mr. 4	Mr. 5	Mr. 6	Mr. 7
w	x	y	w	x	y	w
x	y	z	x	y	z	x
y	z	w	y	z	w	y
z	w	x	z	w	x	z

	Total Points	
w	18	15 ←
x	19	14
y	20 ←	13
z	13	

current state of the theory. Some are still edging along the sides of the cavern following the difficult paths that remain from the optimistic route, while others have already accepted a position at the bottom of the hole and are trying to construct some stairs which might lead out.

II. THE GENERAL POSSIBILITY THEOREM

Problem Formulation

At this point everyone should agree that something strange and perhaps unexpected is going on. Furthermore, the possible ramifications are very broad. If the concepts, which help us speak about how we feel whole societies, politics, and even worlds should behave, do not work at all for the simple case of a society with a handful of people with just a few alternatives, then perhaps we apply them at the global level only because we do not really understand them. The simple cases are a natural proving ground for any tools which might be applied to the more complicated.

Now exactly what are the facts and what is being called into question? The facts are that several commonly accepted means of providing social choices from among a field of contenders have some unusual properties. The behavior of these methods does not sit well with our intuitive notions of social preference, and we wish to know what type of system, if any, would sit well with us.

Social Preference

Perhaps the first step is to try to provide a precise statement of our intuition. At the base is some concept of social preference. Any method of social choice should yield the socially most preferred alternative—the "best" option in the eyes of society as a whole. The immediate temptation is to begin to define the social preference directly: what determines the list of priorities, what special considerations need to be included, etc. Such arguments and discussions are enlightening and useful, but anyone who has ever engaged in such a discussion knows that for some reason they never end. Perhaps by using a very clever insight first used by Arrow, we can avoid all of that. Without agreeing on whether society prefers x to y or not, we can all agree on the following *principles* of social preference.[1]

I. *Preference Transitivity.* If society prefers option y to option y, and it prefers option y to option z, then option x is preferred to option z (assuming of course that no relevant consideration has changed in the interim).

II. *Indifference Transitivity.* If society is indifferent between option x and option y, and it is indifferent between option y and option z, then it is indifferent between option x and option z.

III. *Value/Feasibility Separation.* The social attitude, preference or indifference, between x and y does not depend upon what other options are feasible.

IV. *Universal Domain.* The social attitude, preference or indifference, between every pair of options is always defined, even though there may be a great deal (all possible) of conflict among the opinions (rankings of options) of individual members of the society.

Thinking about the examples we have already reviewed will help us begin to understand these principles. The first example shows that majority rule as a way of determining the social preference violates the first principle. The "modified majority rule" and the Borda count examples violate the third principle. The fourth principle simply says that we expect the concept of social preference to make sense in the particular cases (and other cases as well) where individual members of the society have the rankings as given in the examples. More specifically, it means that we expect the social preference to be defined for every array of individual rankings. If you don't like the implicit assumption of individual transitivity, we can expand the domain to include the cases where individual preferences can be intransitive as well.

As it turns out, these are very strong principles. We will ultimately consider doing away with all of them. But, before that happens, let's show why they are intuitively reasonable and how they are implied by the way we normally think about normative social philosophy.

The first three principles are usually accepted as reasonable at the individual level of cognition. Instances of cyclical individual preference or indifference are items of great curiosity (Tversky 1969; Lichtenstein and Slovic 1971), especially if the individual exhibiting the cycle is willing to accept it. Violations of these principles are considered unusual and rare at best. The third principle simply demands that the *concept* of social preference between alternatives has an existence independent of the concept of feasibility of alternatives. It says we do *not* have to be aware of what we are *able* to do *before* we can even discuss what we would like to do. The fourth principle forces us to take a stand on behalf of society as a whole, even though individuals within society have conflicting desires.

Some see the first three principles as following almost axiomatically from the word "best." They would maintain that society should have what is best and that if x is better than y and y is better than z, then it follows that x is "best," clearly better than both y and z. Here we have the first principle with the concept "better" substituted for the word "preference" in the principles.

Concepts of social welfare similarly imply such principles. If the social welfare is greater with option x than with option y, and if social welfare is greater with option y than with option z, then it follows from the concept "greater" that social welfare is greater at x than at z. We thus have derived Principle I, Preference Transitivity. Principle II, Indifference Transitivity, is similarly trivial. Principle III, Value/Feasibility Separation, follows since the level of social welfare generated with option x is generally considered to be independent of whether option y was or was not feasible. So we can see that concepts of social welfare necessitate acceptance of these principles.

The list can be multiplied. Most concepts regarding the normative aspects of social choices utilize these principles *plus* many more. To reject these three would be equivalent to rejecting any social philosophy which implies them. So, it would seem that if we adopt at least these we can proceed. But recall we have already been warned that the analysis below will strongly suggest that these three principles are exactly what we cannot accept. Even though it may *seem* as though we have said nothing but the obvious, we have already descended into the cavern.

Normative Content of Social Preference

So far we have said very little of a normative nature. We have said that we are willing to channel normative demands through a concept of social preference, but we have not made any normative demands. For example, should the social preference have anything to do with individual preferences? How should the social preference be defined?

Almost any libertarian philosopher would demand that if a concept like social preference is to be used, then it should have some systematic connection with individual attitudes. For example, if *everyone* preferred option x over option y, then at least some would maintain, society should not be indifferent between the two options or perversely prefer y to x. That is the famous Pareto Principle. It is actually stronger than the principle we will use.

V. *Responsive*. For each pair of alternatives, x, y, there is a pattern of attitudes, ranking R_1 for person number 1, ranking R_2 for person number 2, etc., such that y is not preferred by society to x, given that the pattern of attitudes $(R_1, R_2, \ldots, R_n)$ prevails.

For some this would seem to be a very minimal sovereignty condition. Most of us would readily demand much more. It simply says that no option is preferred by society to any other option, regardless of the pattern of individual rankings. People's preferences prevail over all other considerations. The social preference is "responsive" to individual citizens. If one accepts the Pareto Principle, then one clearly accepts this principle, since the Pareto Principle states one of the circumstances, unanimity, when the pattern of preferences necessarily outweights other considerations.

Process

Before continuing let's check our location. We are attempting to understand the paradoxes above and see if we can find a process, a method of making group decisions, which does not have such paradoxical results. Our first principles attempt to make clear what constitutes "paradoxical behavior." The principles are a type of *minimal* expectation about system performance. The strange behavior of the examples above is in violation of these principles.

How can we find those processes which do not have paradoxical properties? There are literally millions of processes. In fact, by making small alterations in procedures, there are literally millions of variations of any one process. How can we hope to even *list* them all, much less examine the behavior of each under a variety of circumstances?

This almost overwhelming task can be solved by a two-step approach. The first step is to consider processes only in terms of behavior patterns. If many different systems of institutions always behave identically under identical circumstances, then there is no need to study them all. We need only study one from the set, recognizing that all others in the set are behaviorally equivalent. So the idea is to solve first the simpler problem of finding behavior patterns consistent with our principles. Then, having identified the behavior we want, we can attempt to find institutions and rules which induce that behavior.

Consistent with this plan, the first step is to identify what types of behavior are common to all systems. For example, if we define the outcome or outcomes in case of a tie to be the *choice* of the system, then the following two properties seem sufficiently obvious. (1) The *choice* resulting from any system must be one of the feasible options. (2) The *choice* resulting from any system depends in part on the attitudes, preferences, and wants of the people in the system. All systems have both properties.

A third property, which appears to be common to all processes, deserves the status of a principle. People's attitudes about the infeasible alternatives do not affect the outcome of the process, the *social choice,* unless they affect their attitude about the feasible. The choice, at this point, need have nothing to do with a social *preference.* We will name the principle accordingly Independence of Infeasible Alternatives.

Notice that some new concepts have formally entered with this and the last postulate: (1) the set of feasible options, and (2) social choice. There are two different concepts of "feasible set" floating about. The first comes from economics and is based upon physical and technical considerations. The infeasible options are those which one can imagine, but are impossible given the resource base and technology. The second is more akin to parliamentary processes whereby the "feasible" alternatives are those which are in some sense under consideration. The first type of set will be called the *feasible set* and the second type will be called the *contender set.*

The *social choice* is the option that results from the process. Naturally any chosen option must be a feasible option. We can avoid many problems later if we adopt a convention now regarding ties, ill-defined procedures, and even perhaps uncertainty of outcome. To allow for all these possibilities, we do *not* demand that the social choice necessarily be a single option. We can say the choice is a *set* of options as long as we understand that this means one option from the chosen set will ultimately be the outcome, and we need not even develop a term for the latter.

With these ideas in mind we can talk about a *social choice function,* denoted as $C(v, R_1, \ldots, R_n)$. For any actual or imaginary process it designates, for each feasible set v and each array of individual rankings $(R_1, \ldots, R_n)$, the set of options that are outcomes (the "chosen" outcomes). With this notation we can now formally state the principle.

VI. *Independence of Infeasible Alternatives.* Suppose, where $(R_1, \ldots, R_n)$ is an array of rankings, one for each individual, and $(R'_1, \ldots, R'_n)$ is a different array such that for each individual i = 1, 2, \ldots, n, R_1 and R'_1 are identical over all options in the feasible set v, then

$$C(v, R_1, \ldots, R_n) = C(v, R'_1, \ldots, R'_n).$$

The principle says that if the feasible set remains the same and the outcome changes, then the change in outcome must have been due to a change in someone's attitude about some of the *feasible* options. We used the Borda count example. If only $\{w,x,y\}$ are feasible, the points one through three are assigned. If someone's preference for the fourth option, z, changes, it does not affect the numbering of the three feasible alternatives, and thus the social choice is not affected. Furthermore, if the social choice over the feasible set $\{w,x,y\}$ changes, it could be due only to a change in assigned numbers, and thus be due to an altered ranking.

This axiom, which Arrow called Independence of Irrelevant Alternatives, is, historically speaking, the most controversial of all the postulates listed. Much of this controversy is due to a mistake in Arrow's own explanation and defense of the axiom, which differs from the one we are using here.[2] It would be grossly misleading to indicate that all of the controversy is over. For example, we can easily think of procedures which violate the axiom. How then can we say in seemingly bold contradiction that all processes satisfy it?[3] Rather than following this interesting argument here, we will postpone the discussion for a special section later [not included here].

Rational Social Choice

Perhaps it is so trivial that it need not be mentioned that any normative theory of social choice demands a correspondence between what society prefers and what is actually chosen. But if there has been truth in advertising and we are now going down a dead-end road, then we had better be clear about what we have done so we can find our way back.

The principle states that the option that results from the operation of the social process is the socially most preferred of the feasible options, and if there are several options feasible and equally good at the top of the social ranking, then any one of them can result.

VII. *Rational Choice.* If v is the set of feasible options $(R_1, \ldots, R_n)$ are the individual rankings and if $C(v, R_1, \ldots, R_n)$ is the resulting social choice, then $C(v, R_1, \ldots, R_n)$ = the set of options in v which are best, or tied for best, according to the social preference.

The Problem

Is there a process which does not behave in a paradoxical way? Is there a process that chooses in accord with some conception of a social preference? The answer is yes, but *all* examples are of a particularly distasteful sort. In order to be clear we need to add some summary definitions.

Theorem Statement

Let E be a *universal set of options*. These are all the options you can imagine, whether feasible or not. Just put them together and call them a set. Clearly it is going to be big, but that is OK.

A *social preference definition* is a function which attaches to each pattern (n-tuple) of rankings of E, one ranking for each of the n individuals, a single ranking of the options of E for society. From the first four principles, Preference Transitivity, Indifference Transitivity, Value/Feasibility Separation, and Universal Domain, it makes sense to talk about a social ranking over all of the options of E. Principle V, Responsive, indicates that its particular form is going to be functionally dependent upon individual rankings. Thus, how we define the social preference depends, in part, upon the pattern of individuality preferences, and Principle VI will assure that these are all that count.

A social preference definition is *dictatorial* in case there is an individual i_o such that either $\left\{xP_{i_o}y \text{ implies } xP_sy \text{ for all x,y and regardless of the rankings of the other individuals}\right\}$ or perversely $\left\{xP_{i_o}y \text{ implies } yP_sx \text{ for all x,y and regardless of the rankings of the other individuals}\right\}$. A dictator is an individual whose preference dictates the social preference. By checking his preference *alone* you can determine the social preference. The implication of the dictator's ranking can be either positive or negative. If the implication is positive, then when he ranks any x over any y, the options are ranked the same way in the social preference. If the implication is negative, then whenever he ranks any x over any y, the social ranking between the two options is the *opposite*.

We can now state a theorem based upon Wilson's (1972) version of the famous *Arrow General Possibility Theorem*.

Theorem. If E has at least three options and $C(v,R_1,\ldots,R_n)$ is the choice function of some process (thereby satisfying Principle VI, Independence of Infeasible Alternatives) and if $C(v,R_1,\ldots,R_n)$

    i) is defined for all finite subsets of E (any subset of E can be a feasible set);

    ii) is connected through Principle VII, Rational Choice, to a social preference definition;

    iii) the social preference definition satisfies Principles I, II, III, (the preference axioms) IV, Universal Domain, and V, Responsive;

then either

   iv) the social preference definition is dictatorial, or
   v) for all x and all y, xI_sy regardless of individual rankings.

That is a mouthful, but what does it mean? It probably means that if you are in agreement with Principles I through VII, then you necessarily have what some would regard as a strange definition of social preference. Either you have defined society to be always indifferent, or your conception of the social preference is defined in terms of the attitude of a single individual who is either always favored, since if he ranks x over y so does society, or always disfavored, since if he ranks x over y society ranks y over x.

There is no question about the validity of this result. The theorem is true. All of our principles seemed reasonable enough, so what is the trick? The answer to that question is simply not in. Each step of the argument must now be retraced with a great deal of care. This reexamination process has been the subject of a great deal of attention.

Implications

Before we go to all that trouble, however, let's look at the stakes. Some, like myself (Plott 1972) would claim that the concept of social preference itself must go. Buchanan (1954a, b) was right in his original criticism of Arrow, that the concept of social preference involves an illegitimate transfer of the properties of an individual to the properties of a collection of individuals. For me, the Arrow theorem demonstrates that the concept of social preference involves the classic fallacy of composition, and it is shocking only because the thoughts of social philosophers from which we have developed our intuitions about such matters are subject to the same fallacy.

In order to see how extreme this position is, we should investigate first how broadly the theorem can be interpreted, and investigate second the various implicit ways in which our principles of preference can appear. The first problem, that of interpretation, shows up in the following criticism:

A theory of committees and vote tabulation processes has nothing to do with a whole society, with its history, heritage, legal system, rights, etc. It is to whole societies and social systems that the concept of social preference applies.

There is a two-headed answer to this. First, one would expect that concepts like social preference applicable to large complex societies are also applicable in the special case of a simple one. If your ideas get you into trouble in the special case of a small uncomplicated society such as a committee with well-defined options, they will by definition get you into trouble in the general case.

Secondly, the charge is based upon an unnecessarily narrow view about what has been demonstrated. To be sure, the examples involved committees and committee processes, but nothing about the formulation limited the interpretations to these. An option or social alternative could be a complete description of the amount of each type of commodity, the amounts of various types of work done by each individual, the amount of each type of resource used by each firm, the production level of each firm, the type of government agencies and the services provided by each, etc. An option can be a very complicated thing, but its degree of complexity negates none of the arguments above unless it bears on the interpretation of one or more of the principles.

The set of feasible options could be a *consumption possibilities set* and the process could be a competitive process, a capitalistic process, a socialistic process, or any other kind of process.[4] There is no need, for example, for the process to be directed in that some judge, administrator, or planner uses the defined social ranking to determine the best option and then directs its implementation. The process could be any type of game, voting process, market process, political process, etc., as long as the institutions are designed so that the resulting outcomes, equilibriums, winners, etc. are always, as dictated by Principle VII, Rational Choice, "best" according to the social preference ranking. We conclude that there is nothing about the analysis which precludes the application of our results to whole societies.

"Even if the framework does apply to whole societies, what difference does it make? No one really accepts or uses the idea of a social preference anyway, so no one cares if there are deep logical inconsistencies. The whole enterprise is simply an exercise in logic." It is this line of criticism that we will now attempt to refute by demonstrating that many commonly used concepts are equivalent to the concept of a social ranking.

One does not have to look far to find concepts like social needs, group wants, etc. These are simply expressions of priorities and are thus rankings of options. In other words, they all imply the same technical properties as preference. Ideas about what is good for society are no different. If option x is better for society than option y and option y is better for society than option z, then option x is better than option z. The word "preference" does not appear, but this is clearly a statement of Principle I with "better" replacing "preference." All of the arguments apply without modification. The key observation here is that possibly different substantive concepts, e.g., the "preferred" as opposed to the "best," have the same technical properties, and these technical properties cause the problem.

Even more formalized concepts suffer from the same difficulty. Take for example the concept of economic welfare. To different options one attaches a number, perhaps computed from certain types of economic considerations, indicating the level of economic welfare. Certain forms of cost-benefit analysis are attempts to operationalize such a formula. But indicators of social welfare clearly imply a ranking of social options according to the numbers which indicate the levels of welfare. The ranking satisfies all of our principles of social preference, and thus the theorem stands as a criticism of any such formula. The only admissible definitions of welfare are those which are dictatorial.

Rawls (1971) has diagrams which give rather explicit shapes to the social ranking. Society is better off with one distribution of primary goods over another if the worst-off person is better off. Since this ranking satisfies all of our principles of social preference it follows that, if he is theorizing about processes, thereby picking up the remainder of our principles, his system has the same problems as do all others. In this particular case it seems as though the only admissible definition of the worst-off person, a definition which he does not supply, is that the worst-off person always remains the same person, even in the extreme case in which he has acquired all the primary goods in society (Plott 1974).

So, we can see that social choice theorists have a potential audience larger than themselves. The major results do have profound and broad implications.

NOTES

1. Formally speaking, we need more principles than the ones listed (which the reader will probably implicitly assume anyway): (i) for all x, xI_Sx; (ii) for all x and y, xI_Sy impliess yI_Sx; (iii) xP_Sy and yI_Sz implies that xP_Sz; (iv) for any x and y we have one of xP_Sy or yP_Sx or xI_Sy. We also need an important Principle O which states that a social preference exists.

2. Arrow incorrectly claims that the Borda count *violates* the axiom. The mistake, which was first discovered by Plott (1971), was based on a confusion of this axiom with Principle III above which is, as we have already seen, violated by the Borda count.

3. Suppose only those who prefer Lincoln to Johnson (neither is feasible), get to vote in the next election. If preferences for these infeasible alternatives change, then the voting population and thus the outcome changes, even though no one's ranking of the feasible options changes. This process does not satisfy Principle VI.

4. The term comes from economics. It refers to all possible ways in which final consumption goods can be distributed among members of society, given that the only limitations are resources and the production capacity of the society.

13 • Introduction

A collection of articles on social choice theory that did not include one by Kenneth Arrow would be like *Hamlet* without the Prince of Denmark. We have chosen a fairly recent one, addressed to a nonspecialist audience, in which Arrow reflects on later developments in the field which, it would scarcely be an exaggeration to say, he single-handedly invented with *Social Choice and Individual Values.*

In one respect, the article is perhaps a less than completely happy compromise between popularization and technicality in that it refers to several bodies of work, giving the names of the people who have done it, but does not offer citations to their work or explain in any detail what they did. However, a good solution lies at hand. Any reader who wishes to follow up the ideas mentioned by Arrow can do so by consulting a review article by Amartya K. Sen (1977), which has a comprehensive set of references and constitutes a major feat of synthesis.

In the present collection, however, we are concentrating on the leading ideas in the literature, and in particular, on their relation to the problem of rationality in society. In this context, Arrow's article is useful inasmuch as it focuses attention on precisely that problem.

Following the unnumbered introductory section, which raises the issue of collective rationality, the article falls into two parts. The first (sections I, II, and III) lays out some basic ideas about ordinal and cardinal utilities and about preference aggregation. The second part (sections IV and V) takes up two possible routes out of the negative results of the Arrow theorem. The first is a relaxation of the conditions for a social preference ordering. The second is the admission of one of two kinds of interpersonal utility comparison: comparison of differences in utility and comparison of levels of utility.

Arrow's treatment of these themes does not seem to call for any explication, but we should like to offer a few comments, two minor and one major, beginning with the minor ones. The first is an amplification of Arrow's remark in the last paragraph in section IV that "too many alternatives may be treated as indifferent" if all the alternatives in a social preference cycle are treated as indifferent. Work by Cohen (1979), McKelvey (1976, 1979) and Schofield (1978) has shown that this conjecture of Arrow's is only too sadly correct. It is easy to find quite plausible configurations of preferences such that *all* the feasible alternatives will lie in the cycle. Except for stringently defined special cases, for example, a policy space of two dimensions will generate a cycle among all points in the two-dimensional space including even those that are Pareto-dominated, that is to say, less preferred by all parties than some alternative. It may be recalled that Plott gave an illustration of a cycle including a Pareto-inferior alternative. But the significance of this result is to show that even highly structured sets of preferences are vulnerable to the problem. It has been known since the work of Duncan Black (1958) that no cycles can occur when all preferences can be arrayed on one dimension (i.e., when preferences are "single peaked"—see the Barry selection that follows). The next most constricting general condition that might be laid on individual preference orderings is, obviously, that they should be capable of being arranged so that all can be represented in a two-dimensional space. The proof that this severe restriction on domain does not avoid cycles that include all alternatives, including Pareto-dominated ones, is therefore important in suggesting that not much can be expected in general from less coherently related sets of individual preference orderings.

The second minor point is one that will be of interest primarily to those familiar with John Rawls's *A Theory of Justice* (1971) and Rawls's subsequent articles. The last two paragraphs of Arrow's paper appear to imply that Rawls's difference principle should be stated in terms of utilities. The principle will then demand the achievement of maximin utility by social institutions: that is to say, economic arrangements should be such that the worst-off person (or more precisely the representative member of the worst-off social group) is as well off as he can possibly be made. But any careful reader of Rawls is likely to find this extremely puzzling, since Rawls spends a great deal of time insisting that the difference principle is to be defined over the allocation of primary goods—paradigmatically, income—and not utility.

The solution to the puzzle is simply that the reader is right and Arrow is wrong. Arrow's assimilation of Rawls's theory to one in which a "social choice criterion" is defined in terms of utility speaks eloquently of the hold over economists that this mind-set enjoys. The error is quite standard in economists' writings on Rawls (see for example Sen 1970, 1974). Many economists genuinely find it impossible, it would appear, to think seriously about criteria that are not defined in terms of utility. Two ideas have come to assume the status of unchallenged and unquestioned axioms: (a) that what is "better for society" must be some function of what makes the individuals in it "better off," and (b) that how well-off individuals are should be construed as a question about their utility. Yet such a position—dubbed by Sen "welfarism"—is far from self-evident and conflicts with widely held views about the importance of individual rights. (See for a recent discussion Schick

1980. The welfarist assimilation of Rawls is criticized on pp. 80-82.)

The major point that deserves some comment is the treatment given in section I of the Arrow paper to questions about the "meaningfulness" of statements about utility. Here it is necessary to grasp another intellectual peculiarity of economists, namely their extraordinary attachment as a profession to a kind of epistemological doctrine—naive verificationism or operationalism—that no longer finds favor with philosophers, physical scientists, or social scientists in other areas. According to this doctrine, any statement is meaningful if and only if it is possible to specify a set of observations that would verify it; and the meaning of the statement is exhausted by the specification of these observations.

The crux, when the question is one of the meaningfulness of assertions about utility, is usually thought of as coming when we wish to make interpersonal comparisons of utility—to say, for example, that A is happier than B, or that a lollipop gives more pleasure to A than it gives to B. But we can see Arrow's verificationist allegiances coming out with striking clarity in his discussion of the meaningfulness of cardinal utilities when attributed to a single person. Arrow, it will be noted, says that "careful epistemological analysis of the meaning of quantitative statements of this kind [how much one alternative is preferred to another] . . . shows that they *really assert* that statements of the following form are meaningful: 'the preference for x over y is just as strong (or intense) as the preference for z over w.' " And after setting out an interpretation of strength of preference in terms of lotteries, he writes: "Hence, intensity of preference can be given an operational definition *and is therefore meaningful.*" (Our italics in both quotations.) But clearly many "cardinal" statements are quite meaningful though not comparative—for example, "This toothache is bad." And it seems grotesque to suggest that the *meaning* of a comparative statement—I like downhill skiing a bit better than cross-country skiing and cross-country skiing a lot more than jogging—is given by hypothetical choices among lotteries. Perhaps these attitudes should be expected (with a lot of qualifications about attitudes toward risk) to give rise, in a perfectly well-organized, consistent person, to a certain pattern of choices among lotteries. But the content of the statement is, obviously, a comparison of the qualities of the various experiences, rated in terms of their relative enjoyability.

It is worth noticing, incidentally, that there is something fairly bogus about the whole idea that choices have some sort of privileged evidentiary status, since actual choices are rarely used in the establishment of the economists' cardinal utilities. What in fact the economists usually talk about is offering people hypothetical choices and asking them how they *would* choose if the offer were real. So the actual evidence is, in the end, no more than verbal expressions. But then why should some complex verbal response about choices among lotteries be regarded as better evidence than a direct expression of intensity of preference or a statement about the strength of one's likes or dislikes? This is an issue that becomes even more pressing when we move on to Arrow's treatment of interpersonal comparisons, as we shall now see.

Arrow's discussion of interpersonal comparisons introduces no new methodological ideas: he talks of comparisons being "objectively verifiable" when they are comparisons of level, and thus "meaningful," whereas "cardinal-difference comparisons are not allowed as meaningful, partly on the grounds that the implied cardinality of individual preference has no verifiable meaning." Clearly, this is, once again, absurd inasmuch as it implies that we can never "verify" (in any sense of the word that matters) that your having your leg crushed is more painful than my having my finger pricked with a pin. The use of language to communicate with one another presupposes that we can meaningfully say things of this sort, and we, of course, do it all the time. Once again, we may observe (with increasing curiosity as to what is going on) that Arrow thinks that statements reducible to assertions of preference are somehow more "verifiable" than the far more natural and understandable comparisons that our language is well-equipped to permit. But this time it is not merely that the choices are not actually offered, so that we have only verbal expressions of hypothetical preferences to go on. The problem here is that even in principle the choices could not really be offered. There is no way in which anybody except God (and even then there are some tricky logical problems involving personal identity) could offer you a real choice between your circumstances *and tastes, character, and so on* and somebody else's. We can never, therefore, hope to have more than a verbal protocol expressing a hypothetical choice. But why, we must ask, should such a verbal expression be regarded as more "verifiable" than a statement such as "I think X has a better life than I do" or "I believe that X is happier than I am"? In either case, we can verify that the person said it.

The only way in which it seems possible to reconstruct the thought processes lying behind this fondness for "extended sympathy" is by supposing the thought to be as follows: a preference is a preference, and can be neither true nor false; but a statement about happiness is a statement that appears to be about the world, in which case we need to worry about truth conditions. But of course, preferences may be well- or ill-founded, and ill-founded preferences are of no great interest. If we ask how we would set about answering the very curious question "Would I rather be me, with my tastes, character, and opportunities, or X with his?" it is hard to see how we could do anything other than ask if we think X is happier, gets more out of life, and so on, than we do. Thus, the idea that anything is gained by posing the question in terms of what one would prefer is an illusion.

A more technical discussion and an attempted defense of "extended preference" may be found in Arrow (1977b). This article also sets out more fully the idea that "coordinal invariance" can lead to a Rawlsian maximin—defined, however, in terms of utility (see also Strasnick 1976a, 1976b and, especially, 1979). Although Arrow treats the result as surprising, it is surely obvious as soon as one thinks about it that, if we have information only about utility levels and none about utility differences, any social choice criterion that can be formulated to make use of the information must be stated in terms of either the maximum or minimum utility level, since nothing can be done with the intermediate ones. If we then reject maximax (making the best-off as well-off as possible) on the basis of a weak principle of equity, we are left with maximin. This is no big deal and in no sense "proves" Rawls's conclusions, since it follows purely from the particular form of the limitations imposed on the admissible utility information, plus the assumption that nothing *except* utility information is to go into the "social welfare function."

Rawls's own derivation of maximin, incidentally, requires the assumption that levels are knowable, but proportions of people at different levels are not. This is clearly parallel to the assumption that levels are knowable but not differences. Both deny us the possibility of trading off one person's utility (or amount of primary goods) against another's and thus drive us toward maximin or maximax (see Barry 1973, for a discussion of Rawls in this context).

13

CURRENT DEVELOPMENTS IN THE THEORY OF SOCIAL CHOICE

Kenneth J. Arrow

The theory of social choice, as it has developed in the last thirty years but with earlier history reaching back into the eighteenth century, seeks to analyze the concept of rational choice as it extends from the individual to a collectivity. The concept of rationality it has typically worked with is minimal in nature, being confined to imposing what may be termed formal conditions. The theory is correspondingly general in its application.

Narrowly construed, the scope of the theory is the analysis of the conditions under which some mechanism or rule can be found which permits a collectivity (government, social organization, labor union, business) to arrive at decisions which, in some way or another, reflect the decisions desired by its members. It is therefore a normative theory of elections and legislative choices. More broadly, it can be interpreted to provide one aspect of any normative judgment about interpersonal relations which is based, in some measure, on the satisfaction of individual needs. A theory of justice, such as Rawls's, in which the truth-value of a proposition of the form "state x is just" or, still more in the spirit of the theory, "state x is more just than state y," depends on the truth-values of propositions of the form "state x is better for individual i than state y," or "state x is fairer to individual i than state y," for each individual i, is an example of social choice falling within the purview of the general theory.

Reprinted from *Social Research,* Vol. 44, No. 4, 1977, pp. 607-622 by permission of the author and the New School for Social Research, © 1977 by the New School for Social Research.

Unfortunately, the main results of the theory so far have been negative. That is, if we impose some reasonable-sounding conditions on the process of forming social choices from individual preferences, it can be demonstrated that there are no processes which will always satisfy those conditions. Most recent research has been devoted to seeking ways of overcoming this difficulty. Although there is no thoroughly satisfactory resolution, and there probably can never be a truly all-embracing one, some of the recent contributions are illuminating and very likely hopeful.

In the first section, I will remind the reader of some fundamental formal criteria for rationality in preferences and choices, of the recurring controversy whether preferences have a cardinal as well as an ordinal significance—that is, does it make sense to speak of intensities of preferences—and of the possibility and meaning of interpersonal comparability of preferences. In Section II, majority voting is analyzed as a means of social choice. The reasons it might be judged desirable are stated as criteria for social choice mechanisms. The famous paradox which arises in extending majority voting to choice among more than two alternatives is stated. Section III is a statement of the central result in the theory of social choice, that the paradox arising in majority voting is a general phenomenon which holds for all social choice mechanisms satisfying some reasonable conditions.

The first three sections restate results known by 1952. The remaining summarize current attempts to get around the central paradox. Section IV examines a weakening of rationality requirements for social preference. Section V explores perhaps the most fundamental reorientation, that of strengthening the rationality conditions for individuals so as to admit certain kinds of interpersonal comparisons. In one direction, we are led to classical utilitarianism; in another, to criteria closely resembling those of Rawls.

I. PREFERENCE, CHOICE, AND RATIONALITY

The paradigm of rational choice, as it has been elaborated most especially by economists, is the confrontation of a fixed preference pattern over potential alternatives with a varying set of opportunities. There are many alternative states the chooser might conceivably choose among. Only a limited subset of the alternatives is available at any particular time. Thus an individual can conceive of the alternative consumption patterns available to him at an income of $50,000 a year even though his present annual income is only $10,000 and his effective choices correspondingly limited. It is postulated that the chooser has preference between any two alternatives, to state (in words or actions) which he prefers to the other. (Economists find it necessary to be concerned with the possibility of indifference between two alternatives, but I will ignore indifference for this exposition.)

In any concrete choice situation, only a limited number of alternatives are actually *feasible*; the other conceivable or *possible* alternatives are not available, typically because they would require more resources than exist. Then it is assumed in this paradigm that the chooser selects that one of the feasible alternatives which is preferred to all the others.

This sketch leads to an operational interpretation of preference: it is hypothetical choice from a pair of alternatives. That is, the statement "state x is preferred to state y" is interpreted to mean "state x would be chosen if the only two feasible states were x and y."

A formal requirement of rationality applied to preferences and the choices based on them is that the preferences constitute what is known technically as an *ordering*. Specifically, a relation among alternatives is said to be *complete* (or connected) if, for every pair of alternatives, one is preferred to the other; the relation is said to be *transitive* if, for any three alternatives, say, x, y, z, if x is preferred to y and y to z, then x is preferred to z. The last is a natural consistency requirement among choices made from differing feasible sets. A relation among alternative states is an *ordering* if it is both complete and transitive

There is an intuitive and long-held view that more can be said about a preference than its mere existence. We can, it is held, make quantitative statements, by *how much* is one alternative preferred to another. Careful epistemological analysis of the meaning of quantitative statements of this kind, especially as developed by mathematical psychologists such as R. Duncan Luce and Patrick Suppes, shows that they really assert that statements of the following form are meaningful: "the preference for x over y is just as strong (or intense) as the preference for z over w." Clearly, if preferences are measurable, such statements are meaningful; and the converse can be shown to be true.

If such quantitative statements are meaningful, the preference system is said to be *cardinal*; if only simple preference statements of the form "x is preferred to y" are allowed, the preferences are said to be *ordinal*. Both viewpoints have been defended vigorously. The cardinal preference view has received considerable support from comparing uncertainties about alternatives, an analysis which originated with Daniel Bernoulli in the eighteenth century and has been developed in important ways by Frank Ramsey and by John von Neumann and Oskar Morgenstern in the twentieth. Suppose an individual is offered the following two alternative uncertainties: (a) a 50-50 chance of getting alternative x or alternative w; (b) a 50-50 chance of getting alternative y or alternative z. If x were preferred to y and w to z, we would expect that the first would be chosen. To make the choice interesting, therefore, suppose x is preferred to y but z is preferred to w. Suppose further the individual in fact chooses uncertainty (a). Since (a) is derived from (b) by replacing y by x and z by w, it is plausible to interpret the preference (a) over (b) as meaning that the intensity of preferences for x over y is greater than the intensity of preference for z over w. Hence, intensity of preference can be given an operational interpretation and is therefore meaningful.

The issues are complex and unresolved; for example, as a counterargument, it can be argued that intensities of preference relevant to choice among certainties should not depend on attitudes toward risk. I merely want to indicate that some case can be made for the cardinalization of preferences.

If preferences among pairs of alternatives can be given quantitative significance, then we can, equivalently, assign numbers to the alternatives themselves in such a way that higher numbers are assigned to more preferred alternatives and that the differences in numbers between two alternatives measure intensity of preference. That is, we can find a utility function, $U(x)$, assigning a number to each alternative x with the following properties: (1) $U(x) > U(y)$ if and only if x is preferred to y; (2) $U(x) - U(y) = U(z) - U(w)$ if and only if the intensity of preference for x over y is the same as the preference for z over w. This is done by specifying arbitrarily two alternatives, x_o and y_o, with x_o preferred to y_o, and choosing the utility difference between them to be 1. Then the utility difference between any two alternatives can be compared with this standard difference; if, for example, x is preferred to y more intensely than x_o to y_o, then the utility difference must be greater than 1. It can be shown, under certain technical conditions, that there is a way of measuring this utility difference as a unique number. The system is completed by taking an arbitrary alternative whose utility is 0.

Notice that the origin and scale unit of the utility function is arbitrary, an act of choice by the measurer. In measuring length, the unit, but not the origin, is arbitrary; but in measuring temperature by conventional scales (Fahrenheit or Celsius), both are arbitrary.

If preferences are only ordinal, then, under certain conditions, we can still find a utility function with property (1) above. However, any other function which numbers the alternatives according to the same ranking is also a utility function. In technical terms, cardinal utility functions can be subject to *positive linear* transformations—that is, if $U(x)$ is a utility function with properties (1) and (2), and $V(x) = a\,U(x) + b$, for any $a > 0$ and any b, then $V(x)$ also has properties (1) and (2). Ordinal utility functions, on the other hand, can be subject to monotone transformations—that is, if $U(x)$ is a utility function satisfying (1), $F(u)$ is an increasing function taking real numbers into real numbers, with $F(u) > F(u')$ whenever $u > u'$, and $V(x) = F[U(x)]$, then $V(x)$ also satisfies (1).

Logically separate from the issue of cardinality is that of interpersonal comparability. Historically, however, the two have been linked in the development of utilitarianism, particularly by Jeremy Bentham and, in a more rigorous form, by Francis Y. Edgeworth and Henry Sidgwick in the latter part of the nineteenth century. The utilitarians assumed that preference intensities of different individuals could be compared—that is, it was meaningful to make a statement of the form "the intensity with which individual 1 prefers x to y is equal to the intensity with which individual 2 prefers y to x" and similar statements. These interpersonal comparisons of preference intensities presuppose cardinal preference for each individual, but the converse is not true. Each individual might have cardinal preferences, yet they need not be interpersonally comparable. As noted above, the unit for an individual's measure of cardinal utility is arbitrary; if the unit can be chosen independently for each individual, then no comparison across individuals is valid. To turn the statement around, interpersonal comparability of preference intensities requires that the utility unit be the same for all individuals.

Curiously, interpersonal comparison of preference intensities, or cardinal-difference comparability, to use a slightly shorter expression, does not require comparability of utility levels. Utilitarianism does not require any statement of the form "individual 1 is better off under x than individual 2 is under x (or y)." Yet it does not seem unreasonable that if it is permitted to compare the preference gains of movements from one state to another, it is certainly permissible to compare the absolute levels of satisfaction. Of course, it can be argued that even if comparisons of levels are admissible in the sense of being objectively verifiable, it may still be true that they should be disregarded. This is a standard utilitarian viewpoint; even if individual 1 is worse off than individual 2 in a well-defined sense, one should not transfer income from 2 to 1 unless the improvement in 1's welfare is greater than the loss in 2's.

In recent years, there has come to be a growing suggestion that interpersonal comparisons of level of the form just discussed are permissible and should be the basis of social choice. Cardinal-difference comparisons are not allowed as meaningful, partly on the grounds that the implied cardinality of individual preference has no verifiable meaning. The ideal experiment underlying interpersonal ordinal comparisons is that of changing places or extended sympathy: "would individual 1 rather be individual 2 (with all his characteristics) in state y than himself in state x?" A statement of preference of this kind can be represented by a utility function which can itself be subject to monotone transformations; but the transformation must be the same for all individuals. These comparisons are sometimes called *co-ordinal*. Co-ordinal comparisons are required for John Rawls's "difference principle"; they have also been studied and advocated by a number of writers, Suppes, Serge-Christophe Kolm, the present author, and, more recently, Peter Hammond and Steven Strasnick.

II. MAJORITY VOTING AS SOCIAL CHOICE

Suppose there are a large number of conceivable alternatives, but only two are actually presented. These alternatives might, for example, be candidates for elective office; everyone living (or satisfying certain broad conditions of age and citizenship) is eligible, but only two are actual candidates.

We are seeking a procedure which will work for any set of preferences of the individuals in the collectivity, the *voters,* as we may call them. We do not know in advance what these preferences may be. We want to lay down some conditions that we would expect a good social choice procedure to have.

First, it will be assumed that we wish to treat candidates equally; the social choice procedure should not have a built-in bias toward one alternative or another; this condition will be referred to as *Neutrality.* Second, we wish that all voters should be treated equally; we are seeking to model democracy. This condition will be referred to as *Anonymity.* The first of these is not always desirable, but the basic social choice dilemmas are not resolved even by relaxing it or indeed by relaxing the condition of Anonymity unless we go to the extreme of permitting one individual to be a dictator, in which case, of course, the social aspect of the problem disappears.

Now we come to a more basic assumption: the social decision between the two feasible alternatives should depend *only* on the preferences of the voters between them. Preferences among infeasible alternatives or between feasible and infeasible alternatives should have no bearing on the outcome. This condition is usually known as the *Independence of Irrelevant Alternatives.* It is satisfied by every election procedure. It is far from indisputable. But there is clearly merit in it. If Adams and Black are the only two candidates, why should it make any difference what the voters think of Clark? Further, if preferences about irrelevant or infeasible alternatives counted, then the voters might have an incentive to misrepresent their preferences about them; since the infeasible alternatives will not in any case be adopted, they can misstate their preferences without fear of their being adopted.

One more crucial and controversial condition: the preferences of the voters are taken to be ordinal; all that can be asked or are taken to be meaningful are preferences between the two candidates.

Finally, a condition which, while important, is hardly controversial: the social choice procedure should reflect positively the preferences of the voters. Thus, if there is some set of preferences according to which Adams would be elected and if one voter changes his mind so as to favor Adams more highly, then surely Adams should still be elected. This condition may be termed *Positive Response.*

It is not hard to see that these conditions uniquely specify one social choice procedure, that of majority voting, as first pointed out by Kenneth May in 1952 [reprinted in this volume]. Independence of Irrelevant Alternatives and the ordinality of preferences together imply that the only information that can be used in making the social choice is the list of voters who prefer Adams to Black and the list with the opposite preference. Because of Anonymity, however, only the numbers of voters of the two preferences count. Positive Response implies that, if Adams were elected by a certain number of voters, he would be elected by any greater number (and similarly with Black). Now suppose that a bare majority prefer Adams (assume an odd number of voters to avoid ties) but Black were chosen. Now imagine all voters reversing their preferences. By Neutrality, Adams would now have to be chosen, but he now has less votes than he did in the previous case, a contradiction. Hence, it must be that Adams is elected when a bare majority support him and therefore when any majority support him, and similarly for Black.

Majority voting is then a satisfactory social choice mechanism when there are two alternatives. If we maintain the identification of preference with (possibly hypothetical) choice from a pair of alternatives, we would endow the proposition "x is socially preferred to y" with the meaning "a majority of the voters prefer x to y." But we have suggested that a preference relation, to be regarded as rational, should be an ordering, that is, both complete and transitive. The majority preference relation is certainly complete. But it is not necessarily transitive, and this exemplifies the fundamental paradox of social choice.

That majority voting need not be transitive was first shown as long ago as 1785 by Marie de Caritat, better known under his title of nobility, the Marquis de Condorcet. Suppose there are three voters, Asher, Brown, and Castro, and three candidates, Adams, Black, and Carter. Suppose Asher prefers Adams to Black and Black to Carter, Brown prefers Black to Carter and Carter to Adams, and Castro prefers Carter to Adams and Adams to Black. Then two of the three voters prefer Adams to Black, two prefer Black to Carter, and two prefer Carter to Adams. If we interpret social choice as the outcome of majority voting, we should have to say that Adams is socially preferred to Black, Black to Carter, and Carter to Adams. Social preference can cycle.

To avoid misunderstanding, it is not claimed that majority preference is necessarily intransitive. If our voters had different preferences, the majority preference might in fact be an ordering. For example, if Asher and Brown had the same preference rankings as before, but Castro had the ordering, Carter, Black, Adams, then the majority preference ordering would be Black, Carter,

Adams, and Black would also have a majority over Adams. But the point is that the system of pairwise majority voting can lead to a cycle in social preferences.

III. THE GENERAL IMPOSSIBILITY THEOREM

The result of the last section can be stated in a somewhat formal way: Suppose we have a social choice procedure, capable of making choices from any finite number of alternatives, which uses only ordinal information on individual preferences and satisfies the conditions of Independence of Irrelevant Alternatives, Positive Response, Neutrality, and Anonymity. Then the implied social preference relation is not necessarily an ordering.

This statement contains most of the philosophical significance of the Impossibility Theorem of social choice. However, since Neutrality is not such a transparent desideratum and even Anonymity might be challenged, it is worth noting that the general theorem weakens both requirements very considerably. Neutrality can be replaced by the requirement that every social choice is in fact permitted by the social choice procedure:

Non-Imposition. For every pair of alternatives, x and y, there is some set of individual preferences such that x will be chosen over y and some set of preferences for which y will be chosen over x.

For example, we usually want to require the *Pareto* (or *Unanimity*) principle: If every individual prefers x to y, then the social choice will be x (and vice versa).

Similarly, Anonymity, a requirement of full democracy, can be replaced by the following very minimal condition:

Non-Dictatorship. The rules of the social choice procedure are not such that there is one individual whose preferences completely determine social preferences for every pair of alternatives.

The contradiction found earlier still holds with these weaker conditions on the social choice procedures.

General Impossibility Theorem for Social Choice. Suppose there is a social choice procedure, capable of making choices from any finite number of alternatives, which uses only ordinal information on individual preferences and satisfies the conditions of Independence of Irrelevant Alternatives, Positive Response, Non-Imposition, and Non-Dictatorship. Then there will be some set of individual preferences such that the resulting social preference relation is not an ordering.

As a somewhat technical note, it might be remarked that Non-Imposition and Positive Response together imply the Pareto principle. On the other hand, the Impossibility Theorem remains valid if the conditions of Positive Response and Non-Imposition are replaced by the Pareto principle.

IV. A WEAKENING OF THE SOCIAL RATIONALITY CONDITION

There has been a large literature devoted to exploring ways of avoiding the unpleasant implications of the Impossibility Theorem. In this and the following section, I will present just two, which seem most promising to me.

One possibility is to weaken the requirement that the social choice procedure yield a rational outcome in the sense defined here. There are several possible weakenings. I will concentrate here on just one, weakening the requirement that the choice made from a set of more than two alternatives be completely determined by the preferences among pairs. It is natural to require that the alternative chosen, if there are, say, three alternatives, be preferred to each of the other two. In view of the difficulties found, however, it may be a requirement that will have to be dropped or at least weakened.

To discuss the proposals, it will be necessary to introduce now the idea of *indifference* among alternatives. I will maintain the assumption that individuals are never indifferent (this is in no way a necessary assumption and is made here solely for expository simplicity), but we will admit the possibility that society may in some sense regard several alternatives as indifferent. That is, it does not care which one is selected. This means that for a given set of alternatives, it may have a *chosen set*; some of the feasible alternatives are selected out as being superior to those not in the chosen set, but no preferential distinction is made among the alternatives in the chosen set.

The proposal, due to Donald Campbell and to Georges Bordes, is simply to regard the alternatives in a preference cycle as indifferent. In the previous example, Adams, Black, and Carter would have to be regarded as indifferent, as is indeed a reasonable solution in this case. There might have been many more candidates, and the three candidates so far mentioned might have been preferred to them by majority vote without a cycle. In that case, the three candidates would have constituted the chosen set.

This principle can be applied to any way of forming social preferences, in particular to majority voting. The procedure will always produce what is called a *weak ordering:* (1) for any pair of alternatives, either one will be preferred to the other or the two are indifferent; (2) for any three alternatives, x, y, z, if x is preferred or indifferent to y and y preferred or indifferent to z, then x is preferred or indifferent to z. A weak ordering ranks all the alternatives, but it permits ties at some of the ranks.

The full principle of rationality in relating choice in a set of alternatives to preferences among pairs can be restated as follows: If T is a set of alternatives and S a subset (that is, consists of some but not all of the alternatives in T) and if one or more of the chosen elements in T belong to S, then the chosen set from S consists precisely of the chosen members of T which remain after cutting the set of alternatives down to S. If, in particular, S contains two members of T, at least one of which is a chosen element, then the principle states that a chosen element of T must be preferred or indifferent to any element. The Campbell-Bordes social choice procedure does not satisfy this condition but does satisfy the weaker one: If T is a set of alternatives and S a subset, and if one or more chosen elements in T belong to S, then the chosen set from S is included in the chosen elements in T belonging to S (but might not contain all of them). In the example, T is the set of all three candidates, and all three are chosen in T. If S consists of Adams and Black, then the chosen alternative is Adams, while both Adams and Black are chosen alternatives in T which belong to S.

The Campbell-Bordes procedure of treating alternatives in a preference cycle as indifferent (technically known as taking the *transitive closure* of the preference relation) also satisfies another weak rationality condition, which Bordes terms "minimality": it is impossible to find a subset of a chosen set such that every alternative in the subset is preferred to every feasible alternative not in the subset.

The main danger in the Campbell-Bordes procedure is that too many alternatives may be treated as indifferent. Nevertheless it does provide an interesting resolution of the social choice paradox with what appears to be a relatively slight weakening of the condition of rationality of social preference.

V. INTERPERSONAL COMPARABILITY

The oldest critique of social choice theory and indeed of some of the doctrines of social welfare in economics from which it sprang is that it disregards intensity of preference. Even with two alternatives, it would be argued that a majority with weak preferences should not necessarily prevail against a minority with strong feelings. The problem in accepting this criticism is that of making it operational. Theoretically, is there any meaning to the interpersonal comparison of preferences intensities? Practically, is there any way of measuring them, that is, is there any form of individual behavior from which the interpersonal comparisons can be inferred?

Rawls's maximin or difference principle is based, as already noted, on a different kind of interpersonal comparison, not involving intensities. His position is that the criterion for choosing x over y is that the worst-off individual in x is better off than the worst-off individual under y. The two worst-off individuals need not be the same. To make his principle meaningful, it is required that we can make interpersonal ordinal comparisons as discussed in Section 1. If they are permitted, then for each of the states x and y, it is possible to determine the worst-off; and for these two individuals it is possible to compare the well-being of one in state x with that of the other in state y.

Recent work of Peter Hammond, Steven Strasnick, C. d'Aspremont, and Louis Gevers has greatly clarified the relation of these concepts to social choice theory. Assume that for each individual we have a utility function over all possible alternatives. As was seen in Section 1, this can always be found for each individual preference, but the utility function might be meaningful only up to certain transformations monotone or positive linear according as preferences are construed to be ordinal or cardinal; further, the transformations might be required to be the same for all individuals or permitted to vary independently among them, depending on the assumptions about interpersonal comparability.

A social procedure now assigns to each set of utility functions, one for each individual, a social preference relation, required to be an ordering. It is possible to state the conditions of Independence of Irrelevant Alternatives and the Pareto principle in such a way that they make sense in the present formulation. Thus Independence of Irrelevant Alternatives could be stated as follows: Consider two different sets of utility functions for the individuals i, U_i and U'_i, and suppose that for two given alternatives, x and y, they coincide, so that $U_i(x) = U'_i(x)$ and $U_i(y) = U_i(y)$ for individuals i. Then the social preference as between x and y should be the same if the utility functions are U_i as if they are U'_i.

If we assume ordinal preferences and no interpersonal comparability, as we have been assuming, then we can state the requirement in the present language as the condition that the social choice remain unchanged if the utility function for each individual is subject to a monotone transformation which may differ from individual to individual. We know that in this case no satisfactory social choice procedure exists.

Suppose we assume cardinal preferences but no interpersonal comparability. In this case, social choice should be invariant under a separate positive linear transformation of each utility function. Again, no satisfactory social choice procedure exists, as has recently been demonstrated by Ehud Kalai and David Schmeidler.

As is perhaps not surprising, some form of interpersonal comparability is needed to secure positive results. The most obvious case is that of cardinal-difference comparability, as defined in Section 1. Here the corresponding invariance condition is that social choice not change if there is a positive linear transformation of the utility functions with the *same* linear coefficient—that is, if, for each i, U_i is replaced by $U'_i = a U_i + b_i$, $a > O$. Then straightforward analysis shows that the resulting criterion is the classical utilitarian sum of utilities—that is, one alternative x is preferred to another, y, if and only if $U_i(x) + U_2(x) + \ldots > U_1(y) + U_2(y) + \ldots$.

The most recent work has been based on admitting interpersonal comparisons of level rather than of differences. Then the social choice criterion must be invariant under the same monotone transformation of all utilities functions. To be more explicit, suppose F(u) is a strictly increasing function which assigns to each real number u a real number F(u). If U is replaced by $F(U_i)$ for each i, the social choice should be unaltered. This property has been named *co-ordinal invariance*. It turns out, remarkable, that the only social choice procedures satisfying the stated conditions and co-ordinally invariant are the Rawls maximin rule, to choose x over y if $\min_i U_i(x) > \min_i U_i(y)$, and the maximax rule, to choose x over y^i if $\max_i U_i(x)^i > \max_i U_i(y)$. (The notation, $\min_i U(x)$, for example, means the smallest value of $U_i(x)$ as i varies over individuals—in other words, the smallest utility of any individual if x is chosen.)

This result provides an unexpected connection between social choice theory and the Rawls principle. It remains to be seen whether the interpersonal comparisons required are indeed useful tools of social inquiry.

14 • Introduction

The paradigm created by Arrow has brought into being an entire subject—social choice theory—and within this field, there has been an increasing tendency for technical developments to be pursued without very much critical reflection on the underlying assumptions. In the first few years after the publication of *Social Choice and Individual Values* in 1951, however, Arrow's way of formulating his questions was challenged in a number of papers and it is the issues raised in this controversy, about the very significance of Arrow's work, that most concern us here.

We are reprinting a critique, by Ian Little, that challenges Arrow's approach with a good deal of philosophical sophistication. At the same time, it should be noted that Little is working from within the same basic philosophical position as was Arrow, namely, logical positivism. In particular, he does not challenge Arrow's denial of the meaningfulness of interpersonal comparisons of utility and he endorses the idea that "value judgments" are equivalent to expressions of preference rather than assertions that are capable of being true or false. Nevertheless, within these shared assumptions, Little makes a number of telling points against Arrow's way of conceiving the significance of his own work.

In the second edition of his book, Arrow added a new chapter, "Notes on the Theory of Social Choice," in which he replied to these critics; in a section entitled "What is the Problem of Social Choice?" (Arrow 1963, pp. 103-109), he refers to Little's article, and also to papers by Bergson (1954), Kemp (1953), Buchanan (1954a), and Tullock (1962). We cannot here discuss Arrow's reply in detail: we would recommend that the reader consult it. However, we may say that we do not believe that Arrow shows any sign of having really grasped the point of the criticisms of, at any rate, Little and Bergson, so we do not think that what he says about them begins to constitute an adequate response.

The single most penetrating and fundamental statement in the article by Little comes almost at the end of section II, when he says "that it is foolish to accept or reject a set of ethical axioms one at a time. One must know the consequences before one can say whether one finds the set acceptable—which fact sets a limit to the usefulness of deductive techniques in ethics or in welfare economics." This methodological caveat was remarkably prescient, though neglected. At the time it was issued, Arrow's proof was perhaps the only significant example of the genre. But since then, deductive techniques in ethics and welfare economics (or in its successor, social choice theory) have become the common currency. In philosophy we have, for example, Rawls (1971) and Ackerman (1980); in social choice theory, a whole host of theorists, among whom Sen (1970, 1976) has perhaps gone furthest in turning the subject into a branch of axiomatic ethics. All of them tend to argue as if we had ethical intuitions about quite formally expressed principles, and what Little is emphasizing is that we do not. We have to see such principles at work, in conjunction with others, before we can begin to decide whether to accept them or not. Nobody has any immediate views about the desirability of, say, the independence of irrelevant alternatives, and we should refuse to be bullied by a priori arguments to the effect that we would be "irrational" not to accept it.

The axiom in the Arrow system on which Little concentrates his fire is what might seem on casual inspection to be the most innocuous of all, namely, nondictatorship. As Arrow points out (1963, p. 56), the nondictatorship condition has the implication "that no individual can be a dictator for even one pair of alternatives; i.e. there is no individual such that, with the given social welfare function, the community automatically prefers a certain x to a certain y whenever the individual in question does so." Yet, as Little observes, "the community" might well back a poor man's preference over the disposition of some newly available good over the preferences of a number of richer claimants for a share. Indeed, a quarter century after Little wrote this, a student of Arrow and Rawls at Harvard produced an interpretation of the reasoning behind Rawls's difference principle (that the worst-off be made as well-off as possible) that involved precisely the move considered here by Little, namely making the worst-off member of a society a "dictator" in the Arrow sense (see Strasnick 1976b).

Little's attack on the universal acceptability of the nondictatorship condition is central to his two primary objectives in the article. The first, which is pursued in section II, is to argue for the proposition that Arrow's theorem is not, as he supposes, a continuation of the development of welfare economics that culminated in Abram Bergson's (1938) formulation of the idea of a social welfare function. Rather, it is concerned with a quite different problem, namely, that of aggregating the preferences of all the members of a society to form a single judgment of "society" about "social welfare." The reader may find it useful, in working over this section of Little's article, to turn back to the discussion of Pareto's distinction between ophelimity and utility in the introduction to the selection from Baumol. For what Little is arguing here can be expressed quite well in those terms. Welfare economics, he suggests, has been concerned with ophelimity. "Let us suppose that each chooser orders different economic states strictly according to what he himself gets in each state." Then, we can (following Pareto) "isolate in principle an infinite number of 'Pareto-optimum states,' each of which is defined by the impossibility of selecting any alternative state which is higher on one man's order and lower on no one's." As we have seen, there is nothing internal to the Pareto principle that allows us to choose between these optima. The Bergson social welfare function was proposed as a way of picking a unique optimum. It was in fact purely formal: it simply said that the economic welfare of a society (i.e., the desirability of a state of affairs from an economic point of view), should be construed as some function of the ophelimities of its members, that is to say, the utility derived by each individual in the society from consumption. This idea is of no practical use, and nobody has ever found any real life application for the Bergson social welfare function. But it was an internally consistent way of specifying a unique optimum. Little's argument in section II of the paper is that a social welfare function in Bergson's sense is an ethical judgment made by a given individual about what makes societies better or worse. It does not entail any aggregation of the judgments of different people about what makes societies better or worse. Yet that is the problem addressed by Arrow in the guise of a further analysis of the idea of a social welfare function. Bergson (1954) made a protest similar to Little's.

The second objective, which is pursued by Little in section III, is to argue that Arrow's whole discussion is flawed by the failure to distinguish between a judgment about social welfare and an actual process (a constitution) for social decision-making. This is related to the first objective, and both are related to the attack on the nondictatorship condition, in the following way. If, as Little has contended, a social welfare function should be construed as a rule (adopted by somebody) for getting from information about individuals' tastes and consumption patterns to a ranking of states of affairs, this question immediately arises: what, then, is the status of a social welfare function as conceived of by Arrow? Little argues that it is the result of a confusion. On the individualistic premises that Little shares with Arrow, it makes no sense to say that "the society prefers x to y." Only people can have preferences—not collectivities. A social welfare function that takes individual judgments about what is socially preferable and amalgamates them into what purports to be a "social" judgment is, Little bluntly says, "nonsense."

The connection between this claim and the attack on nondictatorship can now be made clear. Every individual, Little argues, must, as a matter of logical necessity, be a "dictator" when it comes to making ethical judgments. We may, of course (and almost always should), take account of how others as well as ourselves fare in alternative social states, and we may well (though we need not always let them override our own views of the matter) take account of the preferences of other people for alternative social states. But once we have done all that as well as we can, we have a judgment of our own, and that is "dictatorial" in the sense that it is not put forward simply as a contribution to some process in which similar judgments by others are aggregated with it to form some sort of superior "social" judgment. We could, of course, if we chose, commit ourselves in advance to adjusting our own judgment so as to make it coincide with the result of such a process of aggregation. But that would be in effect to say that right and wrong are a matter of majority vote—a proposition not logically absurd, but morally obtuse in the extreme.

"All voting is a kind of gaming, like checkers or backgammon, with a slight moral tinge to it, a playing with right and wrong, with moral questions." Thus wrote Thoreau in his essay on civil disobedience (Thoreau 1970, p. 460). If voting were really a way of settling on a "social welfare function," this would be true. But it is not. It is a way of taking social decisions—a quite different matter. I may, for any of a variety of reasons, agree that (some) collectively binding decisions should be taken by aggregating formally expressed preferences (i.e. votes). Little emphasizes pragmatic reasoning: for most people, there is no chance of being a dictator, so one may as well settle for having one vote along with everybody else. This is not, however, the only way of arriving at an endorsement of collective decision-making by voting. One may take the view that as a matter of equity the power to influence collectively binding decisions *ought* to be distributed equally among all citizens. The crucial point is that in neither case is anyone committed to the view that what emerges from the process of aggregating votes has anything to do with maximizing social welfare. The outcome is the outcome, and it may have nothing apart from that to be said for it.

Arrow's theorem is valid and significant as a proof that there is an inherent difficulty in carrying out the operation of amalgamating votes into a unique outcome that in some sense reflects the preferences fed into the process. This, of course, brings Arrow's theorem back more firmly to the paradox of voting which lies at the heart of the proof: the fact that with three voters and three alternatives an intransitive ordering may be generated by majority voting. The difficulty is a real one, and, as we shall see in the last two selections, has extensive ramifications. But it should not be taken for more than it is. Little's article cautions us against supposing that it undermines the possibility of individual men and women making coherent and sensible judgments about what would, or would not, enhance the welfare of society.

Note that, on p. 269, the statement that the Arrow theorem holds for $m > 1$ is incorrect. This should read $m > 2$.

14

SOCIAL CHOICE AND INDIVIDUAL VALUES

I.M.D. Little

The purpose of this article is to discuss the implications of Professor Arrow's conclusion that "if we exclude the possibility of interpersonal comparisons of utility, then the only methods of passing from individual tastes to social preferences which will be satisfactory and which will be defined for a wide range of sets of individual orderings are either imposed or dictatorial."[1]

Since Arrow's work may not be generally familiar, I will first give a brief summary of the central theorem.

I. THE ARROW THEOREM

Imagine that there are n possibilities ($n > 2$) and m choosers ($m > 1$). Each chooser is deemed to have a self-consistent set of preferences ranging over all the possibilities and is assumed to choose or vote accordingly. Coalitions and bluffs are out of court; no one tries to be clever; everyone doggedly consults his own unswerving faith.

The problem is to find whether a self-consistent collective order of the possibilities, which obeys certain "conditions of correspondence" with the individual orders, is conceivable. So that the problem will be reasonably

Author's Note: ... I am indebted to P. A. Samuelson, to G. Warnock, and to H. Brotman for various helpful comments on a draft of this article.

Reprinted, by permission of the author and The University of Chicago Press, from *Journal of Political Economy*, Vol. 60, 1952, pp. 422-432, © 1952, The University of Chicago Press.

difficult, it is stipulated that there are at least three possibilities such that no conceivable set of individual orders thereof is ruled out a priori.

The "conditions of correspondence" laid down by Arrow can be formulated as follows:[2]

1. If one possibility rises or remains still in the order of every individual, then, *ceteris paribus*, it must not fall in the collective order.

2. If the removal from or insertion into the set of possibilities of a certain possibility x results in no change in any individual order of the remaining possibilities, then it must cause no change in the collective order of those possibilities. This condition is named the "independence of irrelevant alternatives."

3. For all x and y, x must not rank above y in the collective order, regardless of the individual orders. This is called the condition of "nonimposition."

4. The collective order must not coincide with the order of any one chooser, regardless of the orders of the other choosers. This is called the condition of "nondictatorship."

Arrow has proved that no consistent collective order satisfying these conditions is conceivable. In his terminology no satisfactory social welfare function is possible. By "satisfactory" is meant "satisfying the arbitrary conditions above." By "social welfare function" is meant "a process or rule which for each set of individual orderings for alternative social states (one ordering for each individual) states a corresponding social ordering of alternative social states."[3] In this definition the possibilities are interpreted as the different possible states of society. A "social state" is defined thus: "The most precise definition of a social state would be a complete description of the amount of each type of commodity in the hands of each individual, the amount of labor to be supplied by each individual, the amount of each productive resource invested in each kind of productive activity, and the amounts of various types of collective activity."[4] The process of proof need not detain us here.[5]

II. RELATION OF THE ARROW THEOREM TO "WELFARE" ECONOMICS

Let us suppose that each chooser orders different economic states strictly according to what he himself gets in each state. As is well known, this assumption enables one to isolate in principle an infinite number of "Pareto-optimum" states, each of which is defined by the impossibility of selecting any alternative state which is higher on one man's order and lower on no one's.

Bergson suggested that this comparatively useless theoretical result could be improved on only if an "economic welfare function" were postulated. What has this Bergson function to do with the Arrow function described above?

As I understand it, Bergson's welfare function was meant as a "process or rule" which would indicate the best economic state as a function of a changing environment (i.e., changing sets of possibilities defined by different economic transformation functions), *the individuals' tastes being given.* It may at once be noticed that Arrow's condition 1 above is inapplicable if tastes are given. Consequently, if I have interpreted Bergson's meaning correctly, then Arrow's result has no bearing on the possibility or impossibility of such a function.[6]

Arrow has a different interpretation. Thus he writes: "The ethical system is a rule which defines the Social state chosen from a given environment *as a function of the tastes of all individuals.* If, for a given set of tastes, the environment varies we expect that the choices will be consistent in the sense that the choice function is derivable from a weak social ordering of all social states. Thus the Bergson Social Welfare Function has the form of a rule assigning a social ordering to each possible set of individual orderings representing tastes."[7]

I should agree that we must expect that, in principle, for a given set of tastes, as the environment varies, the choices will be consistent in the sense that they are derivable from a weak ordering. In other words, all logically possible social or economic states (not merely all scientifically possible ones) must be ordered. Then, as the scientific possibilities change, different states are selected as best. This is my idea of a Bergson function; or, if it is not what Bergson meant, it is what I think he should have meant. This conception has two important points of difference from Arrow's conception. First, tastes are given. If tastes change, we may expect a new ordering of all the conceivable states; but we do not require that the difference between the new and the old ordering should bear any particular relation to the changes of taste which have occurred. We have, so to speak, a new world and a new order; and we do not demand correspondence between the change in the world and the change in the order.

The second important difference is that my interpretation of a Bergson function requires only that there should be an order. It does not require that it should be an order such that anyone would want to say of it that it represented the choices of society. To call an ordering a social ordering at all implies that one approves of the order, or of the mechanism (if any), through which it is determined by the individual choices or preferences. This is, of course, because "social" is a persuasive word. In discussing the logic of welfare economics there is no need thus to involve one's self in political philosophy. Thus the so-called "social welfare function," postulated by welfare economists, should on my view be regarded as a social ordering *only* in the sense that it orders states of society. Whether or not it is possible that such an ordering may be, in some further sense, a social ordering is a question we can, for the moment, leave on one side; we return to it later. The essential point here is that none of the advantages claimed for theoretical welfare economics, as a result of introducing such a function, depends in the least on the ordering of economic states being an ordering by society.[8] Instead of writing, with Bergson, $W = W(U_1, \ldots, U_n)$, we can write $W_i = W_i(U_1, \ldots, U_n)$ $(i = 1, \ldots, n)$. There is no need, so far as pure theory is concerned, to introduce a further (social) welfare function of the form $W = W(W_1, \ldots, W_n)$. We can deduce the whole effective corpus of welfare economics from, say, $W_{10} = W_{10}(U_1, \ldots, U_n)$—remembering only to put "in the opinion of individual No. 10" after "welfare" whenever we use the term.

Arrow wants to go much farther than this in two directions. He wants a "process or rule" which will produce a social ordering as a function of the tastes themselves. As I have tried to indicate, neither of these requirements really has anything to do with what is commonly thought of as welfare economics. Traditionally, tastes are given; indeed, one might almost say that the given individuals are traditionally defined as the possessors of the given tastes and that no sense is attached to the notion of given individuals with changing tastes (certainly the individual's "economic welfare" is not supposed to be comparable before and after a change of taste).

Quite apart from condition 1, Arrow's other conditions are defined in terms of changing tastes. Nevertheless, it is condition 1 which is crucial, because the other conditions have analogues if tastes are given. Condition 2 need merely be modified to read, "The removal from or insertion into the set of possibilities of a certain possibility x must cause no change in the collective order of the remaining possibilities." For, if the entry or exodus of a possibility *did* cause a change in the individual orders of the remainder, we should be faced with a new set of tastes which would require a new "master"-order,[9] which, on my view, need not bear any relation to the old order. Condition 3, called "nonimposition," can be modified to state simply that there must be some conceivable set of individual orders which precludes any given "master"-order. In this form, "nonimposition" is a traditional assumption of welfare economics equivalent to the postulate that if someone prefers x to y and no one y to x, then x is better than y. Condition 4 ("nondictatorship") must also, if tastes are given, be modified to the effect that the "master"-order must not coincide with that of any one individual if this order is exactly reversed for all others.[10]

While we must conclude that Arrow's work has no relevance to the traditional theory of welfare economics, which culminates in the Bergson-Samuelson formulation, it remains, of course, true that his wider conception may have advantages of its own. Let us therefore examine his conditions on their own merits.

First, consider condition 1. Suppose that we have three individuals (defined independently of their tastes) and that the orders of three possible states are xyz for Mr. A, zxy for Mr. B, and yzx for Mr. C. Let the "master"-order be zxy. Then, let there be a change of taste such that z rises or remains still in each order, letting the orders become xzy for Mr. A, zxy for Mr. B, and yzx for Mr. C. Condition 1 requires that z remain top of the poll. But, looking at the matter from an Olympian point of view, one can ask, "Why on earth should it?" Could not, for instance, A's change of taste as between y and z justify a higher weighting of his first choice, so that xyz should become the "master"-order? There is, indeed, nothing in Arrow's theory which prevents us from supposing that the rise of z in the first order is due not to a change of taste on the part of an ostensibly defined Mr. A but rather to the substitution of a new individual for Mr. A. There is then even less reason why one should accept the view that z must remain top of the poll. I may want to attach a high weight to the new man's tastes.

Take now condition 2, called the "independence of irrelevant alternatives." Arrow himself gives an example which throws some doubt on this condition. He writes: "Suppose that there are just two commodities, bread and wine. A distribution, deemed equitable by all, is arranged, with the wine-lovers getting more wine and less bread than the abstainers. Suppose now that all the wine is destroyed. Are the wine-lovers entitled, because of that fact, to more than an equal share of bread? The answer is, of course, a value judgment. My own feeling is that tastes for unattainable alternatives should have nothing to do with the decision among the attainable ones; desires in conflict with reality are not entitled to consideration, so that condition (3) . . . is a valid value judgment, to me at least."[11] It is, however, easy enough to argue the other way. Thus I can argue that if sacrifices must be made in an equalitarian society, then they should be equal sacrifices. But if the wine-lovers got only an equal share of bread, they would lose more heavily than the bread-lovers. What one would think in an actual case would depend so much on so many circumstances. At all events, I know that I should hate to commit myself a priori to Arrow's value judgment.

Condition 3 (nonimposition) needs no comment, since it has been discussed *ad nauseam* in the literature.

As put by Arrow, condition 4 ("nondictatorship") appears eminently acceptable. In his formulation, Tom is a dictator if, for all x and y and "regardless" of the orderings of others, "Tom prefers x to y" implies "x is higher in the master-order." What Arrow evidently has in mind is that if no change in the orders of others can upset the coincidence of Tom's and the master-order, then it would seem reasonable to call Tom a dictator. Here I should agree. But, when we discover that this condition, if combined with the others, produces the consequence that no more need be known to dub a man "dictator" than that his ordering of any pair of alternatives has prevailed against the reverse ordering on the part of everyone else, we may well begin to feel uncomfortable.

Take an example. Let there be three men and two alternatives, x and y. Let the orders be xy for Tom and yx for both Dick and Harry. The conditions then preclude xy as the master-order. The two (economic) states may be such that in y Tom has one piece of manna, while Dick and Harry both have ninety-nine pieces; in x Tom has three pieces and Dick and Harry both have ninety-eight pieces. Might not then the master-ranking xy be desirable? Use of the word "dictatorship" suggests that Tom's preference for x over y somehow causes society to choose x. But, in fact, the coincidence of Tom's and the master-order may be a result of his poverty and not of his power. The plausibility of the "nondictatorship" condition may come partly from the ambiguity of the word "imply." In ordinary language it carries a suggestion of causation. But in logic "p implies q" means no more than "not both p and not q." Thus poor Tom is deemed dictatorial merely because it happens to be the case that society agrees with him and not with the plutocrats. This may be an absurdly limited example (there being only three men and two alternatives), but, presumably, Arrow intended his conditions to be perfectly general. He does, it is true, find this sort of consequence paradoxical;[12] but he draws no conclusion from the paradox. The conclusion, to my mind, is that it is foolish to accept or reject a set of ethical axioms one at a time. One must know the consequences before one can say whether one finds the set acceptable—which fact sets a limit to the usefulness of deductive techniques in ethics or in welfare economics.

It is evident that Arrow has introduced a most interesting logical framework for possible critiques of the behavior of economic systems under conditions of changing tastes and changing income distribution. He fills out the framework with a set of value judgments which yield him entirely negative conclusions. The fact that I have argued that I can see no reason to accept, and some reasons not to accept, his conditions does not, of course, imply that I think that any generally acceptable set of value judgments, which would turn the logical framework into something useful, is likely or even possible. In fact, I think the opposite, as should become clear from what follows.

III. THE GENERAL VERSION OF THE
ARROW SOCIAL WELFARE FUNCTION IN ITS
RELATION TO ETHICS AND POLITICAL PHILOSOPHY

In the preceding section it was supposed that each individual ordered states solely according to what he himself would get. Everything else which individuals thought significant could play its part only in determining the form of the function which would produce the "master"-ordering from these original orderings. But of course there is no need to suppose this. In general, Arrow assumes that the individuals take more into account than their own utility when compiling their original orders; more, indeed, than other people's utilities or welfare. In fact, quite generally, we may suppose that they arrange all states in order of what they regard as ultimate desirability, taking every-thing they know and feel to be significant into account. We shall call such an ordering a value ordering, although, of course, many of the discriminations made would not really be felt sufficiently strongly to be called value judg-ments. The problem, then, is to form a "master"-ordering; in Rousseau's language the problem is the well-known one of discovering the general will.

We must now make an important distinction which Arrow fails to draw. He calls his function both a social welfare function and a decision-making process. He believes that "one of the great advantages of abstract postula-tional methods is the fact that the same system may be given different interpretations permitting a considerable saving of time." Yes, but we must be careful not to give such a system a nonsensical interpretation, and it will be my contention that to interpret it as a social welfare function *is* to give a nonsensical interpretation.

Imagine the system as a machine which produces a card on which is written "x is better than y," or vice versa, when all individual answers to the question "Is x better than y?" Have been fed into it. What significance are we to attach to the sentence on the card, i.e., to the resulting "master"-order? First, it is clear that the sentence, although it is a sentence employing ethical terms, is not a value *judgment*. Every value judgment must be *someone's* judgment of values. If there are n people filling in cards to be fed into the machine, then we have n value judgments, not $n + 1$. The sentence which the machine produces expresses a ruling, or decision, which is different in kind from what is expressed by the sentences fed into it. The latter express value judgments; the former expresses a ruling between these judgments. Thus we can legitimately call the machine, or function, a decision-making process.

But what would it mean to call the machine a social welfare function? One would be asserting, in effect, that if the machine decided in favor of x rather than in favor of y, then x would produce more social welfare than y or simply be more desirable than y. This is clearly a value judgment, but it is, of course, a value judgment made by the person who calls the machine a social welfare function. Thus, in general, to call the machine a social welfare function is to assert that x is better than y whenever the machine writes the sentence "x is better than y." Now we may suppose that the individual who calls the machine a social welfare function is one of those who has fed his own value order into it. It is clear that this person must be contradicting himself unless the "master"-order coincides with his own value ordering. It follows that if the machine is to be called a social welfare function, then anyone who is called upon to accept or reject the principles on which it is built (i.e., the conditions of correspondence) must refuse to accept any principle which insures that the "master"-order will necessarily not coincide with his own. This is because the conditions of correspondence determine the "master"-order and because by calling the machine a social welfare function the person in question has accepted the "master"-order. (It should be noted that accepting or rejecting a value sentence entails agreement or disagreement with the corresponding value judgment.) In other words, it is inconsistent both to call the machine a social welfare function and to accept the condition of non-dictatorship.

This may appear very surprising. First, it may be objected that, as in the case considered in the previous section, a rich man may, like Bernard Shaw, easily *prefer* a state which yields him more manna but at the same time *disapprove* of it because he is an equalitarian and would therefore accept a rule which named as best a social state which yielded him less manna. This objection does not, however, apply in the case under consideration, because in this most general version it is presumed that the individual orders take the welfare of others into consideration. He would therefore *not* rank as higher the state which yielded him more manna.

It is true, of course, that, in the initial ordering, one thing which a person cannot take into consideration is other people's valuations, which he may very well regard as highly significant, if he is a tolerant sort of person. Even worse is the fact that valuations are expressed in value statements, whose whole purpose is to influence other people's value judgments and behavior. It would consequently be surprising if an individual were entirely uninfluenced by the verdicts of others. Indeed, when a working agreement is reached, it is usually partly, if not wholly, the result of this kind of mutual influence. These are difficulties which Arrow does not seem to face. Nevertheless, they can, formally at least, be side-stepped. Thus we can suppose that we can have as much revoting, or rearrangement of individual orders, as the individuals want when they learn the opinions and verdicts of each other. Accordingly each order is, so to speak, a deadlock order. It is the individual order resulting when all persuasion has been used, and after an indefinite number of straw votes.[13]

Second, it will be objected that I may regard x as better than y but still be willing to submit to a ruling which proclaims y as society's choice. But it can easily be seen that this, though true, is no objection, for it interprets the machine as a decision-making process. I am not maintaining that there is anything inconsistent about accepting the nondictatorship condition when the machine is *thus* interpreted. The acceptability of the conditions of correspondence, given the decision-making-process interpretation, will be discussed in the next section.

Third, some people might not find convincing my statement that the sentences which the machine produces cannot themselves be regarded as value judgments. They may think that judgments do not necessarily require someone to judge. Though I believe it to be a nonsensical supposition, let us suppose, for the remainder of this section, that the machine *does* produce value judgments.

Now if I think x is better than y, and the machine announces that y is better than x, I have three choices. First I can say: "I was wrong; y is better than x." Thus Rousseau claims: "When therefore the opinion that is contrary to my own prevails, this proves neither more nor less than that I was mistaken."[14] Rousseau's remark can be taken to mean merely that I was wrong in that my original vote was a guess at the general will which, *ex hypothesi,* is the majority decision. But Rousseau is nothing if not inconsistent, and the remark could be taken as an appeal to some mystical standard of right and wrong. But since few philosophers now believe that value judgments can be verified or falsified (i.e., be said to be true or false in any objective sense), and since the fact that they cannot be thus verified is the whole basis of Arrow's work, this choice can be dismissed. Second, I can say: "I have changed my mind. I now wish to assert the same value judgment as the machine; y is better than x." It is quite clear that we can dismiss this as a possibility for everyone; for if everyone always changed his values to be in conformity with the machine, no problem could arise. There would always be unanimous agreement in the end, however perverse the machine was. Third, I can say "To hell with the machine; x is better than y, whatever it says." If I always did this (and how could I do anything else, since, remember, we are supposing that all other people's values are already known; indeed I have taken into account everything I think significant!), then I should naturally have refused to accept the condition of nondictatorship. It is in the nature of value judgments that the only order which I can fully accept is one that coincides with my own, regardless of the orders of other people. In other words, no one can consistently accept the condition of "nondictatorship." At all events, it is sheer nonsense to say, "A is better than B, but everyone else claims B is better than A; therefore, since I don't want to be a dictator, B is better than A." Yet this is what acceptance of condition 4 would imply in this general case. Once again we are back at the conclusion that condition 4 makes nonsense of any interpretation of the Arrow system in ethical terms. In my opinion, this makes the title "social welfare function" a dangerous misnomer.

Arrow presumably thinks differently, though it is difficult to be sure of this from his book. Thus, having shown that a "social welfare function" satisfying his conditions is possible if individual orders happen to be of a certain form,[15] he proceeds to a brief discussion of some of the politicoethical systems which various philosophers have vainly proposed and rightly says that they are based on some idea of an initial consensus of values; he then writes: "The results ... show that the condition of unanimity is mathematically unnecessary to the existence of a social welfare function, and we may well hope that there are still other conditions [i.e., conditions as to the form of the individual valuations] ... under which the formation of a social welfare function will be possible."[16]

The very use of the phrase "social welfare function" suggests that if such were possible, then somehow an objective moral code would have been erected. Political philosophers used to worry over the question "Why ought I to obey the state (or society, or the general will)?" The pseudo-puzzle of how one can both be free and be subject to law is a variant of the pseudo-puzzle of how duty and self-interest can be reconciled. The philosophers tried to show that it was always really in one's own interest to abide by whatever the "objective" code might be. Since, plainly, conflict must arise, at least in the absence of complete initial consensus, and since such consensus was obviously absent, they invented the doctrine of a metaphysical consensus. When people actually (i.e., really) disagreed about some matter affecting the common interest, they were really (i.e., metaphysically) agreeing. Rousseau, who was first responsible for this nonsense, found some difficulty in explaining how one found out what people were really metaphysically agreeing about when they disagreed; i.e., he found some difficulty in explaining the circumstances under which one could be sure that the general will had expressed itself. We may illustrate all this with a few quotations: "The problem is to find a form of association which will defend and protect with the whole common force the person and goods of each associate, and in which each, while uniting himself with all, may still obey himself alone, and remain as free as before."[17] "Each of us puts his person and all his power in common under the supreme direction of the general will." [18] "Whoever refuses to obey the general will shall be compelled to do so by the whole body. This means nothing less than that he will be forced to be free."[19] "The general will is always right and tends to the public advantage."[20]

It is but a very short step from here (a step which Hegel took) to maintain that acceptance of the social order (or obedience to the state) is really only self-obedience. Arrow's problem clearly has so much in common with Rousseau's that it seems worthwhile to point out again the insidious danger of this approach. Modern totalitarian philosophy may be not altogether unjustly fathered on Rousseau.

Ever since the objectivity of utilitarianism was called in question, economists have been searching for that old philosophers' stone, a scientific ethic. Recently many philosophers, those of the linguistic school, have given up the search, because they have realized that any attempt to define ethical terms is necessarily also an attempt to lay down a moral code; i.e., any supposed definition of an ethical word in nonethical terms is itself an ethical judgment. Thus, in view of the undoubted fact of disagreement about values, any assertion that such-and-such a given value statement is "objectively true" is itself a value statement which persuasively twists words like "objective" and "true" in an attempt to get the given value statement accepted.

We can have an "objective" ethic only when there is universal agreement. But when there is universal agreement ethics will have ceased to exist, since all moral judgments will have become futile and redundant. One does not tell people that they ought to do what they are doing or will do anyway. If everyone agreed, there would be no need to try to change other people's values and behavior, which is the primary use of value statements. In Utopia, not only will the state have withered away, but also all morality; and naturally, since it is Utopia, not only all morality, but also welfare economics.

IV. THE GENERAL VERSION OF THE ARROW SOCIAL WELFARE FUNCTION IN RELATION TO POLITICS AND DECISION-MAKING

We indicated in Section III that the so-called "social welfare function" must be interpreted not (as the name might seem to imply) as a social welfare function but as a decision-making process. The question arises whether one can consistently accept Arrow's conditions, given this interpretation.

The importance of the distinction between a value order and a decision order, for our purposes, is as follows: In a given community, or committee, as many value orderings as there are individuals may coexist. On the other hand, as between two alternatives there can be only one effective decision. Thus we may all have our conflicting opinions as to whether we ought to go to war or not. But the decision to do so or not to do so is unique and binding for everyone. Where values are concerned, everyone must be a "dictator" (i.e., the logic of value judgments is such that one cannot consistently *accept* any value ordering which differs from one's own); where decisions are in question, everyone cannot be a dictator, in Arrow's sense, unless there is unanimity.

Thus an individual will often be prepared to accept a decision which goes against him, because the same decision-making process (or "procedure," for short) will be used for making many other decisions between other alternatives, some of which will go in his favor. This is, of course, true; but it is not an answer to the problem of why acceptance of Arrow's conditions does not imply inconsistency. I may be prepared, of course, to accept decisions which go against me because it is unwise to rebel against an established procedure with established sanctions. But this does not explain why, when I am free and still without my chains, I should accept certain a priori conditions to which any social contract must conform—a priori conditions which rule out all procedures which would ever decide in my favor against everyone else. To explain this, we require, I think, the hypothesis that, among the very limited number of procedures which would stand any chance of being established, none would make me dictatorial in Arrow's sense, together with the hypothesis that all such procedures would determine social states higher on my valuation than anarchy.

It may be suggested that the matter is much simpler than this and that I am making possible acceptance of the conditions depend too much on expediency and not enough on high moral purpose. Thus it may be said that, although one values x above y, one might prefer to accept a procedure which would yield y, if the only way to get x were to impose one's will on society.[21] This is true; but it is not a sufficient reason for accepting Arrow's condition of "nondictatorship," which, barring the name, contains nothing about power or force. This is not, of course, Arrow's fault, given his technique. It springs from the fact that causal and power relations are not logical relations. Thus, since "dictatorship," in the ordinary sense, involves the idea of causation, it cannot be adequately described in terms of implication. Even so, one must add that it is probably true that most people would attach intrinsic demerit to a procedure which ever allowed a minority of one to win.

To sum this up: One may say that expediency might, in most situations, counsel one to accept condition 4 as applied to procedure. It may also be widely acceptable on moral grounds. Indeed, conditions 3 and 4 might be said to contain the bare essentials of democratic procedures—but, perhaps, only the barest essentials, since there is nothing in them to prevent, say, a minority of two in a million from carrying the day.

We may now briefly consider conditions 1 and 2, taken in conjunction with the others. It would seem unlikely that anyone would want to attach intrinsic merit or demerit to them. Consequently, one may suppose that individuals would decide whether or not to accept them on the basis of whether, in conjunction with the remaining conditions, they would be likely to admit or exclude procedures more or less likely to lead to higher or lower states more or less often than alternative procedures. Thus the value of such conditions of correspondence would be derivative, though not derivative solely from one's own present, or even expected future, ordering, but also from a consideration of probable changes in other orderings as well (e.g., if I disapproved of drunkenness very much and thought the taste for gin on the increase, I might not wish condition 1 to be satisfied for states involving alcohol). The chief difficulty with any such "conditions of correspondence" is that, for both logical and factual reasons, it is exceedingly difficult to see what they involve one in. Nevertheless, Arrow's conditions undoubtedly have some prima facie plausibility, probably mainly for the reasons of expediency discussed above.

V. CONCLUSIONS

It was first concluded that Arrow's system is quite different from, and has little relevance to, traditional welfare economics. Second, it was found that it cannot without inconsistency be interpreted as a critique of social welfare functions. Last, we found that it, and no doubt similar deductive techniques, are in principle applicable to decision-making processes. Whether, in this sphere, Arrow's conditions of correspondence are sufficiently acceptable as minimum conditions for a satisfactory democratic decision-making procedure for it to be said that he has proved that consistent decisions cannot be reached via such procedures must be left an open question. Some people will no doubt think that such a proposition requires no proof. Others will think that the essence of democracy is something which must escape definition in terms of any functional relation between decisions and individual preferences.

NOTES

1. K. J. Arrow, *Social Choice and Individual Values* [1951], p. 59.

2. Arrow actually has five conditions, but his first condition is not comparable with the others in that it merely sets the requirements for the problem indicated above, i.e., that the collective ordering be a true self-consistent ordering and that individual orders should not be unduly restricted a priori.

3. Arrow, *op. cit.,* p. 23.

4. *Ibid.,* p. 17.

5. See *ibid.,* pp. 51-59.

6. I am indebted both to the Rockefeller Foundation and to Samuelson for a conversation with the latter in which he pointed out this divergence between his concept of the Bergson function (as elaborated in his *Foundations of Economic Analysis* [1947] chap. viii) and that of Arrow.

7. *Op. cit.,* p. 72. Italics mine.

8. It is, incidentally, clear from Samuelson's work (*op. cit.*) that he would agree with me about this.

9. I shall, where necessary, refer to a "master" order throughout the rest of this article, in order to try to avoid begging questions about the nature of the order.

10. This form of the "nondictatorship" condition is, in any case, a consequence of the above conditions. See Arrow, *op. cit.,* pp. 53-54.

11. *Op. cit.,* p. 73.

12. E.G., *ibid.,* p. 55.

13. This consideration alone would seem to limit the applicability of the Arrow theorem to a very small society. Moreover, it is quite reasonable to suppose that no such deadlock, or equilibrium, set of orders would ever result, especially in a large society. The dynamics of value formation may imply that values are, as a result of mutual influence, in a state of permanent flux.

14. *Social Contract* ("Everyman" ed. [1950]), p. 94.

15. So-called "single-peaked" preferences. See Arrow, *op. cit.,* chap. vii, Par. II.

16. *Ibid.,* p. 83.

17. Rousseau, *op. cit.,* p. 14.

18. *Ibid.,* p. 15.

19. *Ibid.,* p. 18.

20. *Ibid.,* p. 25.

21. It should be noted that to formulate this suggestion at all it is necessary to assume that the "social states" contain only descriptions of the goods accruing to each individual. It presupposes that the procedures have intrinsic, and not merely derived, merit or demerit. In other words, since we are now dealing with decision-making processes or mechanisms, means may be valued apart from the ends attained by them. This distinction of "ends" and "means" could not, of course, arise when we were considering (or, rather, trying to consider) the function as a social welfare function. There cannot be procedures or mechanisms (means) for working out what is right or wrong. Means are, in the present context, means of arriving at a decision. It should be noted, however, that "means" usually refers to social states which would necessarily precede some more distant social state aimed at. In this sense, the means are part of the ends in the present discussion: the individuals in willing the ends necessarily also will the means; they order the alternative future chains of social status.

15 • Introduction

The following paper by Kurt Baier was originally written in response to one by Kenneth Arrow, entitled "Public and Private Values" and published as part of the proceedings of a symposium. We have not included the piece by Arrow because we judged it to be less interesting than the one that we have reprinted. The reader who wishes to consult it can find the reference in the first footnote. However, the general framework should already be familiar by this time, and Baier himself restates in his own contribution the particular points in Arrow's article that he chooses to comment on.

Baier's paper follows naturally from the previous one by Little. He also is concerned with probing the significance of Arrow's result, and, like Little, concludes that it is overstated by Arrow. In particular, he takes up an issue raised only in passing by Little, namely, the fact that Arrow is so indiscriminate in allowing "preferences" of any nature to enter into his "social welfare function." As Baier observes, once we see the kind of bigoted, envious, or otherwise objectionable desires (for example, the desire to keep others down) that can enter into a social welfare function as construed by Arrow, we are much less likely to worry about the fact that a consistent "social" ordering is not always going to be possible.

15

WELFARE AND PREFERENCE

Kurt Baier

Arrow's Impossibility Theorem is generally considered surprising and embarrassing.[1] For it appears to prove the impossibility of something widely held possible and desirable: a formula for translating the will of the people into social policy; or more technically, a formula for aggregating individual preferences concerning alternative states of society into corresponding collective, or social, preferences, such that the application of this formula always yields determinate (transitive) social preferences that satisfy at least the minimal, and surely very reasonable, requirements of democracy.

The problem raised by Arrow's Impossibility Theorem is much the same as that posed by the well-known voting paradoxes. Arrow himself formulates it as follows: "There are three alternatives, A, B, and C, among which choice is to be made. One-third of the voters prefer A to B and B to C, one-third prefer B to C and C to A, and one-third prefer C to A and A to B. Then A will be preferred to B by a majority, B to C by a majority, and C to A by a majority."[2] Each individual may have a perfectly consistent (transitive) set of preferences yet the group preference, as determined by a majority vote, is inconsistent (intransitive). Hence in some cases this method of arriving at social policy will not yield determinate results.

Author's Note: Work on this paper was made possible by a research grant from the Carnegie Corporation of New York and the International Business Machines Corporation to the Department of Philosophy of the University of Pittsburgh to undertake a philosophical study of American values. I have greatly profited from helpful criticisms by David Braybrooke, Martin Bronfenbrenner, and Nicholas Rescher.

Recently, it has been shown[3] that the intransitivity of such results is due to a certain contingent matter of fact about the tastes of the individuals whose preferences are being aggregated: the results are intransitive if and only if "the profiles of preference orderings," that is, the patterns formed by the individual orderings of possible social states, lack certain specific features, such as "singlepeakedness."[4] However, since the reasonable democratic conditions imposed on the aggregating formula (Pareto Principle, Citizens' Sovereignty, and Non-Dictatorship) are all designed to insure dependence of the resulting social choice on that profile, it is not surprising that this profile is always reflected in the social choice. Is it really surprising then that the shape of some such profiles is reflected in the intransitivity of social preferences? On the face of it, this would seem to be no more surprising or paradoxical than the fact that an equal division of voters on some issue should show itself in a "contradictory social decision." In such cases there is then no genuine (transitive) social will or preference, however genuine (transitive) the individual wills or preferences may be.

All the same, it may be said, it surely is surprising when an individual has intransitive preferences. Why then is it *not* surprising when a *group* consisting entirely of individuals with transitive preferences has social preferences that, though quite adequately reflecting the individual transitive preferences, are themselves intransitive? It will help to make it completely clear why it is so surprising when individual preferences are intransitive. Note in the first place that, strictly speaking, what is intransitive is not *preferences* but *expressions of preference.* For, as economists define "preference," a person's real or genuine preferences (logically) cannot be intransitive, even though his expressions of preference are so. From the fact alone that his expressions of preference are intransitive, it does not of course follow that his preferences are intransitive; and in the economists' sense of "preference" such a consequence would be impossible. Thus, he may at t_1 *express* a preference for A over B, at t_2 for B over C, and at t_3 for C over A, and yet he may *have* genuine (transitive) preferences in relation to A, B, and C. For there may be an explanation of why his expressions of preference are intransitive. Perhaps the explanation is that he wishes to deceive someone about his real preferences, or that he has changed his mind or that he is unaware of the inconsistency. In any case, *his expressions of preference,* being intransitive, do not *express preferences.* Hence if he has genuine preferences, they must be different from what he says they are. In such a case, three questions arise: (1) whether or not he has any genuine preferences; (2) if so, what they are; and (3) what exactly is the explanation of the intransitivity.

The test of whether there is an adequate explanation of the intransitivity comes when he is confronted with it. If he gives an adequate explanation and withdraws one of the expressions of preference in favor of another that would make the set consistent, then we may assume that he has real or genuine preferences and that they are what he says they are. If he persists, then we are inclined to assume that he has no real preferences and that he is irrational. The irrationality must be ascribed to him, not to his preferences for, since preferences are by definition transitive, he has none. This point is not unimportant for it shows that having (transitive) preferences is one of the (minimal) achievements of a rational ordering of behavior. A greater achievement of such rational ordering would lie in having not just preferences, but rational preferences; not just dispositions to make consistent (transitive) choices, but dispositions (transitively) to choose what is really preferable for one, and not what is merely erroneously thought to be so.

Now, sometimes an individual's expressions of preference are intransitive because he is unaware of that intransitivity. This is *surprising* because we so confidently expect people to achieve transitivity in their expressions of preference. The surprise lies in the rarity of this deviation from the norm. Such a deviation is also *embarrassing* to the individual because he has been caught out in a performance that falls *below* the norm. Our surprise turns to alarm when the person so caught out, instead of being embarrassed, persists in his intransitive expressions of preference. For then he convicts himself not merely of lack of competence but of a high degree of irrationality, or perhaps worse. However, a person lays himself open to the charge of failing to achieve transitivity in the expression of preference only if, at the time of expressing a preference, he knows or should know what these expressions are, and so knows or should know whether they are transitive or intransitive. But a society, unlike an individual, cannot know what its (collective) preferences are until they have been "constructed" by the aggregation, in accordance with some chosen formula, of individual preference orderings. For there is not, of course, a "moi commun," a conscious common self analogous to an individual, and capable of knowing his (collective) preferences prior to and independently of the results of the aggregation procedure. And so at the time of constructing the collective preference there is no one whose failure to achieve transitivity of the expression of (collective) preferences would be censured or could cause a surprise. But what about afterwards, when the intransitivity of the results has transpired and the citizens nevertheless persist in their original choices? Is there not then cause for surprise, embarrassment, or even alarm? The problem is to see whose failure could give rise to it.

Let us retrace our steps. When someone proclaims that a certain person, whether himself or another, prefers oranges to pears, pears to bananas, and bananas to oranges, he lays himself open to the charge that his expressions of preference are intransitive. Such a charge amounts to one or other of the following three things. (1) That he has failed accurately to state what he actually does; that is to say, that, contrary to what he implies, he either does not really choose bananas in preference to oranges but actually chooses oranges in preference to bananas. (2) That he has failed to note and state the limiting conditions under which he makes the choices he implies he makes; that is to say, that, contrary to what he implies, he does not *always* prefer oranges to pears and so forth, but rather prefers oranges (and pears) to bananas only under some conditions, e.g., when he is thirsty, and prefers bananas to oranges when he is hungry. (3) Or, lastly, that he has failed to note that he does not have any settled preferences at all.

Now, such a failure amounts to inadequate self-knowledge or inadequate expression of it. It can be corrected by withdrawing one or the other of the inconsistent expressions of preference, or by the appropriate modification of (imposition of limiting conditions on) both of them, or by the abandonment of the word "preference," which amounts to an admission that the individual does not *have* (settled) preferences in this matter.

The parallel failure in the case of social preference would clearly be the expression, by an official or a social scientist, of the society's preference ordering of the alternative social states open to it. Such an expression would be in the nature of an imputation to the society of a certain preference ordering and, by implication, of its adoption of a certain social policy. Such an imputation is faulty if it fails to correspond to the policy actually adopted. However, the mere fact that the expression is intransitive or that it fails to correspond to one of the reasonable conditions imposed does not render it faulty since it may be the case that the employment of the aggregate procedure does in fact yield such results. For the reason already given, the parallel with the case of individual preferences here breaks down. For on the view so far presented, the social scientist and the official have merely the task of recording the collective will of the people. If that will, when aggregated, turns out to have the characteristics mentioned, then neither the scientist nor the official is at fault. If their function is merely to ascertain and record, the unsatisfactoriness, from some points of view, of what they find cannot be blamed on them. An individual differs from a scientist and an official, as so far conceived, in being not merely an observer and recorder, but a molder of his own preferences and behavior.

By now it should be perfectly clear that the cause of the surprise and embarrassment engendered by Arrow's theorem does not lie in the discovery of the inability of given scientists or officials to get the popular will right. The embarrassment rather lies in the content the popular will occasionally has and in the underlying implication of certain strands in democratic thought that the popular will is always *sacrosanct* and that, even if it is not, there are no clear principles available for dividing popular preferences into the more legitimate ones that must be reflected in social policy and the less legitimate that need or must not.

To repeat, the surprise and embarrassment are due not to the discovery of someone's ignorance or incompetence, but to the discovery of the very real possibility of an irreconcilable conflict between two basic democratic desiderata of social policy, conformity with the popular will and the requirements of fairness, as formulated in Arrow's axioms (Pareto Principle, Citizens' Sovereignty, Non-Dictatorship, and Independence of Irrelevant Alternatives). Given these (very reasonable) formulations of these desiderata, some possible, even likely, profiles of individual expressions of preference will not result in a determinate (transitive) collective preference ordering, satisfying all of Arrow's conditions. Thus whether we get satisfactory social decisions does not depend solely on democratic procedures, the good will of bureaucrats, and adequate scientific homework, but also on suitable tastes and attitudes of would-be-democratic citizens. Put in its simplest form, the lesson of Arrow's proof is that if we want consistent social policies, then officials may be required to choose without possible objective guidance between policies that are fair but unrepresentative of the popular will, and policies that are representative of the popular will, but unfair. In the remainder of this paper I want to suggest another alternative. It involves conceiving of Arrow's conditions, not as axioms, but as criteria or desiderata, that is, as prima facie principles. If we conceive of them in this way, we are prepared for occasional incompatibilities between them. We then do not ask which of these conditions should be altogether abandoned. We ask merely which of them should be set aside on those occasions and only those when they come into conflict with one another.

If I am right in what I have said so far, then we need only to find principles for settling the conflict between such desiderata for those occasions on which such conflicts arise. Indeed, the very technique for determining social policies, which employs the four (or five) desiderata spelled out by Arrow, itself rests on further value assumptions that must not be treated as wholly inflexible. But the more flexible they are the less embarrassing is the necessity to accept social policies that occasionally fail to satisfy all of the desiderata in question, provided only that there are principles determining when to set aside or in what manner to modify these assumptions. I have space for the discussion of only one of them. I mean the assumption that social action should be designed to maximize or at any rate increase the satisfactions of the members of the society, irrespective of the states of affairs, events, or activities from which they derive these satisfactions. If this were not accepted, then the axiom of citizen sovereignty would not be so plausible, for then we might grant that not all of the individual preferences need be reflected in the social preference orderings.

Here we may with profit examine one of the natural extensions of this assumption that is supposedly in conflict with one of the axioms necessary to Arrow's proof. I mean the assumption that since an individual must (presumably by the definition of "intensity of preference") derive greater satisfaction from developments based on a preference of greater intensity, social action should reflect not only individual preferences but also their relative intensities. It is widely held that this assumption, and the extension just mentioned, are sound, that a consideration of such "irrelevant" alternatives (those not actually open to the society) would enable us to determine not merely the preferences of individuals but also their intensities and that, since these should be taken into account in determining social policy, Arrow's axiom of the Independence of Irrelevant Alternatives should be waived. This would of course have the further consequence of removing Arrow's impossibility.[5] It is, however, a highly questionable value assumption that the collective preference ordering should *always* reflect not merely individual preference orderings but also their intensities. No doubt there are plausible cases, as when a minority prefers its principle much more passionately than the majority prefers a contrary alternative.[6] But suppose Jones, a wealthy man, is passionately opposed to any increase in the living standards of the poor and therefore passionately prefers policies that leave the poor in their miserable and apathetic state or make it worse. Is a social policy that does not adequately reflect the intensity of these preferences really worse, less fair, less democratic than one that does? Thus even if it is correct that by taking into account "irrelevant" alternatives, one can determine the intensities of individual preferences, still the main argument for relaxing Arrow's axiom of the Independence of Irrelevant Alternatives falls to the ground, because it is not morally defensible to argue that intensities of individual preferences *should* in all cases be reflected in social policies. On the other hand, it does seem true that in some cases, such as that of the minority just cited, the intensity of their preference should be taken into account. Hence neither the retention of the axiom of the Independence of Irrelevant Alternatives nor its replacement by some axiom of the Dependence on Irrelevant Alternatives would seem satisfactory.

Let us then return to the discussion of the basic value assumption: that social action should be designed to maximize the satisfactions of the members of the society, irrespective of the states of affairs, events, or activities from which these satisfactions are derived.

The point at issue is an old one. Many liberals reject the evaluative assumption just mentioned and insist that although social action should indeed aim at maximizing individual satisfactions, it should also take into account wherein individuals find their satisfaction. Liberals attempt to draw a distinction between those states, developments, and actions that affect an individual and that therefore are *his business* or *legitimate concern* and those that do not and therefore are not. Arrow denies that this distinction *can* be drawn. One need have no illusion about the ease of drawing it to find fault with the grounds for this contention put forward by Arrow.[7] It is of course true, as he says, that mankind is interdependent, but from this it does not follow that we cannot draw a line between what is and what is not a person's business. It does not seem true that "if my satisfaction is reduced by somebody else's poverty (or, for that matter, by somebody else's wealth), then I am injured in precisely the same sense as if my purchasing power were reduced."[8] Surely the wealthy man is not injured by the poor man's increase in income in the same sense in which he is injured by a reduction in his own purchasing power. In one case there is an economic (causal) connection between the poor man's getting more money and the rich man's having less purchasing power, attended by various psychological and other satisfactions and frustrations following upon these complex changes. In the other case there are only the psychological satisfactions and frustrations caused by the knowledge of the unwanted improvement in the poor man's condition.[9] The difference between the two lies in the fact that the former change affects the purchasing power of the rich man, whether or not he knows of that change and its causal impact, the latter affects him only by way of knowing of it. There is thus a meaningful way of distinguishing between the consequences of social actions that do and those that do not actually affect third persons. Hence if we are liberals and democrats and so subscribe to the view "that every individual should have the opportunity to find his own way to personal development and satisfaction,"[10] then we can draw a further evaluative inference. We can infer that social actions should not reflect Jones's preferences as between the ways in which other individuals should seek or not seek their satisfaction, unless such seeking causally affects Jones's own opportunities. Arrow's examples are a mixed bag ignoring these important distinctions in liberal ethical and political thought. Thus, the example of the rich man's objection to social action improving the poor man's lot cannot (unlike the poor man's objection to the converse case) be based on considerations of injustice or even self-interest but simply on ill will. Such preferences, liberals might argue, need not, indeed should not, be reflected in social policy. Much the same is true for those differences in sexual taste that (assuming that they have no other socially undesirable causal consequences) when dwelt upon in the imagination may arouse disgust, anxiety, or anger. However, the same does not hold for Arrow's third case, a person's being disturbed about discriminations against Negroes, for discrimination is itself social policy differentially affecting classes of individuals, permitting or encouraging some individuals to seek their own satisfactions in ways that diminish the ability and opportunity of others to find theirs. Democratic and liberal theory need not treat in the same way these two kinds of frustration at, or dissatisfaction with, the way others find their satisfaction.

If social policy is to promote social welfare and social welfare is to be determined by aggregating, in accordance with a "constitution," the preference orderings of all members of the society, each member will naturally be vitally concerned not only about the formula of the constitution but also about the "raw material" to which this constitution is applied. For the constitution transforms all individual preference orderings into the social one. Such a transformation implies that the social preference will normally be different from each individual one. As far as each individual is concerned, the constitution sets aside his own preferences to accommodate those of others with whom he lives in the same society. Since social policy is, and often must be, enforced, each citizen will want to insure the "legitimacy" of the other persons' expressions of preference that are taken into account. He will hope not only that others refrain from forming illegitimate coalitions or from illegitimately modifying the expressions of their preferences lest such modifications of their *real* preference orderings jeopardize the representation of his *real* preference orderings in the social preference ordering, but he will also hope that the preferences of others in matters that are none of their business be regarded as illegitimate and therefore not taken into account.

Our misgivings about the judgment that all preferences indiscriminately *ought* to be taken into account increase when we ask ourselves why this assumption should have been thought acceptable in the first place. Of the considerations apparently at work, two stand out, both unsound.

One of them is that by indiscriminately allowing all preferences to be aggregated, the difficulty of determining their legitimacy has been bypassed. But this is clearly not so. The decision to include all is tantamount to the judgment that all are equally legitimate and should therefore weigh equally, or in proportion to their intensity. However, as we have seen, this may sanction a policy that obligates a person to act against, for instance, his preferences in food, housing, sex, and so forth, because a majority (though directly unaffected by his doing so) intensely *dislikes* the thought that he should indulge them.

The second consideration seems to be this. It seems self-evident and generally accepted that governments *ought* to promote the social welfare. Moreover it is contended that social welfare is determined by the social preference ordering (sometimes called social-welfare function) as determined by the aggregation of individual preference orderings in accordance with a constitution. Hence the necessity of this enterprise. Hence the embarrassment when it is found impossible.

It is, however, doubtful whether governments *ought* in all situations and circumstances to promote social welfare. It is in any case a value judgment that is widely rejected, and that cannot therefore be defended on the ground of consensus. For many would maintain that when social welfare conflicts with certain higher aims or claims, such as Christian spiritual values, the free-enterprise system, basic human rights, international treaty obligations, and the like, then government policy ought to promote these higher ends and adhere to these higher principles even if such adherence fails to promote social welfare. The doctrine of basic human minority rights, of international treaty obligations, and international law is surely as much a part of the democratic tradition and quite as respectable in itself as the doctrine of citizen's sovereignty. If Arrow's proof tends to show that rigid adherence to the doctrine of consumer sovereignty could be self-stultifying, this need not be an embarrassment to rational democrats. They need only be prepared to substitute for *unconditional* adherence to the principle of consumer sovereignty adherence to it, *other things being equal,* and to include among the several exempting conditions the case in which expressed individual preferences turn out to aggregate into an intransitive social preference. We (as detached thinkers) may then agree that in such a case public officials should be allowed and required to select, by some other criterion, the policy that is best and we may advocate the inclusion of such a provision in our "constitution."

A second doubt is more radical. It arises not merely in exceptional cases when individual preference patterns aggregate into an intransitive social preference, but also in the standard case in which no such difficulties occur. It questions the very idea of determining social welfare through the aggregation of individual preference orderings of alternative possible social states. The main objection is that, as the economists use the term "welfare," the sentence "Governments ought, other things being equal, to promote the welfare of the society they govern" does not express the plausible value judgment ordinarily expressed by these words. Economists define "welfare" in terms of "preference," except that by "preference" they do not mean preference but "the order of priority in which a person chooses from a given set of alternatives." Thus if for example someone chooses to court financial ruin rather than let his daughter marry a wealthy member of a certain racial minority, then quite irrespective of why he chooses he *prefers* (in the economists' sense) the former to the latter. Ordinarily, we should contrast a choice made from preference with one made for religious or moral reasons. In the latter case our high-principled father chooses financial ruin, not indeed because he *prefers* it to the mixed marriage but because he feels he ought to choose it and *despite the fact that he prefers the other.* Even if we waive the question of preference, it would not be at all convincing to claim that the person who, for religious or moral reasons, chooses (prefers) financial ruin, thereby promotes his welfare. Yet that is what economists would have to say, in their technical senses of "preference" and "welfare." Now, there is of course no objection in principle to using a technical sense of "welfare" and "preference." But we must remember (which in practice is very difficult) that the reasons we normally have for favoring the promotion of welfare will not then always apply to cases of "welfare" (in the technical sense).

What is true for the welfare of individuals is true, by and large, also for the welfare of a society. Just as the actual choice pattern of an individual, however well informed he may be, is not identical with the promotion of his welfare, so *a fortiori* the "aggregation" of individual choice patterns into a so-called social-welfare function can hardly always be identical with social welfare. Now, in the case of an individual we often know what would promote his welfare (his interest, his good, his advantage) without knowing whether he would choose to do it. The explanation is of course that individuals, even when they have full information, often choose for reasons other than that they wish to promote their welfare. Thus, an individual's welfare is not constituted by his choice pattern even when he has full information. It would be really surprising if his actual choices, determined by his loves and hates for others, by moral, legal, and other considerations, by his inclinations, desires, impulses, and passions, were always to coincide with his choices based solely on his interest, good, or welfare, i.e., his nonerroneous judgments of what is in his interest, is for his good, or promotes his welfare, etc. But we could use even his actual choice patterns (or his nonerroneous declarations of intention to make certain choices) as perfectly reliable guides to what constitutes his interest, good, or welfare only if we could rely on the regular occurrence of this miracle. By parity of reasoning we could use a choice pattern based on aggregation of individual choice patterns as a guide to social welfare only if the two coincided or if social welfare was nothing but (nothing but another word for) the aggregation of individual choice patterns. Coincidence here would be even more miraculous than in the case examined above; particularly if one bears in mind the different possible bases of individual choice patterns just mentioned, e.g., those based on an individual's judgment (nonerroneous or otherwise) of what promotes his own welfare (Rousseau's Will of All) or based on an individual's judgment of what promotes the welfare of the society (Rousseau's General Will) or based on anything whatever (the economists' "preferential choice").[11]

Could it be that social welfare is *nothing but* the aggregation of individual choice patterns in accordance with a certain constitution? This is a tricky question that it would take a lengthy examination to settle. Here it must suffice to say that on the face of it, it does not seem so. We can point to a few rather obvious cases of promotion of social welfare, e.g., the raising of living standards, general health, life expectation, personal and economic security, education and amenities, lowering of the rate of violent crimes, elimination of dangerous and illness-causing types of work, and so on. And it is clear that we know that these are cases of the promotion of social welfare even though we do not know whether these are developments favored by the individuals of a given community, or whether there is a "constitution" that would aggregate individual preference orderings into a social choice pattern favoring these things. The epistemological basis for saying that some development promotes social welfare would thus seem to be other than the individual choice patterns and the "constitution." "Social Welfare" can thus hardly mean the same as "social choice pattern derived from individual choice patterns in accordance with a reasonable constitution." But if it is granted that social welfare neither normally coincides with nor means the same as "social choice pattern derived by a certain method," then we should no longer feel quite so dependent on this particular method nor quite so embarrassed by the proven impossibility of always insuring its successful use.

Of course, the impossibility of aggregating individual preference orderings into social ones remains unaffected. But if social welfare cannot and therefore need not be determined by such an aggregation, then the impossibility is not troublesome and embarrassing. If what we determine by such an aggregation is not social welfare but merely social preference, we need not be embarrassed if aggregation of individual preferences in accordance with a formula satisfying Arrow's reasonable conditions does not produce *any* social preference orderings, i.e., produces an *intransitive* expression of social preference. For whereas we might well be surprised and embarrassed by the discovery that frequently no social policy was capable of promoting social welfare, we need not be surprised or embarrassed by the discovery that sometimes no acceptable aggregation of individual preferences will yield such a social policy, or indeed any social policy. For where no such settled social preference exists, officials can reasonably be authorized to decide, on the merits of the case, whether to implement any social policies or instead to allow social developments to take their own course; and if they decide the former, also to decide, on the merits of the case, which of Arrow's conditions should be set aside to make it possible to arrive at a social policy. Such a solution would be objectionable in serious matters but not in matters of *mere* preference.

NOTES

1. For a full discussion, cf. Kenneth J. Arrow, *Social [Choice] and Individual Values,* 2nd ed. (New York, London, and Sydney: Wiley, 1963); *idem,* "Public and Private Values," [1967] (henceforward to be abbreviated as PV); R. Duncan Luce and Howard Raiffa, *Games and Decisions* (New York, London, and Sydney: Wiley, 1957),

Ch. 14; Jerome Rothenberg, *The Measurement of Social Welfare* (Englewood Cliffs, N.J.: Prentice-Hall, 1961), or James M. Buchanan and Gordon Tullock, *The Calculus of Consent* (Ann Arbor, Mich.: University of Michigan Press, 1962), especially Part III and Appendix 2; Robert A. Dahl and Charles E. Lindblom, *Politics, Economics, and Welfare* (New York: Harper, 1953); David Braybrooke and Charles E. Lindblom, *A Strategy of Decision* (Glencoe, Ill.: Free Press, 1963).

2. PV.

3. E.g., D. Black [1958] *The Theory of Committees and Elections,* Cambridge, England; see also PV.

4. For details, cf., e.g., Luce and Raiffa, *op. cit.,* p. 332, and all of section 14.7.

5. Cf. Luce and Raiffa, *op. cit.,* pp. 335-38; also Robert A. Dahl, *A Preface to Democratic Theory* (University of Chicago Press, 1956), especially Ch. 4.

6. Robert A. Dahl, *op. cit.,* p. 90.

7. PV.

8. PV.

9. For a similar distinction, see H.L.A. Hart, *Law, Liberty, and Morality* (Stanford University Press, 1963), pp. 38-48.

10. PV.

11. We can now put the difference between the economists' and the ordinary use in this way: "preferential choice" ordinarily is a certain subclass of the class of choices, namely, those based on preference as opposed to other reasons, but as the economists use it, it is any freely made choice whatever it is based on.

16 • Introduction

After autocracy and anarchy perhaps the most important social choice rule historically has been some version of majority rule. It is widely considered the best rule despite its being subject to cyclic majorities. It meets all of Arrow's conditions except condition O, although if individual orderings violate U in relevant and often plausible ways, there can be no cyclic majorities and the rule will meet condition O (see further the paper by Barry and the introduction to it reprinted here). No rule can meet all of Arrow's conditions but, as Luce and Raiffa (1957, p. 357) note, "some seem to fail in better ways than others." Merely being subject to intransitivities seems to be among the best ways to fail.

Given its importance, it is not surprising that one of the earliest extensions of the Arrow literature was the axiomatic treatment of majority rule in the following paper by Kenneth O. May. May's result is essentially a possibility theorem: he proves that certain conditions are necessary and sufficient for majority rule to be the social choice rule. His conditions are commonly listed as four, although he first restricts his consideration to the field of rules that work by paired comparison, that is, rules that meet Arrow's condition I (independence of irrelevant alternatives). Hence, majority rule meets condition I plus the following four conditions: decisiveness, anonymity, neutrality, and positive responsiveness. Condition I says that the rule works only on pairs of alternatives. Decisiveness requires that it must always choose a winner (there may be a tie, but the rule cannot simply fail to decide). Anonymity requires that the rule must not depend on the labeling of individuals (a majority voting system in which I have two votes and everyone else has one violates this condition). Neutrality requires that the rule not depend on the labeling of alternatives (the U.S. Supreme Court rule that a lower-court decision is affirmed if the Supreme Court splits evenly over it violates this condition). Positive responsiveness requires that if x defeats or ties y, and then one individual's preference changes in favor of x while all others keep their initial orderings, then x defeats y. This last condition says that ties can be resolved by the change of a single vote. The rule for juries that the verdict must be unanimous for conviction or acquittal violates this condition if we stipulate that a jury is indifferent if it reaches a split decision. Hence, if a jury is split 6 to 6 and someone has a change of mind to yield a split of 7 to 5, the rule still yields indifference and is therefore not positively responsive.

Note that May shows his conditions are independent in the sense that any one of them can be violated while all others are met by some decision rule. May has extended his results in a later paper (May 1953) to show that his four conditions are completely independent in the further sense that for any subset of them there exists a rule that is consistent with that subset but which violates the other conditions.

Despite its visual impact, this is an accessible and clear paper which succinctly settles a significant, well-defined point and which is deservedly considered a minor classic.

16

A SET OF INDEPENDENT, NECESSARY, AND SUFFICIENT CONDITIONS FOR SIMPLE MAJORITY DECISION

Kenneth O. May

The problem of the relation between group choice and individual preferences has been stated by Kenneth J. Arrow in terms of a "social welfare function" that gives group choice as a function of the preferences of the individuals making up the group.[1] One of the conditions that he puts on this function is that group choice concerning a set of alternatives must depend only upon individual preferences concerning the alternatives in that set.[2] In particular, group choice in the presence of just two alternatives depends only upon individual preferences with respect to this pair of alternatives. Since it follows that the pattern of group choice may be built up if we know the group preference for each pair of alternatives, the problem reduces to the case of two alternatives. We shall be concerned with the method of choice by simple majority vote, in order both to elucidate the nature of this familiar institution and to throw further light on Arrow's interesting results.

We assume n individuals and two alternatives x and y. Symbolizing "the ith individual prefers x to y" by xP_iy and "the ith individual is indifferent to x and y" by xI_iy, we assume that for each i one and only one of the following

Author's Note: The author is indebted to K. J. Arrow, L. G. Field, D. Siplfe, and several referees for reading the draft of this paper and making helpful comments.

Reprinted from *Econometrica*, Vol. 20, 1952, pp. 680-684, Copyright © 1952 by the Econometric Society.

holds: yP_ix, yI_ix, or xP_iy. With each individual we associate a variable D_i that takes the values -1, 0, 1 respectively for each of these situations. Similarly, for the group, we write $D = -1$, 0, 1 according as yPx, yIx, or xPy, i.e., according as the group decision is in favor of y, indifference, or in favor of x.

The function in which we are interested is of the form

(1) $$D = f(D_1, D_2, \ldots, D_n).$$

It seems appropriate to call it a *group decision function*.[3] It maps the n-fold cartesian product $U \times U \times \ldots \times U$ onto U, where $U = \{-1,0,1\}$.[4] We are going to make four very weak assumptions concerning this function and show that they form a set of independent necessary and sufficient conditions that it be just the familiar method of making group decisions by simple majority. In order to define this method precisely, we let $N(-1)$, $N(0)$, and $N(1)$ stand respectively for the number of -1's, 0's, and 1's in the decision function. Then "simple majority decision" means a decision function that yields $D = -1,0,1$ according as $N(1) - N(-1)$ is negative, zero, or positive. An equivalent definition is that $D = -1,0,1$ according as ΣD_i is negative, zero, or positive.[5]

The first condition that we put on the group decision function is that each set of individual preferences leads to a defined and unique group choice.

CONDITION I: *The group decision function is defined and single valued for every element of $U \times U \times \ldots \times U$.*
We might describe this condition by saying that the method must be decisive and universally applicable, or more briefly *always decisive*, since it must specify a unique decision (even if this decision is to be indifferent) for any individual preferences.

The second condition is that each individual be treated the same as far as his influence on the outcome is concerned. This means that in $f(D_1, D_2, \ldots, D_n)$ we could interchange any two of the variables without changing the result.

CONDITION II: *The group decision function is a symmetric function of its arguments.*
This condition might well be termed anonymity, since it means that D is determined only by the values of the D_i that appear, regardless of how they are assigned to individuals as indicated by subscripts (names). A more usual label is *equality*.

The third condition is that the method of group decision does not favor either alternative.[6] A precise way of stating this is that if the names of x and y are reversed, the result is not changed. If the names x and y are interchanged, preferences are indicated by different values of the D's. It is a matter of interchanging -1 and 1 wherever they occur as values of D_i or D, since yP_ix, yI_ix, xP_iy become with the new names, xP_iy, xI_iy, and yP_ix. There is no change as far as 0 is concerned since the relation of indifference is assumed to be symmetric, i.e., yI_ix if and only if xI_iy. Thus if we have a statement about alternatives labeled in one way, we get an equivalent statement by interchanging x with y and 1 with -1. But x and y do not appear in the decision function (1). Accordingly, if we have a true statement about this function, we must get another true statement from it by replacing each D by its negative. Another way of justifying this is by considering that we might have decided in the first place to assign the values -1 and 1 in the opposite way, and we do not want this to make any difference. Accordingly:

CONDITION III: $f(-D_1, -D_2, \ldots, -D_n) = -f(D_1, D_2, \ldots, D_n)$.

For obvious reasons the mathematical term "odd" does not seem convenient in this context, and we describe this property as *neutrality*.

The final condition that we place on the decision function is that it respond to changes in individual preferences in a "positive" way. By this we mean that if the group decision is indifference or favorable to x, and if the individual preferences remain the same except that a single individual changes in a way favorable to x, then the group decision becomes favorable to x. More precisely:

CONDITION IV: *If* $D = f(D_1, D_2, \ldots, D_n) = 0$ *or* 1, *and* $D'_i = D_i$ *for all i* $\neq i_o$, *and* $D'_{i_o} > D_{i_o}$, *then* $D' = f(D'_1, \ldots, D'_n) = 1$.

We call this *positive responsiveness*. It is slightly stronger than Arrow's Condition 2.[7]

We now state our theorem.

THEOREM: *A group decision function is the method of simple majority decision if and only if it is always decisive, egalitarian, neutral, and positively responsive.*

It is easy to see that Conditions I-IV are necessary. Simple majority decision as defined always gives a unique result. Also II holds since the value of the decision function depends only upon $N(-1)$ and $N(1)$ and is therefore independent of the position of the -1's, 0's, and 1's in f. Thirdly, the definition of simple majority decision remains unchanged under an interchange of 1 and -1, so that III is valid. Finally, a change of one vote breaks a tie, so that IV holds.

To show that Conditions I-IV are sufficient, we notice first that II implies that the value of f depends only upon the set of values of the variables and not upon their position in the function. Hence it depends only upon $N(-1)$, $N(0)$, and $N(1)$. It is easy to see that

(2) $\qquad\qquad N(-1) = N(1) \qquad \text{implies } D = 0$.

For suppose that in this case $D = f(\{D_i\}) = 1$. Then from Condition III, $f(\{D'_i\}) = -1$ where $D'_i = -D_i$. But $f(\{D'_i\}) = f(\{D_i\})$ because of the equality of $N(-1)$ and $N(1)$ and the fact that $-0 = 0$. This violates the uniqueness required by Condition I. Similarly, $D \neq -1$, and the only other possibility is $D = 0$. Suppose now that $N(1) = N(-1) + 1$. Then by IV and (2), $D = 1$. By induction, using this result and IV, $D = 1$ for $N(1) = N(-1) + m$ where $0 < m \leqslant n - N(-1)$. Hence

$$(3) \qquad\qquad N(1) > N(-1) \quad \text{implies } D = 1.$$

From this and Condition III

$$(4) \qquad\qquad N(1) < N(-1) \quad \text{implies } D = -1.$$

Since (2)-(4) are just the definition of simple majority decision, the sufficiency is proved.

Since we have exhibited a function satisfying Conditions I-IV, they must be consistent. To show independence, it is sufficient to exhibit functions that violate each one while satisfying all the others. We indicate such a function for each condition, leaving it to the reader to verify that each does satisfy all but the specified condition.

(I). $D = 1$ for $N(1) - N(-1) \geqslant 0$, $D = -1$ for $N(1) - N(-1) \leqslant 0$.

(II). $D = -1, 0, 1$ according as $D_1 + N(1) - N(-1)$ is less than, equal to, or greater than zero. (A kind of plural voting.)

(III). $D = -1, 0, 1$ according as $N(1) - 2N(-1)$ is less than, equal to, or greater than zero. (The familiar two-thirds majority rule.)

(IV). $D = -1, 0, 1$ according as $N(1) - N(-1)$ is greater than, equal to, or less than zero. (A more familiar example is the rule for jury decision in which $D = -1, 1$, or 0 according as $N(-1) = n$, $N(1) = n$, or otherwise.)

Arrow's "Possibility Theorem for Two Alternatives" asserts that simple majority decision satisfies his Conditions 2-5 applied to two alternatives [Arrow, pp. 46-48]. It follows that our Conditions I-IV imply his Conditions 2-5. That his are actually weaker conditions may be seen by noting that the example above for which Condition III fails satisfies his Conditions 2-5.[8] In Arrow's terms our theorem may be expressed by saying that any social welfare function (group decision function) that is not based on simple majority decision, i.e., does not decide between any pair of alternatives by majority vote, will either fail to give a definite result in some situation, favor one individual over another, favor one alternative over the other, or fail to respond positively to individual preferences. The fact that Arrow's conditions are still weaker emphasizes the importance of his result that his conditions are incompatible with transitivity [Arrow, p. 59].

So far we have been concerned only with a single pair of alternatives. Suppose now we have a set of alternatives and that each individual when confronted with any pair either prefers one or the other or is indifferent. For each pair we can construct a decision function. According to the remark made at the beginning of this article, if we accept Arrow's Condition 3, we can build up a function that gives a set of group preferences corresponding to each set of individual preferences. It follows that any social welfare function that satisfies our Conditions I-IV and Arrow's Condition 3 must be constructed in this way. As is well-known, a social welfare function built in this way may lead to group preferences that are nontransitive even if the individual preferences are transitive [Arrow, pp. 2-3, 59]. Nontransitivity of group preferences follows *a fortiori* if the individual preferences are nontransitive. Accordingly any social welfare function satisfying Conditions I-IV for each pair of alternatives will lead to intransitivity unless the possible individual preferences are severely restricted.

NOTES

1. Kenneth J. Arrow, *Social Choice and Individual Values*, Cowles Commission Monograph No. 12, New York: John Wiley and Sons, 1951, p. 23.

2. See Arrow, p. 27. The realism of this condition may be questioned, but we introduce it here to provide the link between Arrow's work and the results of this paper.

3. This terminology seems appropriate since group decision functions, as here defined, and the familiar statistical decision functions are both members of the family of functions whose values are decisions.

4. The cartesian product $U \times U \times, \ldots \times U$ is the set of all different ordered n-tuples $(D_1, D_2, \ldots, D_n)$ whose elements are members of U. Each member of the cartesian product represents a possible set of individual preferences.

5. Our "simple majority decision" is the same as Arrow's "method of majority decision." See Arrow, p. 46. The function is the same as the so-called "signum function of ΣD_i.

6. There are many situations where this neutrality is not desirable. It goes without saying that our purpose here is to illuminate the formal characteristics of simple majority decision and not to assert any special value or universality for the stated conditions.

7. See Arrow, p. 25. His condition might well be called positive monotonicity, since it requires merely nonnegative responsiveness.

8. See Arrow, pp. 26-30. It is also evident that Arrow's Conditions 2-5 do not imply either Conditions II or IV.

17 • Introduction

The following two papers, by Douglas Rae and by Philip Straffin, form a complementary pair. Rae, in the earlier paper, proposes to determine which collective choice rule would be the one chosen by voters sensibly wishing to maximize the agreement between the collective choice and their own individual preferences. His conjecture is that bare majority rule is best (or most *responsive*) in the long run if voters do not know the likelihood of their being in the majority on issues that come up. This conjecture was proved by Taylor (1969) and a somewhat more general version of it is proved by Straffin in the paper following Rae's here.

One might informally convince oneself that the theorem is valid by noting an important difference between a bare majority and a decisive group of any other size. A bare majority is the only size for which the losers can never outnumber the winners. Hence, the chance that one will be among the losers is minimized with bare majority rule. Such a deduction obviously requires that one expect the preferences of oneself and everyone else to be randomly distributed over the issues likely to come to vote (or that one argue from the principle of insufficient reason that randomness is as good a guess as any). If I thought that the only issue likely ever to come to vote was how to distribute my property, then under Rae's assumptions about individual motivation I should prefer that the social choice rule be unanimity. Under unanimity, I would effectively have veto power.

What we have included here is a small part of Rae's paper. The remainder of the paper comprises two principal parts. The first is an exceedingly long argument in support of the theorem, an argument based on example rather than on proof. The tedium, inelegance, and eventual inconclusiveness of that effort can be instructively compared with Taylor's (1969) straightforward proof of the theorem and with the brief, elegant proof of a stronger version of the theorem in Straffin's selection reprinted here.

In the second additional part of his paper, Rae considers the problem of choosing a social choice rule in societies whose members have preferences that are asymmetric or that are patterned rather than random. An example of an asymmetric preference is the belief that it is better to have a legal system that often fails to convict the guilty than one that occasionally convicts the innocent. Such a system of course violates May's condition of neutrality between alternatives in any pairwise choice. Examples of patterned preferences are societies that are split by class or ethnic conflicts. One patterned preference that worried the constitutional convention in Philadelphia in 1787 was the division of American states into large and small states. As it has worked out, there have been almost no issues of significance over which preferences have depended on the sizes of states.

If preferences are asymmetric or patterned, the optimal decision rule in the view of a given individual may no longer be bare majority, but may rather be an overlarge majority. However, there are significant differences in the implications of asymmetric and patterned preferences. The latter might lead me to prefer overlarge majorities simply from Rae's "criterion for choice between decision rules." Asymmetric preferences, however, require a substantial modification in that criterion: not only expected frequencies of my losing, but also the weight or significance of my losing or winning now matter. To the extent such weights are worthy of consideration now, they should have perhaps also been worthy of consideration from the beginning so that we should have considered intensities of preferences across issues and not only direction of preferences. If we do so, we may be led to adopt different choice rules according to issue. For example, on certain civil liberties issues, we might prefer one-person veto as the choice rule. On many issues, we might prefer very complex multi-institutional decision rules.

Finally, let us note one technical point in the part of Rae's paper that we have included, a point more generally of interest in the problem of majority rule. Rae is concerned with issues taken one at a time, each in a contest with the status quo. We vote yea or nay and move on or stay put. This and the previous point raise again an issue we discussed in our introductory essay to this set of readings. Rae has taken over parts of two of Arrow's conditions: the ordinalism of individual preferences of condition O and the binary comparison part of condition I. On the ordinalism he is explicit: one only wins or loses and there are no variable weights attached to different victories or defeats. His adoption of condition I, however, is only implicit. He weights each election equally and counts as best that system which most often yields agreement between the individual's and society's choices. But how frequently one wins may be far less important than the pattern of one's victories and defeats. In part, this is because different elections are of differing weights. But it is also in part because the various elections may interact so that one may be more concerned with the clustering than with the frequency of victories. One may still conclude that majority rule is the best procedure for making each choice in isolation while adding that over a given cluster of related elections, it might be better to contrive to package them so that choices in one affect choices in others. (One might also consciously choose not to package them in order to force more nearly isolated choices, as many states in the United States have moved their elections for state offices away from presidential election years.) Legislative bodies commonly cluster issues to change results, both for ill and for good.

17

DECISION-RULES AND INDIVIDUAL VALUES IN CONSTITUTIONAL CHOICE

Douglas W. Rae

I

Once a political community has decided which of its members are to participate directly in the making of collective policy, an important question
remains: "How many of them must agree before a policy is imposed on the
community?" Only if participation is limited to one man does this question
become trivial. And this choice of *decision-rules* may seem only a little less
important than the choice of rules in a world so largely governed by
committees, councils, conventions, and legislatures. This paper is about the
consequences of these rules for individual values.

Both the oral and written traditions of political theory have generally
confined the search for optimal (or "best") decision-rules to three alternatives. The *rule of consensus* tells us that all direct participants must agree on a
policy which is to be imposed. *Majority-rule* tells us that more than half must
concur in a policy if it is to be imposed. And the *rule of individual initiative*
(as we may call it), holds that a policy is imposed when any single participant
approves of it. These three decision-rules—"everyone," "most of us," and

*Author's Note: An earlier version of this paper was read at the International Conference
on the Mathematical Theory of Committees and Elections, Vienna, June, 1968. For
helpful criticisms of that earlier version, I thank Jay Casper, Richard Curtis, Robert
Dahl, William Riker, Arnold Rogow, and Michael Taylor.*

Reprinted from *American Political Science Review*, Vol. 63, 1969, pp. 40-53 (some
footnotes omitted) by permission of The American Political Science Association and the
author, © 1969 by The American Political Science Association.

"anyone"—are terribly important, but they cannot be said to exhaust the available alternatives.

The list of alternatives is just as long as a committee's roster. Only for a committee of three would 'consensus,' 'majority' and 'individual initiative' exhaust the possibilities. In a committee of n members, we have n possible rules. Let the decision-rule be a minimum number of individuals (k) required to impose a policy. For a committee of five, we have five alternative values of k: This means, of course, that the number of possible rules is often very large. The U.S. House of Representatives might, for example, choose any of 435 decision-rules; the British House of Commons could choose any of 630 rules; and the Supreme Soviet might choose any of 1300 rules. A committee of n can, in short, choose any of n possible rules. And one can hardly claim to have identified the 'best' decision-rule, whatever his normative standard, unless he has shown it superior to the n − 1 alternatives.

This paper reports one normative analysis of the decision-rules available to a generic political committee.[1] In it, I consider a single, anonymous individual who wishes to optimize the correspondence between his own values, however selfish or altruistic, and those expressed by collective policy. This individual would like to "have his way" as often as possible, by securing the adoption of proposals he likes and the defeat of proposals he dislikes. For him, then, the "optimal" decision-rule will be the one which minimizes the frequency with which he must expect to support a proposal yet have it defeated, or to oppose a proposal yet have it adopted. This is because his values will correspond to collective policy most closely under rules which minimize the frequency with which he is "outvoted" in one of these two ways. And, for him at least, the best decision-rule will be the one which minimizes the expected frequency for these unhappy events. The resulting normative criterion is elaborated in Part II below.

The formal analysis [omitted here] begins with a simple model for the operation of political committees. This is a "null" model in the sense that it presumes very little information about the future. Under it, we know nothing about the (long-run) agenda which will confront the committee, about the ways individuals will evaluate the proposals which do arise, or about the factional structure of the committee. This model serves two purposes. First, it produces a recommendation appropriate to the circumstances of "constitutional choice": If we presume to know very little about an indefinite future, this model rigorously demonstrates the optimality of majority-rule under our individualist criterion. And second, the results of the simple model provide a "baseline" against which to consider the normative implications of additional information about the future. [After this] we consider the consequences of information which would, for example, lead us to expect the formation of a standing minority faction, or a general prejudice for or against government action.

Let me begin by explaining my normative criterion and distinguishing it from three leading arguments about decision-rules—those which rest on the ideals of equality, economy, and "truth."

II. A NORMATIVE CRITERION

Let us suppose that the individual with whom we are concerned has some personal schedule of values. We know nothing about the specific content of his value schedule—its selfishness or altruism, its sophistication or naivete, its generality or specificity—since this individual, whom we may call "Ego," is a purely generic figure. We must, however, suppose that his schedule is complete enough that it leads Ego to like or dislike each proposal which comes before the committee. Accordingly, our major assertion is that Ego would like to optimize the correspondence between his preferences and the policies which are imposed by the committee: he wants to have his way by defeating proposals which his values lead him to dislike and by imposing those which they lead him to like. Our major normative assumption is then:

Value Assumption. Ego wishes to optimize the correspondence between his schedule of values and the list of policies which are imposed.

Now let us suppose that Ego looks ahead and contemplates four events which might occur:

A. Ego's value schedule leads him to support a proposal, but it is not imposed.

B. Ego's value schedule leads him to oppose a proposal, but it is imposed.

C. Ego's value schedule leads him to support a proposal, and it is imposed.

D. Ego's value schedule leads him to oppose a proposal, and it is not imposed.

Ego need not be much of a logician to see that our "Value Assumption" will be best served by the frequent occurrence of events C and D. Since it is also clear that the four classes of events are disjoint, Ego can be sure that a decision-rule which minimizes the summed frequencies of A and B will also maximize the summed frequencies of C and D. Hence, Ego can see that the lower the frequency of events A and B, the higher the frequency of C and D, and the higher the degree of correspondence between his schedule of values and the list of policies imposed by the committee. This leads to a criterion by which Ego may evaluate decision-rules.

Criterion for Choice Between Decision-Rules. One should choose that decision-rule which minimizes the sum of the expected frequencies for (A) in which the committee does not impose a policy which his value schedule leads him to support, and (B) in which the committee imposes a policy which his value schedule leads him to oppose.

This is the normative criterion which underlies our analysis. Each decision-rule will be evaluated by the frequency with which we must, under given assumptions, expect these events to occur if that decision rule is adopted. Our initial commendation of majority rule will imply nothing more than this: under majority rule, the expected (summed) frequency of events A and B is at a minimum, and majority rule is therefore optimal under this criterion. This in turn suggests simply that majority rule maximizes the probability that our (anonymous) individual will "have his way" with respect to a given proposal. And this, in the long run, suggests that majority rule will optimize the correspondence between individual values and collective policies. Since "having one's way" is its central mechanism, we may call this criterion *political individualism.*

The "moral tone" of this position is exactly that of the individuals with whom we are dealing—no better and no worse. Under the criterion of political individualism, we must recommend decision-rules which optimize the correspondence between individual values and collective policies, even if we do not like these values, and even if we do not consider these values "rational" in some larger context.

The best known alternative to this criterion is also independent of the "morality" or "rationality" of individual values: this is, of course, the criterion of *political equality.* While "equality" is a word of many meanings, its most relevant use for present purposes is the rule that, " . . . the weight assigned to the choice of each individual is identical."[2] A minimum consequence of this criterion is that all decision-rules must be defined by the *number* of members who must vote yes if a policy is to be imposed, regardless of *which* members these may happen to be.[3] This criterion is the best-known basis for recommendations of majority-rule. As Neal Reimer puts the case, any alternative rule amounts " . . . to ignoring the majority: to declaring that the minority shall be considered and weighted *unequally.*"[4] In the present analysis, this is taken for granted: we are equally concerned with each individual member, and we define decision-rules without respect to the identities of the individuals voting yes and no. Here we are examining the additional requirement that a decision-rule optimize the expected correspondence between these (equally valued) individual preferences and the policies which a committee adopts.

A second and more restrictive alternative to political individualism is offered by the family of criteria based on the *truth-value* of collective policies. An example is provided by the 15th Century Council of Ferrara, which adopted a two-thirds decision-rule for proposals to alter Church doctrine, apparently on the presumption that this was a hedge against theologically fallacious changes.[5] Another example is held out by Rousseau's first criterion for the choice of a decision-rule: " . . . the more grave and important the questions discussed, the nearer should the opinion that is to prevail approach unanimity."[6] The apparent presumption is that voting is a sort of sampling device for the determination of the General Will: restrictive sampling criteria reduce the chance of a policy inconsistent with the General Will being adopted. Our criterion makes no claim to the optimization of truth values, mainly because such a criterion seems epistemologically indefensible, and because it suggests that past policy is necessarily "truthful," independent of changing circumstances.

Yet a third alternative, much closer to the present criterion, is offered by *economic individualism.* This criterion is embedded in the often fruitful application of economic methods to politics—the works of Olson, and Buchanan and Tullock being important examples.[7] As the latter authors put the criterion, " . . . individuals will, on the average, choose more rather than less when confronted with the opportunity for choice in the political process, with more and less being defined in terms of measurable economic position."[8] In their analysis of decision-rules, Buchanan and Tullock define two cost functions: (1) "external costs," which are defined by the costs a single individual " . . . expects to endure as a result of the actions of others," and (2) "decision-making costs," which are defined by "the time and effort . . . which is required to secure agreement . . . " among the number of people required by a decision-rule to impose a policy.[9] One then looks for a rule which minimizes the sum of these costs.[10]

While this approach is in many respects a powerful one, I have chosen not to follow it here for two major reasons. The first is most important: we are interested in a political problem in its own right, and this must not be submerged in the conceptual (sometimes even ideological) bath of economic individualism. We do not wish, therefore, to conceive the problem of having one's way as a means to success in a larger economic game, but to leave the source of individual values open to the unspecified "value schedules" of individuals. A second, less important reason is methodological: I know of no way to associate costs with decision-rules and at the same time assure that these costs are additive. So, instead, I have chosen to examine expected frequencies for having one's way without subsuming these frequencies under more general cost-functions. While this analysis owes important intellectual debts to these economic models—especially to Buchanan and Tullock—it should not be viewed as a contribution to that tradition.

NOTES

1. The term "political committee" is used here in its broadest sense—to include all bodies which vote on collective policies. This use is illustrated by Duncan Black's book, *The Theory of Committees and Elections* (Cambridge: Cambridge University Press, 1958).

2. See Robert A. Dahl, *A Preface to Democratic Theory* (Chicago: University of Chicago Press, 1956), pp. 67, 84.

3. This requirement is closely related to K. O. May's condition of "anonymity," under which the decision-rule does not depend in any way upon the identification of individual members. See his "A Set of Independent Necessary and Sufficient Conditions for Simple Majority Decision," *Econometrica,* 20 (1952), 680-684 [reprinted in this volume]. May's paper shows that majority rule alone satisfies "anonymity" and three other conditions simultaneously.

4. Neal Reimer, "The Case for Bare Majority Rule," *Ethics,* 62 (1951), 16-32. The cited statement is from p. 17.

5. Thomas Baty, "The History of Majority Rule," *The Quarterly Review,* 216 (1912), 1-28. See especially pp. 22-23. The Council also was tri-cameral: within each chamber, a two-thirds rule prevailed; between chambers the rule of consensus was followed. This is indeed a restrictive decision-rule, and a fine hedge against doctrinal error, *if* we assume the existing doctrine is altogether correct.

6. *The Social Contract,* translated by G.D.H. Cole (New York: E. P. Dutton, 1950), p. 107. Rousseau's second rule was that " . . . the more the matter in hand calls for speed, the smaller the prescribed difference in the number of votes may be allowed to become: where an instant decision has to be reached, a majority of one should be enough." Condorcet actually devised a truth-function theory using probabilistic assumptions [. . .] See *Essai sur l'application de l'analyse à la Probabilité des Décisions Rendues à la Pluralité des Voix* (Paris, 1785).

7. Mancur Olson, *The Logic of Collective Action* (Cambridge, Massachusetts: Harvard University Press, 1965); and James Buchanan and Gordon Tullock, *The Calculus of Consent* (Ann Arbor: University of Michigan Press, 1962).

8. Buchanan and Tullock, *op. cit.,* p. 29. The quotation is one of two interpretations which these authors give to the more general criterion of utility maximization.

9. *Ibid.,* pp. 64, 68.

10. *Ibid.,* p. 70. "For a given activity the fully rational individual, at the time of constitutional choice, will try to choose that decision-making rule which will *minimize* the present value of the expected costs that he must suffer. He will do so by minimizing the *sum* of the expected external costs and expected decision-making costs. . . ." It is not clear that these costs can be added on any single scale. For a commentary on these cost functions see, Herbert J. Kiesling, "Potential Costs of Alternative Decision-Making Rules," *Public Choice,* 4 (1968), 49-66.

18 • Introduction

In the following paper Philip Straffin proves Rae's theorem under
assumptions somewhat more general than those discussed by Rae or used by
Taylor (1969) in proving the theorem. This theorem, again, is that for binary
(aye or nay) choices, bare majority rule is the voting system that maximizes
responsiveness—that is, it yields results that most often concur with each
individual's preferences. Rae assumes everyone will vote aye with the same
probability and that everyone has the same probability of agreeing with the
collective decision. Straffin relaxes the latter assumption and proves more
generally that bare majority rule is the most responsive procedure for all
simple games, which include the symmetric majority rule games as a subclass,
but which also include weighted, or asymmetric, majority rule games as well.

"Majority rule" games is a slight misnomer; "voting" games would be
better because the general class includes games in which some number of
votes less than or equal to the total number available is sufficient to
determine the outcome and that number may be a minority. In symmetric
games, all coalitions of a given size have the same "value," which for majority
rule games means that they all either win or lose (in which cases the values
conventionally assigned are 1 and -1, respectively). In such games, therefore,
all players have equal weight. In asymmetric games, the value of a coalition is
a function of more than merely the number of its members; it also depends
on who the members are because some members are weighted more heavily
and therefore have more "votes" than others. In the terminology now
commonly applied to May's conditions in the paper reprinted here, such a
game is not anonymous, as in the example we gave in our introduction to
May of a body in which I get two votes while everyone else gets one vote
each. If there are 2n of us, a coalition of n of us will win if and only if I am a
member of the coalition.

After settling the issue of responsiveness, Straffin goes on in Arrow's
fashion to consider other desirable properties for social choice rules. He
proposes three properties: rules should be symmetric, proper, and decisive. A
rule is symmetric if under it every voter has the same relation to the set of
winning coalitions in the game; it is proper if no two disjoint subsets of voters
can both be winning (sets are disjoint if they have no members in common);
and it is decisive if it is proper and if the complement of every losing coalition
is winning (the complement of a subset S of the set N is the set of all

members of N not in S, hence N – S). Bare majority rule has all four of Straffin's properties when the number of voters is odd, but when the number of voters is even, majority rule can produce ties and hence fail to be decisive.

The problem of ties for even numbers of voters is a flaw that ordinarily bothers only mathematicians and logicians unless it becomes a practical problem. This problem is often resolved in committees and in legislative bodies by giving their chair only "half" a vote: the chair can vote only to break a tie, never to cause one. This rule is clearly not symmetric in Straffin's sense. If 1 is the chair of the four-member committee 1234, the two-person coalitions 23, 24, and 34 are winners while 12, 13, and 14 are losers. There is no permutation of 1 into anyone else that would preserve this division.

In many electorates, decisiveness is so seldom a problem that one need perhaps not worry about having special devices to achieve it. Indeed, pure ties are practically inconceivable for the simple reason that vote-counting is not sufficiently accurate to yield them. What happens therefore is practical indecisiveness since the declared loser in a very close contest may dispute the count. The value of decisiveness may be suggested by the 1974 New Hampshire senatorial election (*CQ Almanac* 1975, pp. 699-702). In the unofficial tally at election time, Republican Louis C. Wyman led Democrat John A. Durkin by 355 out of nearly a quarter of a million votes cast. Durkin demanded a recount which gave him a ten-vote margin, and he was declared elected. Wyman now contested and the state's ballot law commission of Republican partisans gave Wyman a two-vote margin, and he was declared elected. Durkin now appealed to the U.S. Senate with its large Democratic majority since, under the Constitution of the United States," each house shall be the judge of the elections . . . of its own members." Alas, if the electorate of New Hampshire is indecisive, the Senate is hopeless. For seven months the Senate was at an impasse. Republicans and southern fellow travelers were sufficiently numerous to block Senate floor votes by threat of filibuster, while the Democrats sympathetic to Durkin could have elected him if ever they could have gotten the issue to a vote. As part of the rampant indecisiveness, in the Rules committee a defecting southern Democrat guaranteed 4 to 4 ties on crucial votes over the final 27 disputed New Hampshire ballots. All in all, the total number of people-hours spent by the Senate to dither over that election may have rivaled the number of people-hours spent voting in the New Hampshire election itself. In the end, Durkin agreed to have a new election, which he won by 27,000 decisive votes (p. 928).

Some definitions may be of use to readers of Straffin's paper. In his discussion of "Simple Games and Rae's Theorem" he gives the three conditions that define simple games. These are that the null set, O, is not included among the set, *W*, of winning coalitions; that the set, N, of all voters is included in W (this is equivalent to Arrow's unanimity condition, P); and that if S is a winning coalition and S is a subset of T, then T is also a winning coalition. If S is a subset of T, then T is a *superset* of S.

18

MAJORITY RULE AND
GENERAL DECISION RULES

Philip D. Straffin, Jr.

Suppose that an n-member body must collectively decide whether to accept or reject each of a series of proposals. We might, for instance, think of a society which must decide whether to impose or not to impose each of a series of proposed laws. What decision rule would be best for that body to adopt? To answer this question, we must make precise what we mean by a decision rule, and we must specify the criteria by which we propose to judge a decision rule best.

We should first note that we are dealing only with dichotomous choices: to accept or to reject. Hence we avoid the difficulties surrounding the Arrow Impossibility Theorem, which become relevant as soon as a decision is required among three or more alternatives.[1] Although decisions among many alternatives are very important, many societies and legislatures operate under 'parliamentary procedures' which have the effect of reducing multi-choice decisions to a sequence of dichotomous decisions, at which point our question of how best to make dichotomous decisions becomes applicable.

Among the decision rules which an n-member body might adopt, majority rule has occupied a special place in political theory. An obvious attractive property of majority rule, at least for democratic theory, is its symmetry: it treats all members of the decision-making body alike. Of course, it shares this property with other decision rules. One can, for instance, require approval by three-fifths, two-thirds, or all of the members of the body. Alternatively, one can make decisions by a 'two stage plebiscite': partition $n = mk$ voters into m districts, with k voters in each district. Require approval by a majority (say) of the k voters in each of a majority of the m districts. The 'pure delegate' model of representative democracy is essentially such a two stage plebiscite. We think of each district as electing a representative who votes on each issue in accordance with the wishes of a majority of his constituents, and approval is required by a majority of the representatives. One could also use rules other than majority rule in the stages of the plebiscite, and consider plebiscites of more than two stages.

There are also non-symmetric decision rules. Consider for example:

(1) Dictatorship. One member, D, is chosen from the body, and a proposal is approved if and only if D approves it.

(2) Oligarchy. A subset of $m < n$ members is chosen from the body, and the decision is made by these m members, acting under some decision rule. The remaining members are 'dummies,' and have no say in the decision.

(3) Committee system. A subset of $m < n$ members is chosen from the body and a proposal must be approved by a majority (say) of both these m members, and of the body as a whole.

Although these decision rules are not symmetric, they can effectively be made symmetric by the simple expedient of randomly assigning the distinguished roles to different members of the decision-making body. Thus a decision could always be made by one person, but the identity of that person could vary for different decisions, with each member of the body having equal chance to be 'dictator for a day.' More realistically, the American jury system could be thought of as decision-making by randomized oligarchies of twelve, operating under unanimity rule. In a committee system, randomization is over bills: different bills are sent to different committees. The system would be symmetric if each legislator were a member of the same number of committees, and each committee considered an equal number of equally important bills.

With many possible symmetric decision rules, and all asymmetric decision rules subject to being made symmetric by randomization, can we claim a special place for majority rule? We need a different criterion, and I propose to follow Douglas Rae in proposing a criterion of maximal responsiveness to individual preferences, which will turn out to *almost* select majority rule as a uniquely best decision rule. We must first formalize the idea of a decision rule.

SIMPLE GAMES AND RAE'S THEOREM

The concept of a decision rule can be formulated as follows. Let N be the set of members of an n-member decision-making body. A decision rule must specify which subsets of N can ensure acceptance of a proposal. Thus a decision rule corresponds to a collection W of subsets of N. It is natural to place three conditions on the collection W:

(i) $\phi \in W$
(ii) $N \in W$
(iii) If $S \in W$ and $T \supset S$, then $T \in W$.

A pair (N, W) where W satisfies conditions (i)–(iii) is called by game-theorists a *simple game*. Members of N are called *players* in the game. Sets in W are called *winning coalitions*; sets not in W are called *losing coalitions*.[2] The three conditions specify that the empty set is a losing coalition, the set N of all players is a winning coalition, and all supersets of winning coalitions are also winning coalitions.

One family of n-person simple games is the family $M_{n,k}$ $(1 \leqslant k \leqslant n)$ of 'symmetric majority games.' A subset $S \subset N$ is a winning coalition in $M_{n,k}$ if the number of players in S is greater than or equal to k. Among the games $M_{n,k}$, *majority rule* is the game:

$$M_n = \begin{matrix} M_{n,\,(n/2)+1} & \text{if } n \text{ is even} \\ M_{n,\,(n+1)/2} & \text{if } n \text{ is odd} \end{matrix}$$

In an article in the *American Political Science Review*, Douglas Rae considered the class $M_{n,k}$ and asked which of these decision rules is 'best.'[3] His criterion for choosing a preferred decision rule was

CRITERION I. A 'best' decision rule should maximize the probability that the collective decision will agree with any individual's decision.

Since probabilities are involved, we must specify the assumptions we will use to calculate probabilities. Rae's assumption is that each member of the body will vote in favor of a proposal with probability p, for some p between zero and one.[4] The fact that the same p is used for all members simply means that we wish to consider the abstract question of the design of a political system, and hence we cannot assume special information which would allow us to treat members differently. Rae's theorem is then:

THEOREM. *Judging by Criterion I, under the above probability assumption, majority rule is uniquely best among all $M_{n,k}$ when n is odd. When n is even, $M_{n,n/2}$ and $M_{n,(n/2)+1}$ are equally good.*

It is interesting that this theorem holds regardless of the value of p. We could think of p as representing the 'degree of acceptability' of a proposal. Majority rule is the best decision rule for deciding on highly acceptable (p close to 1) and highly unacceptable (p close to 0) proposals, as well as controversial proposals (p close to $1/2$).

Since Rae's article, there has been considerable interest in elaborating his result,[5] but investigations have always been restricted to the class of decision rules $M_{n,k}$. As we have seen, this restriction to $M_{n,k}$ leaves out of consideration other symmetric decision rules, and all asymmetric decision rules. In the next section, I will prove a theorem which generalizes Rae's result to the class of all simple games. That the class of simple games is considerably larger than the class of $M_{n,k}$'s can be seen from the following figures, due to Shapley:[6]

Number n of players	1	2	3	4	5	6
Number of $M_{n,k}$'s	1	2	3	4	5	6
Number of essentially distinct simple games	1	3	8	28	208	>1500

An added benefit is that the proof for the general case is considerably simpler than Taylor's original proof of Rae's result.

THE MAJORITY RULE THEOREM

On the class of all simple games, we can use without change Rae's probability assumption that all players vote 'Aye' with probability $p(0 < p < 1)$. On the other hand, since we now allow asymmetric decision rules, different players may have different probabilities of the collective decision agreeing with their decision. Hence we must modify Rae's criterion for optimality. An appropriate modification is

CRITERION I′. A 'best' decision rule should maximize the *average*, over all members, of the probabilities that the collective decision will agree with an individual's decision.

For instance, if a decision rule is asymmetric, but members are assigned randomly to positions in the corresponding simple game, as was the case in the situations we discussed in the first section, the average in Criterion I′ is exactly the expected probability that the group decision will agree with any individual member's decision. Our criterion specifies that this expected probability should be maximized. We can now state the

MAJORITY RULE THEOREM. *Judging by Criterion I′, under the Rae probability assumption, a decision rule for an n-member body is optimal if and only if all subsets of more than n/2 members are winning, and all subsets of fewer than n/2 members are losing.*

Proof: Let (N, W) be any n-person simple game. For $0 \leqslant s \leqslant n$, let w_s be the number of distinct winning coalitions of size s. We suppose that every member of N will support a proposal with probability p, for some p between 0 and 1. Define A to be the average probability, over all members of N, that the collective decision of N will agree with an individual member's decision. I will show that

$$(1) \qquad A = (1 - p) + \frac{1}{n} \sum_{s=0}^{n} (2s - n) w_s p^s (1 - p)^{n-s}.$$

To maximize A, one would make w_s as large as possible when $2s - n > 0$, i.e. $s > \frac{n}{2}$, and would make $w_s = 0$ when $2s - n < 0$, i.e. $s < \frac{n}{2}$. Hence the theorem. Notice that the conclusion is independent of the value of p. Also notice that if n is even, A is independent of the value of $w_{n/2}$. We can make coalitions of size exactly $n/2$ winning or losing arbitrarily, without changing the value of A.

To prove formula (1), first suppose that we knew that the members who would support a proposal were exactly those members in some set S of size s. We could then easily calculate the value of A for this case, call it A_S:

$$A_S = \begin{cases} \dfrac{s}{n} & \text{if } S \in W \\[2ex] \dfrac{n - s}{n} & \text{if } S \notin W \end{cases}$$

For instance, if $S \in W$, then the probability of group-individual agreement would be 1 for the s members of S, and 0 for the $n - s$ members not in S for an average value of $\frac{s}{n}$. If $S \in W$ the probabilities are reversed.

Now denote by $P(S)$ the probability that S will indeed be the set of members who support a proposal. Under our probability assumption $P(S) = p^s (1 - p)^{n-s}$. Then for the general case, we will have

$$A = \sum_{S \subset N} A_S \cdot P(S) = \sum_{S \in W} \frac{s}{n} p^s (1 - p)^{n-s}$$

$$+ \sum_{S \notin W} \frac{n - s}{n} p^s (1 - p)^{n-s}$$

Finally, there are w_s winning coalitions of size s, and $\binom{n}{s} - w_s$ losing coalitions of size s, so we get

$$A = \sum_{s=0}^{n} w_s \cdot \frac{s}{n} \cdot p^s (1 - p)^{n-s} +$$

$$+ \sum_{s=0}^{n} \left(\binom{n}{s} - w_s \right) \left(\frac{n - s}{n} \right) p^s (1 - p)^{n-s}$$

$$= \frac{1}{n} \sum_{s=0}^{n} (n - s) \binom{n}{s} p^s (1 - p)^{n-s}$$

$$+ \frac{1}{n} \sum_{s=0}^{n} (2s - n) w_s p^s (1 - p)^{n-s}$$

To get formula (1), just note that the first sum is the expected number of opponents of the proposal, which is equal to $n(1 - p)$. *Q.E.D.*

COROLLARY. If n is odd, majority rule is the unique optimal decision rule, judging by Criterion I'. If n is even, majority rule is one among many optimal decision rules, but all other optimal decision rules differ from majority rule only in how they treat coalitions of size exactly $n/2$.

Some comments are in order about this theorem and corollary. First, we have a justification for majority rule which is independent of assuming that players' roles must be symmetric. Let us call the probability that the collective decision will agree with the decision of some individual member, that member's *agreement index*. Assume for definiteness that n is odd. If we deviate from majority rule in an asymmetric manner, some members' agreement indices may go up, while others may go down. The majority rule theorem says that the total amount of lowering of agreement indices must exceed the total amount of raising. Deviations from majority rule will hurt more than they will help.

Secondly, consider the decision rules discussed in the first section. In the asymmetric decision rules discussed there, the distinguished players (the dictator, the members of the oligarchy, the committee members) will have higher agreement indices than they would under majority rule. However, the other members of the body will have lower agreement indices, and by the majority rule theorem the total loss is greater than the total gain. Thus if roles were assigned randomly, any member's expected probability of having the group decision agree with his, would be lower than it would be under straight majority rule. In a plebiscite of two or more stages, hence in the pure delegate model of representative democracy, every member's agreement index must be lower than it would be under majority rule. The interesting question of how much lower has been treated (for the special case $p = 1/2$) by James Coleman.[7]

ADDITIONAL CRITERIA AND THE CASE OF n EVEN

There are several other reasonable criteria which could be considered in choosing a preferred decision rule. In this section, I will consider three such criteria, all of which are satisfied by majority rule when n is odd. Of special interest, then, will be the case of n even, when majority rule is not uniquely optimal by Criterion I'. One interesting question is whether new criteria might make majority rule uniquely 'best' in this case also. I will be particularly concerned with small even n, where majority rule frequently produces deadlocks.

Although we have fruitfully avoided a symmetry assumption thus far, it is certainly a prime candidate for an additional criterion:

CRITERION II.   A 'best' decision rule should be symmetric.

Thus we would want to restrict our decision rule to lie in the class of symmetric n-person simple games. The key problem is to define 'symmetric' precisely. For instance, the two stage plebiscite certainly seems to be symmetric, but in exactly what sense? The following definition is common in game theory:

Definition. A simple game (N,W) is *symmetric* if, for any two players i and j in N, here is a permutation π of the set N such that

(1) $\pi(i) = j$
(2) $S \in W$ if and only if $\pi(S) \in W$.

Thus the permutation π is required to take i into j and to leave the collection of winning coalitions unchanged. The definition formalizes the idea that i and j should occupy similar positions vis à vis the collection of winning coalitions.[8] It is possible to check that when a game is symmetric in this sense, all players have the same agreement index (under the Rae probability assumption). Hence when Criterion II is satisfied, Criterion I' is equivalent to Criterion I.

Criterion II does restrict candidates for optimal decision rules when n is even. For example, when $n = 4$ there are eleven essentially different decision rules which are optimal by criterion I'.[9] Criterion II rules out all but four:

$M_4 = M_{4,3}$: majority rule

$M_{4,2}$

$B_2 + B_2$:   the four members are divided into two committees and unanimous approval by one committee is required

$B_2^* \times B_2^*$:   the members are divided into two committees, and approval by at least one member from each committee is required.

A third natural criterion will produce M_4 as the unique optimal decision rule when $n = 4$.

Definition. A simple game (N, W) is *proper* if there are no two disjoint winning coalitions.

CRITERION III. A 'best' decision rule should be proper.

The problem with improper decision rules is that if two disjoint coalitions can both ensure acceptance of proposals, they may well accept contradictory proposals. Majority rule is always proper; the last three games above are all improper. Interestingly, when $n = 6$, majority rule is not uniquely optimal even by Criteria I, II, and III:

Example. Let G_6 be the simple game with player set $N = 1,2,3,4,5,6$, where winning coalitions are all those with four or more players together with the following three-person coalitions:

$$123 \quad 124 \quad 135 \quad 146 \quad 156 \quad 236 \quad 245 \quad 256 \quad 345 \quad 346.$$

G_6 satisfies Criterion I′ by the majority rule theorem. You can check directly that it satisfies Criterion III. It is also true, but much harder to check, that G_6 is symmetric.[10] G_6 has one additional property which might favor it over M_6:

Definition. A simple game is *decisive* if it is proper and whenever S is a losing coalition, $N - S$ is a winning coalition.

In a decisive game, no deadlocks are possible. M_6 is not decisive, since if S is any three-person coalition, both S and its complement are losing. You can check directly that G_6 is decisive. If we add

CRITERION IV. A 'best' decision rule should be decisive.

we find that majority rule satisfies Criteria I, II, III and IV when n is odd. When n is even, majority rule satisfies Criteria I, II and III but not Criterion IV. In fact, when $n = 2,4,8,12,16$ there are *no* decision rules which satisfy all four criteria. However, when $n = 6,10,14$ there are such decision rules (similar to G_6).[11]: The general question of which even n admit decision rules satisfying Criteria I, II, III and IV is open.

SUMMARY AND CONCLUSIONS

We have examined the philosophical bases of majority rule as an optimal decision rule for an n-member body making dichotomous decisions. Our major criterion (I′) for an optimal decision rule was phrased in terms of average responsiveness to individual preferences: a 'best' decision rule should maximize that average responsiveness. We proved a theorem which implies that majority rule is uniquely optimal by this criterion when n is odd. When n is even, there are decision rules other than majority rule which are optimal, but they differ from majority rule only in how they treat coalitions of size exactly $n/2$. We introduced other optimality criteria, including an appropriately formulated symmetry criterion, but concluded that by these criteria, for at least some even values of n, we could not claim that majority rule is uniquely best.

NOTES

1. See for example Kenneth Arrow, *Social Choice and Individual Values*, 2nd edition (Yale University Press, 1963) or Peter Fishburn, *The Theory of Social Choice* (Princeton University Press, 1972).

2. The standard reference on simple games is L. S. Shapley, 'Simple Games: An Outline of the Descriptive Theory," *Behavioral Science* 7 (1962), 59-66. Because of the correspondence between (dichotomous) decision rules and simple games, I will use the terms interchangeably.

3. Douglas Rae, 'Decision Rules and Individual Values in Constitutional Choice,' [partially reprinted in this volume].

4. Rae originally assumed $p = 1/2$. Michael Taylor generalized the assumption to any p between 0 and 1 when he proved Rae's theorem in 'Proof of a Theorem on Majority Rule,' *Behavioral Science* 14 (1969), 228-231.

5. See for instance the papers by Richard Curtis, Wade Badger, Norman Schofield, and Charles Plott in Niemi and Weisberg, eds., *Probability Models in Collective Decision Making* (Charles E. Merrill, Columbus, Ohio, 1972).

6. L. S. Shapley, 'Compound Simple Games III; On Committees,' RM 5438PR, RAND Corporation, Santa Monica, 1967.

7. James Coleman, 'Loss of Power,' *American Sociological Review* 38 (1973), 1-17. For $p = 1/2$, Coleman treats the amount by which a player's agreement index exceeds 1/2 as a measure of that player's *power*. He then uses a Stirling formula approximation to show that a two-stage plebiscite (with m and k both large) results in a 20% loss of power, compared to majority rule (page 9 of his article).

8. The two-stage plebiscite is symmetric by this definition. For instance, suppose $m = k = 3$ and the players are $a_1a_2a_3b_1b_2b_3c_1c_2c_3$. The permutation $a_1a_2a_3b_1b_2b_3$-$c_1c_2c_3 \rightarrow b_2b_1b_3a_2a_1a_3c_1c_2c_3$, for example, leaves the winning coalitions unchanged and interchanges a_1 and b_2. Notice that the permutation which interchanges a_1 and b_2 but leaves other players fixed, would *not* leave the winning coalitions unchanged.

9. In Shapley, *op. cit.* (1962) there is a table of simple games with four or fewer players. The eleven optimal ones (by Criterion I') are $e,i,i^*,k,k^*,l,l^*,n,o,o^*$, and p. The notation in the following list in the text is also Shapley's.

10. The collection of winning coalitions in G_6 is left unchanged by the permutations $123456 \rightarrow 214356$ and $123456 \rightarrow 345612$ and enough similar permutations to take any player to any other player.

11. Proofs of these statements may be found in J. R. Isbell, 'Homogeneous Games,' *Mathematics Student* 25 (1957), 123-128.

19 • Introduction

As we have seen, for binary, ordinal preferences, bare majority rule is generally the best voting system for maximizing responsiveness to individual preferences. In "Is Democracy Special?" Brian Barry wants, in the section of the paper reprinted here, "to take this popular idea, see what it presupposes in order to be persuasive, and then ask what should be done where it breaks down." This discussion comprises about a third of his full paper, which more generally addresses the question of whether or not the fact that a law has been passed by a democratic procedure provides a special reason for obeying it. One of the issues pertinent to this question is whether having laws determined by majoritarian procedures is in the interest of typical individuals even though they might not be in the majorities that vote some of the laws. Barry's analysis of this problem is different from Rae's, however, in that it is explicitly cardinalist and therefore consistent with an additive utilitarian position rather than merely a ordinalist one.

Barry proposes two conditions under which to analyze the value to an individual of majority rule: (1) each person in the majority stands to gain as much as each person in the minority stands to lose on average on each issue, and (2) on a given issue each person has an equal chance of being in the majority. By a cardinal variant of Rae's theorem we should expect bare majority rule would be most beneficial to everyone if these conditions could be expected to hold. Barry then (in the paragraph before fn. 6) supposes that the second condition does not hold while the first does. He concludes that "It will still maximize the average satisfaction of all the people one might turn out to be to endorse the majority principle." This conclusion depends on Barry's Rawlsian argument from behind the veil of ignorance (or, alternatively, on an argument from the principle of insufficient reason): one is not supposed to know whether one would actually be in the majority more or less often than the average person. Clearly, however, if one did know, then one might strongly prefer a procedure which required super-majorities if one were sure to be in the minority most of the time. One might suspect, for example, that the well-to-do landowners, lawyers, and financiers who wrote the American Constitution did not choose from behind a veil of ignorance with respect to their probable positions in the society to be governed by that constitution.

Although there is a strong individual interest justification for determining law by majority vote in many plausible actual circumstances of conflicted interests, there is still a problem of what to do about obeying a law that is not in one's interest but which has majority backing. This is a variant on the problem of collective action treated in the first section of these readings: it is in my interest that the collective good of law by majority rule be provided; it is also in my interest that the costs of enforcement be kept low by mutual voluntary obedience; but it is not in my interest to be obedient in particular instances. I may want the collective good but I need not want to "pay" a share toward providing it.

We noted in our introductory essay to this section that, in the provision of a collective good, there may be a cost-sharing procedure that would be a Condorcet winner, that is, a procedure that would defeat every plausible alternative procedure by a majority vote and that also would defeat nonprovision (which is costless). It should perhaps not be surprising that obedience to the majority principle would be a Condorcet winner over plausible alternatives. However, as Barry's discussion makes clear, this need not always be so. It will be so if conflicting preferences are ordered on a dominant single dimension; it need not be so if conflicting preferences are ordered on more than one major dimension. This is an insight that has arisen independently in two modern realms:

(1) In the technical social choice literature it was recognized early that "single-peaked" preferences are not subject to intransitivities when they are aggregated. A set of individual preferences over a set of alternatives is single-peaked if: the alternatives can be arrayed along a single line (say, from left to right) so that each individual is located at a most preferred point on the line; and if for any pair of points to one side of the individual's preferred point, the individual prefers the nearer to the farther point. If we represent preference orderings by relative distance above the line, each individual's preferences will define a curve with a single peak as in Figure 6 in Barry's paper. The condition of single-peakedness can be generalized in various ways, e.g., to include single-troughedness (the social choice literature is plagued with unaesthetic terminology). The generalizations are discussed further in Vickrey's paper, also reprinted in this volume (also see Black 1958, Sen 1970, pp. 161-186). In the example (mentioned in the preface to this book) of the Roman Senate's vote whether to acquit, banish, or condemn to death the freedmen of the mysteriously deceased consul Afranius Dexter, it is not unreasonable to assume that preferences were single-peaked if the choices were arrayed on a line in the order acquittal, banishment, condemnation (or mnemonically A, B, C). Farquharson (1969, pp. 7-8) supposes that the Senate was divided into three groups with the preference orders ABC, BAC, and

CBA. That these are single-peaked follows from the fact that B is not last in anyone's ranking. With BCA added to the list, the preferences would still be single-peaked, but if either CAB or ACB were added they would not be.

(2) In the traditional literature of comparative politics it has often been held that societies divided along more than one dimension—say, along class and along religious or ethnic dimensions—may be unable to develop supposedly stable two-party systems and may be subject to volatile politics.

Barry's paper should present no technical difficulties to the reader. Unlike most of the selections in this volume, it is concerned with to applying the theoretical ideas of the social choice literature to the understanding of actual societies. Such application should help to make clear both the significance and the limits of those ideas.

19

IS DEMOCRACY SPECIAL?

Brian Barry

Martin . . . if government, in the sense of coercion, has hitherto been essential to society, that is because no society has yet been founded on equity. The laws have been made by one class for another; and there was no reason, other than fear, why that other class should obey them. But when we come to imagine an ideal society, would government, in this sense, be essential to it?

Stuart I suppose there would always be recalcitrant people.

Martin Why should there be? What makes people recalcitrant, save the fact that they are expected to obey rules of which they do not approve?

Stuart But make your institutions as just as you like, and your people as public-spirited as you like, there must always be differences of opinion as to this or that law or regulation; and if those differences become acute there must be a point at which coercion comes in. . . .[1]

Social choice theorists often write as if all our problems would be over if (*per impossibile*) we could crack the Arrow General Possibility Theorem. Yet for a single dichotomous choice, the majority principle satisfies all of Arrow's

Author's Note: This essay was prepared during my tenure of a four-week Fellowship at the Australian National University, Canberra, in August/September 1977. I am grateful to the Department of Political Science in the School of Social Studies for facilities and for comments at a seminar at which it was presented. I also acknowledge with thanks comments from James Fishkin, Carole Pateman, Aristide Zolberg and the participants in a Yale Law School workshop.

Reprinted from Peter Laslett and James Fishkin, eds., *Philosophy, Politics and Society*, Fifth Series (New Haven, Conn.: Yale University Press, 1979 and Oxford: Basil Blackwell, 1979), pp. 172-185 and 188-189, some footnotes omitted or shortened, © 1979 by Yale University Press and Basil Blackwell Publisher Ltd.

conditions for a satisfactory system of aggregating preferences into a 'social decision' and other stronger conditions as well. For all this, [. . .] it is perfectly possible for a single dichotomous decision to be one that nobody with any elementary regard for self-preservation would voluntarily submit to. We thus get much deeper into the real problems of politics by asking not what is the best procedure but what one should do about actual decisions, taking account (among other things) of the procedures by which they were reached.

In order to offer any general statements we have to be able to imagine ourselves in all the possible positions that a person might get into, and ask what for someone in this position would be the right thing to do. A dramatic though not essential way of setting up the problem is to say that we are to imagine ourselves behind a Rawlsian veil of ignorance.[2] A person behind a veil of ignorance does not know his or her talents, aspirations, race, sex etc., but must choose principles that will be binding on whoever he or she turns out to be. Unlike Rawls I shall posit (and not suggest that I can derive it from the specification of the choice situation and the notion of rationality) that someone who is looking at all the possible positions he or she might turn up in will be particularly concerned with the protection of vital interests.

The first question to be asked is whether to have laws at all, and, if so, what is to be their status. One possibility is that there should be no rules of any kind. Another is that there should be rules but that they should have only the status of suggestions to aid interpersonal co-ordination. Alternatively, there might be a society in which laws carried sanctions but nobody ever considered anything except the sanction in deciding whether or not to obey the law (just as in our society we buy a bottle of Scotch if it is worth it to us after paying a large sum to the government); or there might be one in which the existence of a law was taken as a reason for obeying it but no sanction was attached to disobedience. Finally, the existence of a law might be taken as a reason for doing what it requires but there might be sanctions against disobedience too.

The question has been set up in classical 'social contract' terms, and the classical 'social contract' answer is that the last of these possibilities is preferable to any of the others: we need stable expectations that certain rules will be generally followed, we want there to be sanctions underwriting the rules, but we don't want people to keep the rules only when the sanctions are sufficiently probable to make obedience the course of action that pays on a prudential calculation. I think in general this is a good answer.

But it is one thing to say that one would wish the standard situation to be one in which people accept the existence of a law as a reason for obeying it. That still leaves open the question whether or not something's being a law should always be taken as a decisive reason for obeying it. And, if the answer to that question is negative, it leaves open the question of particular concern here, whether or not the law's origin in a democratic procedure should make a difference.

The first of these questions does not seem too difficult. Looking at the matter impartially, taking account of all the contingencies in which he or she could be exposed, it is surely apparent that our person choosing principles and institutions would not wish to be committed to unconditional obedience to law. In some cases, open disobedience or rebellion may be right. I shall discuss these later. But I should like to say a word here for ordinary non-heroic disobedience, in other words crime, that is to say law-breaking undertaken for private rather than public ends and with the intention of avoiding detection if possible.

A typical reaction among political philosophers is that 'the ordinary criminal may be viewed as acting primarily out of motives of self-interest—motives which render him morally blameworthy and socially dangerous.'[3] Presumably it is not simply the self-interested motive that makes for a presumption against the moral acceptability of ordinary criminal law-breaking. Most market behaviour is motivated by self-interest but is not normally taken to be *ipso facto* reprehensible. I think that the basic reasons for condemning ordinary law-breaking are that breaking the law causes harm to the victim(s) and that it is unfair to take advantage of the forbearance of others to secure a private advantage. The criminal is, in Rawlsian terms, a 'free rider' on the scheme of social co-operation from which he or she benefits. This rationale, however, fails to apply in two kinds of cases: where nobody is benefited by the actor's forbearance and where the whole scheme of social co-operation is not on balance beneficial to the actor.

We must, as Dr. Johnson exhorted, clear the mind of cant. Will anyone seriously maintain that he or she has ever stopped drinking in a pub at exactly 10:40 p.m. (assuming that the landlord is prepared to go on serving) out of respect for the licensing laws rather than out of fear of possible unpleasantness with the police? There are a whole range of laws whose observance benefits nobody—laws against Sunday entertainment, laws prohibiting off-course betting, laws against contraception and abortion, laws regulating the sexual relations of consenting adults, and so on. There can be no unfairness to others in disobeying such laws, and it is surely significant that people break them on a massive scale without guilt feelings. The 'what if everybody did that?' argument against breaking the law has no force in such a case, as long as 'that' is understood as 'breaking the same law.'[4] For *ex hypothesi* the case is one where disobedience has no ill-effects whatever the scale. And inasfar as mass disobedience has a tendency to bring about the demise of the law as a by-product, that is a plus factor in the reckoning. As Christian Bay has pointed out, the massive evasion of Prohibition in the USA had no high-minded motives 'for the Volstead act was usually evaded in secret, even if Clarence Darrow is said to have referred to bootleggers as fighters for American liberties and predicted the erection of statues to Al Capone in many a public park.'[5] But it still made repeal virtually unavoidable.

These are cases where nobody benefits from forbearance. The other cases are those where there are indeed beneficiaries from forbearance, but there is no mutual benefit. Thus, let us say that the system of *apartheid* in South Africa benefits (at least in the short run) the white minority. It clearly does not benefit the rest of the population and I can conceive of no reason other than concern for his or her own safety why anyone subject to this apparatus of legal oppression should pay it any respect. Published reports suggest that the hundreds of pass-law violators who are processed by the courts each day regard the inevitable fine as an incident of life in an unjust society rather than as the expiation of personal wrongdoing. Turning T. H. Green on his head (the time-honoured treatment for idealists) one may say that force, not will, is the basis of the State, at any rate in its discriminatory aspects.

We now need to face the question whether a law's having been passed by a democratic procedure should provide a special reason for obeying it. A common argument for accepting an outcome reached by a democratic procedure even when you dislike it is that you should take the rough with the smooth: you can't win them all, but in the long run you can expect to win more than half the time because on each issue the majority principle ensures that more people win than lose. I want in the rest of this section to take this popular idea, see what it presupposes in order to be persuasive, and then ask what should be done where it breaks down. [...]

Consider, then, a country in which issues are always dichotomous and in which the following characteristics hold: (1) on each issue, each of those who are in the majority stands on the average to gain as much satisfaction from the law as each of those in the minority stands to lose from it; and (2) on each issue there is an independent probability for each person of being in the majority that is equal to the proportion of the total number in the majority on that issue. The first condition says in effect that the stakes of each person are the same on any given issue (though they may not be the same on different issues). The second says in effect that, whatever we know of a person's previous voting record, we cannot do better than predict he or she has a .6 probability of being in the majority if the majority is 60%, a .7 probability of being in the majority if the majority is 70% and so on.

The second condition entails that, over a period sufficient for a number of issues to come up, decisions made in accordance with the majority principle can be expected to yield approximately equal satisfaction to each person. Adding the first condition we can go further: if we count getting the outcome you want as + 1 and getting the outcome you don't want as − 1, then each person can expect $(x - .5) \times 2$ units of satisfaction, where x is the average majority. (E.g. if the average majority is .7 each person can expect .4 units of satisfaction.) But in addition the first condition alone tells us that the majority principle maximizes average satisfaction, for it can never increase average satisfaction to please fewer people rather than more, given that the average gain of each winner is the same as the average loss of each loser.

If the person choosing from behind the veil of ignorance were seeking to maximize the average of the levels of satisfaction of all the people he or she might turn out to be, the first condition alone indicates that the majority principle is the one to pick. But suppose instead that the person behind the veil of ignorance were to follow Rawls's recommendation and choose a rule for aggregating preferences with the object of making the lot of the worst off of all those that one might turn out to be as desirable as possible. Then, because in the special case stated in the second condition everyone has the same expectation of satisfaction, it would still be best to pick the majority principle. For any other principle lowers the average, and, since everyone's expectations are the same, that means that on any other principle each of the people he or she might turn out to be would be worse off.

Let us take this idea and cash it out into the choice of sanctions for breaking the law and principles about obedience to the law. Obviously, when we say that people get satisfaction from getting a law they want or lose satisfaction from getting a law they don't want, we are speaking in shorthand. What people gain or lose satisfaction from is not the enactment itself but the operation of the law. If those who are in the minority on any law ignore it with impunity, they do not suffer the loss associated with it; but those in the majority do not experience the gain associated with it either, at any rate if the minority is large enough for its disobedience to undermine the law. But in the case as specified there is a net gain from each law (that is, from the operation of each law) and each person stands in the long run to share equally in these gains. Therefore, from behind the veil of ignorance it is advantageous both to support sanctions and to adopt the principle as binding on all that laws which have majority approval ought to be obeyed even in the absence of prudential motives.

Now, by contrast, suppose that the second condition does not hold, though the first still does. It still maximizes the average satisfaction of all the people one might turn out to be to endorse the majority principle. But if one is concerned to avoid the worst threats to one's interests, the majority principle is no longer so attractive. Take the opposite extreme from the atomistic society in which there is no association between one person's vote and any other's and consider a society permanently divided into two rigid groups. Each group always has monolithic preferences, so the same people are always in the majority and minority. The average of all the people one might be is still $(x - .5) \times 2$, though here x is simply the proportion of the whole constituted by the majority group. But the expectation of each member of the minority group is -1, since on every issue they lose.

If in addition we give up the first condition, we can no longer even be confident that the average satisfaction will be maximized by adopting that side on every issue that corresponds with the majority preference. If (as William Riker assumes in his theory)[6] politics is a zero-sum game, so that on every issue the amount gained by those who are on the winning side is exactly equal to the amount lost by those on the losing side (which entails, of course, under the majority principle, that winners always win less per head than losers lose) it would obviously be better to have no procedure for making laws. Anyone who wants gratuitous risks can always gamble privately—there is no point in forcing risks on everyone. And of course if politics is a negative-sum game (as some even more gloomy theorists seem to believe) the case for having no government at all is overwhelming. In practice however, even the worst state is one in which some laws are positive-sum: in South Africa, for example, it is clearly to the mutual interest of non-whites to respect the law against murder—all the more so because the police take little interest in enforcing it.

The upshot of this very crude analysis is that, from behind the veil of ignorance, a person of reasonable prudence would accept outcomes produced in accordance with the majority principle for an atomistic society or a pluralistic society, which we may take as the closest real-life approximation: that is to say, a society in which there are many groups and the relations between them are fluid. In such a society, the majority principle gives each group a good chance of being in the majority over half the time. This description of the pluralistic society is, of course, recognizable as the picture of the USA drawn by the celebrants of the nineteen-fifties. It is probably a fair description of the way the system works for the best-placed sixty or seventy per cent of the adult population. Conversely, the more closely a society approximates to the model of a monolithic majority bloc facing a minority which is always on the losing side, the more a reasonably prudent person would refuse to accept that, if he or she found himself in such a society and in the minority group, he or she would be bound to respect the laws that had been passed by the majority over minority opposition.

The assumption that all issues are dichotomous is a very restrictive and unrealistic one. Let me extend the analysis just one step, to the simplest case beyond: that where all preferences lie on one dimension. [...] In such a case the majority principle picks out one point as the unique one that is capable of gaining a majority in a pairwise comparison with any other. This is the point corresponding to the preference of the median person, in other words the person with exactly as many others on each side. In investigating the properties of the majority principle, then, all we need to do is examine the properties of the median.

Consider first a case in which these three things are true: (1) on any issue, each person experiences the same loss of satisfaction for any given distance between the most preferred outcome and the actual outcome; (2) for each person the loss of satisfaction is linear with distance, in other words it is always true that an outcome twice as far away represents twice as much loss of satisfaction; and (3) on each issue, each person has an independent probability of being in any position that is equal to the proportion of the total number of people in that position.

(1) and (2) here replace the first stipulation for the dichotomous case, that winners and losers gain and lose equal amounts: they say that the same increase in distance away from one's most preferred position results in an equal loss for everyone. (3) is a strict analogue of the second condition. And we get analogous results. Condition (3) guarantees that in the long run everyone can expect to lose the same amount (i.e. be on the average the same distance away from the median), and (1) and (2) guarantee that the overall average loss on each issue is always minimized by choosing the median. What this is really saying (given the first two conditions) is that the total distance from all the points on a line to the median is less than the total distance to any other point. This can be seen intuitively by imagining the people standing along an actual line. You start by standing in front of the median person and then moving away: in whichever direction you move you are adding an equal amount to your distance from some people and decreasing your distance from others by the same amount, but you are going away from more people than you are going towards. It is important to recognize that this is true regardless of the way the people are distributed along the line. Even if most are bunched at one end with a few stragglers out in the distance you still minimize total distance by taking up the median position.

We can therefore say, strictly analogously with our conclusions in the dichotomous case, that someone who was concerned only with maximizing the average satisfaction (or in this case minimizing the average loss of satisfaction) of all the people he or she might be would choose the majority principle (i.e. the median position) purely on the strength of the first two conditions; while adding the third condition (which provides everyone with an equal expectation) would make the majority principle the choice either of a maximizer or of someone concerned to minimize the losses of the person losing the most.

At this point, however, the analogy with the dichotomous case breaks down. In dropping the second condition for the dichotomous case—the atomistic assumption—we went to the opposite extreme and imagined a society with no changing of places at all, and decided that a person of

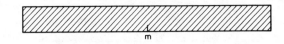

Figure 8.1

reasonable prudence would not endorse the majority principle for such a society. In the one-dimensional case, however, a similar total lack of fluidity in relative positions does not necessarily have such disturbing implications for the majority principle.

Consider the most neutral assumption about the way preferences are distributed: that they are evenly distributed along the dimension. If we plot the density of preferences on the vertical dimension, a distribution of this kind looks as in Figure 1. Now the interesting thing about this distribution is that the median position (marked m) not only minimizes average loss (as does the median with any distribution, given the first two assumptions) but also minimizes the maximum loss of any person. For if we move away from it in either direction, the people at the far end are made worse off than they were when the outcome was at the median.

As may be apparent, a rectangular distribution is not needed to generate this result. Any distribution such that the median point lies half way between the extremes will do it. Therefore all symmetrical distributions—that is to say distributions such that one half of the line is a mirror-image of the other half—satisfy the requirement. Examples are Figures 2 and 3. Of course, the average loss of satisfaction differs between the three distributions: it is greatest in Figure 3, least in Figure 2 and intermediate in Figure 1. The society depicted in Figure 2 has more ability to satisfy its average member than the society in Figure 1, and that in Figure 1 more than that in Figure 3. Failing some realignment of preferences—the rise of a different issue, perhaps—it might be as well for the two groups in the last society to split off into separate polities, or form a federation allowing each the maximum autonomy; or if they are too geographically mingled for that they might at least try *verzuiling* (functional decentralization). But if there *is* going to be one set of policies binding on all of them, the median is the one that anybody choosing from behind a veil of ignorance will have to go for.

The natural reaction to Figure 3 is, I think, to dispute the analysis and suggest that the median position is unlikely to be the outcome. I agree, but mainly because the situation as depicted is so finely balanced. The tension between the two groups would be extreme because so much was at stake: changes in the birthrates or the migration rates, or a little gerrymandering, could so easily swing the outcome a long way to one side or the other. The

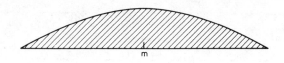

Figure 8.2

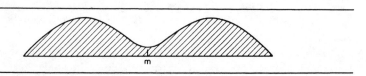

Figure 8.3

reasonably prudent person choosing from behind a veil of ignorance would not, I concede, give unqualified allegiance to the majority principle for a society so evenly balanced between two blocs, with so few people in the region of the median, as in Figure 3. The logic of the situation is illustrated by Figure 4. This shows how once we move off symmetry with a bimodal distribution like that in Figure 3, the median position leaves those in the minority group out in the cold. The average loss is still minimized but the maximum loss is great.

Notice in passing that moving the unimodal distribution of Figure 2 away from symmetry does not have the same kind of drastic results. Figure 5 illustrates the way in which the median shifts a little away from the centre, but not dramatically. A distribution of this kind may be thought of as a rough sketch of a politics of economic interest in an otherwise homogeneous society, where income and status follow a pattern of continuous graduation (as against dichotomous classes) but where the distribution of income and status is in the traditional 'squashed diamond' shape.

How do these results relate to those we obtained for the dichotomous case? We can establish two fairly direct parallels. The atomistic society, in which people distribute themselves randomly on dichotomous issues, is, I suggested, a rose-tinted model of the USA in the 1950s. It might approximate other societies with a fluid social structure, perhaps the USA and other settler societies at a certain stage of development. The one-dimensional model with random placement may be thought of as a somewhat more complex version of the same thing, in which we allow that groups may have a variety of different positions on any given issue. The alternative model of two rigid groups facing one another on successive dichotomous issues approximates the condition of a society with a deep structural cleavage running through it: a

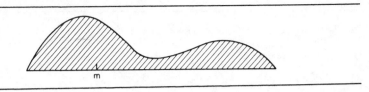

Figure 8.4

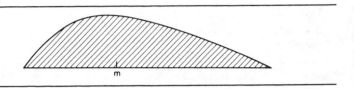

Figure 8.5

division based on ethnicity, language, race, or possibly (where there is a sharp gulf between landlords and peasants or owners and workers) on class. The one-dimensional model with a bimodal distribution refines on this by allowing for a certain range of position within the groups and the possibility of some people holding intermediate positions. But the general implications are much the same as in the dichotomous case: outcomes in accordance with the majority principle may be highly injurious to the interests of the minority group.

Where we get something distinctively new from the one-dimensional analysis is in the case of a unimodal distribution. For we can see here how fixed positions may be compatible with acceptable outcomes. Admittedly the people on the two tails of the distribution will be dissatisfied with the outcomes that the majority principle calls for, that is to say the outcomes preferred by the person in the median position. But what alternative can they seriously propose? Those in the minority group have a good cause for complaint when there is a bimodal distribution and the median person is in the majority group. But with a unimodal distribution any move towards one set of extremists leaves the extremists at the other end even more dissatisfied than they were in the first place. From behind the veil of ignorance it would be inconsistent to say that if one found oneself on one tail of a unimodal distribution one should resist outcomes corresponding to the median position without acknowledging that those at the other extreme should also resist them, for there is no way of distinguishing the two. 'The end I happen to be at' will not do.

Although we started from a defence of the majority principle that was expressed in terms of winning and losing, we have finished up with a case

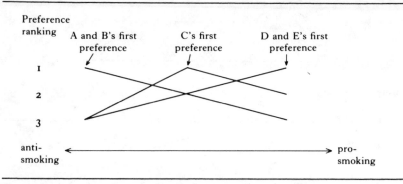

Figure 8.6

where the majority principle can be defended even though the line-up is the same on each question that comes up for decision. That is to say, on each question the same single dimension defines the positions of each of the actors and they find themselves in the same places. We got here by transforming the winning and losing in the dichotomous case into a value of getting the outcome you want and a (negative) value of getting the outcome other than the one you want. We then made a natural extension of that way of thinking so as to accommodate the analysis in one dimension by assuming that the distance between the preferred outcome and the actual outcome provides a measure of dissatisfaction with that outcome. We are thus able to evaluate the median position as an outcome in terms of the distribution of loss of satisfaction that it produces, without any need to refer to winning and losing.

To see that winning and losing is irrelevant, [consider] the set-up depicted in Figure 6, where A and B take one position, C a middle position and D and E the position at the other end of the line. If the final vote on each issue is between C's position and one of the others (which is what we would normally expect) C will always be on the winning side but whether or not A and B 'win' or D and E 'win' depends on the way the choice is structured. If the choice is between the outcome preferred by A and B and the outcome preferred by C, then C, D and E will vote together and A and B will go down to defeat. If the position preferred by D and E is set against that preferred by C, we will get the result that A, B and C combine against D and E. Yet in both cases the outcome is the same: the outcome preferred by C is the one that gets a majority. This simple example illustrates the fallacy of counting up 'wins' and 'losses' where there are more than two possible positions. The only sound procedure is to compare the position preferred by each actor with the actual outcome.

The unimodal model of preference-distribution fits reasonably well the Scandinavian countries, England, New Zealand and Australia. Other countries are not adequately represented by this unimodal model, in which political differences reflect the socioeconomic stratification of an otherwise relatively homogeneous population. Yet at the same time they do not exhibit the radical pluralism of societies such as Guyana, the Lebanon, Indonesia, Nigeria, Cyprus or Malaysia, in which different groups live side by side sharing no common institutions except those of the state. These other societies, of which the Netherlands and Belgium are paradigmatic, have a division between 'spiritual families' (and, in the Belgian case, an ethnic cleavage) but are at the same time sufficiently integrated to have the potential for a politics of socioeconomic interest cutting across these ascriptive lines. An adequate model of preference-distribution in such societies requires two or even three dimensions. However, except for special cases, there is no longer a unique point picked out by the majority principle once we move away from one dimension. There is in general no Condorcet winner, no point capable of gaining a majority over all others. The problem of circularity rears its head once more.

What would be a sensible attitude to adopt towards obedience to law? Although we do not observe people choosing from behind a veil of ignorance, we do see the way they choose in real life and from that we can infer the relative strength of different motives—information that would be needed before an intelligent choice could be made from behind the veil of ignorance. And if we look at the empirical evidence we find that people do in fact tend to deny the legitimacy of a regime—however much it may bolster itself up by appeals to the majority principle—if they find the group to which they belong systematically discriminated against, treated as second class citizens, denied cultural expression or communal organization and generally not dealt with in terms of equal partnership.

It does not follow from that, however, that disobedience should be prescribed from behind the veil of ignorance. We need to examine the evidence. It seems clear that resistance to the majority has in some instances produced a more acceptable outcome, especially where it was backed up by the threat that disunity within the country might result in its loss of independence. If we look at instances where majorities have drawn back from pressing their maximum claims and accepted minorities as equal partners in what has been called 'consociational democracy,'[7] we find that they come about when the minority has established (given the background of the international situation) a capacity to cause trouble to the majority. These conditions can be seen in the stock examples of the conciliation of a minority: the Swiss settlement in 1848 following the Sonderbund war, the Dutch 'pacification' of 1917, the complex Lebanese balancing act and the

Austrian compromise between 'black' and 'red' in 1945. In two cases (Switzerland and Austria) the minority lost a civil war, and in the Lebanese case the possibility of a civil war was (as recent events have tragically proved) too clear to miss. At the same time, in all of them, the international situation was threatening. Switzerland's integrity was threatened by the growing idea that state boundaries should correspond to 'nationalities,' with the prospect that Switzerland might be dismembered and the parts absorbed into national states. The risk to the survival of the Netherlands of harbouring a discontented minority predominantly located on its border with Germany are too clear to need spelling out. The position of the Lebanon has always meant that internal disturbances risked outside intervention—as in the recent civil war. And in Austria the country was under four-power occupation in the post-war period, the withdrawal of the Russians could not be taken for granted, and the country was bordered by states under Russian influence.

There are, it need hardly be said, other situations that are far less favourable to the minority, where the only effect of resistance is to increase the degree of injustice and repression. In such cases, the minority has prudential reasons (though no others) for refraining from resistance, and hoping that some new turn of the wheel of international politics will bring about a more propitious situation, in which the ability to create a disturbance will be a stronger bargaining counter.

NOTES

1. G. Lowes Dickinson, *Justice and Liberty: A Political Dialogue* (London: Allen and Unwin, 1908, repr. 1943), p. 125.

2. John Rawls, *A Theory of Justice* (Cambridge, Mass.: Harvard University Press, 1971), pp. 136-42.

3. Jeffrie G. Murphy, in his Introduction to a book of readings on *Civil Disobedience and Violence* (Belmont, Calif.: Wadsworth, 1971), p. 2.

4. Compare Richard A. Wasserstrom, 'The Obligation to Obey the Law,' reprinted in Bedau, *Civil Disobedience: Theory and Practice* (New York: Pegasus, 1969), pp. 256-62.

5. Christian Bay, 'Civil Disobedience: Prerequisite for Democracy in Mass Society,' reprinted in Murphy, *Civil Disobedience and Violence*, pp. 73-92 at p. 85.

6. W. Riker, *A Theory of Political Coalitions* (New Haven: Yale University Press, 1962).

7. For a critical discussion of the concept, see my 'Review Article: Political Accommodation and Consociational Democracy,' *The British Journal of Political Science*, 5 (1975): pp. 477-505.

Perhaps the most thorough brief survey of the issues implicit in Arrow's theorem is William Vickrey's classic, "Utility, Strategy, and Social Decision Rules." Vickrey explains the background of the theorem, presents a remarkably lucid, short proof of it, discusses ways around the conclusion by relaxing its conditions, and then lays out a problem which, more than a decade later, was to become a, perhaps the, central concern of the contemporary Arrow literature—the problem of strategic manipulation of outcomes by misrepresentation of preferences. (We have reprinted only about half of Vickrey's paper, which goes on to consider numerous other issues from ways of introducing cardinal utility and interpersonal comparisons to the role of economics in the analysis of social choice.)

That every choice rule is subject to manipulation is the argument of the subsequent selection by Gibbard. What Gibbard essentially does is prove Vickrey's conjecture near the end of this selection that if a social choice procedure "is to be immune to strategy and be defined over a comprehensive range of admissible rankings, it must satisfy the independence criterion [condition I]." Before this conjecture, Vickrey shows that if condition I is met so that all rankings can be established by pairwise comparisons, there can be no room for increasing one's effect on the outcome by misrepresenting one's preferences. Since May and others claim that majority rule over binary alternative sets satisfies condition I, one might think that majority rule is therefore safe against strategic manipulation. But we know that majority rule in legislatures is subject to regular manipulation by vote-trading, or log-rolling. Where have we gone awry?

Recall from our introduction to this section of readings that the commonplace problem of majority rule, May's problem in the selection reprinted here, is fundamentally different from Arrow's problem. Arrow is concerned with ordering all possible *complete* states of affairs. Obviously, any two complete states of affairs are mutually exclusive—either one obtains or another does. In actual instances of majority rule, we choose officials or laws from numerous fields of candidates. In the extreme case we vote for dozens of candidates for dozens of offices at once. Hence, we make numerous separate choices under majority rule and the outcomes, our aggregate choices, are not all mutually exclusive.

Now consider May's claim (in the opening paragraph of his selection reprinted here) that majority rule has the attractive property that it is consistent with condition I. This is true only in certain limited circumstances. It is consistent with condition I in Arrow's context because Arrow is concerned with a once-and-for-all choice of the best state of affairs out of all states of affairs. It is not consistent with condition I in typical majority rule contexts in which decisions over various related issues or candidates are taken more or less sequentially even if each election is over a binary choice. In such a context my preference for x over y may be contingent on the outcome of the vote between z and w. My joint preferences might be in the order xz, yw, xw, yz—but in this case, I cannot say I prefer x to y until I know whether z or w will prevail. Note that Arrow's condition U (universal domain) mandates that someone be able to have the joint preference ordering given here. One might assert that such an ordering is individually irrational, in which case Arrow's theorem is severely undercut. But anyone who would assert its irrationality might consider commonplace preferences for combinations of x (roast beef) or y (pastrami) with z (kaiser roll) or w (rye). Not everyone need have the joint preference ordering beef on roll, pastrami on rye, beef on rye, pastrami on roll, but some of us surely do have. Of course, this is a trivial complication compared to what we encounter in fuller and typical circumstances. For example, if we did not hesitate to revolt sensitive palates, we could complicate matters by introducing the third pair, mustard-mayonnaise.

The only way to make majority rule over piecemeal votes on candidates or issues rather than over complete states of affairs consistent with condition I is to stipulate for a given pairwise choice that everyone's preferences over that pair are independent of anything else. But that is a sure way to make our theory irrelevant to the analysis of actual institutions. The independence criterion makes good sense in Arrow's context; it makes little sense in contexts of piecemeal choices, i.e., in actual contexts. And where condition I makes little sense, strategic misrepresentation of preferences may, as Vickrey suggests, make very much sense.

20

UTILITY, STRATEGY, AND SOCIAL DECISION RULES

William Vickrey

A social welfare function can be thought of as an operator which, when fed data relating to the preferences of the individuals in a society, will produce a social choice. Much if not all of welfare economics can be considered to be essentially a search for such social welfare functions having acceptable properties. Arrow's justly famous but often misunderstood impossibility theorem is in effect a signpost warning that certain approaches to the search for social welfare functions lead to a dead end. As a first step in considering the current state of welfare economics, it is important to be clear as to just what roads are in fact impassable: exploration of the possibilities for circumventing the impasse will then be more effective.

ARROW'S THEOREM

From the time of Bentham until fairly recently, the underlying basis of much of welfare economics could be expressed in terms of a social welfare function consisting of the summation of individual utilities over all members of society, and ranking social states according to the magnitude (or perhaps the per capita average) of this sum. Difficulties with cardinal measurement of utility, and particularly with interpersonal comparisons, have led to attempts

Author's Note: I wish to express my appreciation of very helpful comments by Abram Bergson and Robert Dorfman which have helped me clarify a number of points; this, of course, does not necessarily impute agreement to them.

to avoid the use of cardinal utility in the construction of social welfare functions. The notion of a Pareto optimum is, of course, an early manifestation of this tendency. Arrow's theorem is in effect an attempt to examine just how far one can get in constructing social welfare functions that will consider only ordinal preferences.[1]

Arrow's theorem states that if the arguments of a social welfare function are restricted to the rankings of the alternative social states in the preferences of the various individual members of society, then no social welfare function is possible that satisfies certain seemingly reasonable postulates. A set of such postulates, slightly weaker than the set used (or at least than the set actually required) by Arrow in his original presentation, is as follows:

1. *Unanimity. If an individual preference is unopposed by any contrary preference of any other individual, this preference shall be preserved in the resulting social ordering.* (This is, of course, the principle of Pareto optimality.)

2. *Nondictatorship. No individual shall enjoy a position such that whenever he expresses a preference between any two alternatives <u>and all other individuals express the opposite preference,</u> his preference is always preserved in the social ordering.* (This does not of itself preclude an individual's being granted a paramount interest in a limited number of choices, such that his preferences in this limited area are always respected.)

3. *Transitivity. The social ranking given by the social welfare function is in each case a consistent ordering of all the feasible alternatives.* Ties in the social ranking need not be excluded, though in any actual decision-making process some tie-breaking device would have to be resorted to, and the effect of such tie-breaking might better be included in the social welfare function so as to make it yield strict orderings only. If ties are admitted between two or more alternatives, the relation between these alternatives must be one of equivalence with respect to ranking among the alternatives, not of uncertainty, so that if xPy and yIz, then xPz.[2] We reject a function which tells us that x is better than y, but cannot indicate a choice between z and x nor between z and y; if x is better than y, then necessarily z is either better than y or worse than x (or both).

4. *Range. There is some "universal" alternative u such that for every pair of other alternatives x and y, and for every individual, each of the six possible strict orderings of u, x, and y is contained in some ranking of all of the alternatives which is admissible for the individual.* By an admissible ranking is meant one with which the social welfare function is required to be capable of dealing, in combination with other admissible rankings selected on a particular occasion by other individuals. Certain rankings might be excluded, for example because they appear inherently inconsistent by some test, or perhaps because they are deemed contrary to the patent interests of the individual

concerned. This form of the range postulate restricts such exclusions fairly severely: for example, it precludes any restriction on the voting of an individual which would prohibit his ever expressing a preference for a specified x over a specified y, though it does permit the exclusion of certain triplets of the form $xPyPz$. It will be seen later that it is possible to obtain the basic result with range postulates less demanding than this, but more complicated.

5. *Independence. The social choice between any two alternatives shall not be affected by the removal or addition of other alternatives to the field of feasible alternatives under consideration.*

PROOF OF THE ARROW IMPOSSIBILITY THEOREM

A proper appreciation of the scope of the theorem is facilitated by going over a brief proof of the theorem. Such a proof in terms of the above postulates is made possible by introducing the concept of the "decisive set." A set of individuals D is here defined to be decisive for alternative x against alternative y in the context of a given social welfare function, if the function is such that whenever all individuals in D express a preference for x over y and all other individuals express the contrary preference, then the social welfare function yields a social preference for x over y. It can then be shown that by virtue of the transitivity and independence postulates a set that is decisive for any one choice must be decisive for all choices among alternatives covered by the range postulate. A one-person decisive set thus contains a dictator, which is not permitted. But it can be shown that if a decisive set is split into two subsets, one of these subsets must itself be decisive; since the set of all individuals must be decisive by virtue of the unanimity postulate, repeated splitting must eventually lead to a one-person decisive set, violating the nondictatorship postulate.

In detail, the proof is as follows. Suppose D to be a set of individuals which is decisive for x against y. Then by virtue of the range postulate, for each individual in the society there must be some admissible ranking of all of the feasible alternatives within which the alternatives x, y, and u are ranked $xPyPu$, and likewise another admissible ranking in which $yPuPx$. The social welfare function is therefore required to be defined for the case where all members of D have a preference $xPyPu$, while all others have $yPuPx$. But these preferences satisfy the conditions under which the decisiveness of D for x against y is effective, so that application of the social welfare function to this case must yield a social ranking in which x is preferred to y. By the unanimity postulate, y must in this case be socially preferred to u, so that by the transitivity postulate x is socially preferred to u. But in this case only members of D prefer x to u as individuals, while all others prefer u, to x; since in this case the preference of the members of D for x over u prevails in the social choice against the opposition of all of the individuals not in D, and since by the independence postulate this preference must prevail regardless of changes in the individual rankings of y or any of the other alternatives, the set D is also decisive for x against u. Iteration of exactly similar arguments with the members of D voting $zPxPu$ and all others voting $uPzPx$ shows that D must be decisive for any fourth alternative z against the universal alternative u, and a further iteration with members of D all voting $zPuPw$ and others $uPwPz$ shows that D must be decisive for any given alternative z against any other alternative w. Thus a set that is decisive for any one decision must be decisive for all decisions covered by the range postulate.

Again, let D be a decisive set containing two or more persons, let A be a proper subset of D, let $B = D - A$, and let C be the set of persons not in D, if any. Some decisive set D must exist, since at least the set of all persons in the society is a decisive set by virtue of the unanimity postulate. Consider the case where the members of A have the preferences $xPyPu$, the members of B have $yPuPx$, and members of C have $uPxPy$. Since the members of A and B agree in preferring y to u and together form a decisive set, while the members of C have the opposite preference, the resulting social ranking for this case must put y above u. If in addition the social welfare function is made to put x below y, in this case, the members of B will then be the only ones having a corresponding preference, so that B would be decisive for y against x. On the other hand, if the social welfare function does not in this case put x below y, it must by transitivity place x above u, making A decisive for x against u. In either case, one of the proper subsets of D is itself decisive, and a repetition of the argument eventually leads to requiring a one-person set to be decisive, i.e., to contain a dictator.

THE VARIATIONS FROM ARROW'S TREATMENT

While the above treatment follows the general approach pioneered by Arrow, there are significant differences. For example the transitivity postulate is included by Arrow in his definition of a social welfare function, whereas here it is displayed as an explicit postulate subject to questioning in its turn. On the other hand Arrow added another explicit postulate, not directly represented among the above five, which can be termed the "nonperversity" postulate. Stated somewhat loosely, this postulate is as follows:

6. *Nonperversity. A change in the preference expressed by an individual between two alternatives shall never operate to change the social preference in the opposite direction, other individual preferences remaining unchanged.*

The function of this postulate is taken over, in the above proof, by using the unanimity and the nondictatorship postulates in slightly stronger forms than the corresponding postulates used by Arrow. Arrow in effect omitted the italicized words in the nondictatorship postulate, restricting the concept of dictatorship to cases where the dictator is absolutely independent of the choices of others, whereas the postulate in the above form would term a person a dictator even if his expressed preferences could be perversely frustrated, in some cases, by his finding too many individuals agreeing with them. Given the nonperversity postulate, however, the two forms of the nondictatorship postulate are equivalent, so that the two postulates of Arrow, taken together, are stronger than the nondictatorship postulate used here.

Similarly, Arrow's "Nonimposition" postulate merely requires that for any two given alternatives, one is not always to be preferred to the other in the social ranking, regardless of individual preferences; this by itself is a weaker requirement than the unanimity postulate used here. But since the unanimity condition can be derived by applying the nonperversity postulate to the nonimposition postulate, the present set of postulates taken as a whole is weaker at this point also.

On the other hand, Arrow's range postulate as given by him appears to be weaker than that used here: he merely requires that there exist some set of three alternatives such that there exist, among the admissible rankings of all alternatives for each individual, rankings which rank the three selected alternatives in all possible transitive orders. Unfortunately this is not adequate: Arrow errs in assuming that he can restrict his universe of discourse at a crucial point to three such alternatives without loss of generality.[3] For his definition of dictatorship is in terms of choices among all possible alternatives; his proof that a (one-person) set decisive for one choice is decisive for all choices actually holds only for choices within the selected triplet of alternatives, and can be extended to other choices only if the range postulate is correspondingly broadened, as it has been here. This can perhaps be best understood in terms of the following counterexample to Arrow's theorem as presented: consider three persons choosing among alternatives w, x, y, and z, subject to the constraint on the individual orderings that w must be put either at the top or at the bottom of the scale; let the social welfare function place w at either the top or bottom of the social preference scale according to majority rule, and rank x, y, and z according to the preferences of a designated individual from among the three; this individual might be termed a "semidictator." This social welfare function satisfies all of Arrow's postulates as literally given; it fails to satisfy the stronger range postulate presented here.

RELAXING THE POSTULATES

The significance of Arrow's theorem is most readily brought into sharp relief if the various postulates are relaxed one at a time and the possibilities that are thus opened up for the construction of a social welfare function examined. This procedure also serves to show that each of the postulates given is at least in some degree necessary to the proof of the theorem.

Thus waiving the unanimity requirement admits the use of an imposed social welfare function which always gives the same arbitrary predetermined social ranking regardless of individual preferences. Waiving the nondictatorship requirement admits the use of a social welfare function that always makes the social ranking agree with that of some designated individual, who is thus the dictator. In either case the remaining four postulates are satisfied; on the whole, however, functions that violate either the unanimity or the nondictatorship postulates are of relatively little interest: they hardly deserve the name of social welfare functions at all.

INTRANSITIVE SOCIAL ORDERINGS

Waiving transitivity admits, for example, of the use of pairwise weighted majority voting, the weights being such as to make ties impossible while not giving any one person a majority of the weight. This, of course, permits the occurrence of the Condorcet effect, or "paradox of voting," but otherwise the postulates are satisfied. Another possibility under this head is the "Pareto" social welfare function which admits that x is socially preferable to y if and only if some individual prefers x to y while none prefers y to x; in all other cases the social welfare function produces a symmetric relation xJy which can be called "uncertainty" or "indecision" and which lacks the transitivity property of the "indifference" relation. That is, xJy and yJz do not necessarily imply xJz, as contrasted with the indifference relation xIy which is an equivalence relation.

Another possibility is that while in a given case intransitivity occurs, it occurs only among alternatives that are all necessarily inferior to some dominating alternative, so that if the dominating alternative is required to be actually available by some constraint on the nature of the set of feasible alternatives, intransitivity will always be irrelevant to the decision actually to be made. It is not easy, however, to construct instances of this.

RESTRICTIONS ON INDIVIDUAL CHOICE

Rather more interesting are the various ways in which the range requirement can be relaxed so as to permit a social welfare function to be constructed. Here the case most discussed in the literature is that of "single-peaked preferences," where the admissible individual rankings are such that the alternatives can be ordered along a one-dimensional continuum in such a way that starting with the alternative ranked at the top in any given admissible individual ranking, the alternatives will rank successively lower as we proceed in either direction along the continuum. In other words, in any admissible ranking of the alternatives, no alternative can rank higher than any of the alternatives lying along the continuum between this first alternative and the top-ranking alternative. This criterion is likely to be satisfied, for example, when the alternatives represent different amounts to be spent on some program, or when political parties or candidates can be ranged in order from radical to conservative. In such single-peaked cases, weighted majority rule, with suitable restrictions on the weights to prevent ties or dictatorship, provides a class of acceptable social welfare functions meeting the remaining four requirements; the result is the selection of the median alternative.

Less well known is the case of the "single-troughed preferences," which is obtained by simply reversing all rank orders in the preceding case. It also admits the construction of a social welfare function satisfying the four nonrange postulates, but in this case the result is fairly trivial, since the top ranking social choice must be one of the two extreme alternatives at either end of the continuum, which end being determined, for example, by weighted majority rule.

Single-peaked and single-troughed patterns do not exhaust the possibilities, however. Where there are just three alternatives, proscription of any one of the six strict rankings of the three alternatives permits a social welfare function to be constructed as follows: establish as a "standard" ranking one of the circular permutations of the proscribed ranking, e.g., if the proscribed ranking is $zPyPx$, the standard ranking may be either $yPxPz$ or $xPzPy$. Then pairwise weighted majority rule in which the standard ranking is added in to the voting with a weight of just under half of the total weight produces a transitive social ordering satisfying the unanimity, nondictatorship, and independence postulates. This can be described as the case where "one plus God is a majority."

With four alternatives we can have cases where we have neither a cyclical triplet (e.g., $xPyPz$, $yPzPx$, and $zPxPy$) nor single-peaked nor single-troughed patterns. With the following set of admissible orderings: $wPxPyPz$, $wPxPzPy$, $wPzPxPy$, $wPyPxPz$, $xPyPzPw$, $xPzPyPw$, $yPxPzPw$, and $zPxPyPw$, majority rule with weights that preclude ties or dictatorship yields a transitive social welfare function. Since w appears at the bottom of some of the rankings, w must be located, in the single-peaked case, at one end of the sequence along the underlying continuum, but if this were so, then only one ranking with w at the top would be possible; since there are four such rankings, all distinct, representation as single-peaked preferences is not possible for this set of orderings. A symmetrical argument disposes of the single-troughed possibility.

Since w never appears between two other alternatives in the admissible orderings, w cannot enter into a cyclical triplet, and since x never appears as the third alternative among x, y, and z, a cyclical triplet over x, y, and z is not to be found among these orderings.

Thus fairly wide possibilities exist for defining ranges of admissible rankings sufficiently narrower than that specified by postulate 4 to permit one or more social welfare functions to be constructed satisfying the remaining postulates, yet broad enough to cover an interesting range of cases. On the other hand postulate 4 is itself somewhat stronger than is absolutely necessary to support the theorem. Actually, what is required is that the set of admissible rankings be rich enough so that a set that is decisive for one choice, say for x over y, can be shown by a sequence of steps to be decisive for a range of choices wide enough so that if any single individual had the power to enforce any choice of his within this range against universal opposition, this would be considered an intolerably dictatorial position. Now if all six strict orderings among any given set of alternatives x, y, and z are admissible, then decisiveness for any one of them over any other, say for x against y, implies complete decisiveness for any choice within the field of these three alternatives. Accordingly, if we can start from some such triplet of alternatives and proceed to extend the field of alternatives by a "triangulation" process in which one new alternative at a time is successively added to the field of alternatives already triangulated, in such a manner that as each new alternative is added it is possible to find two alternatives already in the triangulated set such that for each individual there exist admissible rankings containing each of the six strong rankings of these three alternatives, one new and two old, then the unanimity, transitivity, and independence postulates together imply that some individual must be a dictator over the field of alternatives thus triangulated. In the range postulate as given, the universal alternative u served as a pivot around which all other pairs of alternatives could be triangulated, but there are many other less stringent forms of triangulation.

If the set of admissible rankings is to be the same for all individuals (i.e., they are all given identical ballots to mark), then it seems a likely conjecture that the possibility of such triangulation may be a necessary as well as a sufficient condition for the impossibility theorem to hold. On the other hand, the admissible ways of ranking the alternatives may well vary from individual to individual. For example some individuals may be considered a priori to have no valid reason for expressing a preference between two alternatives that are indistinguishable in terms of their direct effect on them; or one alternative may be considered to be so obviously or inherently more advantageous to them than the other as to warrant their being precluded from voting contrarily, whether from ignorance or for strategic reasons. If such restrictions are allowed, triangulation seems to be a sufficient but not a necessary condition for the Arrow social welfare function to be an impossibility, and the impossibility theorem may hold in terms of even less demanding requirements on the range of patterns of preference over which the function is to be defined.

Indeed, it may be possible to find cases where rather reasonable constraints on individual preferences make possible the construction of a social welfare function satisfying the other requirements, as generalizations of the single-peaked and single-troughed cases, or otherwise. But the problem of just what specifications of the range will make possible the construction of satisfactory social welfare functions promises to be a difficult one, particularly as varying degrees of partial dictatorship that fall somewhat short of that stipulated in the nondictatorship postulate may also be considered fatally objectionable.

RELAXING THE INDEPENDENCE POSTULATE

A more promising line of inquiry seems to be the consideration of various modifications of the independence postulate. This is indeed the postulate which, together with the restriction of the argument of the function to mere rankings, rules out the more usual Benthamesque welfare functions that are obtained by summing individual utilities. Indeed, it does seem rather prodigal to throw away, in deciding between two alternatives, whatever indication regarding the intensity of individual preferences for one over the other is furnished by the relative rankings of other alternatives, even though these other alternatives may not be actually available, either at the moment, or, indeed, ever.

Once we decide to relax the independence postulate, there are many ways in which a social welfare function can be constructed, many of which adequately fulfill the remaining postulates. For example, the sum of the ranks assigned to each alternative by the various individuals may be taken as indicating the social ranking, as is frequently done in preferential balloting; more generally, some set of values could be assigned to the ranks which might be considered to be more representative of the degree of distance to be expected between the ranks than the mere rank numbers. One attractive way of assigning such numbers would be by doing this in such a way that the resulting distribution of values would approximate a normal distribution with unit variance. Or some kind of sequential elimination procedure could be specified, as in various schemes of proportional representation.

All such schemes will, of course, be open to the objection that the social choice may be affected by changes in the range of alternatives presented to the individuals, even when the selected alternatives are not themselves excluded or included by the change. But this will be true in considerably varying degrees. Where the number of alternatives is small, omission or inclusion of one or two alternatives may be crucial; where the number of alternatives is large, however, omission or inclusion even of a number of alternatives constituting the same proportion of the total number may be much less likely to affect the result. Appropriate selection of the values assigned to the various ranks in the procedure indicated in the preceding paragraph may help to minimize the influence of changes in the range of alternatives offered, and the particular set of values which produces a normal or near-normal distribution may indeed under some conditions be the one that does minimize these effects. To examine this hypothesis in detail, however, would take us too far afield.

STRATEGIC MISREPRESENTATIONS OF PREFERENCES

There is another objection to such welfare functions, however, which is that they are vulnerable to strategy. By this is meant that individuals may be able to gain by reporting a preference differing from that which they actually hold. For example, if there are two groups roughly equal in numbers, with group A ranking the four alternatives in the order $xyzw$, while group B has the preference order $zxwy$, then if both report correctly and the social decision is derived by summing ranks, x becomes the social choice, whereas if the B's, instead of reporting their genuine preferences, report instead the ranking $zwyx$, then z becomes the social choice, and the B's have succeeded in shifting the social choice in the direction of their own preferences by a strategic misrepresentation. In general, whenever intensity of preference is given effect in the social welfare function, whether directly as such or through considering the number of intervening ranks, it will be to the advantage of an individual or group, whenever it can be discerned in advance which alternatives are likely to be close rivals for selection as the social choice and which alternatives are almost certain to be defeated, to exaggerate preferences among the close rivals, at the expense, if necessary, of understating the relative intensity of preferences for or against the less promising ("irrelevant") alternatives, whether this lack of promise is due to technical difficulty or impossibility or simply to lack of general appeal. Such a strategy could, of course, lead to counterstrategy, and the process of arriving at a social decision could readily turn into a "game" in the technical sense. It is thus not for nothing that we often hear references to "the game of politics."

It is clear that social welfare functions that satisfy the nonperversity and the independence postulates and are limited to rankings as arguments, are also immune to strategy. For if some individual prefers x to y, and as a result of his reporting this and other preferences correctly the social choice is nevertheless y, there is nothing this individual can do to improve matters for himself by misrepresenting his genuine preferences, even if joined by others who also prefer x to y, since changing of expressed preferences concerning other alternatives can, by the independence postulate, have no effect on the social choice as between x and y, nor, by the nonperversity postulate, can a change in the expressed preference of this group for x over y, say by some or all of the members claiming to prefer y to x, improve the chances of obtaining x. It can be plausibly conjectured that the converse is also true, that is, that if a function is to be immune to strategy and be defined over a comprehensive range of admissible rankings, it must satisfy the independence criterion, though it is not quite so easy to provide a formal proof for this. Immunity to strategy and independence are thus at least closely similar requirements, if not actually logically equivalent.

Of course, susceptibility to strategy is an objection of varying degrees of seriousness according to the circumstances of the case. Where the number of individuals is large and the social welfare function assigns no outstanding role to any one individual, and where the individuals are unorganized and without systematic knowledge of each other's preferences or advance information as to which alternatives are the more likely candidates for the social choice, no individual may have the knowledge required or the time and sophistication to work out a strategy that will have a significant edge over that of reporting his preferences honestly. But where individuals are few or well organized or well informed, and the number of likely alternatives is limited, the situation may pass from one analogous to perfect competition to one analogous to oligopoly where the process of arriving at a social choice may become a game of strategy with all the uncertainties regarding the outcome that this entails. An analysis of the ways in which a social welfare function might be set up so as to minimize the probable influence of strategy might be interesting, but appears from this vantage point to present formidable difficulties.

NOTES

1. Kenneth J. Arrow, "A Difficulty in the Concept of Social Welfare," *Journal of Political Economy*, LVIII (Aug. 1950), 328-46. *Idem, Social Choice and Individual Values* (New York: Wiley, 1951).

2. xPy means x is preferred to y; xIy means x and y are indifferent alternatives.

3. *Social Choice and Individual Values, op. cit.*, p. 51.

21 • Introduction

The general result in Allan Gibbard's "Manipulation of Voting Schemes: A General Result" is that, in any voting game over at least three alternatives, outcomes are subject to manipulation by misrepresentation of preferences unless the choice is made by a dictator or by chance. An equivalent theorem was simultaneously proved by Satterthwaite (1975). These proofs ended a long line of conjectures and more limited proofs from the time of C. L. Dodgson or, if one wishes to stretch the history, from the time of Pliny. Before Vickrey's conjecture in the preceding selection, the most interesting contributions were those of Dodgson and of Farquharson (1969). Dodgson recognized that point or Borda systems were easily subject to manipulation, as in the example Gibbard gives in his introductory section. Farquharson (1969, p. 63) found such general results as that, in order to best get one's way, in a committee of sincere voters, one should seek power, while in a committee of sophisticated voters, one should shun power.

Gibbard's theorem is based on a game theoretic proof (not reprinted here) that for a generalized game (what he calls a "game form") it is not the case that every player must have a dominant strategy. If I have a dominant strategy, it is a strategy choice in which I do at least as well as I would with any other choice available to me no matter how anyone else plays. (Recall that in standard prisoner's dilemma every player has a dominant strategy: to defect.) If I do not have a dominant strategy, I can generally achieve the best result if I can wait until all others have chosen and then make the choice best suited to take advantage of their choices. If I cannot wait, I can do best if I can accurately guess how others will act, and then choose accordingly. Specifically for present purposes, if I do not have a dominant strategy, then simply voting my true preferences is not a dominant strategy for me, that is, honest voting will not always yield me the best results. Hence, it may be in my interest to misrepresent my preferences (whether it is in my interest in any given instance will depend on how others vote). Gibbard's theorem says that in any nontrivial voting game, at least one player does not have a dominant strategy, from which it follows that every such game is potentially manipulable. Interestingly, once the problem has been recast in these terms, the general result seems almost obvious. Gibbard's great insight is to generalize the problem to the level of the general game and then to have the resolution of the problem for voting games fall out as a special case.

Why does Gibbard's result matter? His answer merits emphasis by restatement here: "It means that no system of decision-making but a trivial one can depend on informed self-interest to make outcomes a function of preferences. If a system does make outcomes a function of preferences, it is in virtue of individual integrity, ignorance, or stupidity, or because preferences are sufficiently predictable that the system does not have to accommodate all possible patterns of preferences." His result overrides Rae's theorem in practice since in actual contexts, as we have noted earlier (pp. 341-342), condition I (independence of irrelevant alternatives) is not generally met even when choices are ostensibly binary (and hence "trivial" in Gibbard's terms) because choices in one election are likely to affect choices in other elections. On the other hand, his result may often be less impressive in large-scale contexts, as Vickrey notes at the end of the last selection: "Where the number of individuals is large and the social welfare function assigns no outstanding role to any one individual, and where the individuals are unorganized and without systematic knowledge of each other's preferences or advance information as to which alternatives are the most likely candidates for the social choice, no individual may have the knowledge required or the time and sophistication to work out a strategy that will have a significant edge over that of reporting his preferences honestly." In such contexts, the logic of collective action in Downs's economic theory of democracy (see Barry's selection in the first section of this volume) may suggest that extensive effort to heighten the impact of one's vote is pointless. Still, one may wonder whether strategic misrepresentation has not occasionally been pervasive even in large-scale elections, perhaps because opinion polls and past experience give some degree of "advance information." For example, in the American presidential election of 1980 there may have been many voters who honestly preferred Independent John Anderson to either major party candidate but who voted for their second choices on the presumption that Anderson could not win—that he was an irrelevant alternative.

Gibbard's result is one of a general class of problems of strategic choosing, or gaming, to which we have become especially alert since the invention of game theory (von Neumann and Morgenstern 1944). In his paper in the first section of this volume Samuelson notes that misrepresentation of preferences is a problem for the public provision of collective goods. This is generally true if payment for the goods is from taxes based on benefits received or if demand for them varies across the population. As in Gibbard's game forms, when taxes depend on benefits one cannot be sure that some beneficiaries are not in fact losers or at least nongainers from the collective provision. Hence, they may have strong incentive to *claim* to be nongainers in any case in order to avoid being taxed to support the provision if exclusion is not easy. And when demand varies across the population, people may exaggerate their demand to ensure that average demand and therefore provision is at the level they prefer. Samuelson recognized already at the time of publication of that paper (1954) that this problem suggested the relevance of the Arrow literature to the understanding of the politics of collective goods.

Before reading Gibbard's paper, one might benefit from brief reflection on the nature of game theoretic representations of individual choices for collective outcomes. Ordinarily in game theory, with payoffs represented by utility numbers, one could immediately say which payoff and therefore which outcome among those available is preferred by any given player. In actual game situations, however, there are only outcomes (e.g., the election of candidate x) and one must infer the associated payoffs to all players. If the outcomes specified distributions of money, we would generally be sure of our inferences about the relative rankings of the payoffs to a given player. If I prefer less money to more, one would assume that something else in addition must be at stake—e.g., my pleasure in taking risks or my concern for equity or vengeance (see Marwell and Schmitt 1975, ch. 3)—or that I am mistaken or irrational. But when the outcomes are not in money or utility terms, we generally cannot be sure of our inferences about others' preferences and often we will have little idea at all except for those others whom we know very well. More importantly for present purposes, if the outcomes are not in money or utility terms, then it will often be plausible to suppose that someone could rank them in any possible order (i.e., to suppose that Arrow's condition U—universal domain—applies to the set of outcomes).

Gibbard's game forms are games in which the outcomes are specified but the associated utilities are not. Hence, I may fail to have a dominant strategy in such a game form only in the sense that my best strategy against one set of rankings of the outcomes by the other players may not also be best for some alternative set of rankings of those outcomes by the other players. As in the proof of Arrow's theorem, condition U is forcefully invoked in this claim. The importance of the claim and the importance of Gibbard's theorem therefore depends on whether or not certain alternative sets of rankings are plausible. In many fundamentally interesting contexts, such as voting for candidates for various offices, the plausible variety among individual orderings is sufficient to yield the prospect of strategic misrepresentation of preferences.

21

MANIPULATION OF VOTING SCHEMES: A GENERAL RESULT

Allan Gibbard

I. INTRODUCTION

I shall prove in this paper that any non-dictatorial voting scheme with at least three possible outcomes is subject to individual manipulation. By a "voting scheme," I mean any scheme which makes a community's choice depend entirely on individuals' professed preferences among the alternatives. An individual "manipulates" the voting scheme if, by misrepresenting his preferences, he secures an outcome he prefers to the "honest" outcome—the choice the community would make if he expressed his true preferences.

The result on voting schemes follows from a theorem I shall prove which covers schemes of a more general kind. Let a *game form* be any scheme which makes an outcome depend on individual actions of some specified sort, which I shall call *strategies*. A voting scheme, then, is a game form in which a strategy is a profession of preferences, but many game forms are not voting schemes. Call a strategy *dominant* for someone if, whatever anyone else does, it achieves his goals at least as well as would any alternative strategy. Only trivial game forms, I shall show, ensure that each individual, no matter what his preferences are, will have available a dominant strategy. Hence in particular, no non-trivial voting scheme guarantees that honest expression of preferences is a dominant strategy. These results are spelled out and proved in [a section omitted here].

Reprinted from *Econometrica*, Vol. 41, 1973, pp. 587-594, Copyright © 1973 by the Econometric Society.

The theorems in this paper should come as no surprise. It is well-known that many voting schemes in common use are subject to individual manipulation. Consider a "rank-order" voting scheme: each voter reports his preferences among the alternatives by ranking them on a ballot; first place on a ballot gives an alternative four votes, second place three, third place two, and fourth place one. The alternative with the greatest total number of votes wins. Here is a case in which an individual can manipulate the scheme. There are three voters and four alternatives; voter a ranks the alternatives in order $xyzw$ on his ballot; voter b in order $wxyz$; and voter c's true preference ordering is $wxyz$. If c votes honestly, then, the winner is his second choice, x, with ten points. If c pretends that x is his last choice by giving his preference ordering as $wyzx$, then x gets only eight points, and c's first choice, w, wins with nine points. Thus c does best to misrepresent his preferences.

Since many voting schemes in common use are known to be subject to manipulation, writers on the subject have conjectured, in effect, that all voting schemes are manipulable. Dummett and Farquharson define "voting procedure" roughly as "voting scheme" is defined here, and remark, "It seems unlikely that there is any voting procedure in which it can never be advantageous for any voter to vote 'strategically,' i.e., non-sincerely" (1961, p. 34). The definition of manipulability used here is roughly that originated by Dummett and Farguharson. The result they prove, however, applies only to a special class of voting schemes which they call "majority games," not to voting schemes in general.

Vickrey [this volume] makes a related conjecture on manipulability. He conjectures that immunity to manipulation is equivalent to the conjunction of two of the conditions[1] that figure in the Arrow impossibility theorem (1963). Arrow's conditions are jointly inconsistent, and hence from Vickrey's conjecture, it would follow that a scheme satisfying the remaining Arrow conditions is manipulable—almost the result in this paper. Indeed the proof in this paper proceeds roughly by confirming Vickrey's conjecture.

A result such as the one given here, then, was to be expected. It does not, however, turn out to be easy to prove from known results: the proof given here relies on the Arrow impossibility theorem, but not in a simple way. I leave the statement and proof of the results in this paper until later; first, informal elucidation.

II. MANIPULABILITY IN THE WORLD

A way of making decisions can be represented by a variety of mathematical structures. In the next part, theorems are proved about structures of two kinds, called "game forms" and "voting schemes." In this part, I shall argue that the game form and the voting scheme that represent a decision-making system pick out the aspects of the system pertinent to its manipulability.

First, then, let us provide definitions of "voting scheme" and "game form." A voting scheme is a formula by which individual preferences among alternatives completely determine a community choice, or "outcome." A voting scheme, then, is a function of the following sort. Let there be n voters, and let Z be the set of alternatives open to society. Call an ordering of Z *a preference ordering,* and an n-tuple of preference orderings a *preference n-tuple.* ("Orderings" in this paper allow ties.) A preference ordering is thus an individual's account of his preferences among available alternatives, and a preference n-tuple consists of a profession of preferences from each individual. A *voting scheme* is a function which assigns a member of Z to each possible preference n-tuple for a given number n and set Z.

A voting scheme is a special case of what I shall call a "game form," and the theorem on voting schemes is a special case of a general result about game forms which I shall give. A game form, as I shall explain, is a system which allows each individual his choice among a set of *strategies,* and makes an *outcome* depend, in a determinate way on the strategy each individual chooses. A "strategy" here is the same as a pure strategy in game theory, and indeed a game form is a game with no individual utilities yet attached to the possible outcomes. Formally, then, a *game form* is a function g with a domain of the following sort. To each player 1 to n is assigned a non-empty set, $S_1, \ldots, S_n$ respectively, of *strategies.* It does not matter, for purposes of the definition, what a strategy is. The domain of the function g consists of all n-tuples $\langle s_1, \ldots, s_n \rangle$, where $s_1 \in S_1, s_2 \in S_2, \ldots, s_n \in S_n$. The values of the function g are called *outcomes.* A voting scheme, it follows, is a game form such that, for each player, his set of strategies is the set of all orderings of a set Z of available alternatives, where Z includes the set X of outcomes.

Voting schemes and game forms are mathematical structures used to represent flesh and blood systems of decision making which might be instituted. They represent decision-making systems which leave nothing to chance, but let the choice a community makes depend solely on what its members do. Other structures could be used for the same purpose, but here, voting schemes and game forms are especially apt: each, I shall argue, applies to a wide range of non-chance decision-making systems, and each picks out certain aspects of a system which pertain to manipulability.

Game forms apply to the widest range of decision-making systems, and apply to each in a clear-cut way. Every non-chance procedure by which individual choices of contingency plans for action determine an outcome is characterized by a game form. Game forms, then, characterize any non-chance procedure we would consider voting. In representing a system as a game form, each possible way of voting counts as a strategy. In single-ballot voting of any sort, for instance, a strategy would consist of a way of marking the ballot. In sequential voting, a strategy is a way of marking each ballot on the basis of what has gone before. For any such system, it is clear what constitutes a strategy, and what each combination of strategies has as its outcome. It is clear, then, what game form characterizes the system.

For game forms alone, however, there is no such thing as manipulation. To manipulate a system, a voter must misrepresent his preferences. Nothing in the structure of a game form tells us what strategy "honestly" represents any given preference ordering, and hence which strategies would misrepresent it. To talk of manipulation, then, we must specify not only a game form, but for each voter and preference ordering P, we must specify the strategy which "honestly represents" P. Only then can we apply the definition of manipulation as securing an outcome one prefers by selecting a strategy other than the one that honestly represents one's preferences.

Manipulability, then, is a property of a game form $g(s_1, \ldots, s_n)$ plus n functions $\sigma_1, \ldots, \sigma_n$, where for each individual k and preference ordering P, $\sigma_k(P)$ is the strategy for k which honestly represents P. Formally, then, where Z is the set of all alternatives open to the community, each σ_k is a function whose arguments are all orderings of Z and whose values are strategies open to k. Manipulability is a property of a game form in conjunction with an n-tuple $\langle \sigma_1, \ldots, \sigma_n \rangle$ of such functions.

Where a decision-making system is characterized by functions g, $\sigma_1, \ldots, \sigma_n$ as I have indicated, it is characterized by a voting scheme,

$$v(P_1, \ldots, P_n) = g(\sigma_1(P_1), \ldots, \sigma_n(P_n)).$$

For each n-tuple $\langle P_1, \ldots, P_n \rangle$, $v(P_1, \ldots, P_n)$ is the outcome if individuals $1, \ldots, n$ honestly profess preference orderings $P_1, \ldots, P_n$ respectively. Whereas manipulability is not a property of a game form alone, it is a property of a voting scheme alone. Voting scheme v is manipulable if for some k and preference n-tuples $\langle P_1, \ldots, P_n \rangle$ and $\langle P'_1, \ldots, P'_n \rangle$, $P_i = P'_i$ except when $i = k$, and

$$v(P'_1, \ldots, P'_n) P_k v(P_1, \ldots, P_n).$$

For, then, if P_k is k's real preference ordering, given the way the others vote, k prefers the result of expressing preference ordering P'_k to that of expressing P_k.

Note that to call a voting scheme manipulable is not to say that, given the actual circumstances, someone really is in a position to manipulate it. It is merely to say that, given some possible circumstances, someone could manipulate it. A voting scheme is manipulable, then, unless its structure guarantees that no matter how each person votes, no one will ever be in a position to manipulate the scheme.

Manipulability pertains to voting schemes, and in that sense, then, a voting scheme picks out the aspects of a decision-making system which pertain to manipulation. In some cases, however, it will not be clear what voting scheme characterizes a given decision-making system. It will be clear enough what game form characterizes it, but the voting scheme which characterizes it is derived from the game form by means of the functions $\sigma_1, \ldots, \sigma_n$. What are we to make of these functions? They characterize "honest" voting, I have said. That makes sense as long as for each individual k and preference ordering P, it is clear what strategy for k "honestly expresses" P. For many systems of voting, however, it is not always clear what constitutes honesty. A system may give no single clear way to express certain preference orderings.

Suppose, for instance, a club is to vote first on whether to have a party, and then, if the motion to have a party carries, on whether to make it alcoholic. What strategy would count as expressing the following preference ordering: a nonalcoholic party first, no party at all second, and an alcoholic party last? It is not at all clear. Hence, although it is clear what game form characterizes the system, it is not at all clear what voting scheme, if any, characterizes it. Manipulability is most clearly a property of voting schemes, but many real systems of voting are not clearly characterized by any one voting scheme.

In short, then, game forms are more versatile but manipulability pertains more directly to voting schemes. Any non-chance system of decision making is characterized by a game form in a clear-cut way, but manipulability is not a property of game forms alone. It is rather a property of a game form plus the functions $\sigma_1, \ldots, \sigma_n$ which characterize honest voting. Equivalently, it is a property of the voting scheme defined from the game form g and $\sigma_1, \ldots, \sigma_n$. Unless, however, the system prescribes for each preference ordering a way to express it, the choice of functions $\sigma_1, \ldots, \sigma_n$ to characterize honest expression of preferences will be to some degree arbitrary. Hence the choice of a voting scheme to characterize the system will be to some degree arbitrary. Game forms most clearly characterize decision-making systems, but manipulation pertains to voting schemes.

The moral, of course, is that unless a decision-making system prescribes clearly how each voter is honestly to express each possible preference ordering, manipulation of the system is an unclear notion. A voter manipulates the system if, by misrepresenting his preferences, he secures an outcome he prefers. Unless we have clear standards of honest representation and hence of misrepresentation, manipulation makes no clear sense.

Even so, we can prove a general result on the manipulability of decision-making systems, and do so either in terms of game forms or of voting schemes. What we can show is this: however we characterize honest voting in a system, the system as we characterize it will be manipulable. All non-trivial voting schemes are manipulable, so that no matter what voting scheme we choose to characterize a system, the system, as characterized, will be manipulable. Whatever functions $\sigma_1, \ldots, \sigma_n$ we choose to characterize honest voting, honesty will not always be the best policy. The only exceptions are trivial systems—dictatorial systems and systems with no more than two outcomes.

Here is the result put in terms of game forms. A strategy s^* is *dominant* for player k and preference ordering P of the set of outcomes if, for each fixed assignment of strategies to players other than k, strategy s^* for k produces an outcome at least as high in preference ordering P as does any other strategy open to k. For player 1, for instance, s^* is dominant for P if there is no strategy n-tuple $\langle s_1, \ldots, s_n \rangle$ such that

$$g(s_1, s_2, \ldots, s_n) \, P \, g(s^*, s_2, \ldots, s_n).$$

A game form is *straightforward* if for every player k and preference ordering P of the outcomes, some strategy is dominant for k and P. The theorem on game forms says that no non-trivial game form is straightforward.

From that the result put in terms of voting schemes follows. [. . .] A voting scheme, as I have said, is a game form of a special kind, in which the strategies are preference orderings of the alternatives. Now take a voting scheme, and take a voter k and preference ordering P for which no strategy is dominant. Then in particular, honest voting is not a dominant strategy for k and P. Thus if P is k's real preference ordering, then given some possible way the others might vote, k does best to misrepresent his preferences. The voting scheme is therefore manipulable. The result on manipulability, then, can be put in terms either of game forms or of voting schemes, and the result put in terms of voting schemes follows from the result put in terms of game forms.

Some further comments on voting schemes. They characterize a large variety of systems. A voting scheme need in no way be democratic, and it need not guarantee that all individuals count alike. Some voting schemes represent dictatorships, some oligarchies, and some democracies. Nor must a voting scheme treat all alternatives in the same way. A voting scheme might, for instance, allow Jones a special say on what groceries get delivered to him. It might also rule out duels even if everyone wanted one to be fought. Some voting schemes treat all alternatives alike; others do not.

A voting scheme must assign an outcome to every preference n-tuple, not just to some. Murakami (1968, pp. 75-77) discusses group manipulability of structures which do not meet this condition, but as far as I can see, doing so makes no sense. However people vote, something will happen. If some preference n-tuples lead to stalemate and inaction, then inaction is a possible outcome. If someone prefers inaction to the outcome he would secure with honest voting, and he can secure inaction by misrepresenting his preferences, the system is manipulable. Stalemate must be counted as an outcome, and so in discussing manipulability, we should consider a function which assigns a value to every preference n-tuple and not just to some.

Finally, neither voting schemes nor game forms allow ties. Both take single outcomes as values, and for good reason. In questions of manipulability, the final outcome is what matters; manipulation, after all, is a way of securing a final outcome one prefers. Here we are considering decision-making systems in which chance plays no part, and to display manipulation of such a system, we need functions whose values are definite final outcomes.

In this respect, a voting scheme differs from an Arrow "constitution" (1967), which it resembles in most other respects. Both a constitution and a voting scheme take preference n-tuples as arguments, but whereas to each preference n-tuple a voting scheme assigns a single alternative, a constitution assigns a choice function—a function which, for each non-empty set of alternatives, chooses a non-empty subset. Now this subset may have more than one member. Some constitutions, then, allow ties.

Voting schemes rule out ties, for in systems which leave nothing to chance, ties make no sense. A voter misrepresents his preferences in order to secure a decision he prefers, and in the end only one alternative is chosen. In a non-chance decision-making system, it does a voter no good to have an alternative he likes tie for winning place if some other alternative tied with it is actually chosen.[2] To investigate manipulability, we must consider the entire system by which the choice is made, including the system for breaking any ties which may develop. That means considering a system which results in a single choice. Voting schemes and game forms, then, suit the present purpose; some Arrow constitutions do not.

Suppose, though, a system breaks ties by chance. Game forms and voting schemes, I have said, characterize only non-chance decision-making systems. What can we say about the manipulability of systems which make an outcome depend partly on preferences but also partly on chance?

A system which broke ties by chance would not be a voting scheme. It would assign to each preference n-tuple not an outcome, but a lottery among possible outcomes. We might call it a "mixed decision scheme." Let a *prospect* be an assignment to alternatives of probabilities which total one. Then a *mixed decision scheme* is a function which assigns a prospect to each preference n-tuple.

Just as we can talk about the manipulability of a voting scheme, we can talk about the manipulability of a mixed decision scheme. Call a mixed decision scheme *manipulable* unless it is the case that, whenever everyone expresses his preferences honestly in an election, the scheme assigns to that election a prospect each voter likes as well as any prospect he could have secured by misrepresenting his preferences, given the actual votes of everyone else. Whereas, with trivial exceptions, all voting schemes are manipulable, it is easy to find a mixed decision scheme which is not manipulable. Take the scheme which assigns to each alternative the fraction of voters for whom it is a first choice. In other words, each voter writes his first choice on a ballot; a single ballot is drawn at random; and the choice on that ballot is selected. A voter then has every incentive to give his true first choice. If his ballot is not drawn, it makes no difference how he votes, whereas if his ballot is drawn, the voter gets his true first choice if and only if he puts it as first choice on his ballot. His second and lower choices do not matter, for only the choice on the ballot can affect the outcome. Hence the system is not manipulable, and we have established the existence of a mixed decision scheme which is not manipulable, not dictatorial, and can allow a large number of possible outcomes.

That leaves the question of whether any non-manipulable mixed decision schemes are attractive. Exactly what is required for a scheme to be "attractive," I cannot specify. Clearly, though, the scheme I have presented is unattractive; it leaves too much to chance. On the other hand, a system which allowed only occasional ties to be broken by chance might be quite attractive. Work needs to be done on mixed decision schemes. It would be good to identify properties which would make a mixed decision scheme attractive, and to have theorems on the manipulability of classes of mixed decision schemes which, by various criteria, are attractive. No such work is attempted in this paper.

I have argued, then, that in discussing manipulability of systems which leave nothing to chance, we must consider functions whose values are single outcomes—voting schemes or game forms. For systems with an element of chance, we must consider functions whose values are prospects—mixed decision schemes. There exists a non-manipulable mixed decision scheme, but whether any non-manipulable mixed decision schemes are attractive in any way remains to be seen.

Back, then, to the topic of this paper: voting schemes which leave nothing to chance. Every voting scheme is dictatorial, limited to one or two possible outcomes, or subject to manipulation. Why should that matter? It means that no system of decision making but a trivial one can depend on informed self-interest to make outcomes a function of true preferences. If a system does make outcomes a function of preferences, it is in virtue of individual integrity, ignorance, or stupidity, or because preferences are sufficiently predictable that the system does not have to accommodate all possible patterns of preferences. For suppose a system accommodates all possible preference patterns, and makes outcomes a function of preferences. Then where v is that function, v is a voting scheme, and unless trivial, is manipulable. Hence for some k and $P_1, \ldots, P_n$, let $x = v(P_1, \ldots, P_n)$. Then for some y, yP_kx, but given the preferences of everyone else, for some P'_k, if k's preference ordering were P'_k, the outcome would be y. Thus if k acted as if his preference ordering were P'_k, the outcome would be y, which would be more to his liking than the outcome he actually secures. The way k actually acts, given his preferences, is not the way which best promotes k's interests. The way k acts, then, must depend on something other than informed self-interest—perhaps ignorance, integrity, or stupidity. No straightforward appeal to informed self-interest can make the outcome a non-trivial function of preferences regardless of what those preferences are.

I have argued, then, that game forms and voting schemes are the best subjects for manipulability theorems on non-chance systems of decision—making, and that the theorems proved here have regrettable consequences.

NOTES

1. *Independence of irrelevant alternatives* and *positive association,* which Vickrey calls *non-perversity.*

2. Vickrey [this volume] makes roughly the same point.

Epilogue

"When I make a word do a lot of extra work like that," said Humpty Dumpty, "I always pay it extra."

"Oh!" said Alice. She was too much puzzled to make any other remark (Carroll, 1976, p. 214).

I. INTRODUCTION

A theme that unifies many of the pieces reprinted here is that of rationality. Both the prisoner's dilemma and the Arrow general possibility theorem are thought to throw up some problems for the concept of rationality. More specifically, it is believed that they exhibit some sort of conflict between individual and social rationality, so that, when the preferences or actions of rational individuals are brought together, the outcome is collectively irrational.

It seemed to us that it might be useful to conclude this volume by backing off from the detailed arguments presented earlier, and offering some more general reflections on the notion of rationality and its use and abuse in contexts such as those of the prisoner's dilemma and the Arrow theorem. We shall begin in the next section by offering some speculations about the reasons for the rise of the concept of rationality to such a central place in the way people think about human action and human society. Then, in the third section, we shall take up the notion of a paradox, since this term has been used freely to characterize both the idea that the pursuit of individual self-interest may be collectively self-defeating and the idea that the aggregation of consistent individual preferences may give rise to an inconsistent collective preference ordering. In the fourth section, we shall apply this apparatus to the literature on social welfare functions, including the Arrow theorem. Then, in the fifth section, we shall take up the prisoner's dilemma. The concluding section returns to the general question of rationality in the light of the discussion.

II. THE VOGUE OF RATIONALITY

In former times, actions were likely to be condemned as sinful or wicked, and beliefs were likely to be denounced as false or heretical. There are many places in the world where this is still the rule. But in the United States or (to a somewhat lesser degree), in other liberal individualist societies, there is a strong tendency among people with any claims to sophistication to feel that the use of such strong terms as these would involve them in writing a check on a metaphysical bank account that they are not at all sure has enough funds in it to cover the draft. Among them—among us, if you prefer—the term "irrational" is one that rises most readily to the lips.

It is scarcely too much to say that rationality has displaced both truth and morality as the ultimate criterion for judging both belief and conduct. Even if we do venture to use terms like "true," or words out of the moral vocabulary such as "just," we are liable to construe them in some way that derives them from the more basic concept of rationality. Common sense might suppose that it is rational to believe things because they are true, and rational to do things because they are just. But we are more likely to reverse the relations and say that truth is what it is rational (in ideal conditions) to believe, and that principles of justice are what it is rational (in ideal conditions) to adopt.

Rationality, on the view proposed here, becomes prominent as a criterion in default of any other agreed premises from which people may argue. To appeal to rationality seems to require fewer presuppositions than does appealing to any other consideration. The question is, of course, whether the concept of rationality can stand the strain that this imposes on it. Are we entitled to expect that such a stripped-down criterion can do everything for us that we might have hoped to get out of richer concepts? The argument to be developed here is that any such expectation is unrealistic. The idea that the prisoner's dilemma or the Arrow theorem evince some sort of "breakdown" or "paradox" of rationality should be seen as a reaction to the discovery that the concept of rationality cannot be extended indefinitely to solve all problems of conduct and evaluation.

The thesis that the appeal to rationality constitutes a response to pervasive skepticism is not a novel one. John Stuart Mill put it forward as early as 1834 in general form. Following the Saint-Simonians, Mill distinguished between "organic" and "critical" periods.

> History, on this theory, proceeds in a series of alternating periods. Although the details of the course of events in any period are unique, there are only two kinds of period, the organic and the critical. In an organic period, society is stable and well organized; it is run by those with ability, and united by a widely accepted set of opinions. Those who make and change public opinion are a small but cohesive body—

like the clergy of the Middle Ages—whose views, accepted by the masses as authoritative, provide a framework within which all particular issues may be discussed. In a critical period, by contrast, the men in power are not the men with ability, and the men who form public opinion are not agreed among themselves. Consequently the old bonds of social cohesion begin to loosen. Men start to think for themselves, refusing to accept beliefs on authority. The presuppositions of discussion are lost, and society splits ever more rapidly into factions and parties not united by any common concerns or shared viewpoints. A stable society can emerge only when a new framework of accepted beliefs re-establishes its authority [Schneewind, 1977, pp. 163-164].

Mill argued that "public immorality is worst in sceptical eras, and it is in sceptical eras, when old views are being shaken and are widely seen to be weakening, that philosophy is most likely to be 'in vogue' " (Schneewind, 1977, p. 165). But it is a mistake to blame philosophy, which is a reaction to the breakdown of consensus, for causing it. In any case, the only way to proceed is by more rather than less enquiry into foundations. As Jerome Schneewind has written:

Carlyle, like Hazlitt, distrusted too much reliance on conscious rational thought. Mill, after a short period of submission to Carlyle's influence, reaffirmed the necessity of it. His own period, he thinks, is a critical one; and his own task, as he sees it, is to aid his times as a philosopher, not as a mystic or poet, giving a rational synthesis of beliefs, not an imaginative one. Moreover, there is no going back. The lessons of the critics of the old consensus must be absorbed, and a new set of beliefs must be developed which will be fit to serve as the basis for a new organic period [Schneewind, 1977, p. 165].

If Mill thought that England, France, and Germany showed all the marks of being in a critical rather than an organic period in 1834, it is hard to imagine what he would make of the contemporary United States. He might well, if such a society had been described to him, have doubted if it could avoid a collapse into a Hobbesian "war of all against all." Nor, indeed, would such doubts be farfetched today. In retrospect, anyway, that earlier period seems like one in which, although there was disagreement on the premises, there was a workable degree of consensus on the actual norms of conduct, and this made possible the mutual adjustment of expectations in social life. This practical consensus has eroded a great deal since then. When each person carries around a personal interpretation of the institutions of marriage or parenthood, for example, these institutions can no longer function as matrices defining the basic patterns of social life. Similarly, business affairs cannot be carried on very effectively if each person concerned has a different idea of the stringency and scope of norms of confidentiality, and if the only way of finding out about the norms each acts on (as opposed to professes) is extended observation. The results are, at best, lack of coordination and at the worst, unrestrained conflict. The concept of rationality is pressed into service, as we shall see, in a desperate attempt to plug the gap left by the absence or weakness of social institutions of the traditional kind. It is scarcely surprising that it fails. Societies cannot, any more than individuals, tug themselves up by their own bootstraps.

A more subtle change can be found among the philosophers, one which also has the result of playing up the importance of rationality as a court of appeal. John Stuart Mill, as we have seen, regarded the task of philosophers as being that of laying the intellectual foundations for a new organic age. *Utilitarianism* was intended as such a contribution (Schneewind, 1977, pp. 165-166). So, in a different way, was *On Liberty,* inasmuch as Mill believed that only from a variety of "experiments in living" could a new consensus emerge in the long run on the forms of life that were truly desirable.[1]

Contrast this with the views of recent American philosophers of liberalism. For Mill, lack of agreement on the constituents of the good life was to be regarded as a symptom of social pathology, a temporary and uncomforable state that one should seek to bring to an end as soon as possible. But if we look at the work of John Rawls (1971), Ronald Dworkin (1978), or Bruce Ackerman (1980), we find that the equal intrinsic value of all ways of life is maintained as a cardinal principle. Or, more precisely, it is claimed that the essence of liberalism resides in the refusal to allow social and political institutions to elevate any one way of life over any other. Although each individual may have private views about the relative values of different ways of life, these should be left behind in any discussion of the rules that should be binding in society. The state should be neutral between ways of life.

This idea obviously poses an immediate problem. If no appeal can be made to the value of some way of life that a set of institutions might support and nurture, what can be appealed to? Assuming that the unconstrained pursuit of different ways of life (or indeed the unconstrained pursuit of the same way of life by different individuals) is going to lead to conflict, there must be some authoritative rules to prevent mutual frustration. But on what basis are such rules themselves to be supported?

The answer that suggests itself again involves an appeal to the concept of rationality. For only a concept so devoid of substantive content holds out any hopes of having the desired property of neutrality. Whatever their aims in life, people would prefer, we must suppose, to realize them more rather than less. And they must appreciate that a set of rules rather than a free-for-all provides a better chance of realizing almost any ends. Thus, rationality requires that people settle on a common set of rules to bound their pursuit of different life plans. Of course, it is one thing to say this and another to produce a plausible argument to the effect that rational individuals should agree on some particular set of rules, and accept them as in some sense the best they can hope to get from their own irreconcilable points of view. It would be out of place to ask here how well our philosophers have succeeded with the self-imposed task of supplying such principles. What concerns us here is, once more, the enormous amount of work that the concept of rationality is being made to do.

If this were a book rather than an essay, we would at this point (if we had not already done so) launch into a full-scale treatment of the concept of rationality. For the present purpose, however, we need develop a definition only far enough to cover the points that will be made use of in the rest of the discussion. Let us, therefore, say that, at a minimum, rationality comprises two ideas: consistency and the choice of appropriate means to one's ends, whatever they may be. These ideas may be seen as being united by a conception of irrationality as self-stultifying.

If I contradict myself—in the simplest instance, assert A and not-A—I have not succeeded in communicating anything. Now consider a more complex type of inconsistency. If I say that John is taller than Mary, Mary is taller than Joe, and Joe is taller than John, I have not produced a coherent statement about the relative heights of John, Mary and Joe. There is no way of fitting my three assertions together so as to come up with a consistent ordering of the three in terms of height. Similarly, if I say that I prefer apples to pears, pears to bananas, and bananas to apples, I have not expressed a coherent preference ordering among the three kinds of fruit. Depending where I stop in the cycle of preferences that I have set up, I can put any one of them at the top of the list. Note that I am not saying that they are equally good. Rather, I am saying that each is better than either of the others—which is absurd. Of course, all of us would no doubt turn out to express many inconsistent preferences if we were asked to order enough pairs of things. But when such inconsistencies are pointed out to us we should, if we are rational, admit that something is wrong and be prepared to bring our pairwise judgments into consistency with one another.

It is sometimes suggested that rationality, understood in this sense, is a value that someone may or may not accept. We have no business, it is claimed, criticizing people if they choose not to act according to its precepts. However, a failure to reconcile one's pairwise preferences into a single ordering may, to put the matter at the crassest possible level, be expensive. Suppose that you prefer a Rabbit to a full-size Chevrolet because it costs about the same and is more economical on fuel; and that you prefer a BMW to a Rabbit because it is also fuel-efficient and a good deal roomier; and that you prefer a full-size Chevrolet to a BMW because it is even more roomy, costs a lot less, and spare parts for it are far cheaper and easier to come by. You could lose an awful lot of money to get back to where you began if you acted on your pairwise preferences—and unless you realized what was happening, there would be nothing (except bankruptcy) to prevent you from going round the cycle again and again. To put the point formally, if you prefer A to B, B to C, and C to A, this should imply (otherwise what does it mean?) that you would be willing to give up something (e.g., money) to get from A to B, from B to C, from C to A, and so on, indefinitely. Thus, your cyclic preferences could be a source of continuous income to a sharp entrepreneur. The connection between rationality and elementary prudence in the conduct of one's affairs thus looks compelling.

Let us now move on to consider means-end rationality. Rationality in this sense seems to presuppose rationality in the sense of a consistent preference ordering. As the Cheshire Cat observed to Alice, if you don't mind where you finish up, it doesn't make any difference which direction you go in. The question of choosing an appropriate road arises only when you have some end, or coherently related set of ends, that you wish to pursue. This said, the self-stultifying nature of means-end irrationality is too evident to require much elaboration. If what you want to do is get from Chicago to New York, you will do better by boarding a plane bound for New York in preference to one bound for Seattle. The story can be complicated to any degree once we allow for multiple ends with trade-offs among them and for uncertainty about the way in which alternative acts are connected to alternative outcomes. But the basic idea that it is irrational to act in ways that will not lead to the outcomes that one desires is simple enough and is all that we need for the later discussion.

III. WHAT IS A PARADOX?

It is often suggested that both the prisoner's dilemma and Arrow's theorem are paradoxical. We shall consider the Arrow theorem in the next section and the prisoner's dilemma in section V. To begin with, however, we should try to gain some insight into the nature of a paradox. That will be the business of this section.

The term "paradox" has in recent years come to be thrown around, not merely in everyday speech, but in academic social scientific writings, with a good deal of abandon. One author has recently given the world an entire book with the title *Paradoxes in Politics* (Brams 1976) which includes both the Arrow Theorem and the Prisoner's Dilemma among its paradoxes. In his preface the author writes that "the use of the word 'paradox' in this book should be distinguished from its use in logic and mathematics. In these disciplines, paradoxes, which are sometimes called 'antimonies' [actually, antinomies], describe contradictions between two apparently equally valid principles, or inferences drawn from these principles" (Brams 1976, p. xv). He goes on to say that most of the things treated in the book are not paradoxes in this sense: "I have preferred to highlight the 'surprise' aspects of these paradoxes" (Brams 1976, p. xvi). And this idea is also contained in the subtitle of the book: "An Introduction to the Nonobvious in Political Science."

Any reasoning that goes beyond two or three stages is, however, initially nonobvious; and it is easy to be surprised about matters to which one has not hitherto attended. What makes real paradoxes interesting is that the intellectual discomfort still remains even after one has followed out all of the steps of the reasoning.

The word "paradox" comes from Greek *para* (beyond, contrary to) and *doxa* (opinion) and thus means, etymologically "contrary to received opinion." It is thus quite similar to "unorthodox," though "orthodoxy" carries the sense of "right (or at any rate, established) opinion," whereas *doxa* is neutral on this score. Thus, in one of the most enchantingly eccentric books in the English language, Sir Thomas Browne's *Pseudoxia Epidemica* (or *Inquiries into Vulgar and Common Errors*), the author speaks of "the obscurity of the subject" and "unavoidable paradoxology" as difficulties inherent in his project of exploding what he believes to be commonly held fallacies (Browne 1968, p. 228). However, the kind of thing Browne includes in his "paradoxical" efforts is, for example, the denial "that a Brock or Badger hath the legs on one side shorter then of the other," which, he says, "though an opinion perhaps not very ancient, is yet very general; received not only by Theorists and unexperienced believers, but assented unto by most who have the opportunity to behold and hunt them daily" (Browne 1968, p. 278).

Those who talk about the Arrow theorem or the prisoner's dilemma as paradoxical do not, however, appear to mean simply that they are contrary to common belief. Indeed, it would be difficult to maintain that there *is* any common belief in either matter. The relevant sense of "paradox" is, or ought to be, that used in philosophy: "two contrary, or even contradictory, propositions to which we are led by apparently sound arguments" (Edwards 1967, vol. 5, p. 45). Thus, the famous paradoxes of Zeno the Eleatic purported to show an inconsistency between the deliverances of sense experience and the implications of a belief in the infinite divisibility of time and space. The paradox of the race course, for example, argued that a runner can never reach the finishing line because he must first cover half the distance to it, then half of what remains, then half of that ... and so on *ad infinitum,* so that he approaches closer and closer but never quite gets there (Edwards 1967, vol. 8, pp. 372-374). But this is obviously paradoxical in the sense already discussed in that it conflicts with the common observation that runners sometimes do complete courses. Zeno produced his paradoxes "to enforce predetermined Parmenidean dogmas" (Edwards 1967, vol. 8, p. 378). He apparently wanted to conclude that there really is something wrong with the appearances. Most people, however, at the time and since, have rather accepted that the appearances are veridical in such cases and have therefore either denied the legitimacy of infinite subdivision of space and time (as Aristotle did), or (as is more common now—e.g. Ryle 1954) have argued that infinite divisibility, which is a matter of logic or mathematics, does not entail any physical impossibility of the kind claimed by Zeno. What makes a paradox like Zeno's compelling is that these logically exhaust the alternative responses.

To familiarize ourselves further with this logical point, let us look at one other famous example of a paradox, understanding this again in the sense already specified as a case in which we are inclined to believe that there are good reasons for assenting to propositions that are apparently incompatible or have incompatible implications. The most enduring and troubling of the antinomies (or paradoxes) that Kant stated, and claimed to have solved, is the conflict between physical determinism and human freedom. On one side, the assumption of universal determinism seems to work everywhere it is applied, and it is hard to see how the little corner of the universe constituted by human beings should be an exception. On the other side, we also find it hard to see how we could make moral judgments about people unless we could hold them responsible for their actions; and that seems hard to reconcile with universal determinism. (Kant's version of the antinomy and his solution are succinctly stated in Urmson 1960, p. 206; the reality of the conflict has been recently and forcefully affirmed in a very useful discussion by Bennett 1980.) The point to notice here is that there are again only three possible ways of coping with this conflict of intuitions. One is to say that the conflict is only apparent and that we can have both universal determinism and a kind of human freedom that is consistent with moral responsibility. Kant held one version of this view (though an idiosyncratic one) and empiricist philosophers from Hobbes, Locke, and Hume to the present have held "compatibilist" views. The second approach is to reject universal determinism and maintain that our experience of choosing freely guarantees the falsity of determinism in this regard. The remaining approach is to accept that determinism and responsibility are inconsistent (like those who hold the second view), but to conclude that responsibility is what must be abandoned. All three approaches have difficulties; but what gives the paradox its bite is that they exhaust all of the logically possible types of move.

IV. ARROW'S THEOREM AND THE "PARADOX OF VOTING"

Having made clear the nature of paradoxes, we are in a better position to ask if there is anything paradoxical about Arrow's general possibility theorem. If there is a paradox here, how are we to identify the requisite two intuitions that are (a) hard to give up but (b) at least on the face of it inconsistent? Presumably, one will have to be the belief that preferences can be aggregated in such a way as to satisfy certain minimal formal conditions (like Arrow's), and the other will then be the belief that Arrow's theorem is logically valid. Since nobody is disposed to deny the validity of Arrow's proof (at any rate as given in the revised edition of the book, which clears up a problem that existed in the first), only two of the strategies discussed earlier for coping with conflicts in beliefs are available, and both of these have been tried.

The initial reaction to Arrow's proof was, rather widely, that there must be some sort of catch in it. Attempts were therefore made on all sides to see if some minor fudging with Arrow's formulation of the criteria to be met by any satisfactory "social welfare function" would not solve the problem. If this had succeeded, it would have been possible to hold both that criteria *like* Arrow's (but not exactly Arrow's) should be satisfied, and that Arrow's proof was valid.

However, the upshot of almost three decades of work has been to show that Arrow's proof is quite robust, in the sense that no plausible and nonarbitrary modification avoids impossibility results. The alternative line is to acknowledge that there is a conflict and to simply abandon the expectation that consistent sets of individual preferences can always be aggregated in ways satisfying criteria like those stipulated by Arrow. This is the usual one now taken, and it is certainly the one that we wish to adopt. The only question left is the one that was left open earlier: is there really any paradox here?

We would suggest that the belief that it "ought" to be possible to satisfy Arrow's axioms (or some variant on them) is one that we should be willing to abandon without any great pangs. The idea that there is a paradox rests, in other words, on an intuition that really should dissolve when subjected to serious thought.

The best way to approach the question is probably to try to reconstruct the processes of thought that might tempt someone to believe that there is something paradoxical about Arrow's theorem. If we can then show what is unfounded in the assumptions on which this conclusion is based, we shall have succeeded in what we set out to do.

Let us take, to begin with, the so-called paradox of voting. What this shows, it may be recalled, is that with three or more voters and three or more alternatives, it is possible for consistent individual preferences, when combined, to give rise to cyclical majorities, so that x beats y, y beats z, and yet, z beats x. What is the significance of this? It is true that, if we have never thought about the matter before, we may be inclined to guess that a set of internally consistent preferences will give rise to a consistent ranking of alternatives when the majority principle is applied to them. But surely, as soon as we see an example, we are quite convinced that this initial expectation was unfounded. There is no paradox because, once we have seen the point, we feel no inclination to hold on to our naive belief. We guessed wrong and that is all there is to it.

Or is it? Could one nevertheless manage to find something mysterious in the Arrow theorem that would lead one to say that it really is paradoxical? The answer seems to be that one could, though it would take a fair amount of perversity to do so. The way to arrive at a more lasting puzzlement is to become so entranced with the notion of "social preference" that one fails to realize that it is no more than a metaphor drawn from individual preference and incautiously extended beyond the sphere in which it has a well-defined sense. To say that one outcome is "socially preferred" to another is simply to talk about the results of some decision-making procedure, either hypothetical (i.e., one not actually used for reaching collectively binding decisions), or actual (i.e., an existing constitutional arrangement). There is no reason, once one thinks about it, for expecting to be able to ascribe to the results of such a procedure all the properties that one might reasonably hope to ascribe to an individual's decisions. The air of paradox in Arrow's theorem should dissolve when this is recognized.

Even if we dismiss the suggestion that Arrow's theorem is truly paradoxical, we are still left with the issue of social rationality. Does Arrow's theorem show that there is some sort of irrationality inherent in social (or, as it is often called, collective) decision-making? In thinking about this we need to keep firmly fixed in our minds the fact, emphasized by Little in the article we reprinted here, that there are two quite different senses in which a decision may be said to be social or collective. First, a decision may have a society or, more generally, a collectivity as its subject. Laws, rules, and authoritative decisions of all kinds are, in this sense, social or collective decisions, no matter how they are arrived at, so long as the procedure is the one that bestows legitimacy upon the outcomes. The second sense of a social or collective decision is the one to which Arrow's theorem is directly relevant. In this sense, a social or collective decision is one made *by* a society or collectivity. Since a collectivity is, in Hobbes's terms, an artificial and not a natural person, it can have decisions attributed to it only via some rules for aggregating individual expressions of preference. What Arrow's Theorem shows, then, is that there is no way of coming up with a rule for aggregating these expressed preferences that will guarantee a consistent "social" ordering satisfying a number of conditions that together stipulate certain relationships between the individual preference rankings fed in and the "social" ordering.

What does this negative conclusion tell us about the prospects for rational social decision-making? The answer is that what is closed off by Arrow's result is really quite limited in significance. When we assess the rationality of a piece of social decision-making, we usually focus on its content or on the intellectual processes that went into the decision. Will it do what those supporting it claim it will? Is it based on a sound analysis of the situation? Have alternatives been canvassed in a systematic way? Have the views of the relevant experts been taken into account? Were those making the decision generally open-minded? Did the decision tap some prejudice or personal interest of a key actor? These questions are a mixed bag but they are all concerned, either directly or indirectly, with the rationality of the decision itself. Thus, making use of the distinction between the two meanings of "social decision" that was introduced above, we may say that our interest in the rationality of a social decision usually focuses on its rationality as a decision *for* a society. The rationality of social decisions can be assessed without asking how they relate to the preference rankings of all the members of the society—and almost always is. So can the prudence, worthiness or justice of those decisions. Indeed, it is hard to imagine that any scheme for aggregating preferences—however stupid or vicious—into a social decision in the second sense should be expected to give us outcomes that have any necessary connection with any substantive value. The only value such a scheme could ever have, if it satisfied appropriate conditions (as Arrow's conditions can be satisfied if the preferences fed in bear suitable formal relationships in their structure), would be the procedural one that it did indeed connect the outcome to the preferences in some systematic way.

It is important to bear in mind in this context Baier's caution that "welfare," as it has to be understood within the framework created by Arrow, has no close connection with what we would ordinarily understand by the term. If we are inclined to believe that economists have any expert techniques to offer that put them in an especially advantageous position to advise about what would or would not enhance the welfare of a society, that is because we expect them to have analytical tools (like benefit-cost analysis) that will help to assess in a fairly systematic way the impacts of alternative policies on people: giving some more consumption, imposing inconveniences or health risks on others, and so on. As one of us wrote some years ago: "If an economist were asked about the economic implications of the third London airport and he suggested a method of polling the population of the

U.K. to ask what they thought about it I doubt if he would be paid much" (Barry 1972, p. 248). Yet, as Baier emphasizes, Arrow's "social welfare" is simply constituted out of preferences, without any restriction on their content. That there are problems in constructing a "social welfare function" understood in this way should not give most of us any serious worries, since we never believed in the first place that that was the way in which judgments about social welfare should be arrived at.

V. IS THE PRISONER'S DILEMMA A PARADOX OF RATIONALITY?

The prisoner's dilemma looks like a more promising candidate than the Arrow theorem if we are looking for a genuine paradox of rationality. Even after we have seen exactly how the force of individual self-interest inexorably leads both of the prisoners to confess, we are still liable to feel—as we do not with the "paradox of voting," once we have understood its mechanism—that there is something odd and, yes, *irrational* about the outcome. How can it be that, when each individual in a prisoner's dilemma situation does the best for himself that he can, they do less well for themselves than they would have done if they had all done something different? If one follows this line of thought one may come to be persuaded that there is some sort of incoherence in the very notion of rationality, since the pursuit of self-interest by the means rationally recommended apparently turns out to be self-defeating.

Among the writers whose work is included in this collection, Rapaport most clearly represents the viewpoint just expressed. Unfortunately, in his contribution he does not distinguish sharply between single and multiple plays of prisoner's dilemma games, but it seems clear from what he says that he is prepared to claim that there is something paradoxical about the players of even a one-shot prisoner's dilemma being recommended by the canons of rationality to each play noncooperatively. The same idea has been put forward far more extensively in a book (enthusiastically endorsed by Rapaport) entitled *Paradoxes of Rationality* by Nigel Howard (1971).

Let us examine the idea that there is something paradoxical about the phenomenon of rational self-interested players being advised to defect in a one-shot prisoner's dilemma. We shall restrict the discussion to the case in which the game is played only once because it raises the theoretical issues in the clearest and most acute way. Where the game is to be played an indefinite number of times, then in principle it may be possible for each participant to make his cooperation contingent on that of the others. Thus, in favorable cases, where the number of actors is small enough for the combined threats and promises to be (tacitly or explicitly) communicated, and where it is possible for each to monitor the performance of all the others, it is possible to show that the self-interest of each will lead to universal cooperation, or at any rate a high level of cooperation (see Hardin 1982). In the one-shot case, however, there is no room for these considerations, which depend upon the choice of an actor on this round affecting the choices of others on the next round. (This, of course, oversimplifies many real-life cases, where choices are continuous.) In the one-shot case, the problem of rationality is posed in its starkest form. Hence its particular suitability to our present inquiry.

The argument *for* the rationality of defection is clear enough. Let us assume that the payoff matrix really reflects the relative utilities of the alternative outcomes. Thus, in the original story, let us assume that utility is negatively correlated with length of prison term. This eliminates the possibility that one prisoner may care so much about the welfare of the other, or dislike the idea of testifying for the state against him, that the payoff matrix is not really of the prisoner's dilemma form. If we make the assumption that the payoffs have been correctly stated in utility terms, then it is a simple enough matter to show that a utility-maximizing agent will always defect rather than cooperate. For the particular feature that distinguishes the payoffs of a prisoner's dilemma from those of other games that share some features with it is that defection is the dominant strategy. As we have seen, the point is, in other words, that *whatever* the other player does, one is better off defecting. If he defects too, one minimizes the blow and at least avoids being a sucker; if he cooperates, one can make him the sucker and achieve the best possible outcome of the four that are possible.

If the end is taken as maximizing one's utility, then it looks as though there is an irrefutable case here for saying that means-end rationality requires one to play the noncooperative strategy in a one-shot prisoner's dilemma. What can be said against this conclusion? We can find the argument within the articles collected here in the one by Anatol Rapoport. According to Rapoport, "In the context of nonconstant-sum games like Prisoner's Dilemma actually two concepts of 'rationality' compete for attention, namely *individual* rationality, which prescribes to each player the course of action most advantageous to him under the circumstances, and *collective* rationality, which prescribes a course of action to both players simultaneously. It turns out that if both act in accordance with collective rationality, then *each* player is better off than he would have been had each acted in accordance with individual rationality."

Rapoport's immediately following comments could be made to yield two interpretations of this distinction, both of which are quite intelligible, but neither of which succeeds in impugning the common conception according to which "doing what is for the common good evokes the idea of 'sacrificing' one's individual interest." In a one-play prisoner's dilemma (i.e., the kind of situation presented in the original story) the common conception is exactly right. What Rapoport's two comments show are, respectively: (1) that rationality need not be identified with the pursuit of self-interest and (2) that one-play prisoner's dilemmas are rare and that in most cases of real social interaction there are self-interested reasons for behaving cooperatively. Let us take them up in turn.

(1) Rapoport's first move is to observe that "prescriptions of conduct in accordance with collective rationality are embodied in every ethical system." He goes on: "Such a prescription is spelled out in Kant's categorical imperative." Now, it is correct that the method of what has been called "false generalization" (see Broad 1916, Singer 1961, Lyons 1965, Regan 1980) can be fathered, with some qualifications, on Kant. And this, since it turns on the idea that one should act in a way that would have good consequences if everyone did likewise, obviously ties in with what Rapoport calls "collective rationality." Thus, in the case of the prisoner's dilemma, each prisoner asks himself according to this rule of conduct: "What would happen if the other prisoner behaved in the way in which I am proposing to behave?" (This is often put in the form "What if everybody did that?" [Strang 1960].) Clearly, the best consequences (at any rate for the two prisoners—not perhaps from a wider societal perspective) come about if neither confesses. So the rule prescribes to each in this case that he not confess.

There are two remarks worth making here. The first is that the rule is, it should be emphasized, one of *false* generalization. Even if there is no reason to expect that others will in fact do the same as you do yourself, you should still determine your action by asking what would have the best consequences if everyone did it. So, even if you expect the other prisoner to confess (or, indeed, if you know that he already has confessed), that does not alter the conclusion that you ought not to confess.

Some, though not all, upholders of the principle are uncomfortable with that implication and have sought ways of narrowing its scope. One, which has a good deal of plausibility, limits its application to cases in which each person derives a benefit from the sacrifice of others. The criterion of false generalization is then abandoned and we have in its place the anti-free-rider principle (see Rawls 1958, 1971; Lyons 1965, pp. 164-165). This says that each person should be prepared to do his part in a practice that is mutually beneficial. Thus, to take a stock example from the literature, suppose that there is a patch of grass that will have a path worn across it if more than a few people use it as a shortcut. Assuming that all those concerned would rather have nobody cutting across and an undamaged grass patch than have everyone take a shortcut and have a path worn in it, the principle of false generalization says that the right thing to do is to not walk across—even if so many people are in fact walking across that there is already a path worn. The anti-free-rider principle is more discriminating and says only that if enough others are eschewing the convenience of walking across in order to preserve the grass, you should do so too. This is a matter of "fair play."

Notice that there is no suggestion of causal effect on the actions of others here. If your walking across the grass will damage it only a tiny amount—less than the value to you of walking across—you still ought not to do it, even if it is done at a time when you happen to know that nobody else is looking. The point is simply that, if you are to behave in a morally supportable manner, you should not take advantage of the forbearance of others. In the prisoner's dilemma example, the implication is, plainly, that if you know that the other prisoner has not confessed (or have extremely good reasons for believing that he will not/has not done so), you ought not to confess yourself.

We have isolated a plausible moral principle; but, contrary to Rapoport's suggestion, morality and self-interest do conflict here. An agent who follows the moral prescription in a prisoner's dilemma situation will do less well for himself than one who does not. It is certainly significant that many people will naturally feel that the decision whether or not to confess should turn on what the other party does. What that shows is that many of us do accept the principle of fair play that forbids us to take advantage of the cooperative acts of others. But it does not tell us that there is any question about the best course for a rational self-interested person. It is clearly to confess, even if you know for certain that the other person has not confessed.

It is interesting that even formal treatments of the prisoner's dilemma sometimes make the error of suggesting that the whole problem arises only because each does not know about the actions of the other. Thus, for example, Bartos (1967, p. 230) says that the prisoner's dilemma is a dilemma because of the "temptation" to confess. "If the two prisoners can trust each other (remember, they are not allowed to communicate!) then they both could profit by not confessing. . . . But can they trust each other? The game is constructed so that each prisoner is tempted to double-cross his colleague." The reference to communication here is a red herring: if the players can communicate and are self-interested, then each has an incentive to try to persuade the other not to confess, and to promise that he will not confess himself; but (unless these promises can be made binding, which of course transforms the game) each then should, as a rational self-interested agent, go back and confess.

The point is not one of trust: even if one prisoner is certain that the other will not confess, he still has every (self-interested) reason to confess. Of course, there is something logically peculiar about saying that "if each can trust the other" neither will confess, because if each really can trust the other, each will, as a matter of logical necessity, not confess. This is a trivial implication of the fact that, if A predicts correctly that B will do x, this entails that B in fact does x; so if "trust" means "correct prediction," the two correct predictions, by A of B's behavior and by B of A's behavior, must logically constrain the behavior of A and B. We should avoid taking this purely logical point (which amounts to no more than saying that if neither confesses then neither confesses) as if it expressed a constraint in the real world. To avoid the catch, we should be careful to formulate the relevant propositions taking the actors one at a time. Then it should be clear that it is false to say: "If A can trust B not to confess, it will pay A not to confess," and similarly false when we reverse A and B in the sentence.

Bartos states very plainly the false conclusion as follows: "We have here a situation in which being rational (in the sense of playing it safe, i.e., playing the equilibrium strategy 'to confess') leads to a low payoff, and in which ignoring safety and trusting the other player (i.e., by playing 'not to confess') would increase one's own payoff." Bartos here treats "rationality" as identical with playing a maximin strategy. In a zero-sum game, a maximin (or minimax) strategy is generally optimal for a utility-maximizer. (The case for it does not depend on "playing safe.") But in the prisoner's dilemma, the point is that confession is the dominant strategy. Maximin has nothing to do with it, although the error of supposing that it does is quite often made. There is simply no way in which "ignoring safety and trusting the other player" could increase one's own payoff. It is *always* better to confess.

Any way round this entails a departure from the basic set-up. Thus, suppose that B chooses after knowing what A has chosen, and can somehow convince A that he will match A's choice: B will confess if A confesses, and refuse to confess if A refuses. Then A has a self-interested motive for not confessing. But if B is self-interested too, how can B convince A that he will in fact match a refusal to confess on the part of A? This certainly shows the advantage of being *believed* to be trustworthy. And perhaps a career of having been genuinely trustworthy in the past is the best way of producing the appearance this time. And then perhaps we can add that B has a good reason for trusting A this time because of the advantage to A of keeping his capital of trustworthiness intact or, indeed, because B thinks A simply has that kind of character. But this carries us outside the framework of a one-shot prisoner's dilemma with self-interested parties (i.e., utility-maximizing players whose utilities are captured in the payoffs). Either it makes A a non-self-interested player, whose word is his bond as a matter of principle, or it makes A a long-term self-interested player in virtue of considerations derived from future payoffs in future games outside the single play that is being analyzed.

Clearly, the same move might be made in relation to a one-shot game with simultaneous choice if A could predict perfectly what B was going to do and somehow convince B that he, A, would match B's choice: A will confess if B

confesses, refuse to confess if *B* refuses. This is in essence the same idea, with the additional complication of perfect prediction thrown in.

If we then enable each to predict perfectly the other's choice, we have a "solution" that pulls itself up by its own bootstraps (see Brams 1976, pp. 193-216). But, once again, mutual perfect prediction introduces a purely logical determination of the outcome which is too easily confused with a substantial one.

Nigel Howard's metagame analysis, referred to by Rapoport in his article, turns on the confusion between logical and physical coercion. In effect, each player has to predict the strategies to be followed by all of the others, and they get locked into cooperation by making appropriate mutual predictions. As Howard recognizes (1971, pp. 60-68), this trenches on the "paradox of free will": if actions can be predicted accurately, how can they be freely chosen? The answer is, of course, that a correct prediction does not cause what is predicted to come about (see Ryle's discussion [1954, pp. 15-34] of fatalism). If someone correctly predicts today that I shall leave my house at 9:30 a.m. tomorrow, that simply means that I shall in fact do so: if I were not going to do so, the prediction would not be correct. It does not, however, impel me to do so; nor (unfortunately) does it guarantee that I won't die before then—except, again, in the purely logical sense that if I do die before, then it was not in fact a correct prediction. Of course, if someone is able to predict all of my choices before I make them, I shall be disconcerted. But that is because it suggests he has discovered causal mechanisms that precede my choices and form the basis on which correct predictions can be made. It is not the prediction, but the ability to predict, that constrains (in some sense) my choices.

The second remark to be made is to emphasize that the generalization criterion is an ethical principle. It is addressed to moral agents. That is not to say that what it prescribes is antithetical to rationality. The term "rationality" is one with a broad range of applications and can certainly include acting in accordance with moral principles. The only thing that we must be careful about is not to identify this with the rational pursuit of self-interest. It is, indeed, only to be fitted into the paradigm of means-end rationality at all by the trivial move of postulating an end of acting in accordance with moral principles. But the implication of that is simply that means-end rationality does not exhaust rationality. (One might bear in mind here Max Weber's distinction between *Wertrationalität* and *Zweckrationalität* [see, for example, Benn and Mortimore 1976, pp. 133-134]).

But, it may be asked, what about the point that both parties, by acting morally, do better (from a selfish viewpoint) than they would have done for themselves by acting in accordance with individual rationality? The clearest way to understand what is going on here is to turn around the usual way of talking about a prisoner's dilemma. The aspect that is usually mentioned is that, from the point of view of a given actor, *A,* confessing is better than not confessing, regardless of what *B* does. If *B* confesses, *A* avoids the worst outcome for himself; if *B* does not, then all the better for *A,* who can now get the best possible outcome. Now let us put the matter the other way around and talk about the way in which *A*'s outcomes are affected by what *B* does, given any action on the part of *A.* We can then say that, whichever choice *A* makes, *A* is better off if *B* confesses than if *B* does not confess. If *A* confesses, then *B*'s confessing would save *A* from the worst ("sucker's") outcome that he would be liable for if *B* did not confess; and if *A* does not confess, a confession by *B* would give him the best possible outcome, rather than the middling outcome that is produced by joint nonconfession.

The significance of this can be appreciated if we express it by saying that it is always to the advantage of *A* for *B* to follow a prescription to not confess, and that likewise it is always to the advantage of *B* for *A* to follow a prescription to not confess. Now, if both follow the prescription not to confess, the net result is that both are better off than if both had failed to. But it would be still better for *A* if *B* would follow the prescription to not confess while *A* refused to follow it and confessed instead.

This throws light on Rapoport's conception of "collective rationality" as prescribing a course of action to both actors simultaneously: the best thing for a self-interested individual is for the other player to follow "collective rationality" while he follows "individual rationality" himself. Now if somehow both could be locked into "collective rationality," it is true that both would have good reason for choosing that option rather than being left free. But the essence of the prisoner's dilemma is that there is no mechanism for simultaneously determining the choices in that way. It is, then, simply not true that the prescriptions of what Rapoport calls "collective rationality" have any relevance to a self-interested actor, except inasmuch as he will hope that the other player will be attracted by them, to his own disadvantage.

(2) The second move that Rapoport makes immediately after making the distinction between "individual" and "collective" rationality is also valid in its own terms. But again, it does not in any way imply that, in the original prisoner's dilemma situation, there is any reason for advising a self-interested person to do anything except follow the path of "individual" rationality and confess. Rapoport here switches to a different example and says that the notion of "collective rationality" is "incorporated in every disciplined social act, for instance in the orderly evacuation of a burning theater, where acting in accordance with 'individual rationality' (trying to get out as quickly as possible) can result in disaster for all, that is, for each 'individually rational' actor." This kind of situation is not structurally identical to that of the

prisoner's dilemma, for the choices of the people concerned are not truly independent. If everyone understands that each is watching all the others and that any attempt by one to get ahead of the others will precipitate a rush for the exits, then each really does have good reason (based on "individual rationality") for filing out in an orderly manner. Thus, it is not true here that, irrespective of what the others do, each person is better off refusing to cooperate. Rather, each is better off by cooperating on condition that others do likewise. The structure of the payoff is, formally, that of what Sen has called an "assurance game" rather than that of a prisoner's dilemma (Sen 1967).

Although Rapoport's example is, strictly speaking, beside the point, it is, in a larger sense, highly relevant. For, if we seek to understand why the prisoner's dilemma appears to present a paradox, the best answer is that in real life true one-shot prisoner's dilemmas are very rare. And because of this, we naturally tend to carry into our thinking about them ideas that are relevant to other situations—as does Rapoport here. This may be regarded as fortunate: if each of us could, by pressing a button in secret, kill somebody in a foreign country and get ten thousand dollars, life would probably be considerably more "nasty, brutish and short" than it is already. But, leaving aside science-fiction examples such as this, one might with more validity say that it is no accident that social life is arranged so as to minimize the occurrence of one-shot prisoner's dilemmas. As Luce and Raiffa remark of a typical (artifically created) prisoner's dilemma, "there should be a law against such games" (Luce and Raiffa, 1957, p. 97)—and there frequently is.

VI. CONCLUSION

To return, in conclusion, to the point stated at the beginning of this Epilogue: too much is expected of the notion of rationality. There is no a priori reason to expect that, if people have very diverse ways of conceiving the bases for ranking some states of affairs above others, it will be possible to aggregate these preferences in a way that will satisfy the conditions laid down by Arrow. Similarly, if self-interested people are unfortunate enough to find themselves in the kind of situation represented by the payoffs of a one-shot prisoner's dilemma, there is no reason to expect that they can, by taking thought, avoid an outcome that each judges worse than an alternative that was attainable if both had chosen differently. There is, if we see things straight, no paradox in either case. Nor is there any occasion for weeping and wailing and gnashing of teeth. We should not attach very much importance to the kind of formal rationality embodied in an Arrovian "social welfare function," so we need not worry much about the limitations on the possibility of arriving at one. Substantive rationality—whether or not there are reasons that can be publicly supported for doing one thing rather than another—is much more important. As far as the prisoner's dilemma is concerned, it should be regarded not as a paradox, but as a challenge. The problem is how to devise institutions that will get us out of them.

NOTE

1. This is, however, only one strand of *On Liberty* and there is at some points a celebration of sheer eccentricity for its own sake that jars with this. However, Gertrude Himmelfarb (1974, pp. 79-91) has shown that Mill did not simply abandon his Saint-Simonian or (later) Comtean tendencies and continued, in writings contemporaneous with *On Liberty* or subsequent to it, to stress the importance of attaining a new consensus, though by force of example and conviction rather than, as in previous organic ages, by means of coercive thought control.

Guide to Further Reading

The present book makes no pretense of providing a systematic introduction or a general overview of the fields from which its materials are drawn: game theory, theories of collective action, welfare economics, the theory of public goods, utility theory, and social choice theory. Its focus is on the problem of social rationality as it arises in two kinds of contexts, interdependent decision-making and the aggregation of preferences. We hope, however, that some readers who have reached this point will wish to explore more widely the various subjects that have been touched on here. This guide is intended to help such readers to get started.

After experimenting with alternative ways of organizing the material, we decided in the end that the basic division that would prove most useful and practical would be the level of mathematical difficulty. Our criterion of mathematical difficulty is intuitive rather than technical. It does not turn purely on the kind of mathematical apparatus employed, but also on the ratio of words to symbols, the density of the exposition, and the clarity of the reasoning. Section I discusses treatments that are intended to be introductory. Section II brings in surveys that get more material into a shorter space. Finally, in Section III we offer some advice about journals. These are the major source of publication in all the relevant fields, so anyone who wishes to keep up must get acquainted with them.

I. INTRODUCTORY

Two recent books that provide clear introductions to a wide range of theory in a brief compass are Frohlich and Oppenheimer (1978) and Mueller (1979). Frohlich and Oppenheimer have chapters on "group choice" (e.g., Arrow) and "collective action in unorganized groups" (e.g., Olson). They then discuss ways of getting round the "Olson problem." In a second part of two chapters they analyze electoral competition (e.g., Downs). Each chapter has a list of suggestions for further reading, but the reader should be forewarned before attempting to use these that an extraordinarily high proportion of the names are misspelled.

Mueller's (1979) book also has material relevant to both of our areas. The general issue of collective action is raised in chapter 2 and the problem of estimating the demand for public goods is discussed in some detail in chapters 4 and 5. The Arrow theorem is set out in chapter 10 and the results of May and Rae/Taylor are discussed in chapter 11. The book also covers formal theories of voting and representation and concludes with a discussion of Rawls and his utilitarian critics (chapters 12 and 13). The bibliography is extensive. Mueller's survey tends to be uncritical and is particularly uncritical of the presuppositions of the "public choice" literature, probably because he shares them. This is illustrated especially well by his odd division of the book into "positive" and "normative" sections—as if the work of Buchanan, Tullock, Niskanen, Breton et al. were any less normative in its implications than that of Arrow or Rawls!

Of the books from which we have drawn in making up this collection, several could be read in their entirety without difficulty by anyone who has made it so far: Olson (1965), Barry (1978), Schelling (1978), Baumol (1965), and Hirsch (1976). In addition, two founding works that are referred to in our selections are quite accessible. These are Black (1958) and Downs (1957).

Moving on to systematic introductions to various specific fields let us begin with game theory. A well-known and comprehensive introduction to two-person game theory is Rapoport (1966). A useful general treatment of game theory is Hamburger (1979). Luce and Raiffa (1957) is an early text that is still unsurpassed. It covers game theory, utility theory, and also has a chapter on Arrow. Although much further work has been done, especially on n-person cooperative games, none of the proposed solution concepts is really compelling, and the cautions of Luce and Raiffa about the tenuousness of any "solution concept" that abstracts from everything except payoffs still hold good. Although the book is not easy going, the luminous intelligence that shines through every page makes it repay the effort.

Collective action is analyzed in two recent books. Hardin (1982) is a systematic study of the problems of collective action, which works through the theory in detail, applies it to political action, and considers various kinds of normative structures as ways of coping with the tendency of independent choices to lead to suboptimal outcomes. It does not make use of any advanced technical apparatus. Taylor (1976) is quite difficult mathematically in places but has prose expositions of the theorems and interesting discussions of Hobbes, Hume, and Kropotkin in relation to collective action. The analytical core of the book consists of a rigorous treatment of iterated n-person prisoner's dilemmas, designed to elucidate the conditions under which it is reasonable to expect cooperation.

Another book that contains both mathematical and verbal components—this time in alternating chapters, a mathematical starred chapter following the corresponding verbal chapter—is Sen (1970). This is a lively introduction to post-Arrow social choice theory, with an eye to its relevance to issues in moral and political philosophy.

Feldman (1980) presents a surprisingly accessible and successful "overview of welfare and social choice results unburdened by detail and mathematical complexity" (p. ix). His many short chapters give quick surveys of welfare economics, of its problems with externalities and public goods, and of the problems of voting schemes that one might have hoped would resolve the suboptimalities of market provisions by substituting central, democratic decisions. The chapters on welfare economics, Arrow's theorem, and strategic voting are especially good given their brevity. The chapter on "Fairness and the Rawls Criterion," however, is poor—if Rawls's position were as simplistic as Feldman makes it, it should sooner be ridiculed than refuted. Feldman's discussions of "selected references" at the ends of his chapters provide a useful bibliographic survey of much of the best work in the relevant areas.

II. MORE DEMANDING SURVEYS

Several surveys of the fields covered by this book, especially of the topics of its second section, are useful. The most accessible general survey is perhaps that of Taylor (1975). As a political scientist, Taylor is concerned with the larger implications of the technical issues, from which, however, he does not shy away. Kramer and Hertzberg (1975) cover some of the same ground with greater coverage of the spatial analysis of voting and party alignment and of game theory. Both of these articles are too early to cover more recent work and neither takes up the problem of collective action at significant length. Sen (1977) brings the post-Arrow literature up to the recent past. A comparable general survey of work in collective action would be valuable, but we know of none.

For those who can read long passages without benefit of words, Kelly (1978), Fishburn (1972), and Pattanaik (1971) present highly technical and impressively complete discussions of the Arrow problem up to their time. Fishburn and Pattanaik have themselves contributed many of the recent technical results. Pattanaik (1978) also surveys the literature on manipulability following on the Gibbard-Satterthwaite theorem (discussed in Gibbard's selection here). The speed with which an area of analytical research can progress is attested to by this book so soon after Gibbard's (1973) initial publication on strategic manipulation.

III. JOURNALS

The strongest recommendation we can make to anyone who wishes to keep up with current work, or even to check back on past work on the issues of this book is to consult the *Journal of Economic Literature*. This journal is a bibliographer's delight. It lists all articles on various economic topics published in an extraordinary array of journals, some of which are inaccessible in even very good university libraries, and it prints abstracts of many of the articles. It also indexes them according to various categories for easy searching. Relevant articles will be found especially under "Welfare Theory" (024) and "Social Choice" (025). The journal also reviews books and gives annotated listings of many others. Each quarterly issue includes a few survey articles, several of which from the past decade have been on topics of public choice, game theory, and utility theory and are well worth reading. We cannot recommend the *Journal of Economic Literature* strongly enough. Nevertheless, it is not complete in its coverage of the issues here. It does not systematically include empirical studies of collective action or social-psychological experiments on or accounts of the prisoner's dilemma.

Journals in which one will find work on these issues include most political science journals and virtually all economics journals. Work on the Arrow problem and public goods will be especially in the latter, work on collective action and models of voting behavior, especially in the former. Collective action and prisoner's dilemma gaming occasionally turn up in sociology journals with technical accounts in the *Journal of Mathematical Sociology*. Most prisoner's dilemma gaming is reported in social psychology and occasionally in more general psychology journals, as well as in the interdisciplinary journals below. Several journals conspiciously cut across the disciplines to which these issues are more or less central: the social sciences and philosophy. Five to which one might particularly pay attention are *Kyklos, Public Choice, Journal of Conflict Resolution, Behavioral Science,* and *Theory and Decision.* Contributors to the first two of these are most often economists, to the next two, more generally social scientists, and to the last, commonly philosophers. The *Journal of Conflict Resolution* and *Behavioral Science* are among the best journals for studies on game theory and gaming. *Theory and Decision* occasionally has symposia on relevant topics.

Finally, for the benefit of social scientists who may be unfamiliar with them, we should recommend various philosophy journals. One could begin with *Ethics, Philosophy and Public Affairs, Journal of Philosophy, American Philosophical Quarterly, Nous, Synthese, Philosophical Review, Inquiry, Analysis, Canadian Journal of Philosophy, Philosophical Studies,* and *Philosophia.* In these one will find, for example, extensive discussions of the significance of the Arrow literature for the analysis of justice and of contract and cooperation in prisoner's dilemma contexts.

References

Ackerman, Bruce (1980) *Social Justice in the Liberal State*. New Haven, Conn.: Yale University Press.

Arrow, Kenneth J. (1950) A Difficulty in the Concept of Social Welfare. *Journal of Political Economy* 68: 328-346.

——— (1951, 1963) *Social Choice and Individual Values*. 2nd edition. New Haven, Conn.: Yale University Press.

——— (1967) Public and Private Values, in *Human Values and Economic Policy*, Sidney Hook, ed., pp. 3-21. New York: New York University Press.

——— (1977a) Current Developments in the Theory of Social Choice. *Social Research* 44: 607-622.

——— (1977b) Extended Sympathy and the Possibility of Social Choice. *American Economic Review* 67: 219-225.

——— and G. Debreu (1954) Existence of an Equilibrium for a Competitive Economy. *Econometrica* 22: 265-290.

Arrow, K. J. and F. H. Hahn (1971) *General Competitive Analysis*. San Francisco: Holden-Day.

Baier, Kurt (1958) *The Moral Point of View*. Ithaca, N.Y.: Cornell University Press.

——— (1967) Welfare and Preference, in *Human Values and Economic Policy*, Sidney Hook, ed., pp. 120-135. New York: New York University Press.

Banfield, Edward C. (1961) *Political Influence*. New York: Free Press.

Barry, Brian (1965) *Political Argument*. London: Routledge and Kegan Paul.

——— (1972) Review of *Voting and Collective Choice* by Prasanta K. Pattanaik. *Political Studies* 20: 247-248.

——— (1973) *The Liberal Theory of Justice*. Oxford: Clarendon Press.

——— (1975) Review Article: Political Accommodation and Consociational Democracy. *The British Journal of Political Science* 5: 477-505.

——— (1970, 1978) *Sociologists, Economists, and Democracy*. Chicago: University of Chicago Press.

——— (1979) Is Democracy Special? in *Philosophy, Politics, and Society*, Fifth Series, Peter Laslett and James Fishkin, eds., pp. 155-196. New Haven, Conn.: Yale University Press.

Bartos, Otomar J. (1967) *Simple Models of Group Behavior*. New York: Columbia University Press.

Baty, Thomas (1912) The History of Majority Rule. *The Quarterly Review* 216: 1-28.

Baumol, W. J. (1952, 1965) *Welfare Economics and the Theory of the State*. 2nd edition. Cambridge, Mass.: Harvard University Press.

Bay, Christian (1971) Civil Disobedience: Prerequisite for Democracy in Mass Society, in *Civil Disobedience and Violence*, J. Murphy, ed., pp. 73-92. Belmont, CA.: Wadsworth.

Benn, Stanley I. and G. W. Mortimore, eds. (1976) *Rationality and the Social Sciences*. London: Routledge and Kegan Paul.

Bennett, Jonathan (1980) Accountability, in *Philosophical Subjects: Essays Presented to P. F. Strawson,* Zak van Straaten, ed., pp. 14-47. Oxford: Clarendon.

Bergson, Abram (1938) A Reformulation of Certain Aspects of Welfare Economics. *Quarterly Journal of Economics* 52: 310-334.

——— (1954) On the Concept of Social Welfare. *Quarterly Journal of Economics* 68: 233-252.

Berlant, Jeffrey L. (1975) *Profession and Monopoly.* Berkeley: University of California Press.

Black, Duncan (1958) *The Theory of Committees and Elections.* Cambridge: Cambridge University Press.

Blau, Julian H. (1957) The Existence of Social Welfare Functions. *Econometrica* 25: 302-313.

Blondel, Jean (1963) *Voters, Parties and Leaders.* Harmondsworth: Penguin Books.

Brady, Robert A. (1943) *Business as a System of Power.* New York: Columbia University Press.

Braithwaite, R. B. (1955) *Theory of Games as a Tool for the Moral Philosopher.* Cambridge: Cambridge University Press.

Brams, Steven J. (1976) *Paradoxes in Politics: An Introduction to the Nonobvious in Political Science.* New York: Free Press.

Brandt, Richard B. (1959) *Ethical Theory.* Englewood Cliffs, N.J.: Prentice-Hall.

Braybrooke, David and Charles E. Lindblom (1963) *A Strategy of Decision.* Glencoe, Ill.: Free Press.

Broad, C. D. (1916) On the Function of False Hypotheses in Ethics. *International Journal of Ethics* 26: 377-397.

Browne, Sir Thomas (1968) *Selected Writings,* Sir Geoffrey Keynes, ed. Chicago: University of Chicago Press.

Buchanan, James M. (1954a) Individual Choice in Voting and the Market. *Journal of Political Economy* 62: 334-343.

——— (1954b) Social Choice, Democracy, and Free Markets. *Journal of Political Economy* 62: 114-123.

——— (1967) Public Goods in Theory and Practice: a Note on the Minasian-Samuelson Discussion. *Journal of Law ad Economics* 1: 193-197.

——— (1968) *The Demand and Supply of Public Goods.* Chicago: Rand McNally.

Buchanan, James M. and William C. Stubblebine (1962) Externality. *Economica* 29: 371-384.

Buchanan, James M. and Gordon Tullock (1962) *The Calculus of Consent.* Ann Arbor: University of Michigan Press.

Carroll, Lewis (1976) *Complete Works.* New York: Vintage Books.

Chamberlin, Edward H. (1950) *Monopolistic Competition.* 6th edition. Cambridge, Mass.: Harvard Univesity Press.

Chamberlin, John (1974) Provision of Collective Goods as a Function of Group Size. *American Political Science Review* 68: 707-716.

Clark, J. M. (1923) *The Economics of Overhead Costs.* Chicago: University of Chicago Press.

Clarke, E. H. (1971) Multipart Financing of Public Goods. *Public Choice* 11: 17-33.

Coase, R. H. (1960) The Problem of Social Cost. *Journal of Law and Economics* 3: 1-44.

Cohen, Kalman and Richard Cyert (1965) *Theory of the Firm: Resource Allocation in a Market Economy.* Englewood Cliffs, N.J.: Prentice-Hall.

Cohen, Linda (1979) Cyclic Sets in Multidimensional Voting Models. *Journal of Economic Theory* 20: 1-12.

Coleman, James S. (1966) Individual Interests and Collective Action. *Papers on Non-Market Decision-Making* 1: 49-62.

——— (1973) Loss of Power. *American Sociological Review* 38: 1-17.

Condorcet, Marie Jean Antoine Nicolas Caritat (1785) *Essai sur l'application de l'analyse à la probabilité des décisions rendues à la pluralité des voix.* Paris: De l'Imprimerie Royale.

Congressional Quarterly Almanac 1975 (1976) Washington, D.C.: Congressional Quarterly.

Dahl, Robert A. (1956) *A Preface to Democratic Theory.* Chicago: University of Chicago Press.

——— and Charles E. Lindblom (1953) *Politics, Economics, and Welfare.* New York: Harper & Row.

Dahrendorf, Ralf (1959) *Class and Class Conflict in Industrial Society.* Stanford, Cal.: Stanford University Press.

——— (1967) *Conflict After Class: New Perspectives on the Theory of Social and Political Conflict.* London: Longmans.

Debreu, Gerard (1951) The Coefficient of Resource Utilization. *Econometrica* 19: 273-292.

——— (1959) *Theory of Value: An Axiomatic Analysis of Economic Equilibrium.* New Haven, Conn. and London: Yale University Press.

Deutsch, Morton (1958) Trust and Suspicion. *Journal of Conflict Resolution* 2: 203-264.

Dickinson, G. Lowes (1908, 1943) *Justice and Liberty: A Political Dialogue.* London: Allen & Unwin.

Downs, Anthony (1957) *An Economic Theory of Democracy.* New York: Harper & Row.

Dummett, Michael and Robin Farquharson (1961) Stability in Voting. *Econometrica* 29: 33-43.

Dworkin, Ronald (1978) Liberalism, in *Public and Private Morality,* Stuart Hampshire, ed., pp. 113-143. Cambridge: Cambridge University Press.

Edelman, Murray (1964) *The Symbolic Uses of Politics.* Urbana: University of Illinois Press.

Edwards, Paul, ed. (1967) *The Encyclopedia of Philosophy.* New York: Macmillan.

Ellis, Howard S. and William Fellner (1943) External Economies and Diseconomies. *American Economic Review* 33: 493-511.

Enke, Stephen (1955) More on the Misuse of Mathematics in Economics: A Rejoinder. *Review of Economics and Statistics* 37: 131-133.

Farquharson, Robin (1969) *Theory of Voting.* New Haven, Conn.: Yale University Press.

Feldman, Allan M. (1980) *Welfare Economics and Social Choice Theory.* Boston: Martinus Nijhoff.

Fishburn, Peter C. (1970) Arrow's Impossibility Theorem: Concise Proof and Infinite Voters. *Journal of Economic Theory* 2: 103-106.

——— (1972) *The Theory of Social Choice.* Princeton, N.J.: Princeton University Press.

——— (1974) Paradoxes of Voting. *American Political Science Review* 68: 537-546.

Flood, M. M. (1952) Some Experimental Games. Research Memorandum RM-789. Santa Monica, Cal.: Rand Corporation.

Frohlich, Norman and Joe Oppenheimer (1970) I Get By With a Little Help From My Friends. *World Politics* 23: 104-120.

——— (1978) *Modern Political Economy.* Englewood Cliffs, N.J.: Prentice-Hall.

——— and Oran Young (1971) *Political Leadership and Collective Goods.* Princeton, N.J.: Princeton University Press.

Gauthier, David (1974a) Justice and Natural Endowment: Toward a Critique of Rawls's Ideological Framework. *Social Theory and Practice* 3: 4-26.

——— (1974b) Rational Cooperation. *Nous* 8: 53-65.

——— (1975) Reason and Maximization. *Canadian Journal of Philosophy* 4: 411-433.

——— (1977) The Social Contract as Ideology. *Philosophy and Public Affairs* 6: 130-164.

Gibbard, Allan (1973) Manipulation of Voting Schemes: A General Result. *Econometrica* 41: 587-601.

Goldthorpe, John H., D. Lockwood, F. Bechhofer, and J. Platt (1968) *The Affluent Worker: Industrial Attitudes and Behaviour.* Cambridge: Cambridge University Press.

Gompers, Samuel (1905) Discussion at Rochester, N.Y., on the Open Shop—"The Union Shop Is Right"—It Naturally Follows Organization. *American Federationist* 12: 221-223.

Gouldner, Helen P. (1960) Dimensions of Organizational Commitment. *Administrative Science Quarterly* 4: 468-490.

Groves, T. and J. Ledyard (1977a) Optimal Allocation of Public Goods: A Solution to the "Free Rider" Problem. *Econometrica* 45: 783-809.

——— (1977b) Some Limitations of Demand Revealing Processes. *Public Choice* 29-2: 107-124.

Guyer, M. and B. Perkel (1972) Experimental Games: A bibliography 1945-1971. Communication 293. Ann Arbor: Mental Health Research Institute, The University of Michigan.

Haavelmo, Trygve (1950) The Notion of Involuntary Economic Decisions. *Econometrica* 18: 1-8.

Hamburger, Henry (1979) *Games As Models of Social Phenomena.* San Francisco: W. H. Freeman.

Hardin, Russell (1971) Collective Action as an Agreeable n-Prisoners' Dilemma. *Behavioral Science* 16: 472-481.

——— (1976) Group Provision of Step Goods. *Behavioral Science* 21: 101-106.

——— (1980) Infinite Regress and Arrow's Theorem. *Ethics* 90: 383-390.

——— (1982) *Collective Action.* Baltimore, Md.: Johns Hopkins University Press for Resources for the Future.

Hare, Richard M. (1963) *Freedom and Reason.* Oxford: Oxford University Press.

Harris, Richard (1970) Annals of Politics. *The New Yorker* (December 5 and 12).

——— (1971) *Decision.* New York: Dutton.

Harsanyi, John C. (1962) Rationality Postulates for Bargaining Solutions in Cooperative and Non-Cooperative Games. *Management Science* 9: 141-153.

——— (1977) *Bargaining Equilibrium in Games and Social Situations.* Cambridge: Cambridge University Press.

Hart, H.L.A. (1963) *Law, Liberty, and Morality.* Stanford, Cal.: Stanford University Press.

Head, John (1962) Public Goods and Public Policy. *Public Finance* 17: 197-219.

——— (1968) Welfare Methodology and the Multi-branch Budget. *Public Finance* 4: 405-424.

——— (1972) Public Goods: The Polar Case, in *Modern Fiscal Issues: Essays in Honor of Carl S. Shoup,* Richard Bird and John G. Head, eds., pp. 3-17. Toronto: University of Toronto Press.

Heard, Alexander (1960) *The Costs of Democracy.* Chapel Hill, N.C.: University of North Carolina Press.

Henderson, A. (1948) The Case for Indirect Taxation. *Economic Journal* 58: 538-553.

Hicks, J. R. and R.G.D. Allen (1934) A Reconsideration of the Theory of Value, Parts I and II. *Economica, N.S.* 1: 52-76 and 196-219.

Himmelfarb, Gertrude (1974) *On Liberty and Liberalism: The Case of John Stuart Mill.* New York: Knopf.

Hirsch, Fred (1976) *Social Limits to Growth.* Cambridge, Mass.: Harvard University Press.

Hook, Sidney (1967) *Human Values and Economic Policy.* New York: New York University Press.

Howard, Nigel (1971) *Paradoxes of Rationality.* Cambridge, Mass.: MIT Press.

Hume, David (1978) *A Treatise of Human Nature,* L. A. Selby-Bigge and P. H. Nidditch, eds. 2nd edition. Oxford: Clarendon Press.

Isbell, J. R. (1957) Homogeneous Games. *Mathematics Student* 25: 123-128.

Jervis, R. (1970) *The Logic of Images in International Relations.* Princeton, N.J.: Princeton University Press.

Kapp, K. William (1950) *The Social Costs of Private Enterprise.* Cambridge, Mass.: Harvard University Press.

Kelly, Jerry S. (1978) *Arrow Impossibility Theorems.* New York: Academic.

Kemp, M. C. (1953) Arrow's General Possibility Theorem. *Review of Economic Studies* 21: 240-243.

Kiesling, Herbert J. (1968) Potential Costs of Alternative Decision-Making Rules. *Public Choice* 4: 49-66.

Knight, Frank H. (1921) *Risk, Uncertainty and Profit.* Boston: Houghton Mifflin.

Kramer, Gerald H. and Joseph E. Hertzberg (1975) Formal Theory, in *Handbook of Political Science,* Fred I. Greenstein and Nelson W. Polsby, eds., vol. 7, pp. 351-403. Reading, Mass.: Addison-Wesley.

Laslett, Peter and James Fishkin, eds. (1979) *Philosophy, Politics and Society,* 5th series. New Haven, CT: Yale University Press and Oxford: Basil Blackwell.

Lichtenstein, S. and P. Slovic (1971) Reversals of Preference Between Bids and Choices in Gambling Decisions. *Journal of Experimental Psychology* 89: 46-55.

Lipsey, R. G. and Kevin Lancaster (1956) The General Theory of Second Best. *Review of Economic Studies* 24: 11-33.

Little, I.M.D. (1949) The Foundations of Welfare Economics. *Oxford Economic Papers.* (New Series) 1: 227-246.

——— (1950) *A Critique of Welfare Economics.* Oxford: Clarendon Press.

——— (1951) Direct Versus Indirect Taxes. *Economic Journal* 61: 577-584.

——— (1952a) Social Choice and Individual Values. *Journal of Political Economy* 60: 422-432.

——— (1952b) L'avantage collectif. *Économie Appliquée* 5: 455-468.

Lockwood, David (1958) *The Blackcoated Workers: A Study in Class Consciousness.* London: Allen & Unwin.

Luce, R. D. and Howard Raiffa (1957) *Games and Decisions.* New York: Wiley.

Lynch, David (1946) *The Concentration of Economic Power.* New York: Columbia University Press.

Lyons, David (1965) *Forms and Limits of Utilitarianism.* Oxford: Oxford University Press.

Mackie, J. L. (1967) Fallacies, in *The Encyclopedia of Philosophy,* P. Edwards, ed., vol. 3, pp. 169-179. New York: Macmillan.

MacIver, R. M. (1932) Interests. In *Encyclopedia of the Social Sciences* VII: 147. New York: Macmillan.

MacKay, Alfred F. (1980) Impossibility and Infinity. *Ethics* 90: 367-382.

Margolis, Julius (1955) A Comment on the Pure Theory of Public Expenditure. *Review of Economics and Statistics* 37: 347-349.

Marshall, Alfred (1920) *Principles of Economics.* 8th edition. London: Macmillan.

Marwell, Gerald and David R. Schmitt (1975) *Cooperation: An Experimental Analysis.* New York: Academic.

May, K. O. (1952) A Set of Independent Necessary and Sufficient Conditions for Simple Majority Decision. *Econometrica* 20: 680-684.

——— (1953) A Note on the Complete Independence of the Conditions for Simple Majority Decision. *Econometrica* 21: 172-173.

McGuire, Martin C. (1974) Group Size, Homogeneity, and the Aggregate Provision of a Pure Public Good under Cournot Behavior. *Public Choice* 18, 2: 107-126.

McKelvey, Richard D. (1976) Intransitivities in Multidimensional Voting Models and Some Implications for Agenda Control. *Journal of Economic Theory* 12: 472-482.

——— (1979) General Conditions for Global Intransitivities in Formal Voting Models. *Econometrica* 47: 1085-1111.

Mead, Margaret (1937) *Cooperation and Competition Among Primitive Peoples.* New York and London: McGraw-Hill.

Meade, J. E. (1945) Mr. Lerner on 'The Economics of Control'. *Economic Journal* 55: 47-69.

Meadows, Donella H., Dennis L. Meadows, Jørgen Randers, and William W. Behrens III (1972) *The Limits to Growth: A Report for the Club of Rome's Project on the Predicament of Mankind.* London: Earth Island Limited.

Michels, Robert (1959) *Political Parties,* trans. Eden and Cedar Paul. New York: Dover Publications.

Mishan, E. J. (1957) An Investigation into Some Alleged Contradictions in Welfare Economics. *Economic Journal* 68: 445-454.

——— (1969) The Relationship Between Joint Products, Collective Goods, and External Effects. *Journal of Political Economy* 77: 329-348.

Mitchell, Robert Cameron (1979) National Environmental Lobbies and the Apparent Illogic of Collective Action, in *Collective Decision Making: Applications from Public Choice Theory,* Clifford S. Russell, ed., pp. 87-121. Baltimore, Md.: Johns Hopkins University Press for Resources for the Future.

Moe, Terry M. (1980) *The Organization of Interests.* Chicago: University of Chicago Press.

Moore, G. E. (1903) *Principia Ethica.* Cambridge: Cambridge University Press.

Mueller, Dennis C. (1979) *Public Choice.* Cambridge: Cambridge University Press.

Murakami, Y. (1968) *Logic and Social Choice.* New York: Dover.

Murphy, Jeffrie G. (1971) *Civil Disobedience and Violence.* Belmont, Cal.: Wadsworth.

Musgrave, Richard Abel (1939) The Voluntary Exchange Theory of Public Economy. *Quarterly Journal of Economics* 53: 213-237.

——— (1959) *The Theory of Public Finance.* New York: McGraw-Hill.

——— (1969) Provision for Social Goods, in *Public Economics,* J. Margolis and H. Guitton, eds., pp. 124-144. New York: St. Martin's.

Nash, J. F. (1951) Non-cooperative Games. *Annals of Mathematics.* 54: 286-295.

Neumann, John von, and Oskar Morgenstern (1944, 1953) *Theory of Games and Economic Behavior.* 3rd edition. Princeton, N.J.: Princeton University Press.

Niemi, Richard G. and Herbert F. Weisberg (1972) *Probability Models in Collective Decision Making.* Columbus, Ohio: Charles E. Merrill.

Olson, Mancur, Jr. (1965) *The Logic of Collective Action.* Cambridge, Mass.: Harvard University Press. (Reprinted with a new appendix, 1971.)

——— (1971) Increasing the Incentives for International Cooperation. *International Organization* 25: 866-874.

――― and David McFarland (1962) The Restoration of Pure Monopoly and the Concept of the Industry. *Quarterly Journal of Economics* 76: 613-631.

Olson, Mancur, Jr. and Richard Zeckhauser (1966) An Economic Theory of Alliances. *Review of Economics and Statistics* 48: 266-279.

Pareto, Vilfredo (1896-1897) *Cours d'economie politique*. Lausanne: Rouge.

――― (1935) *The Mind and Society,* trans. A. Livingston. New York: Harcourt Brace.

――― (1980) *Compendium of General Sociology.* Minneapolis: University of Minneapolis Press. (Abridgement of Pareto 1935 by Giulio Farina. English text edited and collated by Elisabeth Abbott.)

Parsons, Talcott and Neil Smelser (1956) *Economy and Society.* Glencoe, Ill.: Free Press.

Pattanaik, Prasanta K. (1971) *Voting and Collective Choice: Some Aspects of the Theory of Group Decision-Making.* Cambridge: Cambridge University Press.

――― (1978) *Strategy and Group Choice.* Amsterdam: Elsevier.

Plott, Charles R. (1971) Recent Results in the Theory of Voting, in *Frontiers of Quantitative Economics,* M. Intriligator, ed., pp. 109-127. Amsterdam: North-Holland.

――― (1972) Ethics, Social Choice Theory and the Theory of Economic Policy. *Journal of Mathematical Sociology* 2: 181-208.

――― (1974) Rawls' Theory of Justice: Some Impossibility Results. Presented at the Public Choice Society Meeting.

――― (1976) Axiomatic Social Choice Theory. *American Journal of Political Science* 20: 511-596.

――― and M. Levine (1975) On Using the Agenda to Influence Group Decision: Theory, Experiments and Application. Social Science Working Paper 66. Pasadena: California Institute of Technology.

Rae, Douglas W. (1969) Decision-Rules and Individual Values in Constitutional Choice. *American Political Science Review* 63: 40-56.

Rapoport, Anatol (1947) A Mathematical Theory of Motivation Interaction of Two Individuals. *Bulletin of Mathematical Biophysics* 9: 17-27.

――― (1959) Critiques of Game Theory. *Behavioral Science* 4: 49-73.

――― (1960) *Fights, Games and Debates.* Ann Arbor: University of Michigan Press.

――― (1962) Some Self-Organizing Parameters in Three Person Groups, in *Principles of Self-Organization,* H. von Foerster and G. W. Zopf, Jr., eds., pp. 1-24. New York: Pergamon.

――― (1966) *Two-Person Game Theory: The Essential Ideas.* Ann Arbor: University of Michigan Press.

――― (1968) Editorial Comments. *Journal of Conflict Resolution* 12: 222-223.

――― (1974) Prisoner's Dilemma: Recollections and Observations, in *Game Theory as a Theory of Conflict Resolution,* Anatol Rapoport, ed., pp. 17-34. Dordrecht, Holland: D. Reidel.

――― and Albert M. Chammah (1965) *Prisoner's Dilemma.* Ann Arbor: University of Michigan Press.

Rapoport, Anatol and Melvin Guyer (1966) A Taxonomy of 2 x 2 Games, *General Systems* 11: 203-214.

Rawls, John (1958) Justice as Fairness. *Philosophical Review* 68: 164-194.

――― (1971) *A Theory of Justice.* Cambridge, Mass.: Harvard University Press.

Regan, Donald (1980) *Utilitarianism and Cooperation.* Oxford: Clarendon Press.

Reimer, Neal (1951) The Case for Bare Majority Rule. *Ethics* 62: 16-32.

Riker, William H. (1962) *A Theory of Political Coalitions.* New Haven, Conn.: Yale University Press.

――― and Peter C. Ordeshook (1968) A Theory of the Calculus of Voting. *American Political Science Review* 62: 25-42.

Ripley, W. Z. (1916) *Trusts, Pools and Corporations.* Boston: Ginn.

Rose, Richard (1967) *Influencing Voters: A Study of Campaign Rationality.* London: Faber & Faber.

Rothenberg, Jerome (1961) *The Measurement of Social Welfare.* Englewood Cliffs, N.J.: Prentice-Hall.

Rousseau, Jean-Jacques (1950) *The Social Contract,* trans. G.D.H. Cole. New York: E. P. Dutton.

Ryle, Gilbert (1954) *Dilemmas.* Cambridge: Cambridge University Press.

Samuelson, Paul A. (1947) *Foundations of Economic Analysis.* Cambridge, Mass.: Harvard University Press.

――― (1954) The Pure Theory of Public Expenditure. *Review of Economics and Statistics* 36: 387-389.

――― (1955) Diagrammatic Exposition of a Theory of Public Expenditure. *Review of Economics and Statistics* 37: 350-356.

――― (1967) Pitfalls in the Analysis of Public Goods. *Journal of Law and Economics* 10: 199-204.

――― (1969) Pure Theory of Public Expenditure and Taxation, in *Public Economics,* J. Margolis and H. Guitton, eds., pp. 98-123. New York: St. Martin's.

――― (1974) Complementarity―An Essay on the 40th Anniversary of the Hicks-Allen Revolution in Demand Theory. *Journal of Economic Literature* 12: 1255-1289.

Satterthwaite, M. A. (1975) Strategy-Proofness and Arrow's Conditions. *Journal of Economic Theory* 10: 187-217.

Schelling, Thomas C. (1958) The Strategy of Conflict: Prospectus for the Reorientation of Game Theory. *Journal of Conflict Resolution* 2: 203-264.

――― (1978) *Micromotives and Macrobehavior.* New York: W. W. Norton.

Schick, Frederic (1980) Toward a Logic of Liberalism. *Journal of Philosophy* 77: 80-98.

Schneewind, J. B. (1977) *Sidgwick's Ethics and Victorian Moral Philosophy.* Oxford: Clarendon Press.

Schofield, Norman (1978) Instability of Simple Dynamic Games. *Review of Economic Studies* 45: 575-594.

Selznick, Philip (1957) *Leadership in Administration.* New York: Harper & Row.

Sen, A. K. (1967) Isolation, Assurance and the Social Rate of Discount. *Quarterly Journal of Economics* 81: 112-124.

――― (1970) *Collective Choice and Social Welfare.* San Francisco: Holden-Day. (Currently published by North-Holland, Amsterdam.)

――― (1973) *On Economic Inequality.* Oxford: Clarendon Press.

――― (1974) Rawls versus Bentham: An Axiomatic Examination of the Pure Distribution Problem. *Theory and Decision* 4: 301-310.

――― (1976) Welfare, Inequalities and Rawlsian Axiomatics. *Theory and Decision* 7: 243-262.

――― (1977) Social Choice Theory: A Re-examination. *Econometrica* 45: 53-89.

Shapley, L. S. (1962) Simple Games: An Outline of the Descriptive Theory. *Behavioral Science* 7: 59-66.

――― (1967) Compound Simple Games III: On Committees. Report RM5438PR. Santa Monica, Cal.: Rand Corporation.

Shils, Edward S. and Morris Janowitz (1948) Cohesion and Disintegration in the German *Wehrmacht* in World War II. *Public Opinion Quarterly* 12: 280-315.

Shubik, M., G. Brewer, and E. Savage (1972) The Literature of Gaming, Simulation and Model Building: Index and Critical Abstracts. Report R-620-ARPA. Santa Monica, Cal.: Rand Corporation.

Singer, Marcus G. (1961) *Generalization in Ethics.* New York: Knopf.

Smith, Adam (1937) *The Wealth of Nations,* Edwin Cannan, ed. New York: Random House.

Snidal, Duncan (1979) Public Goods, Property Rights, and Political Organizations. *International Studies Quarterly* 23: 532-566.

Snow, Charles Percy (1963) *The Two Cultures and a Second Look: An Expanded Version of the Two Cultures and the Scientific Revolution.* New York and Toronto: The New American Library.

Starbuck, William H. (1965) Organizational Growth and Development, in *Handbook of Organizations,* James G. March, ed., pp. 451-533. Chicago: Rand McNally.

Stigler, George J. (1974) Free Riders and Collective Action: An Appendix to Theories of Economic Regulation. *Bell Journal of Economics and Management Science* 5: 359-365.

Stouffer, S. E., E. A. Souchman, L. C. Devinney, S. A. Star, and R. M. Williams (1949) *The American Soldier: Adjustment During Army Life.* Princeton, N.J.: Princeton University Press.

Straffin, Philip D., Jr. (1977) Majority Rule and General Decision Rules. *Theory and Decision* 8: 351-360.

Strang, Colin (1960) What if Everyone Did That? *Durham University Journal* 23: 5-10.

Strasnick, Steven (1976a) Social Choice and the Derivation of Rawls's Difference Principle. *The Journal of Philosophy* 73: 85-99.

––– (1976b) The Problem of Social Choice: Arrow to Rawls. *Philosophy and Public Affairs* 5: 241-273.

Strasnick, Steven (1979) Extended Sympathy Comparisons and the Basis of Social Choice. *Theory and Decision* 10: 311-328.

Taylor, Michael (1969) Proof of a Theorem on Majority Rule. *Behavioral Science* 14: 228-231.

––– (1975) The Theory of Collective Choice, in *Handbook of Political Science,* Fred I. Greenstein and Nelson W. Polsby, eds., vol. 3, pp. 413-481. Reading, Mass.: Addison-Wesley.

––– (1976) *Anarchy and Cooperation.* London and New York: Wiley.

Terhune, K. (1970) Motives, Situation, and Interpersonal Conflict within Prisoner's Dilemma. *Journal of Experimental and Social Psychology* 6: 187-204.

Thompson, E. A. (1968) The Perfectly Competitive Production of Collective Goods. *Review of Economics and Statistics* 50: 1-12.

Thoreau, Henry David (1970) *The Annotated Walden,* Philip Van Doren Stern, ed. New York: Clarkson N. Potter.

Tintner, Gerhard (1946) A Note on Welfare Economics. *Econometrica* 14: 69-78.

Truman, David B. (1951, 1971) *The Governmental Process.* 2nd edition. New York: Knopf.

Tullock, Gordon (1962) in *The Calculus of Consent,* J. M. Buchanan and Gordon Tullock, eds., App. 2. Ann Arbor: University of Michigan Press.

Tversky, Amos (1969) Intransitivity of Preferences. *Psychological Review* 76: 31-48.

Urmson, J. O. (1960) *The Concise Encyclopedia of Western Philosophy and Philosophers.* London: Hutchinson.

Vickrey, William (1960) Utility, Strategy, and Social Decision Rules. *Quarterly Journal of Economics* 74: 507-535.

Viner, Jacob (1937) *Studies in the Theory of International Trade.* New York and London: Harper & Row.

Wagner, Richard E. (1966) Pressure Groups and Political Entrepeneurs. *Papers on Non-Market Decision-Making* 1: 161-170.

Wasserstrom, Richard A. (1969) The Obligation to Obey the Law, in *Civil Disobedience: Theory and Practice,* H. A. Bedau, ed., pp. 256-262. New York: Pegasus.

Weber, Max (1947) *Theory of Social and Economic Organization,* trans. Talcott Parsons and A. M. Henderson. New York: Oxford University Press.

Wilson, R. B. (1972) Social Choice Theory without the Pareto Principle. *Journal of Economic Theory* 5: 478-486.

Wolfinger, R. E., B. K. Wolfinger, K. Prewitt, and S. Rosenhack (1964) America's Radical Right, in *Ideology and Discontent,* D. E. Apter, ed. New York: Free Press.

Wrightsman, L. S., Jr., J. O'Connor, and N. J. Baker (1972) *Cooperation and Competition: Readings on Mixed Motive Games.* Belmont, Cal.: Brooks/Cole.

Index

Note: In order to conserve space, the selections reprinted in this volume are not indexed under their authors' names. Thus, the entries under "Arrow, Kenneth" cover references to Arrow by others (including the editors' introductions) but not to Arrow's own article. The article by Arrow is, however, indexed under other headings, e.g., "Arrow's theorem: Arrow on" and "Rawls, John: Arrow on."

political levies in, 65
and selective incentives, 57-58, 65-66
and social sanctions, 65
and wage rate as public good, 33
Universal domain (Condition *U*), 215-16,
220-25
Gibbard on, 357-66
Plott on, 237
in proof of Arrow's theorem, 221-24,
345-46
restrictions of individual preferences,
326-27, 332-40, 348-51
Vickrey on (range), 341-51
Urmson, J. O., 374
Utilitarianism
Arrow on, 253, 255-56, 262
and Arrow's theorem, 213-15, 218,
223
Barry on, 325
and classical economics, 139, 213
and complementarity effects, 226
and contribution to collective action,
61
Rawls and, 388
simple additive, 139, 213-15, 218, 223,
253, 255-56, 262, 325
as welfare criterion, 213, 279
Utility, 275, 357
cardinal, as lotteries, 85-86, 249-50,
254-55
cardinal vs. ordinal, 85-86, 213-15,
225-27, 254-56, 262
complementarity and, 225-26
coordinal invariance (or comparisons)
of, 251, 256, 262-63
frontier of, 176-77
Gauthier on, 90-105
interpersonal comparisons of, 225,
250-51, 255-56, 261-63, 265, 269
in market analysis, 138
maximization of, 88-89, 90-105
and ophelimity, 139-41, 266-67
Pareto on, 139-41
works on, 390
See also Preferences

Vaccination, 117-18
Value judgments, 265, 275-81
Verificationism, 249-50
Veto, 306. *See also* Consensus, Unanimity

Vickrey, William
on Arrow's theorem, 213, 221, 366n
conjecture on strategic misrepresentation, 341-42, 353, 355, 359
proof of Arrow's theorem, 228
on strategic misrepresentation, 224,
227-28, 341, 342, 352-53, 356, 359
Viner, Jacob, 155n
Volstead Act, 331
Voter's paradox (Cyclical majorities,
Intransitivity of social preference)
Arrow on, 258-61
and Arrow's theorem, 223, 225-26,
228, 268, 284-88
Baier on, 284-88
Campbell and Bordes on, 247, 260-61
and log-rolling, 341-42
and majority rule, 215-16, 219-20,
226, 228, 258-61, 284-88, 297
"minimality" solution to, 234-35,
247-48, 261
as paradox, 232, 234, 239, 241, 253,
287, 375-78
Plott on, 233-34
Vickrey on, 348
See also Condorcet choice
Voting
counting methods in, 219-20, 228n,
235-36. *See also* Borda count
Downs on, 23, 35, 51-55, 59-60, 67-
68, 193-94
"economic" explanation of, 21, 23,
51-52, 53-55, 59-64, 388
and logic of collective action, 21, 23,
51, 53-55
majority rule in, *see* Majority rule
paradox of, 232, 234, 239, 241, 253,
287, 375-78
as preference-aggregating mechanism,
13, 257-59
on public goods, provision of, 129-33,
193-94, 224-25
spatial analysis of, 389
strategic manipulation in, 13-14, 18n,
227-28, 352-53, 355-57, 358-66,
389
Thoreau on, 268
works on, 388-89

Wagner, Richard E., 29

About the Editors

Brian Barry is Distinguished Service Professor of Political Science and Philosophy at the University of Chicago. His undergraduate degree and doctorate were gained at the University of Oxford, where he later spent six years as a Fellow of Nuffield College. He has taught previously at the Universities of Birmingham, Keele, Southampton, and Essex and at the University of British Columbia. He is founding editor of the *British Journal of Political Science* and is currently editor of *Ethics: An International Journal of Social, Political and Legal Philosophy.* His books include *Political Argument* (London: Routledge and Kegan Paul, 1965); *Sociologists, Economists and Democracy* (1970; reprinted Chicago: University of Chicago Press, 1978); and *The Liberal Theory of Justice: A Critical Examination of the Principal Doctrines in a Theory of Justice by John Rawls* (Oxford: Clarendon Press, 1974). He was elected to the American Academy of Arts and Sciences in 1978.

Russell Hardin is Associate Professor of Political Science and Public Policy Studies at the University of Chicago. He studied at the University of Texas, Oxford University, and at the Massachusetts Institute of Technology. He has taught previously at the Universities of Pennsylvania and Maryland. He is book review editor and an associate editor of *Ethics: An International Journal of Social, Political and Legal Philosophy.* His book, *Collective Action,* is forthcoming.

About the Editors

Brian Barry is Distinguished Service Professor of Political Science and Philosophy at the University of Chicago. His undergraduate degree and doctorate were gained at the University of Oxford, where he later spent six years as a Fellow of Nuffield College. He has taught previously at the Universities of Birmingham, Keele, Southampton, and Essex and at the University of British Columbia. He is founding editor of the *British Journal of Political Science* and is currently editor of *Ethics: An International Journal of Social, Political and Legal Philosophy*. His books include *Political Argument* (London: Routledge and Kegan Paul, 1965); *Sociologists, Economists and Democracy* (1970; reprinted Chicago: University of Chicago Press, 1978); and *The Liberal Theory of Justice: A Critical Examination of the Principal Doctrines in a Theory of Justice by John Rawls* (Oxford: Clarendon Press, 1974). He was elected to the American Academy of Arts and Sciences in 1978.

Russell Hardin is Associate Professor of Political Science and Public Policy Studies at the University of Chicago. He studied at the University of Texas, Oxford University, and at the Massachusetts Institute of Technology. He has taught previously at the Universities of Pennsylvania and Maryland. He is book review editor and an associate editor of *Ethics: An International Journal of Social, Political and Legal Philosophy*. His book, *Collective Action*, is forthcoming.